1 MONTH OF
FREE
READING

at

www.ForgottenBooks.com

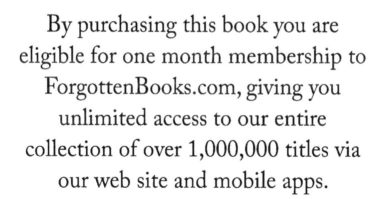

By purchasing this book you are eligible for one month membership to ForgottenBooks.com, giving you unlimited access to our entire collection of over 1,000,000 titles via our web site and mobile apps.

To claim your free month visit:

www.forgottenbooks.com/free1112430

ISBN 978-0-331-36624-2
PIBN 11112430

This book is a reproduction of an important historical work. Forgotten Books uses state-of-the-art technology to digitally reconstruct the work, preserving the original format whilst repairing imperfections present in the aged copy. In rare cases, an imperfection in the original, such as a blemish or missing page, may be replicated in our edition. We do, however, repair the vast majority of imperfections successfully; any imperfections that remain are intentionally left to preserve the state of such historical works.

INAUGURAL ADDRESS

OF

HON. GEORGE F. VERRY,

MAYOR, JAN. 1, 1872.

WITH THE

ANNUAL REPORTS

OF THE

SCHOOL DEPARTMENT, CITY ENGINEER, WATER COMMISSIONER, FREE
PUBLIC LIBRARY, COMMISSION OF PUBLIC GROUNDS, COMMISSION-
ERS OF HOPE CEMETERY, OVERSEERS OF THE POOR,
COMMISSIONER OF HIGHWAYS, CITY MARSHAL,
FIRE DEPARTMENT, CITY HOSPITAL,
AND CITY TREASURER

OF THE

CITY OF WORCESTER,

FOR THE FINANCIAL YEAR ENDING NOV. 30, 1871.

WORCESTER:
PRINTED BY EDWARD R. FISKE, CROMPTON'S BLOCK.
1872.

CITY OF WORCESTER.

In City Council, January 8, 1872.

Ordered:

That the Committee on Printing be, and they are hereby authorized to contract for the printing of 1500 copies of the annual "City Document," to be numbered 26; also for the printing of such number of the Annual Reports of the several Departments of the City Government, for the current Municipal Year, as they shall think advisable.

A Copy, Attest:

SAMUEL SMITH,
City Clerk.

INDEX.

MAYOR'S ADDRESS.

Gentlemen of the Board of Aldermen, and Gentlemen of the Common Council:

Called as we have been by the suffrages of our people to the administration of their municipal affairs, as the chief executive officer of the City Government, I follow the uniform example of my predecessors in giving you such information as I have been able to gather of the present condition of the various departments of the City Government, the various enterprises inaugurated and in process of completion for the permanent advancement of our beautiful city in material and intellectual wealth, and to offer you such recommendations, necessarily crude and incomplete, as have occurred to my own mind, tending to facilitate this desirable object.

It is well for us, in assuming the duties of the administration of government, to remember that the end of all government should be " to secure the existence of the body politic, to protect it, and to furnish the individuals who compose it with the power of enjoying in safety and tranquility their natural rights and the blessings of life, that when public exigencies require that the property of any individual should be appropriated to public uses, he should receive a reasonable compensation therefor, that all officers of government are but the substitutes and agents of the people and are at all times accountable to them, and that the people ought to obtain right and justice freely, without being obliged to purchase it, completely and without any denial, promptly and without delay, conformably to law."

Frequent recurrence and studious adherence to these well digested principles of government, will serve us as a guide and compass in the devious ways through which we shall be called to pass, and the arduous labors we shall be expected to perform.

2

Guided by these principles and inspired by a confidence in the over-ruling Providence of that Almighty Being whose power regulates our destiny and whose blessings have been so conspicuously dispensed to our people, and lighted by the examples of worthy and disinterested service successfully rendered by those who have conducted the affairs of this Municipal Government before us, we may reasonably indulge the hope that when our terms of office shall expire, we shall be able to point to the record of our administration with the assurance that we have added to our constantly accumulating municipal history another chapter of material and intellectual progress, not unworthy of association with those which precede it.

I need not remind you, who are entrusted with these all absorbing cares, that our financial condition will call for your most thorough investigation, and the best efforts which your wisdom and prudence can suggest to provide for the prompt and effectual liquidation of our maturing obligations.

FINANCES.

In dealing with the subject of our financial condition it is desirable that we should possess ourselves of exact and accurate information as to the amount we owe, how our debt is invested, and when it must be paid, together with our present and prospective means of payment. To all our people this subject is of the greatest interest, and as faithful servants it is our bounden duty to deal frankly with reference to it, concealing no fact or figure that shall tend to enlighten, substituting no fact or figure that shall tend to deceive, or by resort to any ingenious complication of calculations, seek to make our financial condition appear in a more favorable light than it deserves to be stated.

A brief history of the progress by which our debt has accumulated, together with some of the causes which have contributed to this result, may not be unprofitable. At the end of the municipal year 1866 our general indebtedness was $303,193.00. Our water debt $155,110.00.

At the end of the municipal year 1869, our general indebtedness was $108,040.07. Our water and sewer debt was $727,018.39. At the end of the municipal year 1870, our general indebtedness was represented to be $383,020, showing an increase during that year of $274,979.93.

This result is mainly attributable to the necessary expenses incurred in building new school houses, opening new streets, cutting down Main street, in the vicinity of Corbett street, and our subscription to the capital stock of the Boston, Barre & Gardner Railroad, having during that year paid assessments upon it to the amount of $104,880. Our sewer and water debt at the end of that year amounted to $1,517,000. The financial condition of the city together with the resources, receipts and disbursements of the treasury for eleven months ending Dec. 1st, 1871, is as follows, as nearly as can be ascertained. The whole amount of our indebtedness as nearly as it can be ascertained at the Treasurer's office is $2,459,900.00.

To this must be added claims against the city in great variety, such as claims for damages to estates, by laying out, altering and widening streets, laying out and constructing sewers, claims for unpaid balances for water and sewer construction, claims not yet reported for work on the high school house. I have been unable to ascertain the amount of these claims so as to make even an approximate statement. This debt, $2,459,900, is disposed of as follows :

```
Funded sewer debt..................................  $499,400
   "    water   "   ..................................   794,500
   "    city    "   ..................................   601,000
Temporary loan...........................  ..................   565,000
                                                         ----------
                                                         $2,459,900
```

The debt has been increased during the past year in the following way ;—

```
Water construction.................................  $100,000
Sewer      "    .................................   245,000
Boston, Barre and Gardner railroad....................   157,320
Soldier's Monument....................................    35.000
Front, Lafayette and Hermon streets..,................    27,500
                                                         ----------
                                                          $564,820
```

The entire sewer debt as far as ascertained is........ $1,072,402 04
The entire water debt as far as ascertained is.......   752,987 98
The Boston, Barre and Gardner railroad investment is.   262,200 00

RESOURCES 1871.

Cash on hand Jan. 2, '71............................	$28,728 28
Received for corporation tax.........................	42,918 47
" taxes....................................	686,933 75
" water rates..............................	53,795 58
" betterments, Chatham and Corbett streets..	5,461 66
Received for betterments on Mechanic street............	6,166 86
Received for betterments on Winter street.............	1,288 29
All other sources not ascertained.....................	

EXPENDITURES 1871.

Paid on sewers, 1871..............................	$245,250 24
" water works, (as reported by treasurer)........	111,200 08
" schools...........................	119,976 00
" highways and bridges......................	139,878 55
" new high school house..................	62,592 61
" old " " "	19,975 47
" Belmont street school house................	7,866 92
" Normal school.............................	15,000 00
Abatement on taxes....:...........................	1,738 69

The other departments are not fully ascertained, but will appear in the treasurer's report.

Our funded debt, which is mostly invested at six per cent., falls due as follows:

FUNDED WATER LOAN.		FUNDED SEWER LOAN.		FUNDED CITY LOAN.	
Due in		Due in		Due in	
1872	$47,500	1872	$50,000	1872	$12,000
1873	68,700	1873	80,000	1873	3,000
1874	119,200	1875	20,000	1874	10,000
1875	133,800	1877	87,600	1875	6,000
1876	79,400	1878	33,600	1876	3,000
1877	18,500	1879	16,300	1877	2,000
1878	27,500	1880	143,000	1878	6,000
1879	14,500	1881	68,900	1879	4,000
1880	11,100			1880	8,000
1881	3,000		$499,400	1881	516,000
1882	12,000			1882	6,000
1885	105,000			1883	10,000
1886	126,000			1884	5,000
1887	1023,00				
1888	5,300				$601,000
	$794,500				

A large amount of the funded city loan of $601,000.00 and of the temporary loan of $565,000.00 has been used in the sewer and water construction.

The real and personal estate belonging to the city, including the waterworks is $1,978,117; 2622 shares Boston, Barre and Gardner railroad at par $262,200; due on Main street school-house, $19,000; due from the state, $15,000. Total, $2,274,317. To this may be added estimated sewer assessments and betterments on streets, the amount of which has not been ascertained.

Ascertained city debt............................. $2,459,900 00
Increase since Jan. 1, 1867....................... 2,022,623 93

TAXATION.

The valuation of our real estate is................. $28,039,150 00
    "   " personal " 10,102,100 00

                                      $38,141,250 00

Rate per cent of tax $17,40 per $1000...............Polls, 11,638.
Amount of state tax.......................... .... $51,075 00
   "   county " 27,639 23
   "   city   " 595,500 00
Overlayings 12,719 52

    Total $686,933 85
Abatement on taxes assessed in 1871, $1,738.69.

PAYMENT OF THE THE DEBT.

The necessary steps should be taken at once to avail ourselves of the means provided by law for raising money for the payment of this debt. Much was done by the last City Government, and much yet remains to be done to accomplish this object, and I trust we shall be able to take the subject up where they have left it, and proceed expeditiously in the performance of this duty.

SEWER ASSESSMENT.

One of the main reliances for the extinguishment of a large portion of this debt has been, and is, the sewer assessment, which was contemplated by the originators of our sewer improvements and expressly provided for in. the statute granting to the city authority to construct sewers. The work of laying sewers under this authority was begun in 1867, and has been steadily continued ever since, but no assessments have ever been made, owing, as I am informed, to the difficulty of adopting an equitable basis of assessment upon those liable to it.

This question is one which must be encountered by the mayor and aldermen of this city at some time, in fact it has already been too long delayed. The people who are to be called upon to pay, are waiting in anxious suspense to know the amount, and the general tax payers are to some extent clamorous that the assessment be made, lest the entire burden of the cost of sewers should be absorbed in the general debt, to be paid by the general tax.

I hope at the earliest practicable moment you will co-operate with me in making this assessment. Upon a careful examination of the subject, I have become satisfied that no arbitrary rule can be adopted, which, strictly followed, will operate equitably to equalize this burden, and while we can hardly hope, owing to the difficulties attending the subject, and the infirmities of human judgment, to do exact and equal justice to all, we should make the effort to approximate as nearly to it as possible.

The act of the legislature, passed March 29th, 1867, under the authority of which our sewers have been constructed, provides, Sec. 4, that "every person owning real estate upon any street in which any drain or sewer may be laid, under or by virtue of this act, and upon the line thereof, or whose real estate may be benefitted thereby, shall pay to said city such sum as the mayor and aldermen shall assess upon him as his proportionate share of the expenditure of the city for drains and sewers."

Section 6 provides that the act shall be void unless submitted to the voters of said city of Worcester and approved by them. On the 16th day of April, 1867, at a meeting duly called for that purpose, the act was approved by a vote of 316 in the affirmative to 49 in the negative.

Section 7 of chapter 42 of the City Ordinances provides that "it shall be the duty of the mayor and aldermen to apportion and assess, according to their best judgment, upon the several persons and estates adjoining the line of any common sewer or adjoining any street or highway in which any such sewer is constructed and deriving benefit from such common sewer, either by the entry of their particular drains therein, or by any more remote means, such sum as said mayor and aldermen shall deem to be his proportionate share of the expenditure of the city for drains and sewers."

These provisions not only authorize, but compel, the mayor and aldermen to make an assessment against persons and estates r fo the purpose of raising a fund to be applied, as far as it may go in payment of our sewer debt, and I think that the duty of making this assessment should at once be entered upon, with a full determination, upon some equitable basis, to complete it at the earliest practical moment, and when completed the assessment should be promptly collected and applied to the relief of our impoverished treasury. It should be a fair and equitable assessment. His Honor, Mayor Chapin, in his inaugural address of 1871, said, "Nothing is more important to the people than a careful and equitable assessment. Much of the reluctance to paying taxes, which is a privilege no one exactly craves, may be traced to a kind of dim certainty that they are not equitably assessed."

It is a proposition which it requires no argument to sustain, that in assessing upon the people a tax for the support of municipal government, care should be taken that the burden fall equally upon all. And in the assessment under consideration this proposition should be constantly recognized, and if it is, our people will, I know, meet cheerfully and heartily the requisitions made upon them in this respect. I think the statute which authorizes the assessment, and the ordinance which makes it the duty of the mayor and aldermen to assess, have, when construed together, furnished the rule by which we are to be guided in making it.

The statute provides that every person owning real estate upon any street in which a sewer may be laid, or which may be benefitted thereby, shall pay such sum as the mayor and aldermen may assess, &c., and the ordinance provides that it it shall be the duty of the mayor and aldermen to assess the several persons and estates, &c., *deriving benefit from such common sewer, either by entry of their particular drains therein, or by any more remote means*, such sum as they shall deem his proportionate share of the expenditure of the city for drains and sewers.

It seems to me to be clear that the assessment contemplated by these enactments is to be based upon and graduated by the benefit derived or to be derived ; therefore no assessment based upon a valuation of the land or by the number of lineal front feet of land which a man may own along the line of any sewer can *alone* form an equitable basis upon which this assessment can be made.

A man owns an estate on Chestnut street, for instance, having 300 feet front; he has a dwelling house upon it; his land is worth $30,000 ; his family consists of four persons; he drains from his house into the sewer. Another man owns in another part of the city, an estate of 100 feet front; upon it he has dwelling houses and tenements which furnish shelter for fifty persons; his land is worth $3000, his dwellings and tenements drain into the sewer. Attempt an assessment based upon valuation or front feet of land, and how soon you depart from the equitable rule of assessment according to benefit derived.

Let those be assessed who derive benefit, either from entering their own particular drains into the sewer, or by any other more remote means," according to benefit received over and above the general benefit which all citizens alike derive from this great benefaction. Such an assessment will without doubt meet the approval and acquiescence of our people. To all citizens of the city the sewers are a general benefit, furnishing as they do surface drainage for the streets, thus preventing in a measure the constant wear to which they are subjected from rains and thaws. And also in a sanitary point of view their general benefits are incalculable. So far then as they are of a general benefit they should be paid for as all general benefits are by the community generally. So far as they are a particular benefit they should be paid for by the individuals particularly benefitted, and according to the particular benefit they receive.

My idea, then, is that so far as one derives benefit from the sewers, other and different from the general benefit derived by all citizens alike, he should be assessed for it, and the balance of the cost of the sewers be absorbed in the public debt. The amount of the sewer debt will be found stated in its appropriate place under the head of finances.

By such means as these, the cost of our sewers, which constitutes the principal part of our indebtedness, will be easily disposed of; its payment will be distributed equitably, and as the debt is now funded with a long day for payment, the burden will fall lightly on those who have to bear it; and those who come after us, and for whose benefit, as well as our own, these improvements are made, will be obliged to contribute their proportionate share of the cost.

⹂ I am aware that there are wide differences of opinion as to the ⹂proper basis for making this assessment, and although I feel entirely confident in the equity and justice of the plan I have suggested, I desire that you shall carefully examine the subject, so that, when you come to a conclusion, it may not justly be said that we have been heedless in the performance of this duty.

SINKING FUND.

The last City Council by an ordinance passed, July 24th, 1871, laid out the ground-work for a sinking fund, the purpose of which is to provide for the payment of our debt. It provides that all balances of money remaining in the treasury at the end of any financial year, all receipts in money on account of the sale of real estate of any description now belonging or which may hereafter belong to the city, all receipts on account of the principal sum of any bond or note now owned or which may hereafter be owned by the city, excepting bonds held in trust for specific objects, all receipts in money on account of assessments for benefit and advantage to estates by reason of the laying out, widening, discontinuance, change of grade or other alteration of streets, and also, of the city tax, the sum of thirty thousand dollars annually shall be appropriated to the purchase or payment of the capital of the city debt.

I would suggest whether in view of our rapidly increasing debt it would not be well to increase the sum to be set aside from the annual tax to fifty thousand dollars. With such active measures as the law authorizes for providing the means of paying our indebtedness, we are justified in taking a hopeful view of our financial condition. Two million dollars of the indebtedness are invested upon long loans at 6 per cent.; the balance of the floating debt or temporary loan we may reasonable hope to take care of without much trouble.

With reference to that part of the debt denominated the water debt, it is confidently believed that the income from this investment will not only pay the interest upon it, and the expense of maintaining the department, but furnish also a sinking fund by which the entire debt may eventually be retired.

George W. Wheeler, Esq., for so long our City Treasurer, hav-

3

ing declined a re-election, now retires from the responsible office he has so honorably filled for twenty-two years. I may be permitted to express my sympathy in the rich reward he enjoys in the benediction of a constituency he has so long and so zealously served, and the hope that the new calling upon which he is about to enter, health and prosperity may attend him.

SEWERS.

In addition to the work necessary to be done to complete the sewers already commenced and in process of construction, I deem it proper to advise you of certain contingencies which may make it necessary to take immediate action, and at a very considerable cost, in order to protect ourselves against the consequences of what has already been done. It is feared, when the waters of Mill brook below Fox's factory are diverted into the new channel that the low lands east of the Providence and Worcester Railroad and south of Lafayette street, will require draining as a sanitary precaution.

The present sewer from what is called the Piedmont district, empties into Mill brook below Sargent's card factory, and when the waters of this brook are diverted, there will be no means of carrying the sewage off. Deposited upon this low land and remaining there it would be likely to breed a pestilence in that neighborhood. It will therefore probably be necessary to extend that sewer through this low land, so as to connect it with the main sewer at or near Cambridge street.

It may also become necessary to provide a remedy for the mischief which our sewage is in danger of doing to the waters of the Blackstone river, into which it is in great part conveyed. Complaints, whether well or ill founded, are not infrequent from those who reside and do business along its valley that the stream is greatly polluted from this cause. If these apprehensions are well founded, the business of providing a remedy will deserve, as I have no doubt it will receive, your earnest and immediate attention. No argument is necessary to enforce the performance of the duty of self-preservation which we owe to ourselves. None should be needed to enforce the performance of that other duty " So use your own as not to injure another," which we owe to our neighbor.

The subject of providing means for utilizing our sewage has been heretofore discussed, and has been recommended as a profitable enterprise in a pecuniary point of view. Of this I have no knowledge, but I am advised by the City Engineer that a plan of utilizing the sewage can be adopted which is feasible, and which will at the same time relieve the Blackstone of the nuisance complained of, which plan will be submitted to your consideration if it shall be your pleasure to desire it. I would therefore recommend that an investigation of these matters be, as soon as practicable, entered upon with a view of providing a remedy, if one is required.

With the duty of providing for the payment of our present debt, and the liability there is that we shall almost immediately be obliged very considerably to increase it for our own self-protection, both in a sanitary and pecuniary point of view, it will be for you to consider whether it is the part of wisdom or prudence to undertake to put down any new street sewers during the coming year.

The following statement shows the amount of work done on sewers and Mill brook, and the cost of construction :

Of the work of arching and walling Mill brook, there remains 340 feet between Lincoln square and Court mills, and between Green and Cambridge streets, including both streets, 1336½ feet. Since the commencement of the work there has been built, year by year, the following amount of work :

In 1867 by Adam Dawson & Co.......... 1364 feet.
In 1868 by E. B. Walker............... 820 "
In 1869 "   "   .... 1571 "
In 1870 "   "   ... . 387 "
In 1870 by Dawson, Tank & Ingerson...... 1765.5 "
In 1871 by E. B. Walker............... 3043.5 "
        Total...................... ——— 8951

Of the above is open canal............... 4647 feet.
"   "   covered by arch........... 4078.9 "
"   "   " 5 street bridges...... 225.1 "
        Total... .... ——— 8951

Amount paid on Mill brook to 1871 .... $383,294 55
        in 1871 to Nov. 30.......... 75,721 37

Cost to Dec. 1, 1871........................ $459,015 92

This amount does not include sums paid for damages to estates, if any, paid by the Treasurer, without passing through the office of the City Engineer.

The balance of all contracts on sewers left over from 1870 were finished early in the season. The contracts for sewers for 1871 were awarded to H. B. Leach & Co., of Philadelphia, and to Leach & Son. Those let this year have not all been finished. Messrs. Leach & Co., and Leach & Son have now to finish 14,350 feet.

The amount of sewers now laid in the city is as follows :

Laid up to 1871...................... 95,465 feet.
    in   "   32,644   "
            Total....................
                                      128,109 ft.   or 24½ miles.

This includes all sewers which were laid previous to 1867 which are denominated " Old Sewers," and includes also two common stone drains used for sewerage purposes. The cost to Dec. 1st has been as follows :

Paid to Jan. 1, 1871................. $443,857 25
        Dec. 1, " 158,242 48
            Total.................... $602,099 73

This may vary from the treasurer's figures, for the reason above given under Mill brook. In each case the amount of cost given only includes bills audited up to Dec. 1, and is exclusive of any estimate of unpaid balances to the several contractors, on unsettled contracts, which will probably amount to $21,000.

The number of private drains now entering the public sewers is 1199; the number of drains entered this year is 383; the number of buildings on the line of the sewers is 2322. Connected with the sewers are 440 catch basins and 967 man holes. The basins hold about three and one-half cubic yards each, as an average, and the amount of sand, gravel and rubbish caught annually, by all these basins, carried in by showers and rains, cannot be less than about 5000 cubic yards, equal to about one acre three feet deep, or a building lot 200 feet square and three feet deep.

Our sewers need constant attention in order to prevent damages which may result to them from becoming clogged, and from other causes, and from damages which may accrue to others from their overflowing. They need frequent cleaning out, especially after heavy showers and storms. There is at present no officer of the city to whom this duty is especially assigned, and with our twenty four miles of sewerage there is no officer who can devote to this business the time necessary for it, without neglecting other important duties. I suggest for your consideration the propriety of appointing a person to the discharge of this duty, who shall also perform the duties of Water Registrar, which is also a service much needed.

WATER.

The operations of the Water Department for the past year have consisted mainly in finishing, as far as practicable, the reservoir dam, as ordered by the City Council, in laying water pipe, adding hydrants and service supplies and setting gates. The slopes of the dam will need dressing up in the spring, at a cost of about $1000. The grubbing has not all been accomplished and will need to be continued the present year.

The amount of water pipe laid during the last year was 35,200 feet. Thirty-eight hydrants and 504 service supplies have been added, and ninety-seven gates set, making the whole number of service supplies 3330. The City Council authorized the borrowing of $54,500 to be appropriated to the water department. The disbursements of this department during the eleven months to December 1st, have been as follows:

Reservoirs.........................	$41,388 74	
Real estate........................	4,632 65	
Construction.......................	66,338 95	
Total.....................		$112,360 34

As reported by the City Engineer.

There is also due and unpaid for work in this department about $8000. Cost of maintenance about $25,000.

Receipts—Water rents, $53,795.58; received for putting in water pipes to be credited on water construction account, about $8000.

A petition signed by quite a number of our citizens was presented to the last City Council, representing that under the present arrangement of our water supply the means were inadequate to furnish water to numbers of our citizens residing upon the higher lands, and praying that measures might be taken to remedy the difficulty. This petition received some attention from the committee to whom it was referred, but no result having been reached, it will probably require your attention. To supply this want it will require the laying of new service mains from the reservoir, a plan thought to be desirable by some, furnishing as it would another line of service mains, thus insuring a supply in case of accident to the present one.

The necessity and feasibility of this enterprise, the plans suggested for its accomplishment, the probable cost (about $167,000) together with other information connected with the subject, you will find in two communications made by the City Engineer in response to instructions from the joint standing committee on water, which will be embodied in the report of the engineer, and to which I respectfully refer you.

The subject of an additional supply of water for the city is one, which, if the demand continues to increase in the future as it has in the past, must sooner or later require the attention of the City Government, but I refrain at this time from entering upon its consideration.

HIGHWAYS.

It is incumbent on the public authorities to lay out and construct all such highways as the public necessity and convenience may require, and after that to keep them in a safe and convenient condition for public travel. We all know how much complaint has justly been made, within the last few years, of the deplorable condition of our streets and highways, and how much blame, naturally enough, has attached to the Highway Commissioner on account of it. But I think when we consider what various departments of our public improvements our streets are put under contribution to furnish accommodations for, how independent of each other these various departments are, and that upon the orders of any committee of these various departments, in the prosecution of the various enterprises committed to their charge a street may be dug up, blocked up, and rendered impassable half a dozen times a year, the wonder is, not so much, that they are in such miserable plight, but rather that they are in as good condition as they are.

There are seven different commissions, which have authority over the streets, as our mode of managing the various departments of the public work is at present constituted, viz: the committee on highways, the committee on sidewalks, the committee on lighting streets, the committee on water, the committee on sewers, together with the gas company and the horse railroad company. Each of these commissions is conducted and managed separately and independently of the others, without harmony or concert, and in the excavations necessary for laying pipes and sewers in the streets, and in many other ways, each incurs the expense of performing its work, when, if properly managed and conducted under one head, with one board of executive officers, a very great portion of the expense of doing the work might be saved, the work be better done, and the streets and highways kept in better repair. Thus, if a sewer, water and gas are to be introduced into a street, there is no reason why the work of excavation might not all be done at once.

I am of the opinion that the work now conducted under the direction of the joint standing committee on highways, the joint standing committee on sewers, the joint standing committee on water, the joint standing committee on sidewalks, and the joint standing committee on lighting streets, should all be committed to the direction of a Board of Public Works. I have not undertaken to state all, or nearly all, the reasons which force themselves on the mind in support of this change. The great enterprises of improvement which we are in process of establishing, calling as they do for the disbursement of more than half a million dollars annually, require more exact, systematic and judicious methods of execution than would ordinarily be required in enterprises of lesser magnitude. The old methods are entirely unsuitable. One executive head, to whom the people could look for a faithful execution of the duties of these various committees, would tend to create a sense of responsibility on the part of this department directly to the people, and would, more than anything else, prevent the enormous waste, which, by the best possible management under our present system, can not be entirely avoided, the work be better done, and the discomfort and inconvenience to the people, necessarily incident to the prosecution of these enterprises, very greatly lessened.

Having carefully examined this subject, and feeling the responsibility I assume in recommending this change, I am urged to do it by a sense of obligation to my constituents, and I can but express the hope that you may be so impressed with the desirability, not to say absolute necessity, of this reform, that it will receive your early attention, and that we may begin our operations of the spring under a newly organized administration of these affairs.

I may be permitted to add that I see no reason why the authority to inaugurate this change does not, under our ordinances, reside in the City Council, and that we need no new legislation to enable us to effect it. But if we should, it could probably be easily obtained, and the objects to be gained by the change are of sufficient importance to authorize the effort.

The following is a condensed statement of the operations of the Highway Department together with its property, resources, and disbursements for eleven months ending Dec. 1, 1871.

NEW STREETS.

Work has been done, as per order of the City Council, upon twelve different streets, six of which have been completed.

Amount expended by the city, a part of which, under the betterment act, has been or will be assessed upon abuttors, $19,946.98.

Amount of streets surveyed is 19,130 feet, or $3\frac{3}{4}$ miles nearly.

SIDEWALKS.

Curbstone, gutter and crosswalks have been laid upon forty-seven different streets, as per order of City Council, to wit:

Amount of new curb set...............	22,370 feet.	
" curb reset...................	6,939 "	
" return curb set.............	1,114 "	
" circle curb set.............	422 '	
Total number of feet set...........		30,845 feet.

Equal to 5 84-100 miles.

	SQUARE YARDS.	
Amount of cobble paving, new	10,832 6-10	
" cobble paving relaid	6,284 8-10	
" crosswalk paving, new........	2,725 1-10	
" crosswalk paving relaid	1,057 9-10	
Total amount of cobble paving laid..		20,900 4-10

FEET.
Amount of flagstone, new............. 5,613 5-10
"   flagstone relaid............ 50 4-10

Total amount of flagstone laid...... 5,663 9-10
Number of long corners............... 68
"   short corners.............. 101
Cost to city..................... $43,795 03

A part of the return curb, corners, flagstone and cobble paving has been furnished to private parties and has been charged accordingly. The number of feet of sidewalk grades set is 78,141, or nearly 15 miles.

SIDEWALKS—PRIVATE EXPENSE.

There have been laid for private parties 31 concrete and 481 brick and stone sidewalks and driveways, using 1054½ thousand brick, covering an area of 20,073 square yards of new brick walk and 2987 square yards of old walks relaid, making total number of square yards of brick walks laid during the season 23,061, costing

For brick and stone walks.............. $32,904 45
For 2438 square yards concrete walk..... 1,952 31

Total cost to parties:......... $34,854 76

Bills of which have been returned to City Treasurer for collection.

BLOCK PAVING.

Main street has been paved with small granite blocks, on that portion of the street near the estate of the late Ethan Allen, suspended in part last year, to admit of the construction of a sewer, an area of 951 1-10 square yards at $3.57 per yard, amounting to $3396 66. Also from Austin street to Chandler street, an area of 1729 6-10 square yards. Average cost per yard $3.61.— Amounting to $6245.30.

Myrtle street from Main to Southbridge street, an area of 420 square yards. Average cost per yard $3.29, amounting to $1383.35.

Union street under, between and fifty feet each side of the Boston & Albany, and Worcester & Nashua Railroad Companies' bridges an area of 722 6-10 square yards. Average cost per yard $3.49, amounting to $2522.30.

Pleasant street from Main to Chestnut, an area of 2156 **square**

4

yards. The small granite blocks have been laid in place of the rough cobbles with which the street was paved.

Average cost per yard, deducting the value of cobbles removed, $3.08, amounting to $6643.15.

SUMMARY OF ABOVE.

Total number of square yards laid during the season, at expense of the department, 5979 3-10. Average cost per square yard, $3.38. Total amount expended under the above orders, $20, 190.76.

An order was passed October 2, for paving Front street, north of the street railway track, between Church and Hibernia streets, with small granite blocks, and for the removal of the railway track to the center of the street, after it is widened under the decree for doing the same. The stone have been secured and are now on hand for doing the work, but the delay in the removal of the buildings made the execution of the order impracticable the past season. The work can be begun early the coming spring.

EXPENDITURES.

Salary, including clerk hire and teams for personal conveyance...................................	$2,291 67
Labor pay roll......................................	38,897 35
Live stock, horses and oxen, bought and exchanged	1300 50
Hay, grain, straw, etc.............................	4379 18
Shoeing	695 81
Tools and repairs.................................	3060 65
Lumber	1976 01
Worcester fire department, use of teams..............	1532 50
Labor, breaking roads, moving buildings, hired teams...	14,721 21
18,738¼ ft. curbstone, average cost per foot 53c........	9921 96
425½ ft. circular curb " " " 82c........	348 85
179 11-12 ft. deep " " " $1.50.........	268 87
2549¼ feet flagstone, " " " 25c.........	887 31
750 feet North river flagstone, including freight.......	244 13
Border covering and wall stone......................	311 24
2161¼ tons cobble paving stone at $1.00	2161 25
100 long corners.................................	501 50
20 short "	58 00
4089 8-10 square yards granite paving blocks at $2.60..	10,633 48
373 6-10 " " " " 2.25..	840 60
9976 pieces " " " "	545 56
Amount carried forward..................	$95,577 63

Amount brought forward...............	$95,577	63
Storage of block stone.................	70	00
1156 1-10 thousand bricks, including freight, at $13 70.	14,845	55
C. O. Richardson, setting curb, paving.&c...........	18,995	58
J. J. Randall, concrete paving..................	1,834	70
Powder, coal, fuse, &c...................	128	52
Water dep't, water at stables 2 years............	90	00
Freight on beach stone....................	72	50
Cement, pipe, &c.....................	253	77
Printing report 1870, blanks &c...............	44	60
Lime and cement......................	45	50
Advertisements for paving blocks.............	13	41
Expense and receipt books.................	14	00
Gas at stable........................	30	34
Stationary and postage...................	11	11
Filing saws........................	4	00
Medicine and attendance on stock.............	30	85
Incidentals	116	24
Amount advanced on granite paving blocks, now on hand for use another year, to be paid for by the square yard after they are laid.....................	8518	89
Total...........................	$140,697	19

RECEIPTS.

Appropriations:			
For highways.....................	$35,000	00	
For sidewalks.....................	50,000	00	
For block paving..................	20,000	00	
Total appropriations..............		$105,000	00

Sidewalks, private expense, 481 brick and stone walks and driveways..........	$32,902	45	
31 concrete walks................	1,952	31	
Total......................		$34,854	76

Live stock, horses and oxen sold.........	$800	00	
Water dept., labor and materials.........	285	94	
Sewer dept., labor and materials.........	1,463	25	
Public grounds, labor and materials......	275	10	
Schools, labor and materials..........	2,818	90	
Poor dept. for manure..............	300	00	
Fire dept. block paving.............	262	60	
Sundry persons, 102½M brick..........	1,004	10	
Sundry persons, labor and materials......	2,177	32	
Total......................		$9,387	21

Appropriations for new streets :

New Worcester hill......................	$1,344	71
Lafayette street, labor, etc................	1,389	05
Wilmot street labor, etc....................	1,087	70
Washington street, labor, etc.............	1,005	50
Front street labor, etc....................	3,556	62
Hanover street, labor, etc................	3,335	70
Salisbury street, McAdam................	2,456	95
Chandler street..........................	3,698	90
Piedmont street..........................	734	30
Seaver street.............................	281	90
Oak avenue..............................	447	65
Mechanic street.........................	578	00

Total..............................	$19,946	98
Total receipts......................	$169,188	95

RECAPITULATION.

Stock on hand Jan. 1, 1871...............	54,653	00
Stock on hand Dec. 1, 1871...............	58,139	24
Total appropriations.....................	$105,000	00
Excess of stock at close of year............ $3486 24		

RECEIPTS.

Rec'd for labor, etc., new streets...........	$19,946	98
Sidewalks. private expense..............	34,854	76
Livestock, horses, etc., sold..............	800	00
Labor for other departments..............	5405	79
Brick sold sundry parties.:..............	1004	10
Labor and material sundry parties.........	2177	32

Total earnings...............	64,188	95
Total receipts................	$169,188	95

EXPENDITURES.

Sidewalk, city expense....................	$43,795	03
Sidewalk, private expense................	34,854	76
Block paving...........................	20,190	76
New streets.............................	19,946	98
Ordinary repairs........................	21,910	06

Total expenditures.............	140,697	59
Unexpended balance.......................	$28,491	56

OVERLAYINGS.

Unexpended balance................... $23,491 36
Excess of stock........................ 3,486 24

Total...................... $31,977 60

. CHARITIES.

Among the many duties devolving upon us, none are more deserving our grateful attention than caring for the unfortunate
ones whom Providence has committed to our charge.

In our city, however, where labor is the rule and idleness the
exception, where the christian virtues are cultivated and intelligence disseminated, absolute pauperism, which is the consequence of vicious living, is rare. Our dependent poor, as a general rule, are those whom misfortune has overtaken in their pathway of life, and to such the hand of charity is extended with a
full realization " that it is more blessed to give than to receive."

There are many, however, to whom occasional aid is furnished,
which is rendered necessary by the dissolute habits and intempe-
rate life of those who are bound to provide. There is also a large
class of traveling vagrants who force from our charity a precarious
existence, simply by being vagrants. These lodge and are fed at
the station house for a night and then pass on. The thrift with
which our Poor Farm is conducted and the discretion with which
the department of the Board of Overseers of the Poor has been
managed during the past year, is highly commendable.

The report shows that there has been a very noticeable increase
of applicants from among those having military settlements, over
those of former years; and the number supported by the city at
the State Lunatic Asylum, fifteen, is three times as great as that
of last year.

The number having a legal settlement in Worcester, to whom
full support has been given during the year, is 99 ; average number supported at the city farm, 42; number removed to their
place of legal settlement, 45 ; number of state paupers sent to
the Monson alms-house, 57, which is some less than last year.

Temporary aid has been given to 291 families, composed of 863
state paupers, of whom 65 were too sick to be removed. 460
heads of families have applied for and received temporary aid, of
whom 101 had a settlement in this city, and 40 were miscellane-

ously settled. There have been fed and lodged in the station house at the expense of the city 2407 vagrants or travelers. 1120 orders, on various persons, have been issued and disbursed to the several applicants in various amounts as follows:

Cash allowances	$189	00
Fuel	732	75
Groceries	1,404	25
Furniture and clothing	90	26
Medicine, attendance and nursing	594	40
Transportation of paupers	204	71
Burial expenses	262	00
Insane hospital bills	1,560	57
Reform and nautical school bills	593	18
Books, stationary and stamps	117	38
Aid to paupers in other towns	185	32
Miscellaneous expenses	80	10

Total		$6,013 92
Salary of clerk, eleven months	$916 66	
" city physician	641 66	

Total expense of city department,	$7,572 24
Total valuation of the real estate, stock, tools, and household furniture	$50,897 32

In the above valuation of real estate, &c., $600 appropriated for the purchase of twenty-five acres of land recently added to the poor farm, is not included.

The total expense of the amlshouse department has been	$4,826 84	
Receipts from sales and board of truant school,	2,471 13	

Total		$2,355 71
Salary of superintendent and matron		$666 66

Total	$3,022 37
Expenses of city department	7,572 24

Total expenditure	$10,594 61

RESOURCES.

Appropriation by city council	$8,000 00	
Receipts from other cities and towns	1,067 35	
" " the commonwealth	2,183 77	

Total recipts	$11,251 12
Total expenses	10,594 61

Unexpended balance	$656 51

The number of inmates at present at the almshouse is thirty-three, which with the twenty-one boys at the truant school, the teacher, and members of the superintendent's family, make fifty-nine persons.

TRUANT SCHOOL.

The truant school kept at the almshouse, a kind of reformatory institution for the correction of a class of irregularities which develope in children, is in very efficient working condition. It is sustained and supported by an appropriation by the City Government, and may, perhaps, be classed among the list of our charities.

There has been expended in this department as follows ;—

Amount paid for board... , ...	$1,269 32	
Clothing and other expenses..............	409 52	
Instruction and supervision..............	366 66	
Total expenditure.............		$2,045 50
Received for boys labor.................	$93 00	
Net expense.................		$1,952 50
Appropriation	$3,000 00	
Unexpended balance....................		$1,047 50

CITY HOSPITAL.

A new public charity recently assumed by the City Government, under authority of an act of the legislature, approved May 25, 1871, authorizing the establishment of this institution, is the City Hospital.

The purpose of this institution is to provide a hospital for the reception of persons who by misfortune or poverty may require relief during temporary sickness. No example of our predecessors is more worthy our emulation than the spirit manifested by them in so nobly responding to the call for material aid in order to provide this asylum for the homeless and the stranger in our midst, disabled by accident or disease.

The enterprise, although yet hardly under way, has, during the short time it has been in operation, commended itself to the fostering care of the City Government by the relief it has furnished to the destitute and suffering.

The hospital is at present established in the Bigelow Mansion, corner of Front and Church streets, which has been rented for the purpose. The accommodations of the establishment are necessarily limited, and call is made for more commodious quarters.

I refer you to the report of the president and secretary of the board of trustees for suggestions upon this subject, and at the same time bespeak for this charity, which so forcibly appeals to our common humanity, your most generous consideration. It was necessary to incur expense in putting the building in a suitable condition as to the arrangement of its various apartments, and furnishing it for an asylum. The following statement from the report before referred to, shows the force of medical gentlemen under whose supervision it is conducted, the expense already incurred in its establishment and support, and other interesting information with reference thereto.

Previous to the admission of any patients, a board of consulting physicians was appointed by the trustees, consisting of Drs. F. H. Kelly, Merrick Bemis and Joseph Sargent.

Dr. J. G. Park was elected superintendent and resident physician, and subsequently admitting physician of the hospital, his salary being fixed at $700 per annum, in addition to office accommodations and board. Twelve visiting physicians were also invited to serve gratuitously, for two months each, the assignment and distribution of their attendance having been arranged as follows ;

Drs. R. Woodward and J. G. Park from the opening of the hospital to Jan. 1, 1872. For the year 1872, Drs. G. A. Bates and E. Warner from Jan. 1 to March 1 ; Drs. O. Martin and A. Wood from March 1 to May 1 ; Drs. H. Clarke and J. M. Rice from May 1 to July 1 ; Drs. J. N. Bates and G. E. Francis from July 1 to Sept. 1 ; Drs. T. H. Gage and H. Y. Simpson from Sept. 1 to Nov. 1.

Mrs. S. W. Whiting, a lady well fitted by experience and other qualifications, was chosen matron, and her compensation was fixed at $25 per month, in addition to board and room in the hospital.

A cook, a laundress, and nurses of course, must form a part of the *personnel* of the establishment, and their wages are among its necessary expenses. Of the number who have received the benefit of the hospital to December 1—sixteen in all—eight were males and eight females. Seven were natives of this state, one of Vermont, one of North Carolina, five of Ireland, one England and one Scotland. One was a clergyman, five were mechanics, one a laborer, one a child; of the females, five were house-keepers and three domestics. The trustees have the pleasure to acknowledge the receipt of several very acceptable donations, contributing some of them to the comfort, and others to the cheerfulness of the wards of the hospital.

From Edward L. Davis, pictures; from Mrs George Thrall, bed linen; from J. D. Chollar, sofa bed; from Dr. George A. Bates, pictures; from Mrs. Charles Tenney, pictures and sick chair; from Kinnicutt & Co., hardware; from H. Woodward, pictures.

Some of the above named articles are of the value of $30, or more, and whatever of them is least in a pecuniary point of view deserves honorable mention here, as an evidence of kindly sympathy for those whom sickness or misfortune consigns to a public hospital. From the organization of the board of trustees, in July last, down to the 1st of December, 1871, their expenditures have been as follows:

On the building..........................	$1,428 25	
Furniture, bedding, etc..................	1,890 64	
Total.......................		$3,318 89
Grocery bills, Oct. and Nov..............	$83 39	
Provision bills...........................	137 62	
Drugs and medicines.....................	63 00	
Payroll.....................:.............	214 76	
Incidentals...............................	42 76	
		$541 53
Total		$3,860 42

Small sums, for board, &c., amounting in the aggregate to less than $25, have been received by the trustees; but this money having been all appropriated towards defraying the incidental expenses, as set forth above, does not require to be more formally accounted for in this place. The estimated expenses of the hospital, on its present basis, for the coming year is in round numbers $6000.

5

Let me not dismiss this subject without a word of thanks to the individuals who have so generously contributed towards the equipment of the hospital.

SCHOOLS.

There is no duty which a member of the City Council assumes upon accepting the office which is more clearly to be discerned than the duty of promptly, liberally and with open hand providing the means of education to every child within the limits of his municipal jurisdiction. This duty is taught by the example of our forefathers, who early inculcated the idea, now by all intelligent communities conceded, that an enlightened and educated people are the bulwark and safeguard of a free government.   It is commended by the example of our illustrious predecessors in this municipal government.   It is so completely enforced by the arguments, addresses, writings and opinions of the most learned men of the present time, that the subject requires no additional confirmation from me.

The law intends that every child in our community shall have the right to an education freely, that every child shall be compelled to avail himself of this right, and that neither avarice, ignorance, poverty nor disinclination shall be permitted to stand in the way of the effectual accomplishment of this purpose.

Recognizing this idea, our school board, by thorough and exhaustive research, have attempted to seek out those children who have not voluntarily availed themselves of the means of an education, and by such authority as the law affords, compelled such as they have found to go to school.   In this way more than 100 children, who, for one reason or another, were being deprived of the means of an education, have within the past year been added to the schools.   By this effort, by the constant immigration of children from abroad, and by the ordinary and natural increase of our resident population, the necessity for additional school accommodations is beginning to be seriously felt.

More than a year ago, a petition was presented to the City Council, asking that the Mechanic street burying ground be appropriated as a site for a school house, at *that time* represented to be necessary to supply a demand for further school accommodations.

This application, for some reason, has met with no response, although I am informed the necessity is constantly increasing.

It may, perhaps, be supposed that when the High School House shall be occupied, this pressure will be relieved, but I believe it will be found that even with the accommodations which the High School House will afford to the High School, (for it is intended to accommodate none but the various departments of that school) the other schoolhouses will be insufficient suitably to accommodate our present numbers. And when it is remembered that certain rooms now occupied for school purposes are pronounced by physicians to be unsuitable and unhealthy, that some of the rooms are already overcrowded, that our numbers requiring school accommodations are steadily increasing, that additional accommodations for the drawing school, required by law to be furnished as a branch of our educational system, are required, and that by the sale of the schoolhouse on the common we are deprived of our accommodations there for two hundred of our pupils, the need for further school room becomes more and more apparent, and leads to the conclusion that if not absolute now, it will probably become so by the time it can be furnished, even if we should begin at once to provide for it.

The law makes the school committee " *the original judges of the necessity of having additional accommodations.*" Common courtesy would seem to dictate that their judgment should be re-respected, and when they represent to us by petition that the necessity exists, and ask for the means of supplying it, ours should be the more grateful, as it is the less responsible, duty of granting the request. A carefully prepared report as to the feasibility of the plan of appropriating this burying ground for school purposes, may be found on pages 48, 49, 50 and 51 of the City Document for 1871. I recommend the matter for your consideration.

I cannot pass from the consideration of this subject without commending to the attention of all the report of our able and efficient Superintendent of Schools. It will be gratifying to know that a system of personal supervision as to the ability, progress and capacity for progress of each individual pupil in the graded schools has been organized, so that advancement to the meritorious is assured, and the constant effort is to keep our schools in the most effective working condition.

An evening drawing school for adults has been organized and
is in successful operation at the Belmont street school house.   It
furnishes to mechanics and artizans a course of instruction much
required and highly prized.   The need of such a school as this
became more apparent as the advantages of the Technical school
became more generally known.   The last City Government -ap-
propriated $2,500 for furnishing room and instruction for this
purpose.

The following statement shows the operations of this department during the past year :

RESOURCES.

Appropriated by city council.............	$125,000	00
Received from state and school fund......	2,013	76
" for articles sold...............	580	68
" from non-resident scholars.......	10	10
" for school books collected in taxes.	87	80
Total.....................	$127,692	34

ORDINARY EXPENDITURES.

Salaries of teachers.....................	$83,973	23
" superintendent and secretary.....	3,850	00
Fuel...................................	7,529	68
Books and apparatus...................	1,264	46
Janitors and cleaning..................	3,824	46
Repairs	4,353	80
Furnishings	728	86
Furniture	461	12
Printing and advertising...............	743	28
Rents................................	519	50
Miscellaneous.........................	859	29
Total	$108,137	35

EXTRAORDINARY EXPENDITURES.

Furnishing Belmont street school house, nine rooms, and nine rooms in other buildings, including furniture, heating apparatus and pianos	$7,494	74
Books and apparatus for new schools......	625	00
Furnishing for new schools..............	265	00
Furnishing two new school rooms in Lamartine street house,....................	427	26
Amount carried forward,.....,	$8,812	00

Amount brought forward......		$8,812 00
New school rooms and stage in Belmont street house................................	898 86	
New out buildings at Pond district........	700 82	
Grading lot—Ledge street house—balance..	193 50	
Ledge street stages, ante-rooms in hall—balance.......................:......	137 72	
New fence, New Worcester school house lot —balance	80 79	
New fence, Providence street school house—balance	78 48	
Woodland street stage and ante-rooms.....	95 94	
Expense on normal school................	81 25	
Insurance on school buildings............	103 40	
Concrete in basement of New Worcester school building......................	176 00	
Curbstone and sidewalks in street in front of Sycamore street and Washington street school houses...........	219 90	
Total.......................		$11,578 66
Total expenditures of the department for eleven months.....................		$119,715 98

The month of December would add but a small amount to this sum, except one more month's salaries.

The whole number of persons who have received instruction the whole or a part of the year is 9941, being a gain over the last year of 521.

The average number belonging to the schools the past year was 7024, being a gain over the last year of 639.

The average daily attendance was 6323, being a gain over last year of 790.

The whole number receiving instruction at the close of the year was 7145, being a gain over the previous year of 488.

The above figures include the evening and the drawing schools. The number in the day schools was as follows :

Whole number of different scholars registered, 9052 ; average number belonging, 6588 ; being a gain of 379.

Average daily attendance, 5945 ; being a gain 342.

Number in actual attendance at the close of the year, 6700 ; being a gain over last year of 228.

The number of schools at the close of the year, including four evening and one drawing school, was 141 ; an increase over the close of last year of 14.

The whole number of teachers at present employed in the public schools, including seven in evening and drawing schools, not employed in day schools, is 158; being an increase over the close of last year of 12.

The average cost per scholar on the average number belonging was $15,39.

There is over $1,000,000 of property in the possession of this department.

The High School House is now nearly completed, although there will be much to be done in the spring in the way of grading, turfing and ornamenting the grounds, fencing, etc. It is indeed a most commodious edifice, supplied with modern conveniences, arranged and divided into suitable apartments for study and instruction, equipped with a laboratory, library, etc., and in architectural design, elegance of finish and completeness of arrangement, is an object of local pride and admiration. It is perhaps the best and most expensive school house in Massachusetts. It will, when completely finished and equipped, cost not far from $200,000.

In the equipment of this institution the donation of our worthy citizen, Wm. Dickinson, Esq., of the bell, at a cost of $1000, the donation of our late mayor, Hon. Edward Earle, of the clocks, also at a cost of $1000, and the donation of Hon. Stephen Salisbury, of a grand piano, at a cost of $1200, have been most timely and reflect great credit upon the munificent donors. The grateful acknowledgement of our citizens, and of this City Government, are due to these gentlemen for their magnificent presents.

FREE PUBLIC LIBRARY.

The circulating department of the Free Public Library contains about 9,500 volumes and is constantly being increased by the addition of rare and valuable works of art, science and literature, as well as the lighter reading for pleasure seekers, as the means of the institution will warrant. It has also been the recipient by various donations during the year, of 415 volumes and 519 pamphlets and papers. Its advantages are being availed of by our citizens to an extent which shows how great a benefit this provision for the intellectual wants of our people promises. Between January 1st, and December 1st, 1871, the library has been open 281 days and there have been given out 62,954 volumes, making a daily average of about 224 volumes. The number of persons who have availed themselves of this privilege has been 2,019 in eleven months, against 1654 for the whole of the year 1870.

·The Green Library contains about 14,000 volumes. This is intended as a consulting library, and having, as it does, an available annual income of more than $1500 for the purchase of books, additions are being constantly made of the most elaborate and substantial works.

The officers in charge of this department have shown a most commendable appreciation of the wants of our busy working community of inventors, artizans and mechanics by making a liberal provision for their wants. To this numerous and highly intelligent class of our community, it will be a pleasure to know that arrangements have been made for the receipt of the new weekly volumes of specifications and drawings of patents issued at the patent office at Washington. These volumes are quite too expensive for individual subscription, are very elaborate in their drawings and specifications, and valuable for consultation and examination.

One feature of the Green Library, under its present management, deserves the highest commendation.

The librarian endeavors so to acquaint himself with the books of the library as to be able to direct all inquirers to the sources of information which they seek, thus furnishing a guide to the treasures of the collection. This is a most valuable service, and its appreciation is attested by the great numbers who have occasion to avail themselves of it.

The valuable library of the Worcester District Medical Society is also placed in the library building and is accessible to all, under the same rules which govern the use of the books of the Green Library. Probably more than 7,000 persons have sought information from the Green Library during the eleven months to December 1st. Certainly, this institution of individual and municipal bounty commends itself to your consideration in the full appreciation which these facts show it is held by great numbers of our citizens. The financial condition of this institution is as follows:

There are three funds, separate and distinct from each other, from which the library is supported. The Green Library fund, the reading room fund and the city appropriations.

Income for 1871 of Green fund.	$2,630 35	
¼ of income added to fund as per provisions of will........... ....:.....	657 59	
Balance of income appropriated for purchase of books...........................	1,972 76	
Total......................		$2,630 35

RESOURCES.

Cash in hands of city treasurer, Jan. 1, 1871	$257 69	
Appropriated for purchase of books....... .	1,972 76	
Total......................		$2,230 45

EXPENDITURES.

Expended for purchase of books..........	1,006 36	
Paid taxes ou bank stock...............	110 98	
Total........................	1,117 34	
Unexpended balance in treasury,	$1,113 11	

READING-ROOM FUND.

Bonds six per cent................................		$10,650 00

RESOURCES.

Balance last year........................	$191 60	
Interest...........	677 56	
		896 16

EXPENDITURES.

Subscriptions to periodicals and newspapers,	$842 94	
Postage.....................................	1 80	
Total...........................		$844 74
Unexpended balance............................		$24 42

CITY APPROPRIATIONS.

RESOURCES.

Unexpended balance, Jan. 1, 1871..................		$5,073 43
City appropriation, 1871.....................		8,000 00
Dog fund (city appropriation).....................		1,777 50
Total resources.........................		$14,850 93

ORDINARY EXPENDITURES.

Books ...., $1,300 63
Salaries and care of building............. 3,068 48
Other expenses........................ 1,846 00
                                    —————— 6,215 11

EXTRAORDINARY EXPENDITURES.
Alterations and repairs on building........ 4,079 80
                                    ——————
                                              $10,294 91

Unexpended balance.......... .... $4,556 02

POLICE.

From the best information which I can obtain, it is highly
necessary that the police force should be permanently increased.
The regular police force of this city to the middle of October
comprised but thirty men. After the Chicago fire, and when it
was believed that we were threatened with an influx of some of
the worst elements of humanity, the force was increased eight
men.

There are localities in the city, widely separated from each
other, which give the Police officers much trouble and which
require their vigilant attention. It is believed that, for the
proper protection of the city and its inhabitants against law-
lessness and crime, the present force is none too large, and,
unless otherwise advised by your counsels, my purpose is to keep
it up to the numerical standard of thirty-eight men, established
by the recent action of our predecessors.

By comparing our own force with the force of other cities, it
will be seen that ours is considerably smaller in proportion to ou
population, and that the cost of its maintenance is considerably
less.

Providence, with a population of 69,000, has a force of 143
men, at a cost of $139,000.

Lowell, with a population of 43,000, has a force of 38 men, at
a cost of $35,000.

Cambridge, with a population of 39,650, has a force of 50 men,
at a cost of $60,000.

Charlestown, with a population of 30,000, has a force of 36
men, at a cost of $41,000.

Worcester, with a population of 43,000, had a force of 30 men,

6

prior to the middle of October last and 38 men since that time, at a cost, for eleven months, of $25,724.16.

I would also suggest the propriety of providing a lock-up in the vicinity of the Junction depot, and another in the vicinity of Lincoln Square, at a moderate cost, for the temporary detention of offenders arrested in the night. By this arrangement officers would be able to remain more constantly on their beats, instead of occupying their time in conveying prisoners to the present station house.

The following statement will show the operations of this department, for eleven months, ending December 1st, 1871, together with its resources and disbursements.

Total number of arrests	2380
" poor lodgers	2014

The resources of the department have been as follows :

Appropriation by City Council	$28,000	00
Fees on warrants served by officers	4,080	00
Witness fees of police officers at municipal court	1,301	40
Extra duty of officers at balls and theatre	192	75
Collected on warrants for use of city teams	800	00
Total resources	$34,374	15

EXPENSES.

Pay roll of Police	25,042	700
Salary of marshal and assistants	3,529	13
Horse hire for use in department	1,342	50
Special police, July 3d and 4th	131	93
Special police convention Sept. 26th and 27th	291	62
Special police, eight men on duty since Chicago fire	1,078	00
Printing, telegraphing and postage	158	37
Food for prisoners and poor lodgers	206	44
Cleaning lock-up, station and hospital-room	157	11
Repairing in lock-up, station and hospital-room	83	24
Blankets for lock-up, station and hospital-room	23	25
Ice bill for season	19	12
Sundry small bills	34	84
Total expenditures	$32,098	31
Earnings deducted	6,374	15
Net cost of police department	25,724	16
Unexpended balance in favor of the department	2,275	84

FIRE DEPARTMENT.

The operations of this department of our municipal system, during the past year, have been highly satisfactory, the ordinary expenditures of the department within the appropriation, and the loss of property by fire much less than in previous years. The average loss of property by fire during the four preceding years, 1867, '8, '9 and '70, was $43,596 each year. The loss during the eleven months of last year was only $15,865. It is not too much to say that this great diminution in the loss of property by fire is at any rate in part attributable to the excellent organization of our fire department and the ample facilities for extinguishing fires, which we now possess.

The fire alarm telegraph which has been put in operation during the past year, it is believed, has already more than paid for itself by the facility which it has afforded in discovering the location of fires, thus .enabling the fire companies to put themselves on the ground with promptness and dispatch. Its cost was about $17,000, of which the city paid about $14,000 and the insurance companies the balance.

True economy in the management of this department consists in providing ourselves with every facility which the progress of the age can devise for the control of this destructive element. When we reflect upon the fearful conflagrations which have occurred during the past few months in the west, causing as they have such a mournful loss of life and property, we must remember with thankful hearts how mercifully we have ourselves been spared.

The following statement shows the resources and disbursements in this department to December 1st, 1871, not including the cost of the alarm telegraph:

RESOURCES.

Appropriation by city council	25,000 00
Received from highway department for use of drivers and	
horses...........................	1,532 50
Received for hose.......................	3 25
Total amount of receipts.......................	26,535 75
. Expense of the department to December 1st, 1871.....	17,388 73
Unexpended balance...........................	9,147 02

There will be due, Jannary 1, 1872, six months' pay for the men and other expenses, which will amount to about $7000.

Whole number of alarms............................ 37
Estimated loss.......................... $15,365
This department is composed of 3 steam fire engines, 12 men
  each...................................... 36
Five hose companies, 10 men each....................... 50
Two hook and ladder, 20 men each..................... 40
One hand engine(men)............................... 40
Drivers 2
Engineers 5
                        —

      Total of men............................ 173

There is also a hand engine located at Quinsigamond, with a company of volunteers, to whom the city has given during the past year $100. The city also owns six horses, used for drawing engines, and worked on the highways in summer.

UNION DÉPOT.

The last City Government, having been instructed by a vote of the people, made application to the last legislature to provide a remedy for the annoyance occasioned by the passing of railroad trains from the depot on Foster street towards the Junction across the streets and common at grade. This was a source of inconvenience which had occasioned much complaint for many years. The city solicitor, Mr. Nelson, prepared and presented a bill, which not only provided for the discontinuance of railroad tracks through that part of the city, but also for a union passenger station for all the railroads coming into the city. This bill passed both branches of the legislature. It left the railroad companies the option of agreeing among themselves upon the location for this depot, or in case of failure to agree, it provided that a commission, to be appointed by the supreme court, should settle the question.

Failing to agree, the court appointed a commission consisting of three gentlemen of learning, ability and experience, a majority of whom, after hearing the parties, reported in favor of the location on the line of the Boston and Albany road, easterly of Grafton street. This report after a full hearing, was accepted by the court, and it is understood that the Boston and Albany road are now projecting a plan for the erection of a station house at the place designated, sufficient for the accommodation of the various railroad companies.

At the hearing before the commissioners, there was a great diversity of opinion as to the most suitable place for this location but it having been finally, and I suppose it will be conceded, fairly settled by the commission, the great interests of the city require that it should now regarded as a finality, that the contemplated changes in the railroad accommodations be as speedily perfected as possible, so that the changes in business locations, if any, as most probably there will be some, may at once be begun, with a certainty that a settled purpose in this regard has been attained. Our citizens may congratulate themselves in the reasonable expectation of being relieved from the annoyance of which they complained, at no distant day.

Gentlemen of the City Council:

Our systems of water and sewer improvements have been designed and in part executed upon a comprehensive, and I might almost say magnificent scale. These improvements are now and for all time will continue to be a blessing to this community, and the time will come when all who enjoy it will unite in according to those who conceived the plan and had the courage to undertake its execution, hearty and universal commendation.

Such is the universal evidence which the history of enterprises of internal improvement, undertaken and accomplished, furnishes. The roads and aqueducts of Rome live among her imperishable glories, while her greatness as a republic is swallowed up in despotism. In the enjoyment of the advantages which our own improvements afford us, we to-day derive the greatest satisfaction, and for these, future generations who shall occupy these places will bestow their most fervent gratitude. Therefore to pursue to a consummation the purpose of supplying our city with water, and also of completing this arterial system of drainage, ought to be the aim of our city authorities until the work is done.

But how is this to be accomplished? How rapidly are we to pass on? To what depths of indebtedness are we to plunge? Is our accomplishment to have no limit so long as our credit is intact? These are questions that address themselves to practical common sense. A large class of our citizens are of opinion that these improvements should be prosecuted at once to their completion, and that we should continue to build so long as we can continue to borrow. Another large class are of opinion that the course of prudence is to continue to build, but to let our means of paying in some measure control the amount of our construction.

To these opinions the most respectful deference is due. It is for us to evolve from the conflicting evidences, if we can, what is the true course, and, being satisfied, follow it. I suppose it is a conceded fact that the result of the election, which places those of us who are new to government in charge of municipal affairs, was attributable, in part, to a growing sentiment of distrust in the community as to the propriety of recklessly enlarging our obligations without first providing some substantial means of their final payment, in part to an uncertainty as to the amount of our indebtedness, and in part, perhaps, to a suspicion that our improvements were costing us too much. Our constituents are looking to us to solve these problems, and there will be no better time than now to pause and consider what is the true policy, what is best and for the best interests of our city.

These are no holiday pastimes, but labors which call for earnest, honest effort. Having taken upon ourselves the most solemn obligations faithfully to perform the duties of our respective positions according to the best of our abilities, let us assume these responsibilities, determined to perform them openly, frankly, honestly and faithfully, remembering that " except the Lord keep the city, the watchman waketh but in vain."

In conclusion, I desire, in this public manner, to express my thanks to Mr. Mayor Earle, the other officers of the government, and to the heads of the departments for the uniform kindness and courtesy with which they have aided me thus far in the prosecution of my labors.

NEW WORCESTER SCHOOLS.

GENERAL COMMITTEE.—Messrs. Jaques and Draper.

GRADE.	PRINCIPALS.	SPECIAL COMMITTEES.
1st GRAMMAR,	C. H. Munger,	Jaques.
2d "	S. L. Carter,	Jaques.
SECONDARY,	Mary A. Slater,	Draper.
PRIMARY,	Mary A. E. Tirrell,	Draper.

QUINSIGAMOND SCHOOLS.

GENERAL COMMITTEE.—Messrs. Griffin and McCafferty.

GRADE.	PRINCIPALS.	SPECIAL COMMITTEES.
GRAMMAR,	M. J. Wetmore,	Griffin.
SECONDARY,	Anna C. Perry,	McCafferty.
PRIMARY,	L. E. Perry,	Griffin.

UNGRADED SCHOOLS.

GENERAL COMMITTEE.—Messrs. Newton and Whitcomb.

LOCATION.	PRINCIPALS.	SPECIAL COMMITTEES.
ORANGE ST.—Boys,	Geo. A. Adams,	Whitcomb.
" " Girls,	P. E. King,	Newton.

SUBURBAN SCHOOLS.

LOCATION.	PRINCIPALS.	SPECIAL COMMITTEES.
NORTHVILLE,	A. E. Clough,	Woodward.
TATNUCK,	Susan M. Forbes,	Gale.
VALLEY FALLS,	Mary J. Davis,	Ballard.
LEESVILLE,	E. J. Pratt,	Simpson.
BLITHEWOOD,	J. R. Raymond,	Simpson.
POND.	H. M. Johnson,	Simpson.
ADAMS SQUARE,	L. M. Harrington,	Woodward.
BURNCOAT PLAIN,	S. M. Maynard,	Ann B. Earle.
NORTH POND,	E. S. R. Kendrick,	Metcalf.
CHAMBERLAIN,	Clara Manley,	Metcalf.

EVENING SCHOOLS.

LOCATION.	PRINCIPALS.	SPECIAL COMMITTEES.
ORANGE ST.—Young Men's,	C. A. George,	Stone.
ELM STREET—Girls,	L. L. Newton,	Newton.
EAST WORCESTER—Girls,	Annie Brown,	Wheeler.

VOCAL MUSIC.

HIGH, GRAMMAR AND SECONDARY SCHOOLS—E. S. Nason, Teacher.

COMMITTEE—Messrs. Warner, Staples and Newton.

The Committee of Visitation shall exercise a general supervision over the Schools to which they are severally assigned, and shall visit them according to the provisions of the Statutes, not less than once in four weeks, and generally during the week preceding the monthly meeting of the Board, at which they shall report their true condition.—Rules, Chap. 3, Sec. 6.

Though each School is assigned to a special Committee, yet every member of the Board shall deem it his duty to watch over all the Public Schools of the City, to attend their examinations and visit them at other times as his convenience will permit.—Rules Chap. 9, Sec. 9.

SUPERINTENDENT'S REPORT.

To His Honor, the Mayor, and the School Board of Worcester :

In conformity to your regulations, I submit the following as my Fourth Annual Report.

The efficiency of public schools depends largely upon the sympathy and co-operation of parents and citizens. No intelligent sympathy and co-operation can be expected from those who are ignorant of what these schools attempt and what they accomplish. Information concerning them is due the citizen, that he may know how the public funds are expended, and how the foundations of the future city are being laid ; and especially due the parent, that he may know on what principles the education of his child is conducted. This information having been furnished, you may of right expect that your administration of a high public trust shall be carefully inspected. To adapt the schools to the wants and necessities of our city, requires constant and nice adjustment. The test of success or failure is an intelligent public judgment ; and such a judgment is possible only after close examination. Attention is, therefore, solicited to this account of what has been done the past year and what is aimed at for the future, and to the suggestions for still further increasing the efficiency of the public schools.

SUMMARY OF STATISTICS.

FOR THE YEAR 1871.

I. POPULATION.

Population of the city Jan. 1872 estimated,	43,000
Population, census 1865,	30,058
Population, census 1870,	41,115
Number of children in the city between the ages of five and fifteen, returned by the assessors, May 1871,	8,297

II. VALUATION.

Valuation of the city May 1871,	$38,141,250.00
Increase for the year	4,122,800.00
City debt, aside from investments,	372,309.98
City debt including cost of water works, and sewers and investment in B. B. & G. Rail Road,	2,459,900
Value of school houses and lots,	866,200.00
Amount assessed for state, county and city tax 1871,	686,933.85
Rate of taxation,	.0174

Ordinary expense of schools,		$108,137.35
Per cent. of the same to valuation,	.00284	
Per cent. of the same to whole tax,	16	
Amount for fuel, janitors, ordinary repairs etc.,	$20,314.12	
Salaries of teachers,	83,973.23	
Salaries of school officers,	3,850.00	
Extraordinary expense, including, permanent repairs, furnishing new houses $1,000, for Drawing School etc.,		$11,578.66
Amount expended in new houses and lots,		90,435.00
Whole expense for schools including cost of new houses, etc.,		$210,151.01
Amount paid the state towards Normal School,		15,000.00
Amount received from State School Fund for 1871,		2,013.76
Average cost per scholar for all schools for 11 months,		15.39
or a yearly rate of about,		16.78
Same last year,		16.75
Cost of Evening Schools 5-6 the usual time,		1,369.70
Average per scholar,		5.80
Cost of Mechanical Drawing School to March 1871,		1,500.00
Average per scholar, estimated,		6.00

III. SCHOOL HOUSES,

Number occupied Dec. 1870,	33
Number, Dec, 1871.	35

Completed and occupied during the year, Belmont St.
house and High School house, 2
Undergoing repairs, old High School house, 1
Rooms occupied Dec. 1870, 132
Rooms occupied Dec. 1871, 144
Whole number of sittings, 7817
In High School, 400
Additional space for 180,
Grammar schools, 1607
Secondary schools, 1627
Primary schools, 3681
Ungraded schools, 107
Suburban schools, 395

IV. SCHOOLS.

High School, nine rooms, 1
Grammar rooms, four grades 32
Increase, 1
Secondary rooms, two grades, 31
Increase, 3
Primary rooms, three grades, 59
Increase, 6
Ungraded school, for boys, 1
Ungraded school, for girls, 1
Suburban schools, 11

Northville, 2   Bloomingdale,
Tatnuck,   Adams Square,
Valley Falls,   Burncoat,
Leesville,   North Pond,
Blithewood,   Chamberlain.

Evening Schools, 5
Orange St. for boys ; Elm St. for girls ;
Shrewsbury St. for girls ; Summer St. for both sexes ;
Cambridge St. for both sexes.
Mechanical Drawing Classes, at Belmont St. 4

V. TEACHERS.

Male teachers in High School, 4
Female teachers in High School, 5
Male teachers in Grammar and Ungraded Schools, 6
Female teachers all grades below the High School, 133
Male teachers in Evening Schools, 2
Female teachers in Evening Schools, 9
Teachers in Mechanical Drawing Schools, males, 6
Special teacher of Music, male, 1
Graduates of State Normal School, 12
Graduates at our Training School, 33
Former members of the High School, 70

VI. PUPILS.

Number registered in the public schools,		9941
Increase,	521	
Number over fifteen years old,		412
Estimated number from this city in private schools here,		300
Average number belonging to the schools,		7024
Increase,	639	
Average daily attendance,		6322
Increase,	590	
Average daily absence,		702

Number at close of Fall Term, 1870,		6541
At the close of Winter Term, 1870-71,		6448
Decrease,	107	
At the close of Spring Term,		6058
Decrease,	390	
At the close of Summer Term,		6203
Increase,	145	
At the close of Fall Term 1871,		7145
Increase,	942	
Per cent. of daily attendance to average number belonging,		.903
Number perfect in attendance the whole year,		343
Number perfect three terms,		466
Number perfect two terms,		736
Number perfect one term,		1577

Whole number registered in the High School,	379
Boys, 155. Girls, 224.	
Average number belonging,	220
Average daily attendance,	214
Per cent. of daily attendance,	.93
Average age of pupils Jan. 1872,	16 : 10
Number of graduates June, 1871,	23
Average number of pupils to a regular teacher,	27.5

Items similar to the above, relating to the schools of each grade may be found in the secretary's tables accompanying this report. Your attention is also called to the course of study, which has been slightly advanced in each grade; to the questions for the written examinations near the close of the school year in June; to the report of the committee on the Truant School; and to tables showing the number and attendance, and the absence and tardiness of pupils in each of the public schools, the nationality of parents and scholars, the salaries of teachers, the amount expended for schools from 1850 to 1871, inclusive, the value of

school houses and other school property, and to the Roll of
Honor, containing the names of pupils perfect in attendance two
or more terms.

By a recent city ordinance the fiscal year ends Nov. 30th,
instead of Dec. 31st. The ordinary expense given above,
covers a period of only eleven months. It is slightly larger than
last year; while the average daily attendance of pupils has increased 490, and the average number belonging to the schools has
increased 639. Add the expenditure for the remaining month
and the yearly expense would be .0039 of the valuation and .171 of
the entire tax. These ratios, and the cost per scholar, are
almost precisely the same as last year.

SCHOOL HOUSES.

The Belmont St. house was occupied in May last; the new
High School house, the first of the present month. The former
was described in the last report. In this report will be found a
description of the latter, and an account of the exercises at its
dedication. These exercises were representative of sixteen
houses, built and entered within the last six or seven years in
such rapid succession as to leave no time for ceremony.

We have been criticised for opening schools in new houses too
soon; and it is better to have them thoroughly completed in
every part before they are used. But six hundred and thirty
nine pupils, the increase last year, must have room. The only
way to prevent this need is to stop the increase of children and
the growth of the city. Our friends in the City Council have
responded nobly to the yearly call, the last half decade, for a
house like that on Dix street. But if at the first they wait upon
our call only a little, while the children continue to multiply,
they must expect us to hurry them at the last.

No action has yet been taken to build the house on Mechanic
street, called for in last year's report. The only rooms at present unoccupied are two at Quinsigamond, inaccessible from any
other part of the city, two in the attic at Providence street, one
at Sycamore street, one lately finished at Woodland street, and
four in the old Summer street house.

The Front street house has been sold and must be abandoned
next July; the same number of pupils can be sent to Summer

8

street.   The room in the Library on Elm street must be given up,
and the two basements on Dix street ought not to be used.
The pupils might occupy three of the rooms in the old house
on Walnut street, if they were finished.   There remain, then,
two very inconvenient rooms at Providence street, one at Sycamore street, one at Woodland street, and what may be made
ready at Walnut street.   There is now a surplus of pupils in several
schools sufficient to fill half these rooms.   The influx in the
early spring will crowd them to more than overflowing.   Such
is the state of things, after increasing our accommodations last
year by fourteen rooms for about seven hundred children.

Ledge street house and Belmont street are crowded.   Lamartine street is crammed.   What are we to do with the five or six
hundred new pupils, as sure to come this year as the flood tide?
While the city grows she must build.

The old High School house should be put in order, and rooms
fitted up for the evening Drawing Classes.   A house on Mechanic
street, or some neighboring site ought at once to be commenced.
The growing population of the Island, so called, will require more
room before it can be provided.   Close upon the heels of these
enterprises, there are premonitions of an urgent need near Belmont street, especially if the Summer street house is sold.

SCHOOLS.

Early in the year, two new Primary Schools were opened on
Lamartine street, where there is an abundance of the younger
pupils, in rooms fitted up in the hall of that house.   Another .
was opened on Ledge street.   In May the four higher grades
were removed from Thomas street, to Belmont street; two
schools, grades sixth and seventh, from Shrewsbury street, and
one of grade fifth, from Front street, to Thomas street.   By this
means the double primary schools were divided, and two new
ones were opened on Shrewsbury street.   At the commencement
of the new school year, the last Monday in August, another
primary school was opened at Providence street, and the school
of grade seventh was removed to Ledge street.   All the schools
were removed from the old house on Summer street, to Belmont
street, the last double primary school was divided and a new
school was opened, and still another was formed at Thomas street.

A school of grade eighth, was also formed there. In pursuance of the plan adopted for the organization of the schools at - Belmont street, and in all the new and larger buildings, grade eighth was removed from Sycamore street to Woodland street. This arrangement secures a continuous gradation in the larger buildings, and leaves the more central rooms for the smaller pupils. About the middle of the autumn the crowded condition of the schools of grade fourth rendered it necessary to open another on Front street. The large attendance and multiplicity of classes at Northville compelled the opening of a new school there at the same time. As the new house was not ready at the commencement of the year, the High School temporarily, occupied the old Summer street house, all except the large entering class. This was quartered in the two rooms at Providence street, at Sycamore street, and subsequently a section in a room of the People's Savings Bank. All entered the new house on the second inst. The arrangement of our schools in grades may be seen in the course of study, further on. The studies in each grade were advanced last April, when the time of the annual examination was changed to June. The questions, also, for the written examinations at the close of the year, in the grades above the primary, indicate the range of studies in each grade. They are further intended, in some instances to suggest a line of study which may be profitably pursued.

EVENING SCHOOLS.

Two new evening schools have been organized this year; that at Summer street, and that at Cambridge street. There is an increasing demand for these schools; and the attendance is larger than ever before. The majority of pupils need instruction in the most elementary studies. Many are children scarcely fifteen years old, who work by day. Others, especially those at Orange street, are of maturer years, and some are well advanced in their studies. These schools must soon receive much greater attention. Stricter laws for school attendance will soon be enacted. Then the question of Evening Schools and Half Time Schools will become prominent; for there will be men and women to be taught, who see at length the need of the learning they did not acquire in youth; and " the poor ye shall have with you always," whose children must work. In the neighboring city of Fall River, one-half the youthful operatives in the mills, work in the morning and attend school in the afternoon, exchanging places with the other half, who attend school in the morning and labor in the afternoon. An arrangement like this, which the parent might make early in the year, would prevent all hardship in the execution of our law for school attendance. But the evening schools are not for the poorer class of scholars only. Like any other free schools they are open for any who have the desire to improve. These schools have been more encouraged and more successful than elsewhere, in the city of Providence where they were established as early as 1840. Last year in 6 schools with 63 teachers, they had an aggregate attendance of 1649, with an average of 609, for each of the twenty evenings the schools were in session. The sum paid for salaries was $5829, and the entire cost of these schools, which did not occupy the rooms of the day school, was $7000. Says the report "Were all the funds appropriated for public uses as judiciously expended, the tax payers would be more than satisfied."

As an example of steadfast perseverance, the case of a young man is mentioned "who has attended school for three winters, and during all that time has been absent but a single night. He is a printer by trade, and while engaged in his daily work, he has devoted his leisure moments to hard study. He has acquired a good knowledge of the English branches, and has made such proficiency in the Latin and Greek languages, as to be able to enter an advanced class in the Sheffield Academy, where he hopes soon to complete his preparatory course for college. " In another of their evening schools " two young men are preparing to enter college. "

In our evening schools the aid has been given mostly to individuals. They have been classified only in reading and partially in arithmetic. In the new schools an attempt has been made to give oral instruction illustrated with globes and wall maps, in the elements of geography, the continents, oceans, river and mountain systems, the location of principal places, lines of travel, and staple products, the climate, seasons, etc. ; in the outlines of grammar or language, the grand divisions of subject and predicate, with their modifications ; in physiology and hygiene ; and in the more common business forms, as well as in the principles of arithmetic, reading, spelling and writing. The teaching aimed at is concise and clearly illustrated ; and the facts stated should subsequently be written by the scholars in language of their own. This exercise produces a habit of close attention to the teacher, practises the memory, gives skill and accuracy in expressing ideas ; and with the criticism of the teacher upon each performance, it is the very best mode of teaching grammatical construction and spelling, for it is a practice in both. This attempt has been only partially successful, owing to the very limited proficiency of a majority of the pupils ; but the degree of success attained thus far, will warrant a further trial, especially with the more advanced pupils. A better classification, however, and more teachers are necessary for the highest success of these schools.

FREE EVENING SCHOOL FOR INDUSTRIAL AND MECHANICAL DRAWING.

REPORT OF SPECIAL COMMITTEE NOV. 25th, 1871.

To His Honor, the Mayor, and the School Board of Worcester.

The special committee, to whom was referred the question of opening an evening school for Mechanical and Industrial Drawing, in accordance with the statute on this subject, submit the following report :

On the 29th of Sept. 1870, resolutions were adopted by this Board, at the suggestion of a sub-committee who had investigated the subject, authorizing the establishment of an evening drawing school at Boynton Hall. Accordingly applications for admission were received, and a class was opened in October ; but the number who wished to avail themselves of its privileges increased so rapidly, as soon as the nature of the instruction was understood, that a second and a third class was organized in rapid succession. But not all these classes were sufficient to accomodate all who wished to attend ; and many were put off till the next year.

Items of interesting information concerning this school, may be found in the report of the public schools for 1870, and in an address before the social science association, delivered by Prof. C. O. Thompson in the spring of 1871. This school was the first established under the law authorizing such schools. It opened under the most favorable auspices, both because the Institute of Industrial Science located here, furnished able instructors, the necessary apparatus, and rooms fitted for the use of the school, and also because here, to a remarkable extent, the citizens, workmen and others, appreciated such a school.

It was therefore a model which other cities copied largely. The success was a credit to the city, and to those in attendance ; and the progress made by all the classes, was surprising to those familiar with what it was. What was an experiment fourteen months ago—to which we felt our way blindly—is now clear in the light of successful experience.

This school supplies a sensible want, and is seen to be useful by persons of almost every occupation. In connection with these schools, established throughout the state for the first time last year, either originating them, or originating from them, or in part both, a new interest in art education has been awakened ; art education, not only as cultivating the taste for the beautiful in architecture, in gardening, painting, etc., which are its less practical, perhaps higher forms, but also as tending to increase the products of industry, when applied to the varied manufactures of the state. The city of Boston has employed a distinguished teacher from the famous school at Leeds, in England, to superintend this branch of education in her public schools, at a salary of £500 ; and to this sum the state Board of Education adds an equal amount, in the interest of the state. This gentleman, Walter Smith, Esq., addressed the late meeting of the state teachers association in Tremont Temple on the subject ; and his remarks are printed at length in the November number of the Massachusetts Teacher.

He says, very wisely, that this education must begin in the public schools, and that the regular teachers are best situated for doing the work. But at first they themselves must be instructed, and the public interest in this branch of study, must be aroused ; and for these purposes, Evening Schools.

While this subject is receiving such attention throughout the state, it is evident that for us not to move forward is to fall behind ; and in this art educa-tion, so called for want of a less pretentious name, there is opened for cultivation a field whose profit, even in a material point of view, may be seen when we compare the countries neglecting it, with those which ha● given it the proper attention. Our school this year ought to be as much better than the last, as the course to be pursued is clearer in the light of experience.

At a meeting of your committee the propositions made in the last monthly report of the superintendent, relative to this subject were considered. The old High School house cannot be put in permanent order for any school purpose in less than two or three months ; and any temporary patching. up which might be accomplished would subject both the school and the workmen to great inconvenience. To use this house is out of the question.

The hall of the school house on Belmont street, and the ward room in the basement will furnish room for two large classes. A side walk is in process of construction from Lincoln Square to the house. The superintendent of the gas works has promised to carry pipes to the building, and no other expense need be incurred to put the rooms in readiness, except to pipe the house, which can be done at no very large expense, and perhaps, to put doors at the head of the stairs leading to the hall. These improvements are needful, aside from the drawing school, and will be permanent.

In occupying rooms of our own, some furniture will be needed, such as drawing tables, chairs and models. Tables similar to those in use at the Institute can be obtained. At least 100 will be needed, each with a chair such as may be bought for 50 or 75 cents.

A set of models consisting of ten pieces, more fully described by drawings and specifications prepared for this committee, is needed for this class ; a similar set is needed for each of the larger grammar schools.

The teachers employed last year may be secured for the present season at the same rate as last year. And the superintendent has been directed by this committee to engage them subject to the approval of the Board.

He was also directed to advertise for application to be made at his office by any who wish to become members of the proposed class.   *   *   *   *

About three times as many persons have sought the privileges of this school, as had applied at a corresponding stage last year. We are two months behind the time of beginning last year. Our furniture and apparatus are yet to be made.

In accordance with the above suggestions we therefore recommend ; the fitting up and use of the Belmont street school hall and ward-room ; the purchase of 100 drawing tables and chairs ; the purchase of a set of models for this school, and one for each grammar master ; to employ the same teachers as last year ; and to open such classes, to have 30 lessons each, two a week, as the exigencies of the case may require. And to put this subject in definite form, the following is proposed for action :

Resolved—That the superintendent of schools be directed to give notice of the opening of the Evening Drawing Class, in accordance with the foregoing recommendations ; and that he receive applications for membership, and, in consultation with the committee on drawing, organize as many classes as may be required, at a cost aside from furniture apparatus and fixtures, not to exceed $1500.

GEORGE W. GALE, ⎫ *Special Committee*
C. B. METCALF,   ⎬ *on Evening*
E. WARNER.   ⎭ *Drawing School.*

Worcester, Nov. 21st, 1871.

This school was opened in accordance with the above recommendation, December 4th, in the Belmont street house, because the rooms on Walnut street designed for its accommodation, were not ready. Under the direction of the special committee in charge, the sum of one thousand dollars was expended in fixtures for the ward-room and hall of that building and in furniture for the class. The tables in use have a cast iron pedestal with a revolving rod, fastened at any desirable height by a clamp screw, and supporting a small shelf for instruments, besides the leaf which can be placed at any angle. They were manufactured at the Washburn Machine shop at the Institute in this city. A simple set of models was also procured

consisting of ten pieces : sphere, cylinder, cone, pyramid, hexagonal prism, square prism, rectangular box, a hollow square with
sides 2½ inches square, and a ring of the same size 12 inches in
diameter. These, with a large variety of boxes and implements
of various kinds, constitute the apparatus.

Each student provided himself with a.board 18 x 24 inches in
size, four thumb tacks, paper, rubber, and hexagonal pencil of
similar hardness to Faber, No. 3. In addition to the above, the
class in Mechanical drawing require each a T square, adjustable
dividers with pen and pencil, a triangle, a scale, india ink, etc.—
the necessary cost not exceeding $4.50.

The number of persons who entered at the beginning, is 254 ;
of whom 201 were males and 53 females. Their ages were : — 76
from 15 to 20 ; 126 from 20 to 30 ; 36 from 30 to 40; 6 from 40 to
60 ; and 1 over 60. Of machinists there were 46 ; carpenters, 33 ;
teachers, 33 ; and the balance is distributed among 41 different
trades and professions. But since the organization there have
been changes in the classes which modify these figures. Fifty-two
were members of last year's classes. The average number present each two evenings is more than 200.

Four classes were organized :—

I. An advanced class in Free Hand.

II.   An advanced class in Mechanical Drawing.

III. and IV.   Beginners.

The first two, made up largely of last year's pupils, meet on
Monday and Tuesday evening at 7½ o'clock ; the last two on
Tuesday and Friday each week. After the first ten lessons in
Free Hand drawing, the beginners were re-classified about the
12th, inst; sixty took up mechanical drawing ; and two classes
continued Free Hand, one of fifty and one of about twenty.

The course of introductory instruction in free hand is as follows :—"Three lessons in horizontal and vertical lines, and plain
and ornamental forms composed of those lines. Three lessons
in curves. Two lessons in perspective. Two lessons in review.

For the first course of twenty lessons in mechanical drawing,
a good part of the time, say three fourths, is spent in
learning the elements of descriptive geometry. Descriptive
geometry *is* mechanical drawing in one sense ; that is, it is
the method of representing any object in horizontal and

vertical projection in any position. A knowledge of geome- try proper is of incalculable value as a preliminary, but is not indispensable. The problems to be given must be selected with great care ; and the aid of a blackboard so contrived as to show the two planes, is of great importance. The remaining lessons may be devoted to simple or complicated problems in construction, according to the proficiency of each pupil. It will be observed that this method of instruction differs widely from the one usually followed in classes connected with our voluntary organizations. That plan is to give the pupil certain arbitrary rules for producing certain results, and pupils are generally allowed to choose their own studies. This plan contemplates the mastery of the great principles of projection, so that the pupil can delineate any form he wishes, and put it in any desired position."

The mechanical class has gone on to more complicated studies in machine drawing, and the representation of a greater variety of objects. The advanced free hand class takes up more difficult groups, and develops the laws of perspective, shading etc. From the nature of the case the instruction must be general and aim at discipline, rather than specific, for the special benefit of par- ticular classes. It could not aim in forty-four directions at once.

These classes were visited in December by Walter Smith, Esq., late director of one of the best schools of art in England, at Leeds, and now superintendent of this-branch of study for the city of Boston and our own state. He commended the interest and progress of the class, and spoke of an exhibition of the work done in this school and others in the state, which will take place at some central point at the close of the season. A fine collec- tion of samples from the English schools, models, casts, examples, etc., presented by the British government, were at the same time displayed in Natural History Hall. These were visited by a large number of our substantial citizens—machinists, manufac- turers, capitalists, and workmen. Mr. Smith addressed them, and called forth many expressions of the need that has been felt of this kind of instruction, and the advantages to business flow- ing from it. He also addressed the whole body of teachers assembled for the purpose, and imparted a new impetus and a new interest to this regular common school study.

9

THE NORMAL AND TRAINING SCHOOL.

In organization, purpose and number in attendance this school continues as last year. Like all similar schools it has still to contend against the almost universal objection that young ladies have, to seeking a thorough preparation before engaging in the work of teaching. Too often they prefer the crowded ranks of mediocrity and small pay, to the almost vacant eminences in the profession, more difficult of access indeed, but crowded with salaries, honor, influence and extensive usefulness. This school is a constant protest against the round of dull drill and humdrum routine, into which teachers are so tempted to fall, and against the idea that inexperience and incompetency are tolerable in primary schools. The graduates of this school are all employed in the city excepting five ; two have been called to other cities , and two married. Their names are these :

1869, DELIA A. LATHROP, Principal.

Susan M. Buttrick,	Mary T. Gale,	Amanda M. Phillips,
Emma I. Claflin,	Carrie E. Gilbert,	Abbie J. Reed,
Louisa A. Dawson,	Emma J. Houghton,	Mary A. E. Tirrell,
Ellen E. Daniels,	Mary E. Kavanaugh,	Eleanor Watkins,
Eunie M. Gates,	Ella J. H. Knight,	Abbie A. Walls,
	Amelia J. Woodworth.	

1870.   Rebecca Jones, Principal.

Linnie M. Allen,	Julia M. Martin,	Esther M. Rice,
Anetta M. Chapin,	Maggie I. Melanefy,	Esther B. Smith,
Maggie E. Barton,	Mary L. Norcross,	Evelyn E. Towne,
Hattie W. Bliss,	Eliza F. Prentice,	Martha T. Wyman.

1871. Rebecca Jones, Principal.

Emma H. Barton,	Belle Y. Hoyt,	Flora J. Osgood,
Mary V. Callaghan,	Ida A. E. Kenney,	Alice M. Prouty.
Abbie F. Hemenway,	Emma J. Norcross,	

The Exercises of Examination and Graduation, June 28th, 1871, were :

MORNING.—9 o'clock—Opening Exercises.

	In room A.	B.	C.
9:15	Reading,	Reading,	Spelling.
9:35	Language,	Spelling,	Number.
9:50	Number,	Human Body,	Objects.
10:10	Place,	Number,	Reading.
		10:30—Recess.	
10:50	Spelling,	Music,	Animals.
11:05	Form,	Color,	Human Body.
11:15	Plants,	Animals,	Reading.

AFTERNOON.—Dix Street Hall, 2 o'clock.

Music—Chorus.
Essay—"Place, or Elementary Geography," Mary V. Callaghan.
Essay—"Size, Weight, Color, Sound and Objects," Abbie F. Hemenway.
Music—Instrumental—Belle Y. Hoyt.
Essay—"Reading, Spelling, and Writing," Emma J. Norcross.
Essay—"Language." Alice M. Prouty.
"Lesson with Children," Mary V. Callaghan.
Music—Song—Alice M. Prouty.
Essay—"Number," Flora J. Osgood.
Essay—"Form and Inventive Drawing," Belle Y. Hoyt.
"Lesson with Children," Emma J. Norcross.
Recitation—School Economy.
Essay—"Human Body and Animals," Emma H. Barton.
Essay—"Plants and Minerals," Ida A. E. Kenney.
PRESENTATION OF DIPLOMAS.
Music—Class Song.

GRAMMAR SCHOOLS.

The amount of study assigned to each grade of our schools is designed to be .what the average pupil will accomplish in one year. It is the design also, that each room should be occupied by a single class, all of the same grade. This plan has been generally carried out; but from want of rooms, and an excess of pupils in certain localities, it has been necessary to maintain double schools of the lowest grade with an assistant teacher and eighty or ninety pupils in each. All these have now been divided. In the more thinly settled districts on the other hand, at Quinsigamond and New Worcester, for example, there are not enough pupils in each grade to form a separate class; in these cases several grades are taught in one room.

The single class plan encounters the difficulty, that pupils who enter at the beginning of the year have not all the same attainments; for with our new houses, new schools, and growing population in certain sections, they are often collected from several schools; nor have they the same capacity. Some are capable of advancing more rapidly than the majority; others, not so fast. Still others are irregular in attendance, from sickness or less excusable causes, and fall behind. For the dull or the unfortunate pupil to fall back a whole year is discouraging; for the bright active pupil to jump a grade is a difficult feat. Moreover, it has been observed that pupils admitted in the middle of the year, find it difficult to go on with the class they ought to join, especially if they are dull, or backward as is usually the case with such irregular scholars ; and teachers ambitious to do well, very naturally do not desire to receive the dull pupils from the room above or, in the middle of the year, to send their brightest scholars to grace that upper room.

To overcome such evils as these, it was proposed a few years since to go over the studies of a year, in six months ; at the end of that time those qualified were to be promoted to the next grade; the rest reviewed the studies during the remainder of the year. A small class was promoted from each room ; these were scholars least needing the additional stimulus and most injured by it ; many of them subsequently fall back into their original grade. As a result of this effort three pupils entered the High School six months earlier, and at the end of the year joined the regular class from the Grammar Schools ; and of the three, two subsequently dropped out of the school altogether. Had this plan been successful with a majority of pupils it would have shown that the studies assigned for a year were only half enough.

Another remedy proposed is, to place pupils of two or three grades in the same room under one teacher. It is claimed that pupils receive a large part of their knowledge from hearing the older ones recite ; and that every one in the room will be fitted for one or another of the classes. But a scholar below the lowest class or above the highest, would as now be sent to another room ; and evidently the most advanced class could learn from none beyond them. It is at least questionable also how much benefit a boy may derive from listening to a recitation in one class while preparing his lesson for another. It is more than doubtful whether our schools would be more profitable if the classes in three rooms were divided and one third of each given to each of the teachers. The plan has been adopted, however, in some of the western cities. Each teacher is told to select the best pupils and prepare them for promotion as soon as possible. The effect is to expend more effort upon the best pupils who need it least and who from over study are more likely to be injured. And careful observers have seen in it a strong tendency to the "cramming" process which is the great evil of schools.

That our system of grading the schools was not perfect, is seen from those very attempts to improve it. To find a perfect remedy is not easy. In seeking to improve the organization of the schools, the end sought to be obtained by them must not be lost sight of. This end is discipline, development, mental growth and culture, and not the mere memorizing of facts, however numerous and important. This end can not be reached by any mere system, however perfect. It may even be retarded by too rapid progress. No amount of stretching will produce healthy growth in a twig. The gradation of schools is only an aid. For successful work there must be an intelligent teacher—a living force—stationed at every point. Nor should a system be constructed in the interest of scholars irregular, and frequently absent. Their number ought to be reduced by a law which will express the public sentiment on the subject; and for the unavoidable cases, provision might be made by a special school. For remarks on these subjects you are respectfully referred to the last report—titles, School for Special Instruction and Attendance Compulsory.

To give scope and comprehensiveness to the instruction, teachers are directed not only to cover the ground assigned to their own and the lower grades, but also as far as possible to take up collateral subjects, and by oral lessons and reference to things familiar to conduct the pupils over as broad a range as their minds can profitably contemplate. For this purpose, and for others partly specified and partly suggested, as well as to obviate the evils noted above, the Grammar schools have been re-organized upon the plan set forth in the following :—

RESOLUTIONS ON THE DUTIES OF GRAMMAR MASTERS.

To secure a better classification of pupils in the same building, to advance more rapidly those pupils who fall behind their class, and to obtain, as far as may be desirable, uniformity in the methods and plans of instruction and discipline in the several grades of school which occupy the same building, thus uniting them in one system,

Resolved, 1 That the Grammar Master having been provided with an assistant for his own room, shall, under the direction of the superintendent, assume the duties of principal of his own building, and such other rooms as may be assigned to him, and visit them weekly.

2. That he shall make himself familiar with the character, wants, and progress, of each pupil, and promote or send them down, as the best interest of the pupil and the general good may require, taking special care that no scholar lose his courage for want of suitable aid and encouragement.

3. That he shall direct the several assistant teachers in following the prescribed course of study.

4. That he shall report to the superintendent all cases of absence, delinquency, or failure to comply with the rules of the Board on the part of teachers ; and in case of the temporary absence of any teacher in his district he shall let the place be filled by his assistant.

5. That the duties of principal at the Thomas street school shall be performed by the lady teacher of grade eight so far as she may be able to assume them without an assistant in her own room.

EDWARD H. HALL,
GEO. JAQUES,   } *Special Committee.*
E. B. STODDARD,

Worcester, Nov. 7, 1871.

THE HIGH SCHOOL.

In this school in the new house we expect new life, new interest and new prosperity and progress. The indications are favorable. A larger number than ever before has this year been enrolled. A class of one hundred and sixty-five was admitted. The graduating class was larger than any within ten years. There seems a disposition on the part of pupils to be worthy of their privileges. But for the year the average attendance is low. This is in part due to the change of the school year in May and the interruption at the beginning of the Fall term. By the new arrangement of the Grammar Schools access to this school is simple and easy to those who desire it. Admission is governed by the pupil's record as well as by the result of his examination. Any applicant not admitted may rest assured that his best place for study is the Grammar School. The course of study aims to supply the wants of all classes as much as can be expected. The classical man can fit his boy for college here ; the mechanic for the technical school ; the merchant for the counting room ; and a limited choice is left for individual preferences. But here as in all the schools, the aim is and must be, discipline and not special preparation for any particular calling ; the object is to develop men and women, and not to instruct merchants or mechanics, doctors, lawyers, or ministers. For this special training, we now have the Technical School in one direction, and shall soon have the Normal School in another. The first two years in the classical course is the requisite preparation for the Technical School. This course of study appears on a succeeding page.

For many years the law has required that High Schools should be maintained in all the the larger towns of the state ; and from the earliest periods in our history, it has been the aim to raise the rank of the most advanced public schools, to the highest point attainable. This course has commended itself to the popular judgment. It is adopted universally in the states where a system of public schools has been in operation. But the conditions of society are changing; long established customs are from time to time abandoned; new theories of society and of government, the relation of labor and capital, and the rights of women for example, are advocated. The causes which gave rise to institutions long established, often disappear so effectually, that we do not trace to the beneficent influence of those institutions, the absence of the very evils they have eradicated, or see in them the origin of the good we enjoy. It would not be strange if among other things, the necessity for this higher public education should be questioned. It is therefore necessary occasionally to state the grounds for maintaining such a school, that it may receive an intelligent and not a merely traditional support.

For elevating influence upon the other schools the High School is indispensable. In the lower grades reading, spelling, writing, drawing, and the rudiments of arithmetic, grammar, geography, history and music are taught. These are invaluable in the practical affairs of common life; but the study of these branches of knowledge has a still higher value in this, that it leads forward, at every point, to what lies beyond. If the highest point in the public school system were the Grammar School, fewer than now would reach that point, and still fewer would go beyond. The limit of a boy's ambition is seldom reached; it is never surpassed. A knowledge of geography, of history, of arithmetic, creates a thirst for more. That thirst is not to be tantalized by a few drops only. The High School, attractive and attainable, invites to broader fields of study, arouses the ambition and stimulates the dormant energies of boys and girls at every stage below itself; and if they never reach its doors, they at least press further towards them. If any boy is not ambitious to reach this school, he cannot avoid the stimulating influence of another who is striving to reach it. Remove this school, and the usefulness of every other would be greatly diminished. In the second place, one half the three or four hundred pupils in this school could not, probably, obtain the same amount of education by any other

means. There are then about two hundred young people who by
this means start in life with a great and positive advantage.
They enter upon active duty with broader ideas, and powers
better controlled. We each, gentlemen, might have made more
of ourselves could we have enjoyed the privileges afforded the
youth of this generation. It costs the city a trifle to educate
these two hundred children, but the city is paid tenfold by their
intelligent influence as citizens ; and when we consider the value
of a cultivated life, and a mind appreciative of the true, the beautiful
and the good, in the past, all around us, and yet to be hoped for,
the reward appears infinite. And to such culture, the High
School tends. Again, half our teachers are from this school.
They might as well be educated at Academies, it may be said.
So might all education be done in private schools. But *would* it
be done there ? The public doubts, and so provides that it *shall*
be done. A high standard of education among teachers is
immensely important. If a man of the highest literary attainments, familiar with the best method of teaching, and with the
best schools in this country and in Europe, could be placed in
every school room in the land, a degree of progress and improvement would be seen, as marvelous as steam transportation and
telegraphs are in comparison with the old fashioned mail coach.
The intellectual activity thus awakened would show itself in every
shop, factory, and counting room, and at every bench and desk, in
greater skill, new products and increased values ; and the nation
would bound forward on a career of unexampled prosperity.
But these higher attainments among the numerous instructors of
our youth are possible only by raising the standard of universal
intelligence. "No great scholars arise from a nation of dunces ;
no great generals, from a nation of cowards." Shakespeare was
the product of a cultured age ; and Grant is an outgrowth of
American courage. The general excellence among teachers is
due to the High School. Without it the standard would sink to
mediocrity.

And again, besides the advantages to schools, to teachers and
to individuals, the High School is a great and positive benefit to
society ; and this, not only indirectly, by elevating the standard
of education, but by directly providing what is indispensable, a
well educated class. Civilization necessitates that work should

be done in great variety. Some kinds of work demand education that can be acquired in schools. Within the historic period this work of education has lodged in three distinct communities. In the earliest times, each family transmitted to its members the learning and the arts residing within itself. In later times societies and churches, men of like ideas or like faith, handed down the knowledge of their own inventions and traditions to those whom they wished to be their successors. Finally the public, a broader family, the most comprehensive society, takes up the work of education. In these days, the ancient family notion is an absurdity; societies with all harmony within, and no sympathy for outsiders, are an impossibility among busy men. We jump the bounds of party and creed, and we meet as men. Society, undertakes this work of education not from benevolence to the individual alone, but for self preservation. The results of High School culture, the trained boys and girls, are a necessity; therefore the High School must always have a place.

Twenty-three pupils graduated in May; six young gentlemen, and seventeen young ladies. Five had pursued the college course, ten the classical, and eight the English course. The order of exercises at the graduation was as follows:

PART I.

Music.

Latin Oration—Salutatory, · · · Henry Sargent Knight.
English Essay—Unfinished Work, · · Mary Elizabeth Deane.
English Essay—Looking Ahead, · · Annie Dickinson Currier.
French Version from Patrick Henry—La guerre inevitable,
George Woodward Brooks.

Music.

English Essay—Work, · · · · Lucy Lewisson
English Metrical Essay—Life Work, · · Ella Eudora Goddard.
English Oration—Nathan Hale, · · Samuel Adams Souther.

French Play,- -Jour de Mai.

Elizabeth Bacon, Martha Nelson Hooper, Mary Zurviller Coleman,
Nellie Julia Spurr, Kate Amelia Curtis, Ella Eliza Walker,
Alice Elizabeth Griggs.

PART II.

Music.

English Essay—Character, · · · · Mary Olive Hoyt.
German Version from Lamennais—Der arme Verbannte, Maria Louisa Rice.
English Essay—Sunshine, · · · Eliza Jane Seaver.
English Oration—Lessons of History, Charles Rensselaer Johnson.

Music. ·

10

English Metrical Version from Krummacher
                        Death and Sleep,   Emma Caroline Moulton.
English Oration—Memories,   -   -   Frank Edgar Aldrich.
English Essay—Water Lilies,   -   -   Jennie Lea Southwick.
English Oration—Old England and Young America,   Albert Smith Thayer.
                        Music.
    Valedictory Essay—Self Culture.   -   Henrietta Gertrude Aldrich.
    NOTE.—The parts are assigned without reference to rank, and varied merely to add interest to the programme.

    Award of Diplomas—In the absence of His Honor, the Mayor, by the Superintendent of Schools.

CLASS SONG.

WRITTEN BY ELIZA JANE SEAVER.

I.
Our boats, they are resting this side of the bar,
    Where we've coasted for many a day ;
And the zephyrs are waiting to bear us afar,
    Afar from our calm inland bay.
Now a song to the friends who have taught us to guide
    Our barks over life's troubled main,
Who have nerved us to stem the tempestuous tide,
    To work with the heart and the brain.

II.
Our school-life is closed, but our life-work's not done ;
    Far out on the billowy sea
There are rocks,—there are reefs,—there are breakers, beyond;—
    But the Saviour our Captain shall be !
Then quickly and gaily we'll pass o'er the bar,
    Setting out with " well-fortified breast ";
And may each of us carry a freight of great price
    To the gleaming abodes of the blest.

MANUFACTURERS AND EMPLOYERS.

    The proportion of pupils who do not attend school is not large in comparison with that of other cities. The faithful services of the truant officer, and the efforts of teachers, have prevented a great deal of absence. It is believed also that the truant school secures the attendance of many boys at school. Still, much remains to be done to secure for children the full benefit of our schools.

    At the opening of the Evening schools in October many children were discovered who were detained from school and employed contrary to law. The co-operation of manufacturers, and others, was sought in enforcing the law, by means of the following circular, addressed to all who were known to employ children. In

· almost every instance they responded cheerfully and without
· delay. About one hundred were forthwith sent to school in consequence of this circular, and the number now reaches at least
one hundred and fifty. Many of these desired of the superintendent permission to work till spring and then attend school; but
there seemed to be no anthority for thus setting aside a state
law. The parents were in many cases extremely poor. Such
as were in actual want were assisted by the overseers of the
poor. There seemed, however, to be no provision for those who
have no legal residence here. Application for aid was therefore
made to the benevolent section of the People's Club. They
responded at once, and their discriminating committee has
done excellent service in searching out the cases of real need.
Instead of furnishing assistance, they have taken the wiser plan
of interesting some benevolent person in each individual, or
better still, they have encouraged the needy to help themselves.

CIRCULAR.

OFFICE OF SUPERINTENDENT OF PUBLIC SCHOOLS.

WORCESTER MASS.

To Manufacturers, and all Employers of Children.

By the State Law, parents and guardians are required to send to school,
twelve weeks a year, all children between the ages of eight and fourteen years,
under a penalty of twenty dollars for each offence.

And no child under ten years of age shall be employed in any manufacturing
or mechanical establishment. No child between the ages of ten and fifteen
shall be so employed who has not attended some DAY school three months
or sixty school days within the year next preceding such employment, under
teachers approved by the School Committee, under a penalty of fifty dollars
against the employer, and against the parent permitting the employment.
See General Statutes, Chaps. 41 and 41, and Chap. 285 of the Laws of 1867.

The public schools are in session from the first of September to the first of
July, except one week in December, one in February, and one in May. Evening schools, also, are open from October to April.

In a single evening school a dozen children were found the present season
detained from school, and employed in violation of law. There were nearly as
many in each of the others. But these chileren wished to learn, else they would
not have been in the evening school. Ten times as many are kept in ignorance
who care nothing about it.

Prominent causes of this defrauding of the children are the indolence, avarice
or dissipation of parents, poverty and orphanage. To withdraw from such
parents the earnings of childish hands is a penalty only too light; and some way

must be devised for relieving orphans and the worthy poor; but neither of these causes ought to be allowed to keep a child in ignorance.

The school authorities are in duty bound to see that children are not thus cheated; and they rely upon your co-operation and the support of all good citizens in enforcing the laws on the subject in their broadest spirit. They presume that you, not less than they, recognize the right of every child to a fair amount of learning, and the necessity of his obtaining it for the safety of a state where the people rule. And you, perhaps better than they, know that intelligent laborers are the most profitable.

To aid in securing attendance at school you are respectfully requested

I.   To require of all children under fifteen years old, now or hereafter in your employ, a card* signed by their last teacher, containing the name and age of the child, the date of leaving school, and the number of weeks' attendance the year previous.

II.   To examine these cards regularly twice a year, on the first of September and the first of March, to see that the law has been complied with—calling attention to the time by a note in your calendar.

III.   To fix a placard† in some conspicuous place about your factory or counting-room, setting forth the requirements and penalties of the law, and signifying to parties who obtain employment and impose upon you in violation of its spirit that they will be reported to the legal authorities.

These placards will be furnished on application at this office from 8 to 10 A. M., and 12 to 1, or 3 to 5 P. M.

Any influence you may have, directly or indirectly, in informing parents and children of their duty respecting schools will be a public benefit. And parties neglecting the requirements of the laws referred to above will be prosecuted.

By order of the School Board,

ALBERT P. MARBLE,

Sup't. of Public Schools.

Worcester, Nov. 1871.

*This Certifies That

.... Age ....

Last Birthday 187   .

Dismissed from school 187   .

Attended year previous .... weeks,

between 187   , and 187   .

.... School.

Worcester, ... 187   .

.... Teacher.

† To Parents, Guardians and Children.

NOTICE.

The Proprietor of this establishment is liable to a fine of fifty dollars:—

I.   For employing a child under ten years old.

II.   For employing a child under fifteen, who has not attended school three months within a year.

III. Any Parent or Guardian is liable to the same fine for consenting to such employment.

IV. Any person having in his care a child between the ages of eight and fourteen years, who has not attended school twelve weeks within a year, is liable to a fine of Twenty Dollars.

V. Every case of a violation of these laws will be reported for prosecution.

THE SCHOOL YEAR.

The annual election of teachers and the promotion of scholars in all the grades has occurred near the first of May. The short vacation at that season, of only one week, gave no opportunity to secure teachers in place of any who might not continue ; and the general interruption of all the schools at promotion, was followed after a brief term by another interruption at the long vacation.   The election was therefore changed to July, the annual examinations to the last of June, and the promotions to the beginning of the year, the last Monday in August.   The last week in Dec. and Jan. 1st have also been made a vacation, instead of cattle-show-day, and the first two and a half days of Thanksgiving week.

TEACHER'S DRAWING CLASS.

Early in July applications were made by several teachers from this city and neighboring cities and towns for instruction in drawing. Prof. Gladwin of the technical school consented to teach a class, and notice to that effect was accordingly given through the papers. Fifteen or twenty of our teachers and several from other places joined the class, which was maintained at their expense. A similar class will be formed next July, provided the same teacher can be secured. In the early Autumn thirty-four teachers formed a class under the instruction of Mr. E. I. Comins. Including those in the evening classes, which still continue, about half the whole corps of teachers are now perfecting themselves to teach this study intelligently. We shall soon be ready to abandon any mere copying in the schools. Each master has already been furnished with a set of models for object drawing, which will now become general.

WHAT TO READ.

In a recent monthly report to this board the following suggestions were made : "Attention has recently been directed to the books which are read by the older pupils in our schools and to the opportunity for usefulness which teachers have, in giving their pupils a taste for good reading. Some children read books that are positively bad ; many read those that are useless to say the least; while others confine their reading to works of fiction exclusively with an interest which they might just as well find in books far more profitable, if only their reading were well directed and their taste properly cultivated. It would be interesting for any of you to stand at the door of the Public Library on Saturday afternoon and see what books the children read, in some cases such as are wholly unsuited to them ; often, not the best. Even the graduates of the High School would not all be found familiar with the best English writers of prose and poetry, though they read a great deal, no doubt. Why should they not know Prescott, Motley and Irving, Longfellow, Whittier and Tennyson instead of the last writer in the Ledger, Mrs. Southworth or Charles Reade ? The School Committee, parents and teachers should exert a positive influence in this direction ; for here is an important means of education, not to be neglected. The subject was referred to a committee who procured for each teacher lists of valuable books to be read, and a catalogue of the Public Library. The librarian Mr. S. S. Green has kindly furnished every facility in his power to teachers and pupils, to make the library available for their needs . And at a meeting of teachers, many of whom had already accomplished much in the same direction, the means of interesting the children in the best kind of reading were discussed. In the month of May a report of what has been accomplished in each school may be expected.

Children under fifteen years of age are not allowed to take books from the library ; the books are mostly designed for older people. It would be very profitable to organize a department in the library, for the use of children from ten to fifteen years old, to be open Wednesday and Saturday afternoon, and to be used by children on the recommendation of their teachers. The room in the west basement would be convenient for the purpose ; and such a department would tend to a larger use of all the others.

Copies of the Manual of Commerce, containing the description of many products of the earth and many articles in common use, the Childs book of Nature, the Nursery, and Our Youug Folks, magazines, have been placed in the schools. The first two may be used for general information ; the last two, for reading books.

In each of the larger schools there is now a small reference library. A similar library in the High School is of great value and is in daily use.

DONATIONS.

It is pleasant to record this year, as on preceding years, several gifts from liberal citizens, to our schools. A fine toned bell weighing 2000 pounds has been placed in the High School tower. It is rung daily as a signal for all the schools. This is the gift of Wm. Dickinson, Esq., and it is not the first instance of his genarosity towards our schools. An excellent tower clock, and electrine clocks in each room of the house, are the gift of Hon. Edward Earle, added to his untiring labor in the completion of the building. A magnificent grand piano was presented to the same school by Hon. Stephen Salisbury. A large part of the philosophical and chemical apparatus, now located in the convenient rooms provided for it, and put in excellent repair, was mostly a gift from the same gentleman, some years since. The library also receives a yearly addition from the income of the Bullock Fund which has been devoted to that purpose. Such donations have a significance beyond their pecuniary value. They evince a confidence in the schools, and a generous spirit in the community.

OTHER EDUCATIONAL INSTITUTIONS.

Our educational facilities are augmented by the Free Public Library, already mentioned; by the Antiquarian Library containing rare treasures for those capable of using it; and by the valuable cabinet of the Natural History society. A few private schools supplement our work and provide for such pupils as desire to pursue special studies not taught in the public schools, and for those whose attendance is interrupted by ill health.

The Kindergarten is applying the admirable theories of Frœbel, with an infant class too young for the public schools.

The Normal School house, a substantial stone building to be located east of Mulberry street, is now under contract, and will probably be ready for occupancy by September 1873.—another free school for the state.

The Technical Institute is practically for this city an additional free school of the highest order. This institution, and the others, attract hither a large number of students to receive superior instruction and the benefit of our libraries and lectures.

The following circular was addressed to the private schools and other institutions of learning in the city. The reports, are here tabulated.

OFFICE OF SUPERINTENDENT OF PUBLIC SCHOOLS.
WORCESTER, MASS, DEC 18, 1871.

Dear ....

The United States Commissioner of Education, in his last annual report, has suggested the importance of his receiving from the several States, statistics of private and incorporated schools, colleges, and other institutions of learning, as well as of the public schools. This would add greatly to the value of the Report. To furnish these, each town and city must contribute.

You are respectfully requested to fill out the following blanks, so far as they apply to your Institution or School, and return to this office at the earliest opportunity, with any additional statements you choose to make.

Yours Truly,
A. P. MARBLE, Sup't of Schools.

NAMES.	Incorporated.	Value of Real Estate.	Other Funds.	Rec'd for Tuition only	Teachers. Regular.	Special.	Whole No. Pupils.	Average Attendance.
Worcester Co. Free Institute of Industrial Science. C. O. Thompson, Principal.	1865	$200,000	$300.000	$800	8	2	89	87
Highland Military Academy, Boarding School, Young Men. C. B. Metcalf, Principal.		30,000	10,000	7,500	5	2	70	60
Oread Institute, Boarding School, Young Ladies. H. R. Green, Principal.		50,000		9,500	11	2	80	60
College of the Holy, Cross. Boarding School. Young Men. A. F. Ciampi, President.	1865	80,000			9	1	130	
Worcester Academy Boarding School both sexes. J. D. Smith Principal.	1834	100,000		2,400	4	2	99	50
Mrs. Southers School Mrs. F. T. Souther, Principal.	Private, Opened 1864			1,500	2	1	50	24
Kindergarten Mrs. Anna B.Knox, Principal.	Private, Opened Sep. 1871			375	2		32	25
Mrs. Bright's School. Mrs. J. H. Bright, Principal.	Private, Opened Sep. 1871			90	1		15	
Oread Grammar School.	Private,			2000	3	1	55	40
Total.		$360,000	$310,000	$24,165	45	11	620	346

Besides these, there are several private schools numbering from twelve to twenty or thirty pupils each, from which no returns were received.   About one half the whole and average number of pupils in these schools are residents of this city.

IN CONCLUSION.

It remains for me to congratulate you, gentlemen, on the degree of success which has crowned our labors the past year ; and to thank you for the uniform courtesy and kind consideration, which you have shown me.   I bespeak the same for the future.

Respectfully submitted,

ALBERT P. MARBLE.

City Hall, January, 1872.   *Sup't of Public Schools.*

11

SECRETARY'S REPORT.

FINANCIAL STATEMENT.

Appropriated by city council.............	$125,000	00
Received from state and school fund......	2,013	76
" for articles sold...............	580	68
" from non-resident scholars.......	10	10
" for school books collected in taxes.	87	80
Total.....................		$127,692

ORDINARY EXPENDITURES.

Salaries of teachers.....................	$83,973	23
" superintendent and secretary....	3,850	00
Fuel.......................................	7,529	68
Books and apparatus....................	1,264	46
Janitors and cleaning..................	3,824	46
Repairs	4,353	80
Furnishings	728	86
Furniture	461	12
Printing and advertising................	743	28
Rents..................................	519	50
Miscellaneous..........................	859	29
Total		$108,137

EXTRAORDINARY EXPENDITURES.

Furnishing Belmont street school house, nine rooms, and nine rooms in other buildings, including furniture, heating apparatus and pianos	$7,494	74
Books and apparatus for new schools......	625	00
Furnishing for new schools..............	265	00
Furnishing two new school rooms in Lamar-		

Amount carried forward......		$8,384

SCHOOLS.—SECRETARY'S REPORT. 79

Amount brought forward......		$8,384 74
tinest reet house.. *....................	427 26	
New school rooms and stage in Belmont street house..........................	898 86	
New out buildings at Pond district........	700 82	
Grading lot—Ledge street house—balance..	193 50	
Ledge street stages, ante-rooms in hall—balance................................	137 72	
New fence, New Worcester school house lot —balance.........................	80 79	
New fence, Providence street school house— balance.............................	78 48	
Woodland street stage and ante-rooms.....	95 94	
Expense on normal school................	81 25	
Insurance on school buildings.............	103 40	
Concrete in basement of New Worcester school building......................	176 00	
Curbstone and sidewalks in street in front of Sycamore street and Washington street school houses.............	219 90	
Total.....................		$11,578 66
Total expenditures of the department for eleven months.....................		$119,715 98
Unexpended balance, ...		7,976 36

EXPENDITURES OF THE SCHOOL DEPARTMENT.

From time to time we hear of extravagance in the expenditures of this department, and of a demand for reform.

We do not desire to assume that the administration of the affairs of this department is perfect, but we do challenge comparison with any other department of the city government. We assert that, for that great expenditure, the building of school houses, the board of School Committee are not, *but should be*, responsible. Under the provisions of our charter, although as our present Mayor has declared " the School Committee are the original judges of the necessity of having additional accomodations, " yet their responsibility and their powers there end ; they can only call upon the City Council to furnish those accommodations, and their character and all the details of the construction are left solely with them. A school house is needed in a particular locality, capable of accommodating a certain number of pupils. The City Council refers the matter to the committee on

Education of their own bodies. This committee know little or
nothing of what is wanted, except, generally, that they are
expected to cause a school house to be erected. Usually, they
have had no experience in the management or wants of our
schools, they therefore content themselves with securing the
services of some architect, who oftentimes knows as little as
themselves, of these wants to prepare plans and specifications.
These plans and specifications are submitted to this committee,
who issue proposals, and the contract is let to the lowest bidder.
The house is then to be constructed *nominally* under the direction of
this committee. I say *nominally*, for the history of the erection
of our school houses will bear out the statement, that in most
cases, this committee pay little or no attention to the matter, in
many instances no member of the committee ever visiting the
building while in process of construction. The contractors have
the fullest opportunity of completing their contract in the cheapest possible manner. That contractors have taken advantage of
this state of things, is evident to any competent person who will
examine some of the houses so constructed.

I have heard the remark made by a builder, that a man could
bid lower on a school house, than on any other building for the
work required by the specifications of the contract, for the
reason that he could do his work as cheaply, and put in such
material, as he saw fit, as he would not be looked after, and
many things could be left undone which this committee, not
understanding the details, would not discover, even if they made
an examination before accepting the building, which often is
entirely neglected, or made in so casual a manner that defects or
omissions are not discovered. And how can this committee be
expected to pay such close and particular attention to these
matters ? They receive no pay for it, and do not consider
that they were elected for that purpose. They were elected to
legislate, and not as overseers of work ; and besides it is considered by our people that the men who are elected especially to
look after all the educational interests of our city, should be
held accountable, and they are so held in the opinion of the
public, but are entirely ignored so far as the construction of
school houses is concerned. The houses and grounds finally
pass into the hands of the School Board to supply all deficiencies,

oftentimes to make extensive alterations, all to be paid for out of the appropriation for the support of schools. There has not been a house and grounds turned over to this department for the last seven years, concerning which the above statement is not correct. Now this is all radically wrong.

If any set of men are capable, or should be capable of judging what is wanted for the department, and for the interests they were elected especially to represent, certainly the School Committee should be, and should be held responsible therefor. It is a matter in which they have a special interest and the importance of which they are, in the discharge of their duties, made to understand.

A proposition has of late been brought before the City Council to take from the School Board all control over the repairs of the school houses, and the furnishing of supplies for the same, and add these to the duties of a " Board of Public Works, " who are to be charged at the same time with the care of the streets, sidewalks, sewers, water works, gas &c. &c. A board having all these duties would have but little time to attend to the hourly calls for repairs and supplies for thirty-eight school houses and the various wants of one hundred and forty-two schools. They, of course, could not attend to all this, and a necessity would arise for a new officer to be a " Superintendent of Public Buildings and supply agent. "

Such a man could, in time, of course so become acquainted with the wants of the school buildings and schools, as to do this work and attend to all these calls as well as they are now attended to, but such additional expense is not as yet necessary, and will become so only when we have grown to the size of the cities that have such special officers.

The repairs, furniture and furnishings for school houses are now supplied in the most economical manner by persons of many years' experience, and having facilities provided for the especial purpose. No city in the country furnishes its school rooms at less cost, for the quality of the furniture, than does this city. All is manufactured by the day, in our own department shop ; and all ordinary repairs are attended to at the same time, by men who know almost every brick or board in the school houses, and every stove, desk, or other article of furniture in each of the school rooms.

If you had a special officer to attend to this, he would also have to be provided with a base of supplies and some one to attend to the constant calls for the repairs of one hundred and fifty stoves, seven or eight thousand school desks and chairs, hundreds of settees, teachers' desks, tables, water pipes, pumps, broken glass &c. &c. &c.

So long as all these things can be attended to by persons within the department who by long experience are familiar with all the details, it can be done with much more ease, and at far less expense, than it could be by a board overwhelmed with other duties, or by a new officer or officers without that experience, to say nothing of the large additional expense in the way of salaries. I think it will not be unfair, and I certainly do not design to cast any reflections, if I illustrate the comparative economy in such work as done at present in this department, with that done by a committee of the City Council.

The cost of the ordinary repairs of *thirty-seven school houses and furniture* the last year was $4353.80. The cost of the repairs of the City Hall during the same time was $1500, one third as much as for all school houses, out-buildings, furniture and appurtenances. The City Hall is not as large as some of our school houses and is without yard, fences or out-buildings.

If this change is made will it dispense with any present office ? Most assuredly, No ! The School Board must have a Secretary, familiar with the details of the schools, location, grade, state of the schools as to numbers, the location of every street in relation to the houses, the names of one hundred and fifty teachers, the schools in which they teach, the grade of the school, and the qualifications of the applicants for the several grades, to answer innumerable questions for the information of teachers, parents and citizens, keep the records, reports and statistics required by law, the accounts with each teacher and school, audit all bills, procure and furnish all books, maps, charts, &c. &c., for schools, and generally assist the superintendent in the discharge of his duties.

The superintendent cannot do these things, as the educational interests of all the schools, and the internal policy and management in the school rooms, the advice to teachers and scholars, the cases of discipline and attention to the numerous requests, complaints and suggestions of parents and others, the procuring of teachers and substitutes, and numerous other important duties occupy all of his time and attention, without being obliged to attend to the material interests and details.

The amount of labor and responsibility required to successfully manage and care for the instruction of more than 9000 children is little understood and appreciated by a majority of our citizens.

Statistical Table showing the ...ber and Attendance of Pupils in the Public Schools, &c. For the Eleven Months ending Dec. 1st, 1871.

SCHOOLS.	TEACHERS.	Whole number registered during the year.	Males.	Females.	Average number belonging for the year.	Average attendance.	Per cent. of attendance.	Number belonging at the close of the year.	Number of cases of tardiness.	Average to each scholar, for one year.	No. of 1/2 days of absence.	Average to each scholar for one year.	Average age Jan. 1st, 1871.	One Term.
CLASSICAL AND ENGLISH HIGH SCHOOL.														
Walnut St.,	Abner H. Davis,	379	155	224	220.	214.	973	303	525	2.4	1314	6.	16.0	
GRAMMAR SCHOOLS. GRADE IX.														
Belmont St.,	Edward I. Comins,	64	26	38	43.5	41.6	956	45	79	1.6	762	17.5	15.	
Dix "	Addison A. Hunt,	78	36	42	42.	41.6	990	48	22	.5	163	3.9	14.8	
Woodland "	Samuel E. Fitz,	80	31	49	48.7	46.8	961	54	59	1.2	771	15.8	14.3	
Lamartine "	Charles C. Foster,	87	40	47	55.	52.9	981	65	63	1.1	450	8.2	14.5	
Ledge "	Henry M. Harrington,	65	40	25	45.2	43.6	965	43	242	5.4	645	12.0	14.7	
		374	173	201	234.4	227.5	958	255	465	1.9	2791	11.1	14.7	
GRAMMAR SCHOOLS. GRADE VIII.														
Belmont St.,	Vashti E. Hapgood,	42	24	18	37.	35.2	951	41	18	2.0	306.6		14.	
Thomas "	Harriet G. Waite,	65	27	38	43.4	41.6	958	34	99	2.3	736.7		13.9	
Dix "	Sarah E. Dyer,	60	29	31	42.5	40.5	953	42	37	.9	619.1		13.6	
...nd "	Mary F. Wentworth,	52	28	24	39.5	38.	964	43	39	1.0	705.4		14.5	
Lamartine "	Mary E. Eastman,	70	39	31	48.2	45.7	947	51	86	1.8	1002	20.8	13.8	
Ledge "	Mary F. Reed,	63	33	30	47.8	43.8	917	43	318	6.7	1596	33.4	13.8	
N. Worcester	Charlotte N. ...ger,	45	19	26	24.	22.5	937	33	83	3.7	609	25.4	13.6	
So. Worcester	Adella Hills,	57	40	17	24.7	22.4	915	40	132	5.3	926	37.5	13.1	
...and	...ra J. Wetmore,	45	23	22	28.	25.5	910	32	16	.6	995	35.5	13.2	
		499	262	237	335.1	315.2	939	359	828	2.5	7586	22.6	13.7	

GRAMMAR SCHOOLS. GRADE VII.

School	Teacher												One Term
Belmont St.	Mary A. Warren,	75	41	34	50.2	47.5	946	51	162	3.2	1072	21.4	13.6
Thomas "	Ann E. McCambridge,	68	38	30	34.	30.	882	47	300	9.	1596	46.9	13.2
Dix "	Eldora M. Aldrich,	68	38	30	19.	46.9	942	53	83	1.5	1166	23.6	13.3
Woodland "	Minnie S. Fitch,	38	19	19	32.7	31.2	954	37	10	.9	196	18.0	13.4
Ledge "	Joanna F. Smith,	67	38	29	43.	41.8	970	51	112	2.6	484	11.3	13.
Sycamore "	Ann S. Dunton,	62	24	38	42.4	40.8	964	48	59	1.4	648	15.3	13.3
New Worcester	S. Lizzie Carter,	47	22	25	28.1	26.2	934	36	124	4.4	766	26.9	12.
		425	210	215	280.2	263.1	940	323	850	5.0	5928	21.2	13.1

(6, 7, Grade)

GRAMMAR SCHOOLS. GRADE VI.

School	Teacher												
Belmont St.	Sarah W. Phillips,	69	41	28	43.6	38.9	892	52	256	5.9	1866	42.8	12.9
Thomas "	Mary A. Harrington,	50	32	18	41.3	39.	943	46	155	3.8	911	22.1	12.1
"	Laura L. ...n,	51	31	20	32.9	29.8	904	38	202	6.1	1224	37.2	12.3
Dix "	Ellen ...Mr,	57	34	23	44.8	41.2	920	53	112	2.5	1451	32.4	11.11
Elm "	Etta J. Rounds,	56		56	41.2	35.2	853	42	71	2.	2400	58.2	12.11
Sycamore	Carrie A. George,	58	37	21	40.2	38.2	951	52	92	2.3			2.7
Lamartine "	Mary M. Lawton,	52	26	26	44.6	41.9	939	40	41	.9	1080	24.2	12.5
Ledge "	Mary A. Smith,	72	33	39	41.1	39.1	950	53	57	1.4			2.9
Union Hill	Maria P. Cole,	67	38	29	46.	843.	935	50	156	3.4	1200	26.1	12.3
Salem St.	Ellen G. Wheeler,	83	37	46	46.7	136.	932	49	255	5.5	1240	26.6	10.10
	Rebecca ...d,	57	21	36	39.	37.	950	41	106	2.7	792	20.3	13.4
		672	330	342	461.4	426.9	924	516	1503	3.3	13764	29.8	12.4

SECONDARY SCHOOLS. GRADE V.

School	Teacher												
Belmont St.,	Tirza S. Nichols,	64	32	32	50.5	47.	931	50	59	1.2	1365	27.0	10.5
Thomas "	Elizabeth H. Coe,	64	35	29	51.8	48.5	956	51	109	2.1	1317	25.4	12.2
Dix "	Kate A. Meade,	57	34	23	46.5	41.7	897	50	46	1.0	1900	40.9	11.9
Pleasant "	Carrie E. Gilbert,	54	25	29	44.6	41.9	939	51	94	2.1	1069	24.	11.3
Sycamore "	Carrie R. Clements,	72	26	46	43.2	40.2	931	60	73	1.7	1200	27.8	11.6
Woodland "	Mary J. Davis,	71	33	38	49.	47.	959	55	36	1.1	786	16.0	11.9

12

SECONDARY SCHOOLS. GRADE V. CONTINUED.

SCHOOLS.	TEACHER.	Whole Number registered during the Year.	Males.	Females.	Average number belonging for the year.	Average Attendance.	Per cent. of Attendance.	Number belonging at the close of the year.	Number of Cases of Tardiness.	Average to each Scholar for one year.	No. of ½ days of absence.	Average to each Scholar for one year.	Average Age, Jan. 1st, 1871.
Lamartine St.,	Nellie L. ...,	80	49	31	47.	42.3	900	53	136	2.9	1866	39.7	11.5
Ledge "	Charlotte N. Follett,	54	23	31	40.2	36.2	900	42	219	5.4	1592	39.6	11.6
Providence "	...th E. King,	65	25	40	49.3	45.	912	41	364	7.4	1720	34.9	12.1
Salem "	Mary A. E. Adams,	61	20	41	54.7	50.5	923	53	202	3.7	1277	23.3	11.4
Ash "	Helen M. Harlow,	65	35	30	42.2	36.4	867	39	217	5.1	2303	56.9	11.8
E. Worcester "	Harriet Hathaway,	45	22	23	42.5	35.4	846	32	589	13.9	2826	66.5	11.11
Edgeworth "	Hattie E. Clarke,	59	26	33	45.3	40.2	887	34	81	1.8	2030	44.8	11.7
So. ...er	Sarah A. Bigelow,	85	45	40	50.7	42.5	863	62	294	5.8	3247	64.0	11.11
Quinsigamond.	...a C. Perry,	64	29	35	37.8	32.6	863	46	98	2.6	2050	54.2	10.7
		9?0	459	501	699.5	633.2	905	719	2607	3.9	26548	38.0	116

SECONDARY SCHOOLS. GRADE IV.

SCHOOLS.	TEACHER.	Whole Number registered during the Year.	Males.	Females.	Average number belonging for the year.	Average Attendance.	Per cent. of Attendance.	Number belonging at the close of the year.	Number of Cases of Tardiness.	Average to each Scholar for one year.	No. of ½ days of absence.	Average to each Scholar for one year.	Average Age, Jan. 1st, 1871.
Belmont St.,	...ary,	54	28	26	56.	54.	964	52	12	.6	260	13.9	9.11
...as "	...ie F. Knowles,	56	24	32	56.	51.	917	45	51	.9	1995	35.6	10.7
Dix "	Elizabeth E. Daniels,	62	30	32	49.6	40.1	867	52	149	3.0	3790	78.2	10.5
Pleasant "	...ie H. ...as,	65	43	22	50.	44.6	893	56	98	2.0	2138	42.8	10.7
Sycamore "	...nie A. ...en,	58	35	23	49.8	46.6	936	49	97	1.9	1317	26.4	10.8
Woodland "	Linnie M. Allen,	58	37	21	50.9	45.9	902	54	107	2.1	1985	39.0	10.8
Lamartine "	M...da Parker,	90	45	45	54.2	50.4	927	61	86	1.6	1501	27.7	10.3
Ledge "	Margaret M. Geary,	58	34	24	43.	38.	883	55	251	6.0	1980	46.0	10.9

One Term

Teacher	School											
Agnes R. Dame,	Bice St.,	50	26	24	46.8	42.7	914	45	64	1.4	529	11.3 10.1 One Term.
Mary J. ...,	Ash "	52	25	27	48.	44.	937	51	111	2.3	1584	33.0 11.2
Sylvia N. ...,	Ash "	57	32	25	42.	38.	905	47	197	4.7	1592	38.0 10.5
Annie ...,	F. Worcester,	57	39	18	47.	40.	851	44	519	11.0	358.6	11.3
... S. Darling,	E. "	59	37	22	45.	40.	893	45	172	4.3	944.1	10.5
Adeliza Perry,	New Worcester,	51	31	20	45.	42.	880	41	214	4.8	1173	26.1 10.2
Ellen M. Boyden,	So. Worcester,	94	45	49	53.6	48.6	906	71	188	3.5	1970	36.8 11.9
... H. Day,	Front St.,	48	28	20	48.	405	863	43	167	3.5	0.0	10.9 15½ days.
		969	539	430	784.9	703.9	900	82483		3.0	26673	40.8 10.8

PRIMARY SCHOOLS. GRADE III.

Teacher	School											
Mary T. ...,	Bednt St.,	62	23	39	53.	50.1	1949	55	88	1.7	1151	21.7 9.8
Eunie M. ...,	" "	69	31	38	60.	52.6	876	62	112	1.9	2923	48.7 9.5
Rebecca Jones,	Dix "	178	88	90	165.9	143.	862	149	393	2.4	91	54.9 7.11 { Training School Grades 1, 2, 3.
Sarah M. Brigham,	Edgeworth "	76	29	47	57.8	51.3	887	63	388	6.4	2574	44.5 10.2
Julia M. ...,	Mon "	52	26	26	475	42.	884	46	348	7.1	2178	45.8 8.9
Josephine A. Hunt,	Pleasant "	51	24	27	50.	47.	940	43	108	2.2	1182	23.6 8.8
Sarah W. ...,	Sycamore "	60	25	35	48.2	45.	938	56	45	.9	1274	26.6 9.1
Lizzie C. Goodwin,	"	57	32	25	45.1	42.7	946	51	29	.6	992	22.0 8.11
... A. Dawson,	"	76	34	42	61.1	55.9	915	57	190	3.1	2050	33.6 9.11
Eliza F. Prentice,	Ldge "	91	47	44	57.	49.8	874	65	160	2.8	2858	50.1 9.6
Martha J. ...,	Providence "	65	33	32	50.2	46.6	927	54	107	2.1	1422	28.3 9.11
Emma J. Claflin,	Salem "	61	28	33	44.	41.	932	51	100	2.3	1191	27.1 9.
Helen M. ...,	Ash "	57	26	31	54.	49.	907	53	108	2.0	1980	36.7 9.4
My O. ...,	Front "	56	31	25	41.3	36.6	885	45	377	9.1	1847	44.7 9.11
Ella M. McFarland,	E. Worcester,	60	29	31	54.5	45.4	833	45	217	4.	3613	66.3 10.4 1, 2, 3, Grades
Ida A. E. Kenney,	New Worcester,	61	36	25	48.8	43.8	896	52	119	2.4	1980	40.6 7.4
Ann E. Hall,	So. Worcester,	64	34	30	476	43.2	908	53	216	4.3	1725	36.2 9.6
Martha T. ...,	"	71	39	32	48.9	42.9	878	57	327	6.7	2364	48.1 9.2
Leonora E. Perry,	Quinsigamond,	70	37	33	65.3	56.2	859	51	166	2.5	3613	55.3 7. 1, 2, 3, Grades
Abbie A. Welles,	Union Hill,	80	40	40	53.7	45.3	862	49	646	12.0	3335	62.1 7.2 1, 2, 3, Grades
		1417	682	735	1153.9	1029.4	898	1157	4214	3.7	49366	42.8 8.9

INTERMEDIATE PRIMARY. GRADE II.

SCHOOLS.	TEACHERS.	Whole number registered during the year.	Males.	Females.	Average number belonging for the year.	Average attendance.	Per cent. of attendance.	Number belonging at the close of the year	Number of cases of tardiness.	Average to each scholar for one year.	Number of ½ days of absence.	Average to each scholar for one year.	Average Age Jan. 1st, 1871.
Belmont St.,	Susie G. Gale,	70	32	38	50.3	47.5	92.7	58	169	3.4	1098	20.1	8.5
Thomas "	Amanda N. Phillips,	66	30	36	56.	49.	90.0	48	123	2.2	2681	47.9	8.7
Edgeworth "	Susan M. Buttrick,	69	34	35	58.0	51.1	87.0	59	349	5.9	3041	51.7	8.1
Pleasant "	Sarah A. Harrington,	52	31	21	47.1	42.9	91.0	48	77	1.6	1669	35.4	8.
Sycamore "	Emma F. Mh,	56	28	28	42.2	38.2	91.2	51	173	4.1	1588	37.6	8.2
Lamartine "	Mary E. Kavanaugh,	80	38	42	60.1	54.8	91.2	63	195	3.2	2088	34.4	8.8
Ledge "	Esther M. Rice,	83	49	34	52.2	43.3	83.0	54	75	1.4	3533	67.7	8.1
Provdience "	Sarah J. n,	56	34	22	45.	41.9	93.2	46	129	2.9	1537	34.2	8.10
	Evelyn e,	53	33	20	44.8	38.2	85.3	44	191	4.3	2594	57.9	8.5
E. Worcester,	Ĝie E. Putnam,	60	30	30	79.2	44.3	90.0	44	596	7.5	3073	38.8	8.9
" "	Hattie A. Smith,	52	29	23	48.6	44.2	91.1	48	136	5.6	862	33.4	7.10
So. Worcester,	Susan M. Forbes,	59	27	32	48.9	43.8	90.2	50	231	4.7	2014	41.2	8.1
Front St.,	Mary E. k,	66	26	40	55.	49.	89.1	54	371	6.7	2358	42.9	8.3
Ash St.,	Aie J. Reed,	57	20	37	50.2	45.7	94.6	47	87	1.7	1777	34.0	7.1f
		879	441	438	738.4	660.9	90.0	716	2902	3.9	29915	42.1	8.3 (Two Terms.)

SUB. PRIMARY SCHOOLS. GRADE I.

SCHOOLS.	TEACHERS.	Whole number registered during the year.	Males.	Females.	Average number belonging for the year.	Average attendance.	Per cent. of attendance.	Number belonging at the close of the year	Number of cases of tardiness.	Average to each scholar for one year.	Number of ½ days of absence.	Average to each scholar for one year.	Average Age Jan. 1st, 1871.
Belmont St.,	Ida C. Upton,	242	126	116	97.1	83.1	85.9	55	395	4.1	5502	56.7	6.9
" "	Eliza J. Day,	35	14	21	34.	29.6	87.1	35			251	51.7	5.6
Thomas "	Flora J. Osgood,	70	38	32	50.	42.9	85.9	58	237	4.7	1413	28.3	6.8 (6 weeks.)

School		Teacher												Notes
Thomas	St.,	Ide F. Hemmenway,	68	31	37	53.6	47.4	886	44	183	3.3	2438	45.5	7.11	1, 2, Grades.
Edgeworth	"	Hattie W. Ros,	85	47	38	61.	49.1	805	65	203	3.3	4473	73.3	6.10	
Pleasant	"	Emily M- Hsd,	50	28	22	47.5	43.9	924	41	55	1.2	1415	29.8	6.2	
Mason	"	Mary E. Pease,	48	27	21	45.	40.	900	46	311	6.9	1980	44.0	6.8	1, 2, Grades.
Sycamore	"	Nellie C. Hhas,	60	27	33	51.1	45.7	893	43	157	3.1	2138	41.8	5.1 0	
Woodland	"	Maggie I. Melanefy,	79	49	30	60.	52.	867	52	111	1.8	3144	52.4	6.9	1, 2, Grades.
Lamartine	"	Esther B. Smith,	84	43	41	56.	50.6	900	53	199	3.6	1836	32.8	6.4	
"	"	Eliza A. ook,	90	44	46	61.	58.2	954	52	144	2.5	1106	18.8	7.1	1, 2, Grades.
"	"	Belle Y. Hoyt,	68	33	35	57.9	53.8	927	55	128	4.4	794	27.6	6.2	Two Terms
"	"	Mary V. Calleghan,	79	46	33	55.9	50.1	886	67	90	3.2	1025	36.7	5.9	Two Terms
Ledge	"	Mary E. D. King,	60	32	28	65.	53.	815	51	401	6.1	4728	72.8	7.1	
"	"	Alice M. Prouty,	98	49	49	55.	46.	836	60	281	5.1	3546	64.5	7.0	
Providence	"	Harriet A. Harrington,	77	32	45	58.	51.	879	64	422	7.3	2772	47.8	6.4	
Salem	"	Emma H. Barton,	100	49	51	66.5	57.9	871	76	313	4.7	3423	51.5	6.2	
Ash	"	Abby Prtt,	74	34	34	62.	53.	854	67	404	6.5	3528	56.9	5.11	
Front	"	Mattie A. Collins,	73	40	33	96.1	84.3	878	64	456	4.7	4637	48.3	6.3	
E. Worcester	"	Aloysia Raffe,	87	40	47	79.3	66.9	841	72	239	3.0	2318	58.6	5.3	
"	"	Afia J. edf,	78	38	40	46.	40.1	860	52	384	8.3	2519	54.8	6.1	
Adriatic	"	Annetta M. Chapin,	93	50	43	59.7	55.9	936	70	164	2.7	1497	24.9	6.7	Two Terms
So.	Wer		1798	923	875	1318.2	1154.5	878	1242	5277	4.0	56488	46.5	6.5	

SUBURBAN SCHOOLS.

School	Teacher												
Northville	Abbe E. Clough,	60	31	29	44.9	41.3	933	50	163	3.6	1418	31.6	11.8
Tatnuck	My J. Packard,	50	29	21	36.	29.5	819	33	212	5.9	2561	71.1	10.10
Valley Falls	uSie A. Partridge,	77	38	39	43.	37.6	874	39	298	6.9	2128	50.2	7.11
Leesville	Ella J. Pratt,	47	31	16	17.	15.	882	19	137	8.1	788	46.4	8.2
Blithewood	Josephine P. Raymond.	24	13	11	16.	15.5	969	21	102	6.4	191	12.0	9.6
Bloomingdale	Hattie M. Johnson,	73	45	28	37.7	33.6	890	39	82	2.2	1624	43.1	10.2
Adams Square	Lottie M. Harrington,	45	32	13	26.5	22.7	894	35	227	8.6	1103	41.7	10.3
Burncoat	Lizzie M. Vaughn,	29	18	11	15.8	12.2	770	11	218	13.8	1318	83.4	11.1
North Pond	Emma S. R. Kendrick,	46	26	20	31.	27.	871	34	197	6.3	1564	50.5	11.2
Malin	Clara Manly,	23	11	12	19.2	17.2	895	17	63	3.3	784	40.8	11.6
		474	274	200	287.1	252.6	880	298	1699	5.9	13479	46.5	10.3

UNGRADED SCHOOLS.

School	Teacher											
Orange St., Boys,	George A. Adams,	152	152		42.4	38.2	897	34	160	3.8	1722	40.6	14.2
Orange St.,	Persis E. King,	54	48		31.7	27.5	866	33	194	6.1	2012	63.5	11.11
		206	200	6	74.1	65.7	881	67	354	4.8	3734	50.4	13.0

EVENING SCHOOLS.

School	Teacher							
Orange St.,	Carrie A. George,	355	355	169	80.	52.8		85
Elm "	Laura L. Newton,	169		95	46.	37.		45
E. Worcester,	Mary E. McFarland,	95		20	40.	38.		45
Summer St.,	Samuel Souther,	80	60		70.	60.		70
		689	415	284	236.	187.3	881	245

DRAWING SCHOOL.

School	Teacher							
Belmont St.,	Geo. E. Gladwin,	248	186	62	240.	200.		220

AGGREGATE.

High School,	379	155	224	220.	214.	973	237	525	2.4	1314	6.	16.10
Grammar, Grade IX.	374	173	201	234.4	227.5	958	255	465	1.9	2791	11.1	14.7
" " VIII.	499	262	237	335.1	315.2	939	359	828	2.5	7586	22.6	13.7
" " VII.	425	210	215	280.2	263.4	940	323	850	3.0	5928	21.2	13.1
" " VI.	672	330	342	461.4	426.9	924	516	1503	3.3	13764	29.8	12.4
Secondary, V.	960	459	500	699.5	633.2	905	719	2607	3.9	26548	30.8	11.6
" IV.	969	539	431	784.9	703.9	900	811	2483	3.0	26673	40.8	10.8
" III.	1417	682	735	1153.9	1029.4	862	1157	4214	3.7	49366	42.8	8.9
Primary, " II.	879	441	438	738.4	660.9	900	716	2902	3.9	29915	42.1	8.3
" " I.	1798	923	875	1318.2	1154.5	878	1242	5277	4.0	56488	46.5	6.5
Ungraded,	206	200	6	74.1	65.7	881	67	354	5.9		50.4	13.
Evening,	689	415	284	236.	187.3		245					
Drawing,	248	186	62	240.	200.		220					
Suburban,	474	274	200	287.1	252.6	880	298	1699	4.8	13479	46.5	10.3
	9989	5249	4750	7064.2	6334.5	903	7165	23707	3.5	23385	34.6	9.8

The number of cases of absence and tardiness in the Schools that have been in session but a portion of the year are calculated at the rate for a year, in the same proportion as for the time they were in session.

ABSENCE AND TARDINESS.

YEARS.	Average number belonging.	Number of cases of Absence.	Average to each Scholar.	Number of cases of Tardiness.	Average to each Scholar.
1867	5343	189,225	35.6	30.727	5.7
1868	5874	225,284	38.5	29,457	5.0
1869	6097	195,159	32.0	27,422	4.5
1870	6385	216,096	33.7	25,710	4.0
1871	6588	233,852	34.6	23,707	3.5

In the above table the scholars in the Evening and Drawing Schools are not included.

The absence of those scholars who are out of school for two weeks or more at one time is not included in the table, as their names are stricken from the registers and the absence not counted from the time they left until they return.

As the assumption is justifiable, from the examination of the returns of cases of tardiness in the several schools, together with well known facts, that the rule established last year has not been brought to the attention of all teachers, or has not been regarded, it is here repeated.

"At precisely the hour assigned for commencing school, the door of the school-room and dressing-room shall be closed, and all who enter after that time shall be reported as tardy—except such scholars as have the written permission from the Superintendent of Schools to enter at a later hour. No record of tardiness made as above directed shall be canceled, *but must be returned in the term report.*"

Only by following this or some other definite rule, universally, can any approach be made to that uniformity necessary, in order to compare one school with another, and find out where the evil does really exist to such an extent, as to demand unusual remedies.

It will be seen by the above report that there were 23,707 cases of tardiness and 233,852 cases of absence of those accounted as belonging to our schools during the past year. How much this evil has detracted from the usefulness of our schools I will not attempt to estimate. A part of this evil is of course unavoidable; but the great mass of it is without excuse, and should be remedied. This is not all, nor is it the principal evil to be contended against by the friends of education in this city.

The greater evil is the great number of children between the ages of five and fifteen, who are not represented in the average number belonging to our schools, but who are at this age kept at home, put out at work, or allowed to run at large.

The assessors of this city returned the number of minors between the ages of five and fifteen in May last, eight thousand two hundred and ninety-seven (8297). The average number belonging to our public schools the past year was seven thousand and sixty-four (7064) the number belonging to private schools was six hundred and twenty (620) six hundred and eighty four (684) of those in the public schools were over fifteen years of age. How many in private schools, I do not know, and to say nothing of the unascertainable number who are crowded into our schools before they are five years of age, there remains an average of *twelve hundred and sixty-one,* (1261) children in this city between the ages of five and fifteen who do not belong to our schools, or do not make themselves members, by their attendance. Now add the seven hundred on an average who are counted as belonging who are absent each day from school, and we have the alarming fact that in this city there are nineteen hundred and sixty-one (1961) out of school all the time the schools are in session. Is it not a mortifying fact that so many of our citizens so little appreciate the advantages for education so liberally offered to all, by our city and state? Everything possible is done to make our schools attractive, and to induce children to attend.

If we are to maintain our position as a highly educated community, there is still plenty of work to be done by the friends of education among us ; and if all other means fail, the safety of the republic demands that we protect ourselves against the ignorance which is the hand-maid of vice and crime and therefore destructive to all good government ; and that we protect ourselves by more rigid laws and a more rigid execution of them for

CUMPULSORY EDUCATION.

There are many persons, even in the city of Worcester, who look upon the enforcement of the law compelling the education of children as an infringement of the natural rights of parents. While most will admit that children should be educated, yet they are entirely opposed to having a truant officer to execute the law. "They are in favor of the law, on general principles, but are opposed to its execution."

But the practical opposition comes principally from parents' in many cases, idle and dissipated themselves, they desire to live on the small pittance earned by their children, when those children should be in school. There are undoubtedly many cases of poverty where parents really need all their children can earn to "keep the wolf from the door." Such cases should be provided for at public cost: it is a duty the state owe to its children.

But how many there are even among those who stand well in the community, who, if they see a truant officer leading a reluctant urchin to school, denounce the officer and the laws as tyrannical, or think that the boy should be persuaded to go, instead of being, as they express it, dragged along. They forget that powers of persuasion on such are of little avail. The very idea of compelling such a subject to learn to read, write, and cipher is to their minds tyrannical. They shut their eyes to the fact that the country swarms with vast hordes of children, heirs of penury, ignorance and crime, whose parents refuse to give them a chance of education which the public schools offer, but who, nevertheless in a few years demand and obtain as full rights of citizenship as the oldest and wisest men among us.

The state is an association of adults for mutual protection. A child is not a citizen except in embryo, he is utterly destitute of subjective choice and co-operation. The parent alone is responsible to God *and the state* whether it shall continue in ignorance, or whether, when it is of age, it shall take its place in the great association as an intelligent partner, or a brute.

The state in justice to itself should demand of every person claiming the right of citizenship at least an elementary knowledge of his duties; and as this knowledge must come from the volition of the parent, and not of the child, the state should enforce the rights of the child from the parent. So much for the claims of the state; now for the child. The little urchin to whose sensative shrinking from the tyranny which would compel him inside a school-room, and who enlists the enthusiastic sympathy of so many, came into the world without his choice. So far his parents have forced upon him starvation, vice and misery. His whole training has been compulsory. Back of his wretched family life,

13

stands the state power with its mysterious machinery of law and punishments ready to grind him to pieces if he infringe on them. The chances are ten to one that it will so grind him. The mill is ready; first the lockup, then the jail, then the penitentiary, then the gallows. Here all along is compulsion; his only chance of escape lies in the hands of his parents to give or withhold at pleasure, unless the state steps in by her officer. The child has a right to demand that he shall be made able, at least, to read the laws, which at the penalty of his life, he must obey. The question is one which now touches nearly our national life. This country is the receptacle for the ignorant and degraded from every land. It is for us to decide whether they shall be compelled, to accept for their children the help the state offers, to lift them to the level of intelligent beings, or be suffered to leave, like breeding barnacles, a weight and a mass of corruption upon us, which may sink us at last.

TABLE

Showing the Nationality of Parents of Scholars in the Public Schools.

School.	Teacher.	U. S.	British Provinces	Ireland.	England.	Germany.	Scotland.	France.	other countries
HIGH SCHOOL.									
Walnut St.,	Abner H. Davis.	233	56	3					
GRAMMAR, GRADE IX.									
Belmont st.	Edward I. Comins,	32	9	2	1		1		
Dix st.,	Addison A. Hunt,	44	1		1	1	1		
Woodland st.,	Samuel E. Fitch,	50	3	1					
Lamartine st.,	Charles C. Foster,	36	26		3				
Ledge st.,	Henry M. Harrington,	14	28				1		
		176	67	3	5	1	3		
GRAMMAR, GRADE VIII.									
Belmont st.,	Vashti E. Hapgood,	26	10	1	3		1		
Thomas st.,	Harriet G. Waite,	11	21			1	1		
Dix st.,	Sarah E. Dyer,	37	4		1				
Woodland st.,	Mary F. Wentworth,	38	5						
Lamartine st.,	Mary E. Eastman,	23	24	1		3			
New Worcester	Charlotte N. Munger,	20	22		1				
So. Worcester	A. Hills,	16	23		1				
Quinsigamond	Myra J. Wetmore,	17	12		3				
		213	128	2	10	4	2		
GRAMMAR, GRADE VII.									
Belmont st.,	Mary A. Warren,	41	6		4				
Thomas st.,	A. E. McCambridge,	17	30						
Dix st.,	Eldora M. Aldrich,	43	5	2	1	1	1		
Woodland st.,	Minnie S. Fitch,	31	4						
Ledge st.,	Joanna F. Smith,	16	34	1					
Sycamore st.,	Ann S. Dunton,	43	3		1	1			
New Worcester	S. Lizzie Carter,	22	7	4	3				
		213	89	7	9	2	1		
GRAMMAR, GRADE VI.									
Belmont st.,	Sarah W. Phillips,	29	15	2	4	2			
Thomas st.,	Mary A. Harrington,	25	16	3	2				
	Laura L. Newton,	11	26		1				
Dix st.,	Ellen Merrick,	38	7	1	5		1		
Elm st.,	Etta J. Rounds,	14	24	2	1	1			
Sycamore st.,	Carrie A. George,	37	11	1	1			1	1
Woodland st.,	Mary M. Lawton,	31	5	1	1		1		1
Lamartine st.,	Mary A. Smith,	3	40	2	5	1	2		
Ledge st.,	Maria P. Cole,	10	38		1		1		
Union Hill	Ellen G. Wheeler,	31	11	2	2		3		
Salem St.,	Rebecca Barnard,	28	12				1		
		257	205	13	23	6	9	1	2

School.	Teacher.	U. S.	British Provinces.	Ireland.	England.	Germany.	Scotland.	France.	other countries
SECONDARY, GRADE V.									
Belmont st.,	Lizzie S. Nichols,	31	14	1	1	1			
Thomas st.,	Elizabeth H. Coe,	22	27				1		
Dix st.,	Kate A. Meade,	27	17	2	4				
Pleasant st.,	Carrie E. Gilbert,	45	4		1			1	
Sycamore st.,	Carrie R. Clements,	41	17	1		1			
Woodland st.,	Mary J. Davis,	43	10	1	1				
Lamartine st.,	Nellie L. Moore,		42	2	1	8			
Ledge st.,	Charlotte N. Follett,	3	36	2				1	
Providence.,	Elizabeth E. King,	10	27	4					
Salem st.,	Mary A. E. Adams,	29	19	3		2			
Ash st.,	Helen M. Harlow,	12	16		5	2	4		
East Worcester	Harriet Hathaway,		31		1				
Edgeworth st.,	Hattie E. Clarke,	1	30	1				1	
So. Worcester	Sarah E. Bigelow,	18	34	3	3	3	1		
Quinsigamond	Anna C. Perry,	4	37		5				
		287	361	20	22	18	7		1
SECONDARY, GRADE IV.									
Belmont st.,	Esther G. Chenery,	40	6	2	3	1			
Thomas st.,	Abbie F. Knowles,	25	12	4		3	1		
Dix st.,	Elizabeth E. Daniels,	38	7	1	4	1	1		
Pleasant st.,	Addie H. Barnes,	49	2		3	2			
Sycamore st.,	Jennie A. Green,	28	12	3	5	1			
Woodland st.,	Linnie M. Allen,	33	12	4		1	1	1	2
Lamartine st.,	Matilda Parker,	5	37	8	2	6	1		
Ledge st.,	Margaret M. Geary,	6	44	2	2				1
Providence st.,	Agnes R. Dame,	7	28	6	2	1	2		
Ash st.,	Mary J. Mack,	6	40	2	1		2		
	Sylvia N. Stackpole,	13	23	2	3	5	1		
E. Worcester	Annie Brown,		44						
	Tamerson S. Darling,		44		1				
New "	Adeliza Perry,	22	10	6	3				
South "	Ellen M. Boyden,	19	39	8	3	2			
Front st.,	Libbie H. Day,	16	27	1		2	1		1
		307	387	48	30	25	10	1	4
PRIMARY, GRADE III.									
Belmont st.,	Mary T. Gale,	31	10	6	4	2	1		1
Thomas st.,	Eunie M. Gates,	19	32	4	3	3	1	1	
Dix st.,	Rebecca Jones,	89	30	10	12	5	1		1
Edgeworth st.,	Sarah M. Brigham,	5	50	1	1	1	1		2
Mason st.,	Julia M. Martin,	39	2	1	2			1	1
Pleasant st.,	Josephine A. Hunt,	41		1	1				
Sycamore st.,	Sarah W. Clements,	31	21	2		1			1
Woodland st.,	Lizzie C. Goodwin,	34	12	2	2				
Lamartine st.,	Louisa A. Dawson,	5	39	8	2	3			
Ledge st.,	Eliza F. Prentice,	8	51	2	4				1
Providence st.,	Martha J. Morse,	15	24	9	2	1	2		
Salem.,	Emma J. Claflin,	22	22	5		1	1		
Ash st.,	Helen M. Shattuck,	7	40	2		1	1	1	1
Front st.,	Mary O. Whitmore,	3	37	3	1		1		
East Worcester	Ella M. McFarland,		41	1	2				

School.	Teacher.	U. S.	British Provinces.	Ireland.	England.	Germany.	Scotland.	France.	other countries
New "	Ida A. E. Kenney,	20	17	12	2			1	
South "	Ann E. Hall,	17	26	1	9	1			
Adriatic	Martha T. Wyman,	8	30	6	7				
Quinsigamond	Lenora E. Perry,	17	28	2	4				
Union Hill	Abbie A. Welles,	32	11		2	1			
		443	523	79	60	20	10	3	8
INTERMEDIATE PRIMARY, GRADE II.									
Belmont st.,	Susie G. Gale,	35	12	5	3	2	1	1	
Thomas st.,	Amanda M. Phillips,	14	26	3	3	1			
Edgeworth st.,	Susan M. Buttrick,	3	49	1	1	1	1		1
Pleasant st.,	Sarah A. Harrington,	44	1	1		1			1
Sycamore st.,	Emma F. Marsh,	26	22	1	1				1
Lamartine st.,	Mary E. Kavanaugh-	4	32	14	6	5	2		
Ledge st.,	Esther M. Rice,	10	29	3	11				1
Providence st.,	Sarah J. Newton,	7	27	11	1				1
	Evelyn Towne,	12	13	17	2				
East Worcester.,	Carrie E. Putnam,		38	4	3				
	Hattie A. Smith,	1	43	4					
South "	Susan M. Forbes,	9	35	4	2				
Front st.,	Mary E. Trask,	2	45	2			3	2	.
Ash st.,	Abbie J. Reed,	6	30	8	2			1	
		173	402	76	35	13	7	1	5
SUB-PRIMARY, GRADE I.									
Belmont st.,	Ida C. Upton,	41	4	7	2	1			
	Eliza J. Day;	23	12						
Thomas st.,	Flora J. Osgood,	12	30	10	3	1		2	
	A. F. Hemmenway,	16	14	13	1				
Edgeworth st.,	Hattie W. Bliss,	11	48	1	1	2			2
Pleasant st.,	Emily M. Halsted,	39	2	4	1	1			
Mason st.,	Mary E. Pease,	28	8	10					
Sycamore st.,	Nellie C. Thomas,	24	12	2	1				
Woodland st.,	Maggie I. Melanefy,	32	15	1	1	1	2		
Lamartine st.,	Esther B. Smith,	5	24	14	2	7	1		
	Eliza A. Cook,	2	26	15	3	5	1		
	Belle Y. Hoyt,	7	27	13	1	6	1		
Ledge st.,	Mary V. Callaghan,	12	48	2	2	1	1		1
	Mary E. D. King,	7	40		2		1	1	
Providence st.,	Alice M. Prouty,	11	26	20	3				
Salem st.,	H. A. Harrington,	27	22	10	1	2	1	1	
Ash st.,	Emma H. Barton,	19	40	1	3	1	2	1	
Front st.,	Abby Pratt,	3	56	3	2	1	2		
East Worcester.,	Mattie A. Collins,	2	56		1				5
	Aloysia Radcliffe,	2	62	5	3				
Adriatic st.,	Maria J. Metcalf,	5	25	11	3	6			
So. Worcester	Annetta M. Chapin,	19	38	1	4				
		347	635	142	40	35	12	5	8

School.	Teacher.	U. S.	British Provinces.	Ireland.	England.	Germany.	Scotland.	France.	other countries
SUBURBAN SCHOOLS.									
Northville	Abbie E. Clough,	42	4	4					
Tatnuck	Mary J. Packard,	31	2						
Valley Falls	Susie A. Partridge,	13	11	7	7		1		
Leesville	Ella J. Pratt,	I		11	4		3		
Blithewood.,	J. P. Raymond,	18	1	2	2				
Bloomingdale	Hattie A. Johnson,	17	10	6	2			2	1
Adams Square	Lottie M. Harrington,	21	8	2			4		
Burncoat	Lizzie M. Vaughn,	16	13						
North Pond	Emma R. Kendrick,	33				1			
Chamberlin	Clara Manley,	17							
		209	49	30	15	1	4	2	1
UNGRADED SCHOOLS.									
Orange st.,	Geo. A. Adams,	4	29	1					
	Persis E. King,		32		1				
		4	61	1	1				
AGGREGATE.									
High School		233	56	3					1
Grammar IX.		176	67	3	5	1	3		
" VIII		213	128	2	10	4	2		
" VII		213	89	7	9	2	1		
" VI		257	205	13	23	6	9	1	2
Secondary V		287	361	20	22	18	7	1	1
" IV		307	387	48	30	25	10	1	4
Primary III		443	323	79	60	20	9	3	8
Int. " II		173	402	76	35	13	7	1	4
Sub. " I		347	635	143	40	35	12	5	8
Suburban		209	49	30	15	1	8	2	1
Ungraded		4	61	1	1				
		2862	2763	425	250	125	68	14	29

'The parentage oi children in the Public Schools for the last five years is as follows :

	1867	1868	1869	1870	1871
United States,	2448	2617	2742	2704	2862
British America,	224	288	277	387	425
Ireland,	2509	2547	2800	2888	2763
England,	174	209	205	257	250
Germany,	83	86	97	123	125
Scotland,	40	46	45	56	68
France,	10	9	13	9	14
Other countries,	6	20	21	30	29
Total,	5494	5822	6200	6454	6536
United States,	2448	2617	2742	2704	2862
Foreign countries,	3046	3205	3458	3750	3674

The above table does not include the scholars in the Evening or Drawing Schools.

The following tables are brought down to include the last year and republished. They show the rapid growth of the city and consequent expenditures. It will also be seen that the expenditures of the School Department have not increased at so large a ratio as have those of other departments.

The compensation of City Officers is stated as established or reported. Some of them have not been decided upon at present writing, but will not probably vary much, if any, from the figures given.

TABLE,

Showing the number of Schools, Teachers and Scholars, and the amount expended for the same from 1850 *to* 1872.

Year.	Schools.	Teachers.	Scholars.	Expense.	Cost per Scholar.	Expended for School Houses.
1850	35	55	2084	$19,009.11	$ 8.55	$12,282.57
1851	31	55	2037	14,007.65	6.87	11,785.91
1852	31	55	*	19,070.00		4,442.56
1853	33	60	1976	21,162.55	10.71	
1854	35	60	2251	24,505.62	10.81	9,634.26
1855	49	69	2564	29,915.59	11.24	9,813.41
1856	49	67	2520	29,992.00	11.90	2,053.47
1857	55	70	2815	32,280.00	11.82	4,100.00
1858	54	70	2919	30,504.09	10.45	4,346.49
1859	56	71	†3824	35,370.98	9.25	7,915.76
1860	59	76	3983	33,497.00	8.41	
1861	60	80	4023	33,771.00	8.39	9,963.74
1862	62	83	4198	34,581.00	8.28	4,500.00
1863	67	91	4418	36,383.00	8.23	19,191.34
1864	72	93	4537	46,210.00	10.18	
1865	76	94	4720	51,712.00	10.95	15,844.27
1866	84	103	4880	71,101.04	12.64	26,443.66
1867	96	115	5496	75,859.12	13.80	35,043.64
1868	109	124	6112	86,424.52	14.14	47,482.00
1869	116	138	6322	97,651.82	15.44	101,351.87
1870	128	149	6657	‡120,438.60	16.75	138,997.09
1871	141	158	7145	‡119,715.98	15.39	93,254.52

*There is no record of the number of scholars in the scholars for this year.

†Prior to 1859, the average membership of the schools is unknown, and the cost per scholar is reckoned on the average attendance. Since 1859, the cost per scholar is reckoned on the average membership for the year, which accounts for the apparent large increase in the number of scholars, and the apparent decrease of the cost per scholar for the few succeeding years.

The increased cost per scholar since 1863 is accounted for by the large increase in the salaries of the teachers, as well as the increased cost of everything pertaining to the expenditures of the department.

In 1850, assistant teachers in the Primary Schools received salaries of $150 each; they now receive $500. The highest salary paid female teachers in Grammar Schools at that time was $350 ; at present they receive $575 to $800.

As late as 1860, the salaries of female teachers ranged from $250 to $350 ; they now range from $500 to $800, not including the female teachers in the High School, who receive as high as $1000, and we have lost several excellent teachers for the reason that they could command better pay elsewhere.

But large as this increase is, it is more than equalled by the great increase in the salaries of other city officers, and the expense of the supervision of the other departments

‡ This amount includes the cost of permanent improvements in Old Houses.
The number of scholars given is the number belonging at the end of the school year.
The expenses for 1871 are for eleven months only.

TABLE.

Showing the Salaries of Officers of the City Governmeut
in 1850 and for 1872.

1850		1872	
Mayor, - - - -	$600	Mayor, - - -	$1500
Treasurer, - - -	600	City Clerks, - - -	2000
City Clerk, - - -	250	Treasurer, - - -	2500
City Physician - -	100	Auditor, - - -	1500
Highway Commissioner,	600	City Engineer, - -	2500
Assessors ($300 each), -	900	Highway Commissioner, -	2500
Solicitor, - - - -	200	Solicitor, - - -	2500
Clerk of Common Council,	150	City Physician, - -	700
Messenger, - - -	300	Assessors, - - -	3800
City Marshal, - - -	400	Clerk of Common Council,	250
Chief Engineer, - -	150	Messenger, - - -	1100
Sec. of School Board & Visit-		Water Commissioner, -	1200
ing Schools,	498	City Marshal, - -	1600
		1st, Asst. - - -	1150
	$4748	2nd, " - - -	1100
		Clerk of overseers of Poor,	1000
		Superintendent of Sewers,	1200
		Two asst. City Engineers -	2400
		Clerk in Engineers office,	1200
		Drafting Clerk, - -	1500
		Extra Clerk hire, -	5000
		Superintendent of Schools,	2500
		Secretary & Prudential Com.	1700
		Engineer of Fire Department,	500
			$42,900

TABLE
Showing the Expenditures of City Government
from 1850 to 1872.

1850, - - -	$75,304 20			
1851, - -	79,085 25			
1852, - - -	83,984 10			
1853, - -	88,068 87			
1854, - - -	136,644 87			
1855, - -	127,926 30			
1856, - - -	110,673 23			
1857, - -	116,949 19 .			
1858, - - -	99,050 51			
1859, - -	120,633 61			
1860, - - -	124,224 51			
1861, - -	120,551 20			
1862, - - -	128,393 99			
1863, - -	142,666 48			
1864, - - -	127,857 19			
1865, - -	286,846 78	Water, - -	$81,986 86	
1866, - - -	385,889 66	" - - -	107,318 37	
		Sewers, - -	2,118 49	
1867, - -	450,852 77	Water, - - -	87,814 20	
		Sewers, - -	79,745 00	
1868, - - -	543,366 68	Water, - - -	47,448 90	
		Sewers, - -	120,754 82	
1869, - -	845,922 34	Water, - - -	118,673 20	
		Sewers, - -	221,793 88	
1870, - - -	1,438,237 58	Water, - - -	150,463 42	
		Sewers, - -	369,746 00	
1871, * - -	1,245,264 94	Water, - - -	111,282 30	
*Eleven months.		Sewers, - -	254,657 34	

14

Table showing the location, size and value of the School Houses and School House Lots belonging to the School Department.

Location.	Material.	Stories.	Size.	Number of school rooms.	Condition.	Estimated Value.	Size of Lots Sq. feet.	Estimated value per foot.	Amount.	Total value of House and Lot.	Remarks.
Walnut st.,	Brick	3	130 × 87	20	New,	$150,000	31,672	$1 50	$47,508	$197,508	New High School building.
"	"	3	50 × 70	6	Old,	18,000	9,487	1 25	11,849	29,849	Old High School building.
Thas st.,	"	3	75 × 56	10	Good,	20,000	25,000	1	25,000	50,000	Hall in French Roof full size of building.
Dix st.,	"	2	96 × 60	20	New,	32,500	24,000	1	6,000	30,000	Hall in French Roof full size of building.
Woodland st.,	"	2	96 × 60	10	"	27,500	40,000	25	10,000	37,500	Hall in French Roof full size of building.
Ledge st.,	"	2	96 × 62	9	"	40,000	40,670	25	10,167	42,667	Hall in French Roof, also school rooms.
Front st.,	"	2	90 × 60	9	"	30,000	31,440	25	6,288	36,298	Hall in French Roof, two school rooms.
Lamartine st.,	"	2	96 × 60	8	"	26,000	27,000	20	5,400	32,400	Two L's 52 × 21, feet each.
Sycamore st.,	"	4	75 × 52	8	Good,	25,000	12,625	00	12,625	37,625	
Providence st.,	"	3	62 × 50	8	"	20,000	25,000	1 30	17,400	37,400	
Pleasant st.,	"	2	52 × 50	5	"	13,000	58,000	1 50	25,800	38,800	
Salem st.,	"	3	62 × 50	4	"	12,000	17,200	80	6,277	18,277	
Ash st.,	"	3	59 × 51	6	Fair,	13,500	12,555	25	4,020	17,520	
East Worcester	"	2	62 × 30	2	Good,	18,000	18,400	40	4,537	22,537	
Summer st.,	"	2	52 × 30	1	Poor,	5,000	18,150	50	3,624	8,624	Not now in use except for evening school.
"	Wood	1	51 × 48	4	"	100	9,060	50	9,150	121,150	Not occupied.
Front st.,	"	2	22 × 22	2	Fair,	5,000	1,517	15	758	858	House sold, to be occupied until July next.
Mason st.,	Brick	2	67 × 31	2	Good,	6,000	13,200	75	1,980	5,000	
Orange st.,	"	2	44 × 30	4	"	7,500	7,188	12	5,391	7,980	
Southgate st.,	Wood	2	50 × 30	6	"	3,000	25,000	20	3,000	12,891	
New Worces et	Brick	2	45 × 36	1	New,	10,000	14,900	10	2,980	6,600	
Quinsigamond	"	2	50 × 36	1	"	23,000	34,500	10	3,450	12,980	
South Worcester,	"	2	75 × 32	2	"	23,000	29,184		2,918	26,450	
Valley Falls,	"	1	28 × 22	1	Poor,	500	4,988		200	25,918	
Tale,	"	1	25 × 25	1	"	300	5,050		75	700	
Tale,	Brick	1	73 × 30	2	Good,	6,000	34,875	10	1,000	375	
Unn Hill,	Wood	1	38 × 28	1	Fair,	2,000	11,000		1,100	7,000	
Blithewood,	"	1	38 × 28	1	Good,	1,500	1 acre		100	3,100	
Pond Brict,	Bik	1	32 × 30	2	"	3,000	14,000		500	1,600	
Tatnuck,	"	1	43 × 32	1	"	11,500	11,500		300	3,500	L 51 × 33 feet.
Chamberlin,	Wood	1	38 × 22	1	"	1,200	½ acre		100	5,300	L 40 × 33 feet.
Oak Pond,	"	1	40 × 32	1	"	1,600	20,300		300	1,300	
Burncoat,	Brick	1	31 × 32	1	"	2,500	21,500		200	1,900	
Adams Square,	"	1	40 × 32	1	Fair,	2,800	22,360		500	2,700	
Edgeworth st.	"	2	62 × 50	4	New,	17,000	30,760	10	3,076	2,300	Hall in French Roof.
						567,600			233,575	801,175	

OTHER SCHOOL PROPERTY.

3835 Single School desks	$13,412
400 Single School Desks, High School	2,800
1510 Double Desks	6,200
1275 School Chairs	637
750 Teachers' and Common Chairs	600
130 Teachers' Tables	900
80 Teachers' Desks	2,400
145 Clocks	1,400
108 Morning Glory Stoves and Pipe	6,480
18 other Coal Stoves and Pipe ..	450
33 Wood Stoves and Pipe...........	330
85 Coal Hods............................	85
38 Porcelain Kettles..................	10
75 Coal Shovels.......................	10
15 Pairs Tongs........................	8
20 Coal Sieves.........	5
1 Coal Screen.........	8
200 Gross Crayons....................	28
45 Gallons Ink........................	54
55 Ink Jugs...........................	9
70 Ink Fillers.............	30
155 Ink Stands......................	38
220 Brooms...........................	44
260 Floor Brushes....	260
300 Dust Brushes.....................	75
150 Dust Pans......	35
150 Water Pails......................	40
350 Water Dippers....................	35
150 Wash Basins.......................	60
325 Yards Crash.....................	32
210 Door Mats, 3 x 3	315
140 Door Mats, 2 x 3.................	140
170 Waste Paper Baskets............	127
450 Pointers........................	40
50 Dinner Bells........................	60
175 Table Bells........................	45
160 Thermometers..	64
175 Blank Books......................	45
1125 Maps............................	300
6 Setts Guyot's large Maps	300
75 Map Stands......................	150
20 Music Stands......................	40
290 Charts..............................	85
350 Tablets...........................	175
1025 Keys..............................	205
130 Window Openers....................	30
2100 Chalk Erasers....................	315
75 Globes..............................	350
4200 Slates	300
75 Numeral Frames	75
120 Crickets..........................	30
120 Table Covers....	36
Stationery.....	70
30 Setts Mason's Musical Charts..	210
500 Volumes High School Library	750
250 Text Books High School......	200
Philosopeical and other Apparatus at High School...........	3500
1 Grand Piano....................	1200

Carried forward, $50,642

Brought forward,	$50,642
Clocks................................	1000
2 Library Tables	200
8 Teachers' Desks, High School..	308
2 Book Cases, High School.......	290
154 Settees, High School	770
10 Feather Dusters, High School	10
Various articles in Janitor's room, High School......	15
15 large Coal Shovels	15
10 Axes	10
19 Pianos	5150
1 Melodeon	40
240 Settees	1200
5750 Text Books in hands of Teachers, Poor Scholars and in Office,	2300
90 Qua. Dictionaries	450
50 Oca. Dictionaries	100
225 Dictionaries	90
55 Gazetteers	275
60 Manuals Penmanship............	24
155 Object Lessons	155
1 Book Case, Secretary's Room	75
1 Book Case, Secretary's Room.	35
1 Book Case, Sup't's Room.......	40
1 Book Case, Sup't's Room	25
1 Desk, Sup't's Room..............	35
1 Desk, Secretary's room	35
1 Desk, Secretary's Room.........	20
12 Chairs	25
Copy Press	12
Stamp	5
45 Rulers	4
¾ Ream Book Covers...............	6
9 Book Cases......................	300
10 Feather Dusters........	10
6 Goblets, 9 Soap Dishes, 10 Bars Soap, &c.......................	5
2 Wheelbarrows, Hammers, Screw Drivers, Ink Measures, Shovels, Pick, Rake, Lanterns, Wood Boxes, Sinks, &c., ...	250
Desks and Lumber in process of manufacture at Department Shop	2000
40 Boxes Forms......................	100
50 Manuals of Commerce...........	37
50 Childs' Book of Nature.........	25
50 " What to Read, &c."	25
50 Catalogues of Public Library	25
150 Munroe's Manual	50
11 Setts Cyclopædia..................	550
12 Pen Racks.......................	2
18 Setts Animal Charts........... ..	200
200 Tons Coal.......................	1900
45 Cords Wood......................	400
500 Bushels Charcoal..............	87
100 Barrels Kindlings.....	20
40 Mason's Charts..................	235
8 Johnson's Atlas'	160
5 Hall Stoves	300

$65,325

Carried forward, $50,642

Value of Real Estate, $801,175.

Total, $866,500.

TABLE.

Showing the Public Schools of the City, their Grade, the Teachers employed January 1st., 1872, and their respective Salaries.

SCHOOLS.	GRADE.	TEACHERS.	SAL'Y
Walnut St.,	English and classical	Abner H. Davis.	$2300
,,	High School,	Roswell Parish,	2000
,,		Babson S. Ladd,	1200
,,		Latham Fitch,	750
,,		Florence V. Beane,	800
,,		Ann C. Stewart,	800
,,		Mary A. Parkhurst,	800
,,		Mary E. Wilder,	700
,,		Hannah G. Creamer,	1000
Thomas st.,		Edward I. Comins,	1700
"	Grammar IX.	Annie C. Wyman,	500
Dix st.,	"	Addison A. Hunt,	1700
Woodland st.,	"	Samuel E. Fitz.	1700
"	"	Jennie E. Howard,	550
Lamartine st.,	"	Charles C. Foster,	1700
"	"	Eliza J. Wallace,	500
Ledge st.,	"	Henry M. Harrington,	1700
"	"	Minnie F. Whittier,	500
Belmont st.,	"	Vashti E. Hapgood,	575
Dix st.,	" VIII.	Sarah E. Dyer,	575
Woodland st.,	"	Mary F. Wentworth,	575
Lamartine st.,	"	Mary E. Eastman,	575
Ledgde st.,	"	Mary F. Reed,	575
Thomas st.,	"	Harriet G. Waite,	800
Quinsigamond	"	Lenora E. Perry,	575
So. Worcester	" VI. VII. VIII.	Myra J. Wetmore,	600
New Worcester	"	Charlotte N. Munger,	575
Belmont st.,	" VII. VIII.	Mary A. Warren,	575
Thomas st.,	" VII.	A. E. McCambridge,	575
Dix st.,	"	Eldora M. Aldrich,	575
Woodland st.,	"	Minnie S. Fitch,	575
Ledge st.,	"	Joanna F. Smith,	575
Sycamore st.,	"	Ann S. Dunton,	575
New Worcester	"	S. Lizzie Carter,	575
Belmont st.,	" VI,	Sarah W. Phillips,	575
Thomas st.,	"	Laura L. Newton,	575
"	"	Mary A. Harrington,	575
Dix st.,	"	Ellen Merrick,	575
Elm st.,	"	Etta J. Rounds,	575
Sycamore st.,	"	Carrie A. George,	575
Woodland st.,	"	Mary M. Lawton,	575
Lamartine st.,	"	Mary A. Smith,	575
Ledge st.,	"	Maria P. Cole,	575
Union Hill	" VI. V. IV.	Ellen G. Wheeler,	575
Salem St.,	" IV.	Rebecca Barnard,	575
Belmont st.,	Secondary v.,	Tirza S. Nichols,	550
Thomas st.,	"	Elizabeth H. Coe,	550
Dix st.,	"	Kate A. Meade,	550
Pleasantst.,	"	Carrie E. Gilbert,	550
Sycamore st.,	"	Carrie R. Clements,	550

SCHOOLS.	GRADE.	TEACHERS.	SAL'Y.
Woodland st.,	"	Mary J. Davis,	550
Lamartine st.,	"	Nellie L. Moore,	550
Ledge st.,	"	Charlotte N. Follett,	550
Providence.,	"	Elizabeth E. King,	550
Salem st.,	"	Mary A. E. Adams,	550
Ash st.,	"	Helen M. Harlow,	550
Edgeworth st.,	"	Hattie E. Clarke,	550
East Worcester	"	Harriet Hathaway,	550
So. Worcester	"	Sarah E. Bigelow,	550
Quinsigamond	" VI.	Anna C. Perry,	550
Belmont st.,	"	Esther G. Chenery,	550
Thomas st.,	"	Abbie F. Knowles,	550
Dix st.,	"	Elizabeth E. Daniels,	550
Pleasant st.,	"	Addie H. Barnes,	550
Sycamore st.,	"	Jennie A. Green,	550
Woodland st.,	"	Linnie M. Allen,	550
Lamartine st.,	"	Matilda Parker,	550
Ledge st.,	"	Margaret M. Geary,	550
Providence st.,	"	Agnes R. Dame,	550
Ash st.,		Mary J. Mack,	550
"	" III. IV.	Sylvia N. Stackpole,	575
E. Worcester	" IV.	Annie Brown,	550
"		Tamerson S. Darling,	550
New "		Adeliza Perry,	550
South "	"	Ellen M. Boyden,	550
Front st.,	"	Libbie H. Day,	550
Belmont st ,	Primary III.	Mary T. Gale,	500
Thomas st.,	"	Eunie M. Gates,	500
Dix st.,	"	Rebecca Jones,	1200
"	"	Mary L. Norcross,	500
"	" II.	Emma J. Houghton,	500
"	" I.	Emma J. Norcross,	500
Edgeworth st.,	" III.	Sarah M. Brigham,	500
Mason st.,		Julia M. Martin,	500
Pleasant st.,	"	Josephine A. Hunt,	500
Sycamore st.,	"	Sarah W. Clements,	500
Woodland st.,	"	Lizzie C. Goodwin,	500
Lamartine st.,	"	Louisa A. Dawson,	500
Ledge st.,	"	Eliza F. Prentice,	500
Providence st.,	"	M. Jennie Morse,	500
Salem.,	"	Emma J. Claflin,	500
Ash st.,	"	Helen M. Shattuck,	500
Front st.,	"	Mary O. Whitmore,	500
East Worcester	"	Ella M. McFarland,	500
New "	" I. II. III.	Ida A. E. Kenney,	500
South "	" III.	Ann E. Hall,	500
Adriatic	"	Martha T. Wyman,	500
Quinsigamond	" I. II. III.	Amelia M. Walker,	500
Union Hill	"	Abbie A. Welles,	500
Belmont st.,	" II.	Susie G. Gale,	500
Thomas st.,	"	Amanda M. Phillips,	500
Edgeworth st.,	"	Susan M. Buttrick,	500
Pleasant st.,	"	Sarah A. Harrington,	500
Sycamore st.,	"	Emma F. Marsh,	500
Lamartine st.,	"	Mary E. Kavanaugh,	500
Ledge st.,	"	Esther M. Rice,	500

SCHOOLS.	GRADE.	TEACHERS.	SAL'Y
Providence st.,	"	Sarah J. Newton,	500
East Worcester.,	"	Carrie E. Putnam,	500
"		Hattie A. Smith,	500
South "		Susan M. Forbes,	500
Front st.,	"	Mary E. Trask,	500
Ash st.,	"	Abbie J. Reed,	500
Belmont st.,	" 1.	Ida C. Upton,	5C0
"	"	Eliza J. Day;	500
Thomas st.,	"	Flora J. Osgood,	500
"	"	A. F. Hemmenway,	500
Edgeworth st.,	"	Hattie W. Bliss,	500
Pleasant st.,	"	Emily M. Halsted,	500
Mason st.,		Mary E. Pease,	500
Sycamore st.,	"	Nellie C. Thomas,	500
Woodland st.,	"	Maggie I. Melanefy,	500
Lamartine st.,	" I. III.	Eliza A. Cook,	500
"	" I.	Esther B. Smith,	500
"	"	Belle Y. Hoyt,	500
Ledge st.,	"	Mary V. Callaghan,	500
Ash st.,	"	Emma H. Barton,	500
Front st.,	"	Abby Pratt,	500
East Worcester.,	"	Mattie A. Collins,	500
"	"	Aloysia Radcliffe,	500
Adriatic st.,	"	Maria J. Metcalf,	50₀
So. Worcester	"	Annetta M. Chapin,	500
Northville	Suburban.	Abbie E. Clough,	575
"	"	Stella Knights,	500
Tatnuck	"	Mary J. Packard,	575
Leesville	"	Ella P. Newton,	500
Valley Falls	"	Susie A. Partridge,	500
Blithewood.,	"	J. P. Raymond,	500
Bloomingdale	"	Hattie A. Johnson,	575
Adams Square		Lottie M. Harrington,	575
Burncoat		Lizzie M. Vaughn,	450
North Pond	"	Emma R. Kendrick,	500
Chamberlin	"	Clara Manley,	575
Orange st.,	Ungraded.	George A. Adams,	1700
"	"	Persis E. King,	600
	Music Teacher.	E. S. Nason,	1700
			Ev'ng.
"	Evening.	Carrie A. George,	$2.00
"	"	Mary A. Slater,	1.00
Elm st.,	"	Jennie E. Stiles,	1.00
"		Laura L. Newton,	1.50
East Worcester	"	Sarah J. Newton,	1.00
"	"	Ella M. McFarland,	1.00
Summer st.,	"	Lamerson S. Darling,	1.00
"	..	Samuel A. Souther,	1.50
South Worcester	"	Abbie A. Souther,	1.00
"	Evening.	Preston D. Jones,	2.00
Belmont st.	"	Myra J. Wetmore,	1.50
"	Drawing.	George Gladwin,	10.00
"	"	George I. Alden,	10.0C
"	"	Milton P. Higgins,	10.00
"	"	Henry M. Armesby,	8.75
"	"	Edward I. Comins,	5.00
"	"	Edward R. Smith,	3.00

ROLL OF HONOR.

The scholars whose names are found in the following list are worthy of honorable mention for their constancy and regularity in daily attendance.

The roll is made up, first of those scholars who have been perfect in their attendance at school, that is, not absent, tardy, or dismissed at any session of the school during the entire year. Second, of those who, not having been perfect the entire year, were perfect in their attendance for three terms. Third, of those who, not having been perfect in attendance for the year or three terms, were perfect for two terms. We do not give the names of those perfect in attendance for one term, as it would occupy too mnch space, the numbers being 1577.

The number perfect in attendance the entire year, 326
     "   "   "   for three terms, 399
     "   "   "   for two terms, 455

PERFECT THE WHOLE YEAR.

Austin, Mary B.	Boutwell, Leslie B.	Brady, James B.
Adams, Jacob	Bradigan, Louis	Chapin, Lizzie
Allen, James	Bemis, Byron	Clough, Jennie C.
Aldrich, J.	Brown, Michael	Colvin, J. B.
Adams, Frank	Boehmer, Frank	Currier, Edna
Brown, Charles A.	Brown, William	Comstock, Annie
Buckley, Emma	Baker, Albert G.	Caldwell, Ida
Burlingame, Maria	Bancroft, Mary	Chapin, Ida
Booth, Olena E.	Baker, Mary C.	Collins, John
Barrows, Fred	Burns, Jerry	Collins, Timmie
Boyd, Burt	Baudendistel, Louis	Comaford, Mary
Bowen, Mary	Buckley, Nellie	Carter, Carrie,
Booth, Charles	Brown, John	Campbell, Katie
Barrett, Lucy	Brady, Maggie	Cragen, Stephen
Buxton, Etta	Boswell, Emma	Cook, Cleveland
Bullock, Lizzie B.	Broderick, James	Cunningham, Ella
Bemis, Lyman	Barrett, Tommie	Carney, Mary

Clark, Freddie	Gordon, Joseph	Lewis, Charlie
Cahill, Minnie	Goodnow, Willie	Lackey, Ida E.
Cahill, Jimmie	Gavin, James	Lonergan, Katie
Cramer, Mary	Grover, Nellie	Lynch, James
Cooper, George	Gleason Fred	Leonard, Annie
Cunningham, John	Gallivan, Annie	Lynch, John
Cunningham, Tom	Garvey, Mary	Leonard, John
Croak, Dennis	Gorman, Martin	Leland, Eddie N.
Cunningham, Willie	Goss, Mary	Lavery, Dennis
Corliss, John	Goodwin, Francis T.	Love, Emma
Chapin, Marion	Gunderson, Norman	Lawler, Tommie
Chapin, Charlie	Greene, Charlie	Long, Joseph
Crosby, Arthur H.	Greene, George	Love, Aggie
Crosby Justin D.	Hedge, Eddie	Leahy, Annie
Dudley, Fred A.	Hartwell, W.	Mason, Frank
Dusenbury, Walter	Harrington, A. H.	Morse, Charles
Dryden, Ephrasia L.	Holbrook, M. Lizzie	Moody, Stella
Delvey, Chester W.	Henry, Nellie	Mooney, John F.
Dunton, Nellie A.	Hill, Walter	Magoun, H. A.
Dudley, Mary B.	Holman, Arthur	Maynard, W. A.
Denny, Nellie	Hooper, Frank L.	Mason, Leila A.
Doyle, Anthony	Hentz, Josie	McDermott, James
Dryden, Hattie	Hardy, Nellie	Marcy, Arthur D.
Day, Frank E.	Huntley, Isabella	Millea, John
Doran, Michael H.	Hoyle, Alonzo	Marble, Hattie
Delvey, Arthur N.	Heald, Sarah	Mason, Herbert
Dunn, John	Haynes, Herbert F.	Mahoney, Julia
Doherty, Stephen	Hobbs, Wilbur W.	McGone, Maggie
Drohan, Martin	Hagerty, Willie	Moon, Emma
Dupuis Julius	Huntley, Robert	Mason, Joseph
Duggan, Mark	Hunt, Annie	McAuliffe, Michael
Daniels, Mary	Higgins, Tommie	Mossman, George M.
Droghan, Patrick	Hackett, Katie	McDermott, John
Earle, Morris	Holman, Edward	Mahoney, James D.
Estabrook, Fannie	Houghton, Willie	Marshall, George
Eames, Freddie T.	Ittel, Freddie J.	Moore, George E.
Follen, Wm. James	Jones, Eddie	Murphy, Nellie
Fallon, John	Kickham, Alice	McCabe, Sarah
Flaherty, James	Kehler, Lucy	McMahon, Eddie
Fallon, Rebecca	Keyes, George C.	Millea, Willie
Forehand, Freddie	Kelley, Mary	Moore, Nellie
Fay, Nellie E.	Kelley, Tommie	Moore, David
Fuller, Eddie C.	Kidd, Herbert	Murphy, Mary
Finnegan, Michael	Kelley, Katie	Murphy, Jimmie
Fogg, George H.	Kuhl, Henry	Matthews, Lillian
Fernane, Annie	Knight, Jennie E.	Morrisey, Mary
Fitzgerald, Daniel	Lawrence, George	Manley, Charlie
Gordon, Hattie J.	Lowell, C. C.	McCloskey, James
Gill, Florence	Lawler, Nellie	McCloskey, John
Green, Alice J.	Lawler, Joanna	McCabe, John

McDermott, Henry
McManus, Hannah
Murphy, Annie
Mahearn, Michael
Midgeley, Freddie
McGady, Rosa
Mahar, Michael
Mahearn, John
McFarland, Freddie
Needham, Annie
Newton, Emma
Newton, Charles
Nichols, Johnnie
Nichols, Mary
Norton, Flora
O'Conner, John F.
O'Mara, Michael
O'Rourke, Dennis
Overend, Thomas
O'Brien, Willie
Pierce, Arba J.
Pierce, L. D.
Pond, Inez J.
Perkins, Arabella
Powers, John
Phair, Willie
Perry, Helen
Phetteplace, George
Phelps, Willie
Paul, Fannie
Prentice Frank,
Powers, Mary
Pellinger, Charles
Pierce, Jefferson
Palmer, Charles
Pollinger, George
Phelps, Alice V.
Perkins, Willie
Palmer, Mary
Powers, James
Quackenboss, Eddie
Rugg, Georgia

Ross, Willie
Riley, Effie
Richaadson, Willie A.
Rogers, Harry N.
Ross, Hattie
Roberts, Stephen F.
Ready, Mary
Robbins, Willie
Ratigan, Willie
Ranger, Anna
Ryan, Dennis
Reed, Florence
Russell, Willie
Riley, Ella
Reardon, Annie
Robbins, Charlie
Stratton, C. J.
St. John, C. E.
Sullivan, J. A.
Seavey, Charlie H.
Sutton, Clare
Sutton, James
Saunders, Nellie
Sweetser, Charles S.
Speirs, William
Sullivan. Dennis
Stevens, George A.
Stevens, Nellie J.
Smith, Willie
Sutton, Mabel L.
Streeter, Ida J.
Sampson, Alfred
Salmons, Eddie
Sheehan, Edward
Sargent, Cora J.
Styles, Alfred J.
Skinner, John P.
Sweetser, Carrie M.
Smith, Mary
Shaw, Walter
Santon, Lucy
Sullivan, Michael

Sheehan, James
Spitslye, Mary
Sibley, Linus
Spears, Robert
Smith, Thomas
Schofield, Sammie B.
Sweetser, Sammie
Stowell, Charlie F.
Stiles, Sarah
Thayer, Ed D.
Torrey, Louis H.
Taylor, Louise
Thompson, Arthur
Townley, Bennie
Trainor, Eddie
Towne, Addison F.
Troy, John
Thren, Carrie
Thayer, Myra
Volkmer, Willie
Ward, George O.
Wood, H. M.
White, Frank
Whiting, Omer
Whiting, George
Whitmore, George
Woodward, Ira
Whiting, Mary
Weir, Solomon
Wheelock, Herbert
Wesby, Eddie
Wright, Carrie A.
Whalen, Eddie
White, Walter L.
Williams, Edgar A.
Wright, Matilda
Wright, Melissa
Wallis, Eva
Welch. Mary
Weir, Lizzie
Wilson, Sarah M.

PERFECT THREE TERMS.

Allen, Charles L.
Abercrombie, Ella
Adams, Myra
Aldrich, Perley
Adams, Ida L.
Ames, E. Imogene
Allen, Walter P.

Andrews, Lena
Atwood, Nellie
Aubertine, Richard
Barbour, F. A.
Beaman, A. M.
Bardwell, A. R.
Brooks, A. A.

Babbitt, Harry C.
Burbank, Henry L.
Ballou, Hattie L.
Barton, Charles S.
Blanchard, George C.
Buxton, Clara
Blake, Herbert S.

15

Barry, Agnes
Bliss, Bertie
Brady, Nellie
Bixby, Annie
Bean, Hibbard
Bacon, Lucy
Brimbaum, Frank
Buckley, Charles
Bemis, John M.
Blackmer, Jennie
Beaman, Mary A.
Brady, Joseph
Brinkworth, Martha
Brewer, Lizzie M.
Brahm, Maggie
Barber, Clara
Blos, Albert H. J.
Blaisdell, Willis
Bogle, Thomas
Bullard, Freddie
Ballard, Clara S.
Brimhall, Minnie E.
Bigelow, Irving
Bowler, Michael
Butterworth, Martha
Bailey, George
Brosnihan, Mary
Berry, Tommie
Bacon, Florence
Burbank, Thedie
Baker, Jane
Ballou, Willis
Bemis, Abbie
Bowers, George
Buskin, Jerry
Bergen, Emma
Brahm, Caroline
Brahm, Christina
Barker, Hattie
Brosnihan, Naimo
Boyd, Eliza
Bliss, Arthur
Burlingame, Lillian
Chace, E. J.
Childs, Hattie J.
Courtney, Daniel
Cheney, Nellie
Cheney, Charles S.
Connor, Nellie
Cooper, Annie

Childs, Frank
Cooper, Willie H.
Cooney, Bridget
Crane, Fannie M.
Cummings, Mary
Coonan, Willie
Clark, Carrie
Chase, Eddie I.
Coonan, Thomas
Clarke, Alfred
Cahill, Julia
Combs, Jennie
Chapin, Fannie
Conlon, Thomas
Condy, Willie
Coole, Lizzie
Carroll, James
Churchill, James
Creamer, John
Cunningham, Leila O.
Curran, John
Connor, John
Cooney, Frank
Clark, Emma F.
Cunningham, Frank
Carmody, Willie
Campbell, Nellie
Carlton, Carrie
Caniry, Tommie
Colvin, Lewis
Curley, Eddie
Dryden, Martha
Davis, Willie
Dolan, John
Driscoll, Michael
Douglass, Emma
Dawson, Albert
Delaney, George
Doyle, James
Drohan, Mary
Doran, Eddy F.
Doran, Mary E.
Dyer, John
Dyer, Ella
Dean, Willie
Doyle, James
Doyle, K.
Donab, Eugene
Dolan, Eddie
Davis, Otis H.

Davis, Leander
Emerson, Ella J.
Eaton, Alice C.
Eldred, Marion
Ellis, Mary J.
Earle, Charlie
Fales, Abbie
Follet, Carrie
Forney, Henry
Flagg, Jennie M.
Follansbee, Jennie
Flaherty, Martin
Fitzpatrick, Thomas
Fitzgerald, John
Fifield, Mary
French, Mary
Fisher, Freddie
Fuller, Harry M.
Ford, Patrick
Flynn, Eliza
Foley, John, 2
Flemming, Pedee
Foley, Lizzie
Flagg, Luella
Fitzgerald, Mary
Farnham, Estella
Forbush, Emma J.
Gauren, F. A.
Gilbert, W. W.
Gunther, Otis R.
Goddard, M. R.
Gill, Carrie
Guerin, Jennie
Grey, Mary
Gilbert, Walter
Gunderson, M. Louisa
Griswold, Nellie
Goddard, Harry
Gaffney, Bridget
Griggs, John S.
Gunther, Alexander
Goulding, Victor G.
Gauren, Addie
Gilrain, Alice
Garvey, Frank
Gould, Jessie
Gorham, Florence
Goulding, John
Gouche, Delia
Hill, Mary L.

Kickham, Hannah
'Killiher, Mary
Kennidy, Patrick
Kettell, Jennie
Knight, Albert M.
Kimmel, Louise
Keefe, John W.
Keniry, John
Kelley, John
Kneeland, John
Kenney, Maggie
Keyes, Freddie
S. Kyler, Henry
Lewis, W. E.
Lucas, Harry
Loring, Hattie ·
Lawrence, George
Leach, Ellsworth
Lyons, John
Lewis, William
Lavin, John
Le Duc, John
Langlois, Alvina
Lancaster, John E.
Lamb, Alice R.
Lavin, Patrick
Laros, Addie
Luby, Larry
Lafreniere, J.
Lincoln, Marston
Laughlin, Katie
Mawhinney, E. C.
May, Samuel D.
Montrose, Thomas H.
McFarland, Lizzie
Morse, Libbie J.
Magoun, Emma
McNamara, T.
Mara, Michael
Messinger, Charlie
Miles, Jennie
Maloney, Mary
Miller, Henry
McCann, John
Murray, Nettie
May, Eva
Morgan, Ellen
Murphy James
Marble, Willie S.
Mack, Lawrence

Mitchell, Lydia F.
Miles, Mary
Magoun, Jennie M.
Maynard, Alfred
Marsh, Charlie H.
Manly, Dennis
May, Jerry
McLoughlin, John
Murphy, Jennie
Malone, John
McAuliffe, Owen
Mann, Mary
Muzzy, Cora
McDonough, John
McBride, Mary
Mackin, Mary
McManus, Annie
Moore, Joseph
Nelson, Flora
Newton, Arthur
Newton, Georgie
Neylon, Ellen
Newell Eddie
Norcross, Arthur
Norton, John
Needham, Harry
Nugent, Annie
O'Connor, Alice
O'Connor, Eliza J.
Otto, Emma
O'Leary, John
O'Brien, Annie
O'berer, Albert
O'Connor, Eugene
O'Brien, Willie
O'Neil, Katie
O'Mara, Daniel
O'Brien, M.
O'Connor, Hannah
Perry, F. D.
Paul, Lillie
Palmer, Addison F.
Perry, Joseph,
Perry, Eddie
Patch, Fred
Palmer, Horace
Phelps, Alida
Pead, Mary
Perry, Nellie F.
Pierce, Willie

Perry, Helen D.
Phillips, Fannie
Putnam, Henry A.
Putnam, Delia
Prentice, Alfred
Powers, Paul
Putnam, Lizzie
Pero, Eddie
Pierce, Edgar B.
Page, Elvena
Quinn, Daniel
Quirk, James
Reed, Mary
Ross, Eva J.
Richardson, R. A.
Russell, Lucy
Ratigan, Nellie
Rourke, Willie
Robbins, Lillie
Robbins, Nellie
Rivers, Eldridge
Roberts, Georgiana
Reidy, Mary
Riley Phillip
Rourke, Morris
Rollins, Mary
Rice, Lillie
Reardon, John
Riley, Julia
Rourke, Daniel
Reeves, Walter,
Rawson, Nellie
Rice, Jimmie
Rivet, Janet
Rourke, John
Stratton, Edward
Sweetser, Lizzie
Sargent, Henry
Schofield, Flora

Shedd, Mary L.
Smith, Effie C.
Sanders, Willie
Sheldon, Walter
Seavy, Rosa
Sullivan, Thomas
Sampson, Lovina
Sargent, Charlie
Stone, Clara
Shurtliff, Henry H.
Stansfield, Thomas
Sessions, Warren
Sheldon, Theodore H.
Saville, Ellsworth
Sullivan, John
Sullivan, Maggie
Sampson, Mary
Smith, Frankie
Santon, Matilda
Sanders, Alice
Swain, Minnie
Seavey, Nellie
Sullivan, Mary A.
Spring, Joseph
Sullivan, Daniel
Sweeney, Nellie
Sheehan, Cornelius
Smith, Carrie M.
Satchwell, John
Sullivan, Joseph
Sheehan, Mary
Sullivan, Bridget
Sheehan, Agnes
Sexton, Jerry
Sprague, Elmer H.
Tyler, Harry P.
Taft, Jessie
Tibbets, Frank
Thompson, Eliza

Taffney, Eliza
Tainter, Arthur L.
Tew, Mabel
Tooney, Michael
Tapley, Walter
Trainer, Mary
Toole, Daniel
Trombly, Theophilus
Underwood, A. Nettie
Vaill, Mary
Velandey, Stella
Walker, L. E.
Woodward, Jennie
Weir, James
White, Carrie
Wheeler, Fannie F.
Wesby, Herbert,
Woodis, Hattie
Weston, James
Wood, Clara
Willard, Jennie
Waker, Lillie
Winslow, Sammie E.
Willard, Emma
Whittey, Lawrence
Woodis, Henry
White, Frank
Wesson, Frank L.
Woodward, Harry A.
Wilson, Etta
Warren, Nellie
White, Nellie E.
Wunderlich, Freddie
White, Willie
Whitney, Maggie
Warren, Maggie
Wesson, Carrie
Wynn, John
Wilkinson, Frank M.

PERFECT TWO TERMS.

Aldrich, Effie
Allen, Frank H.
Aldrich, Eddie
Allen, Lizzie
Apperson Estella
Allen, Josie
Anderson, William
Anderson, John
Anthony, Eddie
Andrews, Hattie B.

Allen, Nettie
Allen, Mary
Adams, Winthrop
Anderson, David
Allison, John
Arnold, Nellie
Adams, Bennie
Barker, Mary
Barton, Lucy
Buxton, A. A.

Bennett, E. L.
Brooks, Fred A.
Bacheller, Clifford
Bemis, Cora
Brown, Charlie
Bradley, John
Bigelow, Horace
Brosnihan, Katie
Brady, William
Brown, Addie

Briggs, Frank
Burlingame, Harris /
Brooks, Walter
Bush, Ada
Bussell, Daniel
Burlingame, Asa
Buxton, Gertie
Buxton, Ida F.
Bean, Ruthie
Boyden, Walter
Bartlett, Fred
Britt, R. Joseph
Brown, Melia
Bennett, Charles
Ball, Elsie M.
Brinbaum, Emma H.
Buckley, Lizzie
Briggs, Edgar W. H.
Buxton, Etta
Bragg, Walter H.
Baldwin, Cora
Batchellor, Lizzie
Brennan, Thomas
Boehmer, Edward
Ball, Homer
Blake, Charlie H.
Blake, Emogene A.
Blos, Otto
Burke, John
Boyden, John
Burke, James
Bemis, Eddie
Bond, Mattie
Buckley, Nellie
Baker, Willie
Bacon, Florence
Ball, Wilbur
Bennett, Eddie
Booker, Eugene
Buskin, Henry
Brown, Willie
Barnes, Ada L.
Butler, Peter
Barker, Arthur
Barnard, Sarah C.
Carroll, M. E.
Chase, Josie
Cheney, Florence
Crowell, Julia A.
Currier, Herbert A.

Condy, William J.
Chamberlain, Carrie
Cummings, Mattie
Corbin, John
Courtney, Hannah
Cobleigh Hattie
Conner, Emma
Coes, Mary
Cutler, Eddie
Coburn, Ayro
Churchill, Eddie
Cook, Lucian
Converse, Hattie
Clark, Mable
Cooke, Emma
Clarke, Bell
Chapin, Charlie
Carrico, Eddie
Cunningham, Jennie
Coburn, Peter
Cobleigh, Alice M.
Clapp, Florence
Condy, George
Carberry, Mary
Conlon, Andrew
Campbell, Alice
Cragen, Lucy
Connell, John
Conway, Mary
Collins, Julia
Conlon, James
Cummings, Bridget
Chamberlin, Frank B.
Curran, Dennis
Curran, Joseph
Conlon, John
Clark, Frank
Cantwell, Tommie
Chever, Alston
Collins, Mary
Conolly, James
Crowley, Julia
Cooper, Imogene
Cunningham, George
Conner, Michael
Cahill, John
Conley, Ella
Conner Timmie
Currier, Lucy
Croak, Delia

Connell, John
Cantwell, Thomas
Churchill, Fannie
Conlon, Daniel
Cormiskey, Patsie
Clarke, Eddie
Campbell, Owen
Cunningham, Alice
Connors, Daniel
Conlin, Thomas
Clapp, Willie
Croake, Mary
Cook, Willie F.
Doherthy, Mary
Dearborn, Jennie L.
Daniels, Lizzie F.
Dunn, Stephen
Drohan, Nicholas
Dean, Fred
Dearborn, Emma
Desper, Willie
Deland, Etta
Doyle, Johannah
Deveraugh, Maggie
Dolan, Alice,
Dyer, Charlie
Dunn, James
Diemar, Lillie
Doyle, James
Duncalf, Louisa
Doyle, Lizzie
Dwyer, Nellie
Davie, Lulie R.
Donahoe, Daniel
Dean, Delia J.
Davis, Minnie
Driscoll, John
Dowd, Mary A.
Daly, Thomas H.
Desoe, Eddie G.
Deane, Annie
Dudley, Florence
Dansereou, Sarah
Daniels, John
Driffy, Willie
Dean, Ann M.
Delaney, Annie
Degman, Mary
Degman, Patrick
Daniels, Mabel

Decelle, Josephine	Fleming, Peter	Henry, Anita
Deming, Charlotte	Flynn, James	Hunt, Jennie
Donat, Theodore	Fahey, Eddie	Holland, Willie
Donahue, Thomas	Ford, Frank	Hunt, Charles
Delahanty, John	Flynn, Lizzie	Harrington, Elmer W.
Dupuis, Julius	French, Lucy	Hall, Arthur
Dean, Maria	Fawcett, Charlie	Hanlon, Rosa
Day, Patsie	Flood, Eugene	Holland, Lincoln,
Drily, Charlie	Fitman, Willie	Haskell, George H.
Denmovan, Mary	Fisher, Fred.	Hanigan, Edward J.
Duggan, Mary	Fitzgerald, Thomas	Hubbard, Jennie I.
Daly, Katie	Foley, Lizzie	Huntley, Lizzie
Eddy, Frank	Foley, Jerry	Huber, Emily
Eddy, Charles H.	Flynn, Nicholas	Higgins, James O.
Eidt, Carrie	Griggs, Carrie	Heffron, Michael
Everett, Henry	Gunderson, G.	Henry Josephine
Ellis, Carrie	Gay, Clara	Hunt, Lottie
Eccleston, Kate	Gard, Carrie	Holton, George
Ellis, Charles	Gard, Minnie	Holbrook, William B.
Eaton, Willie	Guilfoyle, Timothy	Harrington, Charlie C.
Estabrook, Herbert	Griggs Allie	Harraghy, Katie
Ellis, John	Gaffney, Patrick	Healy, Johanna
Fitch, Frank	Gard, Alice	Hedge, Homer H.
Fitch, Fannie	Goodwin, Clara	Holman, Hattie
Flagg, Ida	Gates, Carrie	Hodgen, George
Flint, Annie E.	Goddard, Dwight	Huff, Albert
Follen, Kate	Gafferney, Jennie	Hutchinson, Lizzie
Fay, Stella K.	Goddard, Alfred E.	Henly, Daniel
Fitzgerald, George E.	Goddard, Carrie	Holmes, Clara
Flagg, Emma J.	Geer, H. Gertrude,	Hickey, Nellie
Fifield, Annie	Gale, John	Henry, Annie
Flint, Charlie	Guild, Flora	Hackett, Julia
Fitzgerald, Thomas	Garfield, Emma	Hacket, Bridget
Fuller, Susie	Glennan, Ellen	Horgan, Ellen
Forbes, Johnnie	Gilrain, Maria	Heron, Katie
Frost, Frank E.	Goss, Hugh	Henry, Paul
Fisher, Harry E.	Garvery, Willie	Henry, Michael
Freeman, Otis	Griffin, Nellie	Herbert, Mary
Fogerty, Willie	Geer, Walter	Herbert, Henry
Flynn, Maggie	Goodney, Mary	Hopkins, Freddie
Flagg, Fred.	Goodney, Johnnie	Hacket, Willie
Flynn, Jerry	Hammond, Jennie A.	Hagan, Maggie
Flynn, James	Hapgood, Mary	Hurley, Daniel
Fallen, Rosa	Higgins, Fred. O.	Hartwell, Georgie
Fallon, Michael	Harwood, C. W.	Holmes, Willie
Finnegan Johnnie	Howe, Edgar	Hanloe, Minnie
Foley, Annie	Hooper, Francis	Horigan, Ellen
Fifield, Alice	Houghton, Mary	Irving, Eddie
Flynn, Charlie	Hakes, Sarah	Jackson Ida J.
Farnham, George	Hopkins, Herbert	Jefts, Arthur W.

Johnson, Annie
Jones, George
Jones, Frank
Jordan, Charlie
Jones, Willie
Johnmary, Willie M.
Johnson, Michael
King, Charles
Kane, Katie
Kingsley, Josie T.
Kelley, Annie T.
Kelley, Mary
Kohlmaun, John
Kimball, Eddie
Kain, Daniel
Kean, Willie
Kelley, John
Kane, Frank
Knight, Arthur
Kettell, Jimmie
Kirby, Scott
Kessel, Joseph T.
Kimmel, Emma
Kabley, Charles A,
Kervin, John
Klingle, Hermaun
Kaney, Patrick
Kirman, Mary
Keating, Michael
Keefe, Nellie
Kelley, Mary
Kinary, Thomas
Knowland, John
Kendall, Herbert E.
Langlois J. F.
Lathe, Alfred
Lewison, Walter
Longley, Alice
Lynch, Christopher
Lovell, George
Lathe, Agnes
Longley, Emma
LaFoye, Joseph
Long, James
Lyon, Carrie
Libbey, Albert W.
Lamb Carrie S.
Leonard, Ella R.
Laughlin, Margaret
Leary, Timmie

Lane, Nellie
Larke, Willie
Learned, Eugene
Leach, Edith
Lowe, Jennie
Lynch, Tommie
Maynard, George
McCann, Sarah A.
McDonald, Thomas
McClennan, Chas. E.
Mead, Minnie
Morgan, Jennie L.
Muzzey, Nellie
Mason, Frank H.
Martin, Mary W.
McAuliffe, John J.
McCormick, Mary E.
Miller, Maggie
McCarthy James
Merriam, Alice
McCann, George
Maynard, Hattie
McGrath, Nellie
Mann, Earnest
McCann, Felix
Murphy, Ella
Malone, Maggie
Messinger, Mary
May, Edward
McGourty, M. Ella
Mooney, Maggie
May, Willie
McKenna Jennie
Miller, Davis
McQueeny, Annie
McAuliffe, John
Mack, Mary
McNeil, Willie
Mack, Nellie
Martin, Peter
Muzzy, Mary
Meyer, Henry
McAfee, Bertha
Matthews, Thomas
May, Ida E.
McNulty, Frank
Midgeley, Alice
Mann, Maggie
Marsh, Mary C.
Murphy, Cornelius

Moffit, Tommie
Monahan, Timothy
McGrath, Rosa
Monahan, Annie
Moran, Eliza
McDonald, John
McGrath, William
McGouty, Alice
Mulcahy, Matthew
Mulcahy, Lizzie
Murphy, Patrick
McCann, Willie
McManus, Henry
Marchessault, Eugenie
McGrath, Mary
Maynard, Charlie
McCann, Charles
MCKindley, John
Mara, John
McKuee, Thomas
McConnelly, Maggie
Morse, Myra N.
Martin, Louis
Nelson, Harry
Newbury, Cora
Newman, Clara
Newbury, Louise
O'Brien, J. M.
O'Neil, James
O'Regan, Louise
Olliver, John
O'Flynn, Thomas
Overend, Walter
O'Neil, Mary A.
O'Rourke, Edgar
O'Leary, Annie
O'Connor, Mary
O'Neil, Abbie
O'Connell, Willie
Odlin, Henry W.
O'Leary, James
O'Brien, Willie
O'Brien, Alice
O'Neil, Thomas
Otto, Hugo
Paul, Estela
Parker, Lizzie
Pendleton, Willie
Phillips, Inez
Putnam, Lizzie

Palmer, Charles O.
Phipps, Arthur
Phetteplace, Nellie
Pond, Sarah
Phelps, Bertha
Poole, Ida
Prouty, Anna
Phetteplace, Carrie
Pickup, Nellie
Phetteplace, Charles
Prentice, Frank
Phelps, Mary
Peters, Willie C.
Patch, Annie
Pero, Louis N. B.
Peacock, Ida F.
Paige, David
Powers, Nicholas
Powers, Jimmie
Powers, Thomas
Pero, Lizzie
Powers, Maggie
Paul, Lutie
Pillet, Napoleon
Putnam, Lilla
Quinlan, Lawrence
Quinlan, Mary A. F.
Quinlan, Mary
Quow, Carrie E.
Russell, Horace
Rourke, Mary A.
Russell, Lucy
Ross, Jennie
Ray, Jennie
Rumery, Henry
Reardon, Mary
Riordon, William
Rose, Marion]
Rice, Ettie
Redican, Katie
Rugg, Edward
Roberts, Asa
Rourke, Mary
Rafferty, Jennie
Rice, Minnie
Rice, Arthur
Reeves, Willie
Ryan, William
Ronin, James
Rafferty, Owen

Rourke, Eddie
Ryan, Mary E.
Reis, George
Reardon, Annie
Reardon, Julia
Reagan, John
Roberts, Mary
Ratican, Katie
Ryan, Mary
Rollins, Emma
Russell, Gertie
Rice, Ellie
Rudy, Frank
Ryan, Mamie J.
Riley, Rosa
Ryan, Minnie
Rogers, Dexter
Rowe, Alice
Riggs, Addie
Reed, Bessie
Ryan, Katie
Russell, Minnie
Rice, Era
Rourke, Charles
Richmond, Emma L.
Robbins, Charlie
Smith, George
Spurr, Fannie
Stone, Agnes
Swain, Lizzie M.
Sawyer, Jennie L.
Sawin, Robert V.
Stimpson, Katie
Sullivan, Daniel
Sherman, Minnie
Shippen, Henry
Shields, Mary
Smith, George 2
Scott, Flora
Sullivan, Willie
Slaughnessy, Willie
Shaw, Charles
Shesman, Mary
Sweat, Emma
Stickler, Raymond
Stowell, Anna
Stamp, George
Sears, Bennie
Spurr, Sammie
Smith, Annie

Sawin, Lelia
Sullivan, John
Smith, Louisa
Spurr, Josie
Smith, Minnie M.
Seaver, Mattie
Stewart, Frank
Servey, Susie
Santon, Josephine
Styles, Katie R.
Spurr, Emma F.
Spaulding, Sarah
Sweeney, Edward
Segur, Charles
Stevens, Alice
Sullivan, Hannah
Smith, Katie
Smith, Julia
Smith, Frank
Stark, Henry
Sullivan, Josie
Sexton, Kate
Sullivan, Patsey
Sweet, John
Sullivan, Michael
Sullivan, Joanna
Slocumb, Samuel
Stott, Mattie
Sweetser, Sammie
Sly, Anna
Sly, Mary
Smith, Mary
Stowell, Eliza P.
Sears, Abbie L.
Temple, Mary
Thayer, John
Tyler, Albert
Tarbell, Minnie
Tyler, Lizzie
Tuttle, George
Taylor, Jakie
Thayer, Sarah
Towne, Emma
Tyler, Laura
Tucker, Albert L.
Tateum, Willie
Tyler, Walter D.
Templeton, Fannie M.
Tyler, Lizzie
Taylor, George S.

Townley, Joseph
Tainter, Augustus
Thayer, Ernest L.
Thompson, Jessie F.
Tarbell, Addie L.
Tibbets, Herbert
Tisdelle, Hattie
Tenion, Mary
Tunncry, Eddie
Tyler, Willie
Thompson, Willie
Traverse, Frank
Troy, Maggie
Trainor, Annie
Tolton, Henry
Toole, Mary
Toole, Daniel
Upham, Freddie G.
Underwood, John
Wheeler, Abbie
Wheeler, Henry
Whipple, Mary
Whitney, H.
Wilcox, L. A.
Williams, F. A.

Woodward, Alice
Woodward, Willie
White, Avery A.
Whitcomb, Harry
Wadsworth, H. M.
Warren, Nathan
Whittemore, Willie
White, Etta
Whiting, Laura
Wesson, Fred
Wardwell, Carrie
Wells, Henry
White, Sarah
Wakefield, Willie
Weixler, Augusta M.
Wheeler, Charles
Wood, Annie S.
Wells, George P.
Woodman, Lizzie
Whitney, Josey
Weir, Jennie
Winn, Mary
Wood, Freddie
Ward, Robert
Warren, Everett H.

Wakefield, George
White, Eddie N.
Woodward, Ralph
Welch, Nellie
Waine, Annie
Ward, Frank
Ward, Freddie
Woodruff, Ella
Whittemore, Jennie
Webb, George
Warren, Ella
Witherell, Charles
Winter, Lizzie
Welch, Daniel
Woodward, Norman
White, Charlie
Wesson, Walter
Watson, Henry
Whittemore, Fred.
Weixler, Arthur
Warren, Herbert
Welch, Thomas
Wheelock, Willie
Whalen, Willie
Woodward, Susie E.

16

Organization of the School Committee.

OF THE

CITY OF WORCESTER,

FOR THE YEAR 1872.

GEO. F. VERRY, President.

ALBERT P. MARBLE, Superintendent.

SAMUEL V. STONE, Secretary.

Members whose term expires January, 1875.	Members whose term expires January, 1874.	Members whose term expires January, 1873.
C. B. METCALF.	HARTLEY WILLIAMS.	EDWARD H. HALL.
GEORGE W. GALE.	G. HENRY WHITCOMB.	ANN B. EARLE.
JAMES McDERMOTT.	JASON CHAPIN.	JAMES DRAPER.
P. J. GARRIGAN.	THOS. GRIFFIN.	JOHN F. MURRAY.
F. J. McNULTY.:	M. J. McCAFFERTY.	SAMUEL V. STONE.
F. P. GOULDING.	LOAMMI HARRINGTON.	EDWARD H. PEABODY.
GEORGE JAQUES.	EMERSON WARNER.	CHARLES BALLARD.
P. EMORY ALDRICH.	E. B. STODDARD.	RUFUS WOODWARD.

SUB-COMMITTEES.

On School Houses—Mayor, Messrs. Stone, Woodward, Gale, Whitcomb and Chapin.

On Books and Apparatus—Messrs. Woodward, Stoddard, Williams, Jaques and Hall:

On Examination of Teachers—Superintendent, and Messrs. Warner, Jaques, Hall, Metcalf and Garrigan.

On Finance—Mayor, Superintendent, and Messrs. Metcalf, Aldrich, Warner. Goulding and Harrington.

On Assigning Visiting Committees—Superintendent, and Messrs. Griffin, Ballard Gale, McNulty, and Ann B. Earle.

VOCAL MUSIC.

Grades Above the Third.—Edward S. Nason, Teacher.

Committee.—Warner, Whitcomb, Garrigan.

The Committees of Visitation shall exercise a general supervision over the Schools to which they are severally assigned, and shall visit them according to the provisions of the Statutes, not less than once in four weeks, and generally during the week preceding the monthly meeting of the Board, at which they shall report their true condition.—Rules. Chap. 3. Sec. 6.

Though each School is assigned to a Special Committee, yet every member of the Board shall deem it his duty to watch over all the Public Schools of the City, to attend their examinations, and visit them at other times as his convenience will permit.—Rules, Chap. 9, Sec. 9.

VISITING COMMITTEES.

The *Roman Numerals* designate the rooms to which members of committees are specially assigned, and the *grades* according to the Course of Study.

CLASSICAL AND ENGLISH HIGH SCHOOL.

COMMITTEE.

Jaques, Hall, Aldrich, Metcalf, Stoddard, Williams, Griffin, Ann B. Earle.

TEACHERS.

ABNER H. DAVIS, *Head Master.*

Roswell Parish,	Florence V. Beane,	Mary E. Wilder,
Babson S. Ladd,	Ann C. Stewart,	Hannah G. Creamer.
Latham Fitch,	Mary A. Parkhurst,	

BELMONT STREET SHCOOL.

COMMITTEE.

Gale, IX, VIII, VII, VI.   Harrington, V, IV, III.   McDermott, II, I, I.

TEACHERS.

IX, Edward I. Comins,	VI, Sarah W. Phillips.	II, Susie G. Gale.
Annie C. Wyman.	V, Tirza S. Nichols.	I, Ida C. Upton.
VIII, Vashti E. Hapgood.	IV, Esther G. Chenery.	I, Eliza J. Day.
VII, Mary A. Warren,	III, Mary T. Gale.	

DIX STREET SCHOOL.

COMMITTEE.

Aldrich, IX, VIII.   Williams, VII, VI.   Griffin, V, IV.

TEACHERS.

IX, Addison A. Hunt.	VII, EldoraM. Aldrich.	V, Kate A. Meade.
VIII, Sarah E. Dyer.	VI, Ellen Merrick.	IV, Elizabeth E. Daniels.

TRAINING SCHOOL.

COMMITTEE.

Hall, III.   Metcalf, II.   Ann B. Earle, I.

TEACHERS.

Rebecca Jones, Principal.

III, Mary L. Norcross.	II, Emma J. Houghton.	I, Emma J. Norcross.

WOODLAND STREET SCHOOL.

COMMITTEE.

Woodward, IX, VIII, VII.   Peabody, VI, V, IV.   Whitcomb, III, I.

TEACHERS.

IX, Sam'l E. Fitz.	VII, Minnie S. Fitch.	IV, Linnie M· Allen.
Jennie E. Howard,	VI, Mary M. Lawton.	III & II, Lizzie C. Goodwin
VIII, Mary F. Wentworth.	V, Mary J. Davis.	I, Maggie I. Melanefy.

LAMARTINE STREET SCHOOL.

COMMITTEE.

Metcalf, IX, VIII, VII.   Stone, V. IV, III.   Garrigan, II, II, I, I.

TEACHERS.

IX, Calvin ⁀C. Foster,	V, Nellie L. Moore.	II, Eliza A. Cook.
Eliza J. Wallace.	IV, Matilda Parker.	I, Esther B. Smith.
VIII, Mary E. Eastman.	III, Louise A. Dawson.	I, Belle Y. Hoyt.
VII & VI, Mary A. Smith.	II, Mary A. Kavanagh.	

LEDGE STREET SCHOOL.

COMMITEE.

Williams, IX. VIII, VII.   Murray, VI, V, IV.   McCafferty, III II, I, I.

TEACHERS.

IX, Henry M. Harrington,	VI, Maria P. Cole.	II, Esther M. Rice.
Minnie F. Whittier.	V, Charlotte N. Follett.	I, Mary. E. D. King.
VIII, Mary F. Reed.	IV, Margaret M. Geary.	I, Mary V. Calaghan.
VII, Joanna F. Smith.	III, Eliza F. Prentice.	

THOMAS STREET SCHOOL.

COMMITTEE.

Ann B. Earle, VIII, VII, VI.   Gale, VI, V, IV.   Warner, III, II, I, I.

TEACHERS.

VIII, Harriet G. Waite.	V, Elizabeth H. Coe.	II, Amanda M. Phillips.
VII, Ann E. McCambridge.	IV, Abbie F. Knowles.	I, Abbie F. Hemenway.
VI, Laura L. Newton.	III, Eunie M. Gates.	I, Flora G. Osgood.
VI. Mary A. Harrington.		

SYCAMORE STREET SCHOOL.
COMMITTEE.
Hall, VII, VI.   Jaques, V, IV.   Aldrich, III, II, I.

TEACHERS.
VII, Ann S. Dunton.   IV, Jennie A. Greene.   II, Emma F. Marsh.
VI, Carrie A. George.   III, Sarah W. Clements.   I, Nellie C. Thomas.
V, Carrie R. Clements.

EAST WORCESTER SCHOOLS.
COMMITTEE.
Whitcomb, V, IV, IV.   McNulty, III, II, II.   Chapin. I, I.

TEACHERS.
V, Harriet Hathaway.   III, Ella M. McFarland.   I, Mattie A. Collins.
IV, Annie Brown.   II, Carrie E. Putnam.   I, Aloysia Radcliffe.
IV, Tamerson S. Darling.   II, Hattie A. Smith.

PROVIDENCE STREET SCHOOL.
COMMITTEE.
Griffin, V, IV.   Ballard, III, II.   Harrington, I, I.

TEACHERS.
V, Elizabeth L. King.   III, Martha J. Morse.   I, Alice M. Prouty.
IV, Agnes R. Dame.   II, Sarah J. Newton.   I, Evelyn E. Towne.

ASH STREET SCHOOL.
COMMITTEE.
Goulding, V, IV.   Jaques, IV, III,   Murray, II, I.

TEACHERS.
V, Helen M. Harlow.   IV & III Sylvia N. Stackpole II, Abbie J. Reed.
IV, Mary J. Mack.   III, Helen M. Shattuck.   I, Emma J. Barton.

SOUTH WORCESTER SCHOOL.
COMMITTEE.
Ballard, VII, V.   Griffin, IV, III.   Goulding, II, I.

TEACHERS.
VIII & VI, Myra J. Wetmore.   IV, Ellen M Boyden.   II, Susan M. Forbes.
V, Sarah A. Bigelow.   III, Ann E. Hall.   I, Annetta M. Chapin,

PLEASANT STREET SCHOOL.
COMMITTEE.
Stoddard, V, IV.   Goulding, III, II.   Peabody, I.

TEACHERS.
V, Carrie E. Gilbert.   III, Josephine A. Hunt.   I, Emly M. Halsted.
IV, Addie H. Barnes.   II, Sarah A. Harrington.

SALEM STREET SCHOOL.
COMMITTEE.
Stone, VI, IV.   Hall, III, I.

TEACHERS.
VI, Rebecca Barnard.   III, Emma I. Claflin.   I, Hattie A. Harrington.
V & IV, Mary A. E. Adams.

EDGWORTH STREET SCHOOL.
COMMITTEE.
Warner, V, III.   Draper, II, I.

TEACHERS.
V & IV, Hattie E. Clarke.   II, Susan M. Buttrick.   I, Hattie M. Bliss.
III, Sarah M. Brigham.

NEW WORCESTER SCHOOL.
COMMITTEE.
Peabody, IX, VI.   Draper, V, I.

TEACHERS.
IX & VIII, Charlotte N. Munger.   IV. Adeliza Perry.   III & I, Ida A. E. Kenny
VII & VI, S. Lizzie Carter.

FRONT STREET SCHOOL.
COMMITTEE.
McDermont, IV, III.   Stoddard, II, I.

TEACHERS.
IV, Libbie H. Day.   II, Mary E. Trask.   I, Abigail Pratt.
III, Mary O. Whitmore.

QUINSIGAMOND SCHOOL.
COMMITTEE.
McNulty, VII & IV. Garrigan, III & I.
TEACHERS.
VII & VI, Leonora E. Perry. V & IV, Anna C. Perry. III & I, Amelia M. Walker.

MASON STREET SCHOOL.
COMMITTEE.
Harrington, III. Hall, I.

TEACHERS.
III, Julia M. Martin.   II & I, Mary E. Pease.

ADRIATIC SCHOOL.
COMMITTEE.
Draper, II. Jacques, I.

TEACHERS.
II, Martha T. Wyman.   I, Maria J. Metcalf.

UNION HILL SCHOOL.
COMMITTEE.
McCafferty, VI. Chapin, I.

TEACHERS.
VI & IV, Ellen G. Wheeler.   III & I, Abbie A. Wells.

ELM STREET SCHOOL.
COMMITTEE.—Murray.   TEACHER.—VII & VI, Etta A. Rounds.

ORANGE STREET SCHOOL. (*Ungraded.*)
COMMITTEE.—Garrigan.
TEACHERS.
Geo. A. Adams.   Persis E. King.

SUBURBAN SCHOOLS.

NORTHVILLE,	VII. Abbie E. Clough,	Wooodward.
	III. Stella E. Knight,	
TATNUCK,	Mary J. Packard,	Ballard.
VALLEY FALLS,	Susie A. Partridge,	Whitcomb.
LEESVILLE,	Ella P. Newton,	McNulty.
BLITHEWOOD,	Josephine P. Raymond,	Chapin.
BLOOMINGDALE,	Hattie M. Johnson,	McNulty.
ADAMS SQUARE,	Lottie M. Harrington,	Woodward.
BURNCOAT,	Lizzie Vaughan,	Chapin.
NORTH POND,	Emma S. R. Kendrick,	Metcalf.
CHAMBERLIN,	Clara Manley,	

EVENING SCHOOLS.

LOCATION,	TEACHERS.	COMMITTEE.
ORANGE ST.—BOYS,	Carrie A. George,	Stone.
	Mary A. Slater,	
	Jennie E. Stiles,	
ELM ST.—GIRLS,	Laura L. Newton,	McCafferty.
	Sarah J. Newton,	
EAST WORCESTER.—GIRLS,	Ella McFarland,	McDermott.
	Tamerson S. Darling,	
SUMMER ST.—MIXED,	Samuel A. Souther,	Williams.
	Abbie A. Souther,	
SOUTH WORCESTER.—MIXED,	Preston D. Jones,	Goulding.
	Myra J. Wetmore,	

EVENING DRAWING SCHOOL—BELMONT STREET.
COMMITTEE.
Gale, Metcalf, Warner.

	TEACHERS.	
MONDAY AND THURSDAY,	Geo. E. Gladwin,	Milton T. Higgins.
TUESDAY AND FRIDAY,	Geo. I. Alden,	Henry M. Armsby.
	Edw'd I. Comins. Ass't.	Edw'd R. Smith, Ass't.

SCHOOL CALENDAR FOR 1872.

Vacation period indicated by full face figures.

JANUARY

Sunday.	Monday.	Tuesday.	Wednesday.	Thursday.	Friday.	Saturday.
	1	2	3	4	5	6
7	8	9	10	11	12	13
14	15	16	17	18	19	20
21	22	23	24	25	26	27
28	29	30	31			

FEBRUARY

Sunday.	Monday.	Tuesday.	Wednesday.	Thursday.	Friday.	Saturday.
				1	2	3
4	5	6	7	8	9	10
11	12	13	14	15	16	**17**
18	**19**	**20**	**21**	**22**	**23**	**24**
25	26	27	28	29		

MARCH

Sunday.	Monday.	Tuesday.	Wednesday.	Thursday.	Friday.	Saturday.
					1	2
3	4	5	6	7	8	9
10	11	12	13	14	15	16
17	18	19	20	21	22	23
24	25	26	27	28	29	30
31						

APRIL

Sunday.	Monday.	Tuesday.	Wednesday.	Thursday.	Friday.	Saturday.
	1	2	3	4	5	6
7	8	9	10	11	12	13
14	15	16	17	18	19	20
21	22	23	24	25	26	27
28	29	30				

MAY

Sunday.	Monday.	Tuesday.	Wednesday.	Thursday.	Friday.	Saturday.
			1	2	3	**4**
5	**6**	**7**	**8**	**9**	**10**	**11**
12	13	14	15	16	17	18
19	20	21	22	23	24	25
26	27	28	29	30	31	

JUNE

Sunday.	Monday.	Tuesday.	Wednesday.	Thursday.	Friday.	Saturday.
						1
2	3	4	5	6	7	8
9	10	11	12	13	14	15
16	17	18	19	20	21	22
23	24	25	26	27	28	**29**
30						

JULY

Sunday.	Monday.	Tuesday.	Wednesday.	Thursday.	Friday.	Saturday.
	1	**2**	**3**	**4**	**5**	**6**
7	**8**	**9**	**10**	**11**	**12**	**13**
14	**15**	**16**	**17**	**18**	**19**	**20**
21	**22**	**23**	**24**	**25**	**26**	**27**
28	**29**	**30**	**31**			

AUGUST

Sunday.	Monday.	Tuesday.	Wednesday.	Thursday.	Friday.	Saturday.
				1	**2**	**3**
4	**5**	**6**	**7**	**8**	**9**	**10**
11	**12**	**13**	**14**	**15**	**16**	**17**
18	**19**	**20**	**21**	**22**	**23**	**24**
25	26	27	28	29	30	31

SEPT.

Sunday.	Monday.	Tuesday.	Wednesday.	Thursday.	Friday.	Saturday.
1	2	3	4	5	6	7
8	9	10	11	12	13	14
15	16	17	18	19	20	21
22	23	24	25	26	27	28
29	30					

OCT.

Sunday.	Monday.	Tuesday.	Wednesday.	Thursday.	Friday.	Saturday.
		1	2	3	4	5
6	7	8	9	10	11	12
13	14	15	16	17	18	19
20	21	22	23	24	25	26
27	28	29	30	31		

NOV.

Sunday.	Monday.	Tuesday.	Wednesday.	Thursday.	Friday.	Saturday.
					1	2
3	4	5	6	7	8	9
10	11	12	13	14	15	16
17	18	19	20	21	22	23
24	25	26	27	**28***	**29**	**30**

DEC.

Sunday.	Monday.	Tuesday.	Wednesday.	Thursday.	Friday.	Saturday.
1	2	3	4	5	6	7
8	9	10	11	12	13	14
15	16	17	18	19	20	21
22	23	24	**25**	**26**	**27**	**28**
29	**30**	**31**				

The 1st, Term begins Dec. 4th, 1871, and ends Feb. 17th, 1872, comprising 10 weeks.
" 2d, " " Feb. 26th, 1872, " " May 3d, " " 10 "
" 3d, " " May 13th, " " " June 28th, " " 7 "
" 4th, " " Aug. 26th, " " " *Nov. 27th, " " 14 "
" 1st, " " Dec. 2d, 1872.
Half Term reports due March 30th, Oct. 19th.
* Assuming that Thanksgiving day will be appointed for the last Thursday in November, as usual.

REPORT OF THE CITY ENGINEER.

To the City Council:

GENTLEMEN : — The city Engineer presents the following Annual Report for the year ending November 30, 1871, to wit:

MILL BROOK.

Operations have been continued upon this important work, during the season making the fifth year in succession since the work was commenced.

Two sections of the work were let, the one for arching the portion north of Lincoln Square, under the extension of Prescott street, and one for a section extending from Green street at a point where the work was commenced in 1867, to the point on Cambridge street where Mill Brook crosses said Cambridge street. The work above Lincoln Square was let to E. B. Walker, of North Oxford, April 22, 1871.

That south of Green street was awarded April 25, to Messrs. Patrick O'Keefe and H. G. Roche.

Messrs. O'Keefe and Roche commenced work May 2. The health of Mr. O'Keefe not proving sufficient to go on with the work, Messrs. E. B. Walker and Brigham Converse assumed their contract at the same rate, and upon the same conditions as it was awarded to Messrs. O'Keefe and Roche. Messrs. Walker and Converse commenced work thereon May 9, 1871.

The city having to put in the wooden flume, to convey the water over the work above Lincoln Square, work was not commenced here by Mr. Walker until June 8. After which dates each job progressed regularly and constantly until the close of the season. The arching above Lincoln Square was completed Dec. 8, 1871. ⹁By a vote of the City Council Oct. 16, 1871, this

17

work was ordered to be extended across Lincoln Square. But
the season being much advanced before this part of the work was
commenced, it was suspended, when it had been carried entirely
under the horse railroad track, when that point was reached,
it was then found impracticable to complete the remainder before
January 1872.

There now remains 55 feet in the Square to be finished. The
connection between the new and old work has been made in a
safe and substantial manner. The lower end has been bridged,
in view of the fact that probably the balance of the work will
be done in two or three years.

The amount of work completed to the present time is as follows, to wit:

		Feet.
1867.	Laid by Adams Dawson & Co.,	1364.
1868.	" " E. B. Walker,	820.
1869.	" " E. B. Walker,	1571.
1870.	" " E. B. Walker,	387.
1870.	" " Dawson, Tank, and Ingerson,	1765.5
1871.	" " E. B. Walker,	3043.5
	Total,	8951.0

The form of construction used in the above work has been as
follows, to wit:

	Feet.
Walled in open canal,	4647.
Covered with an arch,	4078.9
Spanned by 5 street bridges,	225.1
Total,	8951.0

The cost of this work has been as follows,

Paid to 1871,	$383,294 55
" to Dec. 1, 1871,	84,027 74
Expenditure to Dec. 1, 1871,	$467,322 29

To complete the walling and arching from the southerly side
of Cambridge street, to its terminus on the north-easterly side of
Prescott street there remains to be arched in Union street, from
Court Mills to the end in Lincoln Square 340 feet, and of the
work contracted for between Green and Cambridge street 1336.5
feet. On the work between Green and Cambridge streets no
street bridges have been laid this year.

Foundations have been arranged for six. There remains at the lower end to be built next Cambridge street, 127 feet in order to finish the work to the southerly side of the street, including the bridge over it. To put in this section it will be necessary to enclose the work on 3 sides with sheet piling. The Brook will be carried past the work on one side of this piling. To free the foundation from water, it will be necessary to use a steam pump. Across the canal, at all proposed streets, cast iron water pipe has been laid under the bed of the canal, and those not in use at present have been so left as to be ready for future use whenever required, without the necessity of laying them under the water running in it.

No arrangement has been made for the connection of the Piedmont street sewer with this canal, because no plan has been matured by which said sewer shall be extended to the new location of Mill Brook from its present terminus.

This extension will need early attention, or as soon as the present current of Mill Brook is turned into the new channel, as the amount of water then finding its way into the old channel will be entirely inadequate to keep the stream from becoming a nuisance and source of pestilence.

The Plan of this extension will need to include the entire district between Millbury street and the Providence Rail Road, as well as to make ultimate provision for the proper connection of the sewer which must drain the district, the water shed of which follows the valleys around the Adriatic Mills and empties into Mill Brook below the Gas Works.

The matter of building down the foundations of the Boston & Albany Rail Road has not been accomplished, as recommended in the last Annual Report. This has been postponed because all the pumping machinery at the command of the department has been constantly in use the entire season, and further because there seemed to be no immediate haste in the matter, as a late examination shows all the parts of the old bridge to be standing safely and securely in its present position. Still this work needs early attention the coming year.

The quantity of materials moved and used in the construction of Mill Brook, since the work was commenced has been as follows :

103,950	Cubic yards of Excavation
42,611	" " Back filling.
653	" " Ledge Excavation.
24,329	Perch Stone, laid dry.
10,971	" " " in cement.
6,519	" " " in paving.
2,619	Piles driven.
327	Inlets for side sewers.
31	Man holes in the arch.

SEWERS.

The construction of sewers has been continued through the year, the same as in each previous year since 1867.

The unfinished contracts of S. H. Tarbell, George C. Barney and E. S. Knowles, left over from the close of the year 1870 were finished early in the season. The contract for the sewers ordered by the City Council on March 13, 1871, was awarded to H. B. Leach & Co. of Philadelphia, April 20, 1871. This firm commenced work May 9.

The streets in which sewers have been laid the past year, with the number feet, size of sewer, number of man-holes, catch-basins and inlets, are given in the accompanying schedule marked A.

Schedule B gives the streets included in the contracts with Leach & Co. and Leach & Son, and now remaining unfinished.

Schedule C gives all the streets in which sewers have now been laid with the number of feet, size, number of man-holes, catch-basins and inlets.

When Mill Brook from Court Mill to the estate of L. W. Pond shall have been diverted from its present bed into the new arched channel, the following sewers will have to be connected across its present channel, viz:

Central street, Thomas street, Market street, and School street extended from Laurel to Union street.

The expenditure for sewers to Dec. 1, 1871, is as follows:

Paid to Jan. 1	$443,857 25
" in 1871,	159,873 03
Amount,	$603,730 28

The number of private drains now entering the public sewers are as follows:

Entered previous	to 1867,		129
"	in	1867,	6
"	in	1868,	107
	in	1869,	210
	in	1870,	364
	in	1871,	383
	Total,		1199

Schedule D gives the streets upon which sewers have been laid, together with the drains and number of buildings on each.

During the year examinations have been made and investigations entered into relative to the subject of the utilization of the sewage of the city, a report of which will hereafter be submitted.

The care of the present system of sewers is a matter of much importance. There are now built and connected with the sewers 440 catch-basins. These need clearing of the sand, gravel and rubbish carried into them by the rains, from two to three times a year, and many situated upon streets where there are no paved gutters after every heavy shower.

It is necessary that this should be done as often as the basins are filled at least, to prevent the sand and gravel being carried into the main sewers, because it can be removed much more cheaply from the basins than from the sewers where it is liable to be deposited. The average capacity of the catch-basins is about 3 1-2 cubic yards; once full the basins now built hold 1484 cubic yards, and the amount of materials to be moved from them annually will range from 4000 to 5000 cubic yards.

HIGHWAYS.

Surveys have been made preparatory to the making public, or the alteration of the lines in the streets given in the following table;

STREETS LOCATED IN 1871.

NAMES OF STREETS.			REMARKS.
Cedar	Street,	269.78 feet	Relocation from Chestnut to Everet
Chatham	"	639.06 "	Extension from Crown to Newbury
Congress	"	619.34 "	From Crown to Newbury.
Coral	"	1544.23 "	" Grafton to Ætna.
Dix		1159.77 "	" Harvard to North Ashland.
Foster	"	269.24 "	Extension to Waldo.

Hanover Street,	1357.96 feet	Extension from Arch to Kendall.
		Relocation at Junction with New-
Lovell "	1291.78 "	ton Street.
Orchard "	650.12 "	From Arch to Belmont.
Penn Avenue,	1791.67 "	" Grafton to Union Avenue.
Quincy Street,	396.26 "	" Austin to Crown.
Tatnuck "	765.10 "	" May St. to Chandler Street.
Union Avenue,	405.39 "	" Providence to Chapin Street.
Waldo Street,	117.12 "	Extension to Exchange.
Washington, "	492.25 "	From Lamartine to Lafayette St.
Wellington "	1017.22 "	" Main to Chandler Street.
W. Boylston "	3343.00 "	" Holden Road to School House
		line.
Woodland "	3000.00 "	" King to Downing Street.

$$\overline{19,130.09}$$

The number of feet of streets surveyed and located since 1867 is as follows to wit :

1867	1,868 feet	1870	62,582 feet
1868	31,836 "	1871	19,130 "
1869	23,156 "		
			138.572 ft.

Total 26 miles and 1292 feet.

SIDEWALKS.

The number of feet of grades set for sidewalks since 1867 has been as follows :

1867	5,037 feet	1870	39,424 feet
1868	7,876 "	1871	78,141 "
1869	13,139 "		
		Total	143,617 ft

27 miles 1057 feet.

Schedule of streets on which levels have been made for the establishment of grades for sidewalks during the year as follows :

SIDEWALKS LAID OUT IN 1871.

NAMES OF STREETS.		From Main to Oxford street on
Austin Street,	735.0 feet	south side.
Austin "	974.2 "	Both sides from Hawly to Merrick
		street.
Belmont "	2550.0 "	Both sides from Lincoln Square to
		Oak Avenue.
Benefit "	1554.0 "	Both sides from Main to Beacon st.
Central "	2790.8 "	" " " " to Summer st.
Charlton "	1057.7 "	
Chatham "	1302.8 "	Both sides from Crown to Newbury

Chestnut Street.	2770.9	feet.	Both sides from Pleasant to Bowdoin street.
Church "	668.4	"	Both sides from Front to Mechanic
Clinton "	1491.0	"	
Coral "	3107.0	"	Both sides from Grafton to Ætna st.
Crown "	491.0	"	East side from Pleasant to Chatham
Dix	2343.0	"	Both sides from Harvard to N. Ashland street.
Exchange "	1568.1	"	Both sides from Main to Union st.
Hanover "	962.3	"	" " " Prospect to Laurel st.
Harvard "	1069.0	"	" " " State to Highland st.
High "	2141.1	"	" " " Pleasant to Austin st.
Lagrange "	1360.6	"	" " " Main to Beacon st.
Mechanic "	1260.0	"	" " " Union to Bridge st.
Merrick "	1763.0	"	" " " Austin to Pleasant st.
Newbury "	2521.9	"	" " " Chandler to Pleasant
Oak "	696,6	"	
Orchard "	1310.2	"	Both sides from Arch to Belmont st.
			" " " Grafton to Union
Penn Avenue,	3584.0	"	Avenue.
Piedmont Street,	3122.0	"	Both sides from Main to Chandler
Pleasant "	626.8	"	South side from Crown to Newbury.
Portland "	931.0	"	Both sides from Myrtle to Madison
Providence "	5121.2	"	Both sides from Water to Union Avenue.
Quincy "	824.0	"	Both sides from Chatham to Austin
Salem "	2644.5	"	Both sides from Park to Madison st.
Shrewsbury "	790.5	"	North side from Hill to Henry st.
Sycamore "	986.8	"	Both sides
Temple "	2349.5	"	" " " Green to Grafton st.
Thomas "	2463.5	"	" " " Main to Summer st.
Union "	4522.0	"	" " " Mechanic to Market
Vernon "	1893.0	"	Both sides from Green to Patterson
Waldo "	248.0	"	Both sides from Waldo House to Exchange st.
Wellington "	1057.0	"	Both sides from Main to South Irving street
West "	2361.0	"	Both sides from William to Highland street.
Winter "	2203.5	"	Both sides from Green to Water st.
Woodland "	5940.0	"	" " " King to Downing
Total,	78140.8		

MAPS OF THE CITY.

An additional volume of these maps consisting of 41 sheets have been finished during the year. This volume is duplicated, one copy of which is for use in the office of the city engineer and one for that of the assessors. This volume contains 878 lots, and covers an area exclusive of streets of 12,392,517 square feet equal to $284\frac{493}{1000}$ acres.

In addition to this volume there have been finished fourteen duplicate maps of a like character, and a large amount of material collected for additional maps.

On the maps for the use of the office of the city engineer, the sewers are drawn with a representation of all man-holes, giving the elevation of the top of each above mean-tide water, and also the depths of the sewer.

WATER WORKS.

The repair of the works has been as good during the year, as on any previous one, since their construction.

Their efficiency for the usual supply upon the summits of the high lands, upon which distributing pipes have been laid has been constantly diminishing during the year.

During the fall, this evil had increased to such an extent that the Joint Standing Committee on water instructed the city engineer, Nov. 3, 1871 to examine the subject, and report what measures were necessary to be taken to afford the desired relief, as well as to keep up their efficiency upon the lower levels.

In accordance with those instructions, the following Report was submitted upon that subject: to wit:—

To the Joint Standing Committee on Water: Gentlemen:

In accordance with your instructions of Nov. 3, 1871, that the City Engineer report what is necessary in order to carry out the request of Geo. Crompton and 42 others, that measures may be taken to supply the high lands around the city with water, and to make an estimate of the cost of the work, and also to make a statement of the needs of the same as connected with the present works, the following considerations and estimates are submitted.

When the original works built in 1845, were enlarged in 1864, the amount of water assumed as sufficient for the then present and prospective wants of the city for, from 10 to 16 years, was two millions gallons per day. The computations to ascertain the size of pipes required, resulted in adopting the present 16 inch mains. These mains were in capacity twice as large as those recommended for the supply of the city in the project examined and reported upon in 1856 by M. B. Inches, Esq., which project was to bring the water from Henshaw Pond. The main recommended by him at that time as being ample, was 12 inches in diameter, while the amount of water proposed to be supplied was one million gallons per day. The unexpected growth of the city since 1865, which has added to the population a number as large if not larger than that of the whole population in 1848, has so far drawn upon the resources of the water supply as to reach the calculated limits of the capacity of the present mains. This is not only due to the large and natural increase for both domestic and manufacturing purposes, over that of the first years in which the present enlarged distribution was in use, but also to the use of a very large quantity, in a manner at first not contemplated.

The amount of street and other main pipes with the number of service pipes laid in each year since 1863, is given in the following table, to wit:

Date.	Feet of Street Mains Laid.	Number of Serv. Pipe put in.
1864	31.741	29
1865	26.723	207
1866	28.871	284
1867	27.543	388
1868	22.589	504
1869	46.506	673
1870	29.156	581

By this exhibit it will be seen that from 1868 including both years the number of service pipes laid was 1412, and in 1869 and 1870—1254 or in the last years 158 less than in the five previous years.

The amount of street mains also followed about the same ratio of increase. Leaving out 1864 as those laid in that year were mostly the main pipes from Leicester to Austin street, and in the following four years there was laid 105.726 feet and in 1869 and 1870, 75.662 feet. The number of applications for service supplies for the present year is about up to that of 1868. The whole number registered for the year being 488, and the total number attached 3319.

18

The works as projected and enlarged in 1864, continued to fulfill their desired office without much loss of head, until the latter part of 1870, since which time the demand upon the supply has sensibly diminished the effective head.   From 1866 to 1870 the average head at the water shop on Thomas street might be taken at from 70 to 75 pounds to the square inch, or heads varying from 161 to 172 1-2 feet.   Since which time it has been gradually diminished until at the present time the average head may be taken as ranging from 50 to 65 pounds and subject to much and many variations, often going as low as 45 pounds, pressures representing 103½ and 149½ feet respectively.

The premises of the Petitioners lie upon the summit of Union Hill and Grant square, have a head of only 30 feet when the Hunt reservoir is full, at the house of George Crompton and at the square ; and as all motion of water in pipes is only produced or gained by the expenditure of power, and in all works supplied by gravitation, the power is only that of the elevation between the surface of the water at the reservoir and the point of delivery, the power consumed by this motion is a portion of the head itself and causes what is technically termed "loss of head." From the causes before pointed out it results that the petitioners cannot have water upon their premises but a small portion of the day, and that only at night.

This matter was discussed somewhat at length as to its necessity and utility in the annual Report of the Department, and need not be minutely considered at this time.   Only suffice it to say that the mode then pointed out is the only remedy by which the evils and privations complained of can be remedied and these elevations be placed upon the same footing, as regards an effective supply, as is the lower levels in the city.   This mode, as then stated, is to lay an independent main from the Leicester Reservoir, so as to use the whole head of that reservoir, with which to supply these high lands.

This head enables water to be delivered at the house of George Crompton with a head of about 150 feet, and at Grant Square with a head of 130 to 140 feet ; pressure ample both for domestic and fire service.

Before entering in detail upon the arrangement of mains needed for this purpose, one important matter will be mentioned

Of 20 inch pipe, - - - - - - - 1,500 feet,
" 18 " " - - - - - - - - 1,000 "
" 16 " " - - - - - - - 4,800 "
                                              ———————
Total, - - - - - - - - - 7,300 "

While the line from Webster Square to the city hall is 10,400 feet entirely 16 inch pipe, and by taking off a line to Mason street as above suggested a more full advantage can be realized from the arrangement of pipes between the Hunt Reservoir and Webster Square than is now obtained from the present single line, because to the point of supply by adding the new main proposed would be in effect like enlarging the diameter of the present, while the added main would give the double advantage of always having one main open to the city under almost all conceivable circumstances. To add this main is deemed to be an urgent neccessity for the preservation of the value of the present works for fire purposes.

The pipe estimated is the wrought iron and cement pipe now so extensively used on the works for all pressures under 225 feet, and heavy cast iron for all heads over 225 feet.

ESTIMATE OF COST OF HIGH SERVICES.

9,407 feet	16 inch	cement pipe,	at 3 25	$30,605 25
11,183 "	16 "	cast iron "	at 6 00	67,098 00
3,000 "	15 "	" " "	5 50	16,500 00
4,892 "	15 "	cement "	3 00	14,676 00
3,500 "	12 "	cast iron "	4 40	15,050 00
6,825 "	12 "	cement "	2 25	15,356 25
Blasting ledge,				4,000 00
Gates and Branches,				3,500 00

$166,785 50

Respectfully submitted,

PHINEHAS BALL, *City Engineer.*
Worcester, Nov. 17, 1871.

The following report was suggested by the discussion of the foregoing report, and was made in compliance with instructions from the Board of Aldermen. To wit:

Gentlemen: —In compliance with the following order adopted by your Board, Dec. 4, to wit:—

" *Ordered,* That the City Engineer be instructed to make an additional report in print, giving the probable population which the present Water Works will supply, and combining therewith the statement of previous reports on that subject."

The following considerations and extracts from previous reports upon the subject are presented :—

On the subject of the areas of the water shed of the present works, and the basins of some of the adjacent streams, my report to the Committee on Water in 1863 makes this statement :—

" The past season careful surveys in detail have been made of the basin of Lynde Brook, Henshaw Pond, and all of that portion of Kettle Brook above the mill of Samuel L. Hodges, in Cherry Valley.

The basin of Lynde Brook above the outlet of the intervale, on the farm of Mr. Edwin Waite, contains 1,870 acres; that of Henshaw Pond 590 acres ; that of Kettle Brook, as above, 4,200 acres. Thus it will be seen that the basin of Lynde Brook is 3,169 times as large as Henshaw Pond Basin, and that of Kettle Brook only about 2 1–4 times larger than that of Lynde Brook. In general terms the water drained from any basin is directly proportioned to its area, and the amount of rain falling thereon."

A weir was constructed on Lynde Brook and finished on the 19th of March last, which was unfortunately washed away by the very severe freshet of the 26th of March, only six days after its completion, it having proved quite too small to carry so large a quantity of water as then came down the stream. The average amount of water passing down the stream in these six days was 4,845,960 gallons per day, not including but a very small portion of the freshet. From March 25th the stream continued so high that the weir was not reconstructed until the 8th of May afterwards, at which time the gauging recommenced and has been carried forward systematically ever since."

The results of the gauging of the Brook, from May 8th to Nov. 1st have been calculated and arranged in the following table:

DATE.	Time in hours	Number of gallons estimated by the gauge.	Rain fall in gallons, estimated from the rain gauge kept at the Hospital.	Pr. ct. of rain fall.	Inc's of rain fall.	rain fall drained off each month.	Average number of galllons guaged per day.
May,	546	53,730,140	79,420,800	1.56		67	2,361,768
June,	659	15,006,770	60,074,700	1.18		24	546,528
July,	548	131,165,510	448,523,700	8.81		29	5,744,472
August,	757	123,328,550	293,755,000	5 77		42	3,910,008
Sept.	708	56.951,030	130,331,500	2.56		43	1,930,536
Oct.	720	140,153,000	215,352,500	4.23		65	4,671,766
Total,	3,938	520,335,000	1,227,458,200	24.11			3,111,800

Time, 164 1–12 days.   Average amount of flow as estimated by the guage, 3, 111,800 gallons per day; an amount largely in excess of any present want of the city.   Percentage of rain fall drained off from July to November 1st, 48, nearly.   Inches of rain fall during this time, 24.11; being 0.36 of an inch less than the usual average for those months for the last 21 years, as reg. istered at the hospital.   The percentage of rain fall given as drained off in each month is not strictly correct, as each succeed. ing month is affected more or less by the month next preced. ing.

After careful investigation of the subject of the per cent. of the rain-fall, which can be collected from any water shed, and the comparison of many authorities, the amount assumed for basins like those under consideration with the total amount drained off in each year is thus stated in said report:

"An estimate is here given of the amount of water annually drained from these basins, from data derived from the experi. ments just given.   The percentage is assumed at 65, in consid. eration of the steep hilly character of their contour and the impervious nature of their soil, aided by the result of the gaug. ing of Lynde Brook from May 8th to Nov. 1st.   The average annual amount of rain-fall is taken at 46.92 inches, being the amount given as the average of twenty-one years observations at the hospital here.

	Acres.	Gallons drained off per annum.	Gallons per day.
Lynde Brook,	1,870	1,547,686,800	4,240,238
Henshaw Pond,	590	488,307,600	1,337,911
Kettle Brook, above Kent, and from which water may be turned into Lynde Brook,	3,200	2,648,248,000"	

19

Hon. D. Waldo Lincoln as Chairman of the Committee on Water in 1863, in a report to the City Council detailing the doings of the Committee for that year, states the value of Lynde Brook for the purpose of supplying the city with water in these words :

"It is asserted by Professor Silliman as a basis of calculation, beyond question reliable, that the springs and streams of a limited district like this, represent, in the aggregate, only the annual rain-fall—less the amount lost in soaking and evaporation. Adopting and following his calculations and method of reasoning, we arrive at these results. On each superficial acre of ground are 43,560 square feet, upon which a rain-fall of 48 inches (the aggregate annual rain-fall in Worcester for the last twenty years) will precipitate an aggregate of 173,907 cubic feet of water. A cubic foot weighing 62.5 pounds, this is equal 10,869,187 pounds. As the imperial gallon holds 10 pounds of water, this weight corresponds to 1,086,918 gallons. It having been established by Mr. Ball that 65 per cent. of this quantity will flow into the stream and can be stored, we have an amount of water from each acre available for use of 706,496 gallons, and on 1,870 acres, which is the extent of the water-shed of Lynde Brook, 1,321,147,520 gallons, or 3,619,956 imperial gallons a day, which is equal to about 4,223,000 wine gallons for the 365 days of the year."

The observations made in the past seven years upon the amount of water to be relied upon annually from the present works has fully confirmed the conclusions arrived at in the investigations of 1863. In the Fall of 1866 the Reservoir was nearly emptied in order to re-arrange the outlet gate. The work was finished so as to commence filling on the 15th of October. On the first day of January 1867, or in 67 days the Reservoir was filled ; having in this time saved 228 millions of gallons over and above the regular supply of 666 services, an amount exceeding four millions gallons per day.

In the drought of 1870, as is well-known, the amount of water in store was entirely exhausted early in November. The water furnished by the basin was inadequate for the supply until February 18 of the present year, when the Reservoir commenced filling over and above the supply to 2812 services. It was filled May 7, or in 77 days. By the raising of the dam in 1870 its capacity in May last is estimated at 375 millions gallons. On May 7 and 8, there was wasted by estimate 18 millions gallons.

Taking the consumption at two millions gallons per day during this time, and the water collected and wasted would amount to 7 millions gallons per day.

From all these facts it is believed that it is safe to rely upon our present supply as being adequate to four millions gallons per day, provided all the water of the basin is stored.

There now remains the question of how large a population this quantity will amply supply for all its varied uses.

Upon this point the report of 1863, above quoted, makes these statements.

"The usual mode of estimating is to allow a certain number of gallons to each individual enumerated in the population. At the time the Cochituate water works were projected, the engineers assumed that 28½ gallons per day to each individual would be a sufficient allowance. This was assumed because the practice of supplying cities with water, up to that time, had found that quantity to be sufficient.

The following table exhibits the amount of water supplied by the Cochituate water works to the city of Boston from 1848 to 1863.

SUPPLY, INCOME, &C., SINCE THE COMMENCEMENT.

	Amount consumed per day.	Annual income to Jan. 1, of each year.	Water takers. Total number Jan. 1, of each year.	Total No of fixtures supplied as far as registered.	Gallons consumed per day per individual.
1848	Works opened Oct. 25.				
1849	3,680.000		5,200		
1850	5,837.900	$72,043.20	12,108		42¾
1851	6,883.800	98,367.90	13,463		42
1852	8,125.800	161,299.72	16,076		56
1853	8,542.300	179,486.25	16,862	13,594	57¼
1854	9,902.000	196,352.32	18,170		63
1855	10,346.300	217,007.51	19,193		63½
1856	12,048.600	266,302.77	19,998		72
1857	12,726.000	282,651.84	20,806		73
1858	12,847.000	289,328.83	21,602	47,888	72¼
1859	13,175.000	302,409.73	22,414	52,744	72
1860	17,238.000	314,808.97	23,271	59,218	97½
1861	18,189.304	334,544.86	24,316	64,526	99½
1862	16,600.000	364,323.46	25,486	75,216	89
1863		373,922.88	26,289	77,843	

The foregoing table conclusively shows that when once water is introduced, that its use increases from year to year, and probably by the same laws that govern the increase of business, comfort and refinement.

In Boston it is to be remarked, that in 1853, when the takers were 16,862 the fixtures supplied were 31,594 ; and that in January 1, 1863, while the takers had increased 9472, the fixtures supplied had increased 46,294, or nearly five times as fast as the number of takers, showing that from year to year old takers are constantly adding to their fixtures as business necessity, domestic comfort or luxury add the motive, and increased prosperity the means of making the extension.''

The following tabular statement is collected from various recent reports upon the subject of the water supply of various cities named.   The conclusions are deduced from the amount of water supplied :

City.	Date.	Gallons per inhabitant.
Charlestown, Mass.,	1867	41.83
Brooklyn, N. Y., estimated per consumer,	1867	47.19
Cleveland, Ohio,	1866	22.35
Detroit, Mich.,	1867	48.46
Chicago,	—	50.00
St. Louis, estimated per consumer,	1864	54.01
Louisville,	1866	16.81
New York,	1864	62.00
London,	1869	29.00 .
Paris,	1869	24.80
Boston,	1870	60.00
Philadelphia,	1869	50.00

Assuming our supply as equal to four millions gallons per day, and the daily amount per individual as ample to be fifty gallons, then the number of population which can be supplied will be 80,000 ; or at sixty gallons 66,000, and at 70 gallons 57,000.

With any economy in the use of water it is believed that the present supply is adequate for a population of at least 60,000, and for 'purposes not essentially different from that for which water is now supplied, and at the same time it will be seen that there is no surplus for uses for manufacturing purposes beyond the ordinary supply for steam.

Respectfully submitted,

PHINEHAS BALL, *City Engineer.*

Worcester, Dec. 9, 1871.

THE FOLLOWING SCHEDULE EXHIBITS THE AMOUNT OF PIPE LAID AND FIXTURES ON THE WORKS FROM 1863 TO THE PRESENT TIME.

Date.	Feet of pipe laid	Gates set.	Hydrants, public and private.	Service taps.	Service pipe.	Hydrant Branches
1863	27,831			157		
1864	31,741	54	152	29	3,800	
1865	26,723	70	65	207	5,968	1660
1866	26,871	46	36	584	8,082	275
1867	27,543	58	56	388	11,312	430
1868	22,589	47	35	504	13,790	240
1869	46,506	126	45	673	17,202	360
1870	29,156	66	29	581	16,282	232
1871	35,438	80	46	504	11,781	
Totals,	274,398	547	464*	3327	88,219	3197

The expenditures for the year have been as follows:

General maintenance - - - - - -	15,084.85
Pumping " - - - - - - -	9,741.35
General constitution - - - - - -	56,565.23
Reservoir Dam - - - - - - -	41,523.43
Real Estate at Reservoir - - - - -	4,632.67

Income and Expenditures from the works from 1863 to date:

Date.	Assessments received in Cash.	Public Buildings.	Hydrants.	Total Income.	Amount expended in each year from 1863.
1863	2,570.72	included.	not taxed.	2,570.72	35,000.00
1864	3,244.83	"	"	3,244.83	77,425.32
1865	9,542.50	162.00	"	9,704.50	88,701 79
1866	14.0u8.67	276.00	4,800.00	19,084.67	102,066.82
1867	17,311.35	420.00	4,800.00	22,531.35	74,813.05
1868	24,689.94	447.00	5,550.00	30,686.94	32,126.12
1869	31,562,90	403.17	7,550.00	39,516.07	95,131.17
1870	38,310.42	705.00	8,000.00	47,015.42	144,463.63
1871	47,888.98	798.00	8,000.00	56,686.98	102,721.31
Total.	189,130.31	3,211.17	38,700.00	231,041.48	752,449.21

The income and expenditures for 1871 is for only 11 months, as the ending of the financial year has been changed from the first of January to the first of December.

The following fixtures were upon the works and uses made of the water to Dec. 1, 1871.

Buildings supplied	2915	Water Closets	1888
Families "	5484	Set wash tubs	376
Persons using,	29,123	Urinals	207
Offices supplied,	117	Hose	836
Stores supplied,	320	Hot water backs	357
Shops "	227	Horses stabled	1284
Stables ."	328	Cows "	101
Sinks in use	6468	Carriages washed	661
Basins "	1493	Number of taps	14832
Baths "	581		

RESERVOIR DAM.

The raising of this dam has been accomplished during the year in accordance with the order of the City Council.

The contract for the work was continued by the Joint Standing Committee on water, with Messrs. Riley & Smith, upon the same terms and conditions as the contract of 1870. It being considered by them to the advantage of the city so to do. The contractors finished the work Dec. 11, 1871.

The upper gate house was finished Dec. 16. This dam has now been raised 15 feet above the wash as left in 1865.

The roll-way is of solid stone masoney built very substantial, safe and secure.

The lateness of the season did not permit that finish to be made on the exterior slope of the dam which will be required. This is a matter which will need attention early the coming spring, so that the outside slopes may be properly grassed over, and thus be protected from washing by the rains and showers of the season.

The quantity of materials moved and used in the enlargement of the work has been as follows:

8,750 cubic yards of Loam.
6,040 " " Trenches.
91,878 " ." Filling.
2,813 perch of spiling wall laid in cement.
1,335 " other "
397 " dry "
6,429 " paving

This includes all cut and dimension stone work in the two gate houses and roll-way. This enlargement has been done under the superintendence of Mr. Wm. H. Heywood, in a most faithful and satisfactory manner. The land which will be flowed has not been grubbed only partially.

Most of the loose woody refuse has been collected and burned upon all lots bought except that upon the Jos. Bottomly lot. This will be cleared of the wood during the winter, and the brush burned.

It will be necessary to continue the operation of removing, as far as practicable, the woody and organic matters still left upon this ground the coming season. This is urged as a matter of great importance in order to prevent as far as may be, any injurious effect which these substances may have upon the waters stored, when used for domestic and culinary purposes.

The height of the water over the top of the flauge of the outlet pipe in the upper gate house, during the year, is given in the annexed table.

DATE.	Depth above top of outlet pipe.	Remarks	DATE.	Depth above top of outlet pipe.	Remarks.
Jan. 1, 1871,	3.57		June 27, 1871,	27.80	High water
" 16, "	2.37		July 1, "	27.48	of season.
" 19, "	4.35		" 15, "	26.57	
Feb. 11, "	4.10		Aug. 1, "	26.32	
" 17, "	2.92	Commenced	" 15, "	26.90	
Mar. 1, "	11.42	raising	Sept. 1, "	26.00	
" 15, "	16.32		" 15, "	25.24	
Apr. 1, "	22.00		Oct. 1, "	24.14	
" 15, "	23.30		" 15, "	24.66	
May 1, "	24.75		Nov. 1, "	24.00	
" 7, "	27.30	Waste gate ras'd	" 17, "	24.82	
" 15, "	27.60	Reservoir filled.	" 27, "	26.14	
June 1, "	27.10		Dec. 16, "	26.00	
" 17, "	26.00		" 30, "	27.14	

Whole depth of water, from surface of Rollway to top of flauge to outlet pipes, 34.27

On the 30th day of December 1871, the Reservoir lacked 7.13 feet of being filled. This 7.13 feet represents a storage capacity of about 200 millions of gallons, or about 28 millions gallons, less than that of the first reservoir.

The quantity of water which can now be stored is estimated approximately at about 560 millions gallons.

ADDITIONAL SUPPLY.

The question of additional water supply is one of vital importance to every present or prospective interest in the city.

Viewing the rapid growth of the city, and the increased use of water and the facts as stated in the reports of Nov. 17 and Dec. 9, it is appareut that this question from necessity will demand an early attention. The subject is not deemed at the present either inopportune or misplaced, because that whatever may be done in the future, much time must necessarily elapse before any fresh supply will be obtained, and in the mean time the question needs all the various consideration which one of this magnitude demands.

By the Reports above referred to, it is patent that the resources of Lynde Brook have a limit of from $3\frac{1}{2}$ to 4 millions gallons per day varying of course with the seasons.

From the west, and by the present or future mains, there are three methods by which the present supply may be increased.

First, by building a conduit across the ridge which divides the present Lynde Brook Valley at D. Waldo Kent's Mill in Leicester, so as to take the waste floods of Kettle Brook into the present Reservoir when the same is not full.

An arrangement of this nature, fairly used, would not infringe any manufacturing right now existing upon the stream, as it would propose to take nothing from them except the wastage of floods after their own Reservoirs were filled. Its utility would be entirely dependent upon this uncertain annual wastage. Yet in some years the quantity of water which might thus be stored would be of more value than the entire cost of making the conduit across the ridge from basin to basin. It would possess the still further value and advantage of furnishing the means of taking the waters of Kettle Brook through our present mains for the supply whenever the city should find it necessary and for its advantage so to do. The waters of Kettle Brook which could thus be turned into the present system, would be that falling on 3200 acres, or an amount equal to about 7 millions gallons per day. The present Reservoir capacity upon the stream above this point is estimated at about 550 millions gallons.

The waters thus diverted when taken in full control by the city would have to be paid for to the mill owners below, but could thus be taken without further expense.

A still further advantage of this connection would be that in case of a failure of the supply as in 1870, any waters in the reservoirs on Kettle Brook above Kent's, could be bought and conveyed into the present system at once without further expense of pumping or other contingencies. This advantage alone would have saved the city in 1870 from one-fourth to one-half of the cost of the construction of this conduit.

Second, to take and add to the present works Henshaw Pond. This pond has a water shed of 590 acres, and possesses a value equal to about one million gallons per day. The main from this pond could be connected with the present ones on the Leicester road near the house of Mr. Samuel L. Hodges. The outlay necessary to render this source available would be very large in propostion to the advantages obtained by the expenditure.

Third, to add to our present works Parson's Brook by taking it directly into the Hunt's Reservoir. The quantity which would be saved here would amount to perhaps 100 millions gallons per annum. To accomplish this would not cost over $1000 aside from any damage to land or for diverting the waters of said Brook.

In other localities surrounding the city which may be looked to as furnishing an increased supply of water is that of North Pond, so called, which lies in the northerly part of the city and at the head waters of Mill Brook. Levels have been taken and surveys made to ascertain the value of this source. The investigation has led to the conclusion that such a use can be made advantageously of said pond, and at a more reasonable expense than any other available source in the immediate vicinity of the city. The pond lies at an elevation which gives an average head of 60 feet at Lincoln Square and 85 feet at Fox Mill, and about 100 feet upon the entire flat between Millbury street and the Providence & Worcester Railroad.

The city by its purchase of the Fox Mill water power, for sewerage purposes in 1867, became part owner in all the rights, privileges and liabilities in said pond. Thus if any expenditures are made upon the present dam, or other fixtures connected therewith, the city will be liable to pay about one-fourth of the amount so expended.

The present dam at the pond is an old one and has stood the test of many years, a test generally conceded the best as establishing the claim to permanency of any structure. Yet it is well known that many of our citizens have for years been questioning its sta-

20

bility, and ever been skeptical of its solidity. Careful investigations made by the Board of County Commissioners in 1869 and 1870 established the fact that it is unquestionably a structure entirely unsuitable to stand as a restraining barrier between such an amount of accumulated water as is held in its basin, and the destruction of a vast amount of the property, and the probable loss of hundreds of the lives of our citizens living in the valley between Main and Summer streets.

An order was passed by the County Commissioners A. D., 1870, after due notice to, and hearing of all the parties appearing, who are supposed to be responsible for the care and keeping of this dam, and who are interested in the benefits to be derived from its maintainance, directing said owners to rebuild said dam in a manner which shall make it safe, as far as human power can construct it. The owners have taken no notice of this order, and probably do not intend to rebuild said dam.

The dam at the pond as at present constructed, stores the water of only one branch of the Mill Brook stream. There is one brook named Weasel Brook, the waters of which enter Mill Brook just below the present dam. By changing the location of the dam this brook may also be made tributary to the value of this reservoir. Those who live near the dam say that this Weasel Brook supplies a very large quantity of water which now of course flows off in freshets and is of no practical value to any one. J. B. Francis, Esq. of Lowell when he made a careful examination of the dam in 1869, suggested the propriety and pointed out the advantages which would result from placing the dam upon fresh ground in such location as would include this brook within the limits of the Reservoir.

The ground is advantageously situated to carry out this purpose. The cost of a new dam would hardly exceed the necessary amount of expenditure to put the old one in a safe and reliable condition, as ordered by the County Commissioners.

Surveys have been made to ascertain the area of the present pond, the amount of land which would be flowed by the building of a new dam so as to include Weasel Brook, the quantity of water which can now be stored and that when enlarged. These surveys and estimates give the following results, to wit:

The area of the present pond is 228.2 acres and will store about 650 millions gallons.

The additional area added by a new dam including Weasel brook would be 23 acres, and would add 50 millions gallons to the storage capacity.

The cost of a new dam would be about $30,000 to which would need be added the flowage damages for 23 acres of land, and the damages to five mill owners for the right to divert the waters or said brooks and apply them to the supply of the city.

The main from the Pond to the city, would best be carried from Lincoln Square via. Salisbury, Grove, and Holden streets to the westerly end of the Pond, where it crosses Holden street.

This line is about 3700 feet shorter than the line to follow West Boylston street to the Pond at its present outlet.

For a short distance in Holden street the main would have to be laid an extra depth, and for a short distance in the bed of the pond it would be necessary to make an open trench to draw the waters of the easterly end of the pond back to the main.

The distance from Lincoln Square to the Pond by this route is 10.804 feet.

The main southerly from Lincoln Square would best follow Summer, Grafton and Water streets to Millbury street.

The portion of the city which would be supplied from North Pond, would lie along the line of Mill Brook from Lincoln Square southward, including an area in which are located most of the largest takers in the city, as the Machine Shops, and railroad stations, Gas Works &c.

The portion of the city supplied from this source would be isolated from the present distribution by simply closing gates at the junction of such streets as would be changed from one to the other, and by inserting a few in such locations as might need them.

Some objection may be made to this low head as a fire service, as in this district is located much of the most valuable property in tne city.

This may be obviated by opening gates when required, at suitable points between the present and the North Pond mains, and by keeping the waters from flowing back into North Pond by a suitably arranged check valve upon the main above Grove Mill.

This supply under any circumstances would afford ample provisions for the steamers, and would add a source entirely independent of all present means, forming an advantage under some contingencies of inestimable value.

The quantity of water which may be supplied from this source is estimated approximately at 7 to 8 millions gallons per. day. The estimate is derived from the water shed of Mill Brook as given in a report of the Joint Standing Committee on sewers in 1866, in which it is stated to be 5024 acres above Lincoln Square. .

By an examination of the country below the Pond it is adjudged that the area drained into it, including Weasel Brook, is about twice that of Lynde Brook or about 3700 acres.

An incidental advantage resulting from a complete control of this Pond would be the facility with which the present Mill Brook Sewer could be flushed with water at such times as might be found necessary.

The details of construction, as to the kind and form of dam necessary to be built ; the kind and size of pipe best to be used ; the outlet at the pond ; and the necessary improvement of the Basin ; with the filtering apparatus before the outlet ; with an estimate of the cost have not been entered into, and have been studied at present, no farther than was necessary to form a general opinion as to the desirability of adding at some future day these waters to the present system.

In conclusion upon this subject, the statement heretofore made is repeated, that from this source it is confidently believed, that in working up all the necessary details and estimates it will be found that from no source, within reach of the city, can so large an amount of water be obtained by the outlay of so small an amount of means, as from this source.

The Report of the Water Commissioner, giving the details of the operations in his department with an inventory of the materials now on hand together with its appraised value is herewith transmitted.

The present value of the property is $752,023.69.

The nature, amount and disposition of the water investment will be given by the City Treasurer in his Annual Report.

PHINEHAS BALL,
City Engineer.

WORCESTER, JAN. 15, 1872.

SCHEDULE A.

Streets in which sewers have been laid during the year 1871.

Street.	Size. Inches.	Feet of Sewer.	Manholes.	Basins.	Inlets.	Pipe Feet.	Inlets Size.	Contractor.
Allen,	12.	458.5	5	2	2	12.0	12	Leach & Co.
Arch,	18 Oval.	201.5						do.
"	12.	307.0	5	1	1	3.0	12	do.
Austin,	18 Oval.	327.3						do.
"	15.	214.0	4					do.
Beacon,	26x39.	346.8						do.
"	20x30.	734.5						do.
"	18 Oval.	647.5						do.
"	12.	93.0	14	7	7	58.5	12	do.
Belmont,	18x27.	35.0						do.
"	18 Oval.	272.0						do.
"	15 Oval.	425.5	5	2	2	31.5		do.
Benefit,	15.	626.0						do.
"	12.	89.0	7	3	3	51.0	12	do.
" Court,	12.	317.5	3	2	2	9.0	12	do.
Bridge,	12.	182.5	2					do.
Carroll,	20x30.	234.0						do.
"	18 Oval.	103.5						do.
"	15.	277.5						do.
"	12.	187.5	8	6	6	36.0	12	do.
Claremont,	18 Oval.	892.5	9					do.
Davis,	15.	252.0						do.
"	12.	125.5	4					do.
Fountain,	12.	658.5	8					do.
Glenn,	20x30.	142.0						do.
"	15.	663.5	7	3	3	63.0	12	do.
Hammond,	15.	274.0						do.
"	12.	249.0	5	2	2	15.0	12	do.
Hanover,	12.	375.0	2					do.
Harvard,	12.	519.5	4	2	2	22.5	12	do.
Jackson,	26x39.	574.5						do.
"	15.	218.5						do.
"	12.	288.0	8	4	4	105.0	12	do.
King,	18 Oval.	677.0						do.
"	15.	627.5	11					do.
Kingsbury,				2	2			do,
Lagrange,	12.	452.0	4	2	2	12.0	12	do.
Liberty,	18x27.	258.0						do.
"	15.	228.5						do.
"	12.	89.5	6	2	2	13.0	12	do.
Lincoln Square,	18x27.	90.5	4					do.
" "	26x39.	144.0						do.

Street.	Size. Inches.	Feet of Sewer.	Manholes.	Basins.	Inlets.	Pipe Feet.	Inlets Size.	Contractor.
Main,	15.	851.0	7	2	2	34.5	12	Leach & Co.
May,	24x36.	247.0						do.
"	20x30.	216.0						do.
"	18 Oval.	685.0						do.
"	12.	235.5	12	2	2	18.0	12	do.
Mount Pleasant,	12.	284.5	3	2	2	10.0	12	do.
Newport,	12.	414.5	4	3	3	33.0	12	do.
Old Market,	20x30.	507.0	5					do.
Orchard,	12.	615.0	6	2	2	15.0	12	do.
Oread,	18 Oval.	32.5						do.
"	12.	718.5	8	5	5	66.0	12	do.
Palmer,	12.	355.5	4	3	3	21.0	12	do.
School,	18x27.	609.5	6	2	2	6.0	12	do.
State,	18 Oval.	605.0	5	2	2	24.0	12	do.
Summer,	15.	1262.0						do.
"	12.	378.0	14	2	2	54.0	12	do.
Tremont,	12.	225.5	3					do.
Washington,	15.	452.0	5	2	2	9.0	12	do.
Woodland,	15.	119.0						do.
"	12.	71.0	1	1	1			do.
Belknap,	12.	147.0	2					Leach & Son.
Gertrude Avenue,	12.	197.0	2					do.
Gold,	12.	166.5	2					do.
Main,				3	3	48.0	12	do.
New Street,	24x36.	980.0	6					do.
Oread Court,	18 Oval.	271.5	4					do.
Washington,	12.	125.0	1					do.
Austin				2	2	12.0	12	E. S. Knowles
Bowdoin,					1	14.0	6	do.
Cedar,				1	1	9.0	12	do.
Central Park,					4	114.0	9	do.
Charles,				2	2	18.0	12	do.
Cherry,				3	3	24.0	12	do.
Chestnut,				3	3	76.5	12	do.
Clinton,				1	1			do.
Foster,				1	1			do.
Foundry,				1	1	48.0	12	do.
Grafton,				1	1	84.0	15	do.
Howard,				2	2	18.0	12	do.
Kendall,	18x27.	236.0	1	2	2	21.0	12	do.
Laurel,				2	2	9.0	12	do.
Ledge,				2	2	40.5	12	do.
Main,				2	2	45.0	12	do.

Street.	Size. Inches.	Feet of Sewer.	Manholes.	Basins.	Inlets.	Pipe Feet.	Inlets Size.	Contractor.
Millbury,	26x39.	279.5	2	2	4			E. S. Knowles.
Oak,				1	1	6.0	12	do.
Pleasant,				4	4	34.5	12	do.
Plymouth,				3	3	37.5	12	do.
Providence,				1	1	9.0	12	do.
Salisbury,				2	2	54.0	12	do.
Spring,				2	2	6.0	12	do.
Vine,				1	1			do.
Water,				8	8	196.5	12	do.
Washington,				7	8	49.5	12	do.
Exchange,	20x30.	393.0						G. C. Barney.
"	18 Oval.	96.5						do.
"	15.	50.5	5	2	2	15.0	12	do.
Foster,	18x27.	341.0	4	2	2	31.5	12	do.
Main,	18x27.	300.5	2					do.
Madison,	18x27.	410.0	4	5	5	36.0	12	do.
Orange,	15.	150.0						do.
"	12. /	143.0	2	2	2	6.0	12	do.
Park,	18x27.	300.0						do.
"						15.0	12	do.
"	15.	50.5	3	2	2	6.0	9	do.
Salem,	15.	733.0						do.
"	12.	98.5	7	4	4	12.0	12	do.
Home,	15.	432.0	5	2	2	12.0	12	S. H. Tarbell.
John,	15.	99.0						do.
"	12.	352.0	5	1	1	3.0	12	do.
Main,	24x36.	1804.0						do.
"	20x30.	663.0						do.
"	15.	274.0	18	3	3	12.0	12	do.
N. Ashland,				1	1	18.0	12	do.
"						14.0	9	do.
Piedmont,					2	15.0	12	do.
Pleasant,				2	2	18.0	12	do.
Sever,	27x40.	510.0	4	2	2	45.0	12	do.
Wesby,	12.	179.0	1	2	2	18.0	12	do.
Belmont,				2	2	45.0	12	Sewer Dep't.
Central,				2	2	3.0	12	do.
Chestnut,				1	1	21.0	12	do.
Lincoln Square.				2	2	18.0	12	do.
Union,				1	1			do.

SUMMARY OF THE WORK DONE BY THE SEVERAL CONTRACTORS
DURING THE YEAR 1871.

Leach & Co.,	22068.6	203	66
" " Son,	1887.0	17	3
E. S. Knowles,	856.5	7	57
George C. Barney,	3016.5	22	14
S. H. Tarbell,	4313.0	33	13
Sewer Department,	-		8
Totals,	32,141.6	282	161

SCHEDULE B.

The sewers in the following streets are under Contract to
Messrs. Leach & Co., and Leach & Son.

CONTRACTED TO LEACH & CO.,		CONTRACTED TO LEACH & CO.,	
STREET.	FEET.	STREET.	FEET.
Beach,	186.0	Pond,	545.0
Beacon,	200.0	Ripley,	548.0
Brown,	300.0	School,	576.0
Elm,	392.0	Silver,	263.0
Hammond,	254.0	Summer,	300.0
Harrison,	1050.0	Washington Square,	275.0
Harvard,	469.0	Winter St. Place,	267.0
Highland,	700.0	Woodland, •	1160.0
Kingsbury,	967.0		
Larch,	265.0	Amount,	13,034.0
Lincoln,	993.0	CONTRACTED TO LEACH & SON.	
Lyon's Court,	250.0	STREET	FEET.
Lynn,	155.0		
Main,	590.0	Bangs Court,	175.0
Maple,	468.0	Highland St.,	800.0
Maple Place,	200.0	New Street,	340.0
Market,	125.0		
Merrick,	853.0	Amount	1,315.0
Orange,	683.0		

SCHEDULE C.

Tabular statement of the entire sewerage of the City from its commencement to Jan. 1, 1872.

Street.	From point to point.	Date.	Distance.	Size.	Manholes.	Basins.	Inlets.
Main,	Central Exchange to Thomas,	1850	716.0	25x26	4	3	4
Thomas,	Main to Mill Brook,	1850	307.0	26x32	1		
Main,	Central Exchange to Walnut,	1857	104.5	25x26	1	1	2
Front,	Mill Brook to City Hall,	1851	1700.0	26x39	4	5	6
Front & Main,	City Hall to Maple Street,	1855	768.5	26x39	4	5	16
Crown,	Pleasant to Chatham,	1863	355.0	18x24*		1	2
Elm,	Main to Chestnut,		705.0	25x26		1	4
Walnut,	Main to Union Alley,		576.5	21x24*			
Union Alley,	Walnut to Harvard st.,	1860	158.0	14x18†			2
Lexington,	Grove to Mill Brook,		594.0			1	3
Lincoln,	Mill Brook to Kendall,	1866	225.0	20x30			
Main,	Front Street south,	1866	172.0	15 Pipe			
	Amount,		6381.5		14	17	39
Eden,	South from Harvard Ct.,	1867	154.0	9			
Harvard Ct.,	Main Street, west,	"	129.0	15	1		
" "	From 15 to 9,	"	185.0	12	1		
" "	From 12 to near Harvard st.,	"	216.0	9			
Kendall,	Lincoln to Lynde st.,	"	723.5	18x27	2		
Lincoln,	From Linwood Pl. to Kendall	"	362.0	12	2	2	4
Pleasant,	Main to Oxford st.,	"	1412.5	20x30			
"	Oxford to West "	"	518.5	15	8		
Southbridge,	By Sargent Factory,	"	222.0	42x48‡			
"	Gold to Hermon st.,	"	838.0	40x60§			
"	Hermon St., North,	"	779.0	30x45§	5		
Arch,	Summer to Fountain,	1868	294.0	12	3	3	7
Ashland,	Pleasant on curve,	"	52.0	15			
"	" to Elm,	"	412.0	12	3	2	3
Austin,	Main to Irving,	"	641.0	20x30			
"	Irving to Crown,	"	541.0	15			
"	Crown St., to Summit,	"	265.0	12	8	10	14
Bowdoin,	Harvard to Chestnut,	"	316.0	12			
"	Chestnut St., west,	"	34.0	9	3	1	3
Burt,	Mill Brook to Grafton st.,	"	346.0	12	2		
Chandler,	Main to South Irving st.,	"	495.0	20x30			
"	South Irving to Oxford st.,	"	294.0	15			
Chandler,	Oxford to Wellington,	1868	495.0	12	8	7	12
Chestnut,	Pleasant to Pearl st.,	"	282.0	18x27			
"	Pearl towards William st.,	"	614.5	15			
"	From 15 to William "	"	340.0	15 Oval	9	2	2
Crown Ct.,	Austin St., north,	"	197.5	12	2		
Elm,	At West Street,	"				3	4
Foster,	At Waldo "	"				1	2
Gold,	Green to Summit st.,	"	208.0	9	2		
Green,	Mill Brook to B. & A. R. R.,	"	499.0	15			
"	" " "	"	1049.0	15 Oval	10	12	14

*Square Stone Drain.   †Flat stone top, round bottom.   ‡Square stone.   §Two course.

21

Streets.	From point to point.	Date.	Distance.	Size.	Manholes	Basins	Inlets
Harvard Ct.,	From 9 to Harvard street,	1868	61.0	12			
Harvard Street,	Harvard Ct., to Bowdoin st.,	"	93.0	12	1	1	1
Harrison,	Mill Brook to Water st.,	"	117.0	18 Oval	1	2	2
High,	Curve at Pleasant st.,	"	28.0	15			
"	Austin to " "	"	1035.0	12	6	1	3
Houchin Av.	" " Chatham "	"	550.0	18x27	4		
Irving,	Chandler to Austin st.,	"	190.0	15			
"	Pleasant to " "	"	865.5	12	7	2	3
Ledge,	Mill Brook to Water "	"	126.0	18 Oval	1	1	1
Linden,	Pleasant to Elm	"	426.0	12	2	2	2
Lovell Ct.,	South Irving to End of Court,	"	343.0	12	3		
Madison,	Southbridge to Main st.,	"	501.0	30x45§	3	2	3
Main,	Chandler to Austin,	"	358.0	20x30			
Main,	Austin St., to Scott's Block,	"	264.0	18x27			
"	In front of Isaac Davis,	"	139.0	15	7	3	3
Market,	Mill Brook towards Summer,	"	87.0	15			
"	From 15 to Summer st.,	"	162.0	12	1		
Oxford,	" Chandler to Pleasant,	"	1040.0	12	7	2	2
Southbridge,	North to Madison st.,	"	334.5	30x45§	2	6	11
South Irving,	Chandler to Wellington,	"	580.0	15	4	2	4
Thomas,	At Nashua Rail Road,	"				2	2
Wellington,	South Irving to Main,	"	430.0	15			
"	" " " Chandler,	"	368.0	12	8	4	4
William,	Chestnut st., West,	"	193.0	9	2		
Allen's Lot,	From Main "	1869	81.0	40x60§			
"	" "	"	617.0	32x48§	3		
Ash,	Green to Summit st.,	"	214.0	12	2		
Auburn Place,	On curve Kendall "	"	39.0	18 Oval			
" "	Kendall st., north,	"	446.5	15	5	1	2
Austin,	Brook E. to Newbury st.,	"	281.0	18x27			
"	Newbury to Quincy,	"	187.5	15			
"	Quincy to Summit,	"	234.5	9	5		
Beacon,	Hermon to Sycamore,	"	448.0	15			
"	Sycamore to Summit,	"	139.0	12	4		
Boynton,	Salisbury st., south,	"	632.5	18 Oval			
"	From 18 to Highland street,	"	820.5	15	14	5	7
Bridge,	Manchester to R. R. Bridge,	1869	80.0	18 oval	1	1	1
Charlton,	Beacon st. west to Summit,	"	248.0	12	2		
Chandler,	Piedmont to Newbury,	"	325.0	15			
"	Newbury st. east,	"	111.5	12			
"	From 12 to Wellington st.,	"	231.0	9	6		
Chatham,	Houchin av. to Oxford,	"	629.0	15			
"	Oxford to Newbury st.,	"	908.5	12	12	5	7
Clinton,	Chatham st. north,	"	246.0	15			
"	From 15 west,	"	111.0	12			
"	" 12 north and south,	"	366.0	9	9	2	2
Congress,	Newbury to Crown st.,	"	571.0	12	4		
Cypress,	Foster to Exchange st.,	"	352.0	15 oval	4	2	2
Foster,	Union to Waldo st.,	"	607.0	18x27	8	2	3
Front,	At Trumbull st.,	"				1	1
Goddard,	Winter to Green st.,	"	360.0	15	3		
Harvard,	Bowdoin st. south,	"	178.0	12			
"	From 12 south,	"	77.0	9	3		

§ Two course.

Street.	From point to point.	Date.	Distance.	Size.	Manholes.	Basins.	Inlets.
Hanover,	Laurel to Glenn st.,	1869	507.5	40x60§			
"	East towards Liberty,	"	45.0	18x27			
"	West " Orchard,	"	29.0	15	2	4	4
Hermon,	Curve at Southbridge,	"	81.0	40x60§			
"	From 40 x 60 to Main st.,	"	916.5	32x48§	5	5	6
Laurel,	Summer to Hanover st.,	"	376.5	40x60§	2		
"	Brook to summer st.,	"	70.0	30x45	2		
Lincoln,	From Linwood Pl. to Kendall,	"			3	1	1
" Sq.	At Nashua R. R.,	"				1	1
Linwood Plc.	Lincoln to Summit,	"	432.0	12	4		
Lovell Ct.	At end of Court,	"				1	1
Madison,	Southbridge to Portland,	"	147.0	20x30	2		
Main,	South of Hermon st.	"	75.5	40x60§	1	1	1
"	" "	"	186.0	32x48			
Manchester,	Mill Brook to Union st.,	"	690.0	20x30§	6	2	2
Myrtle,	Portland to Salem st.,	"	197.0	12	1		
Newbury,	Austin to Congress st.,	"	687.0	16x24			
"	Congress st. north,	"	21.0	15			
"	Chandler & Congress sts. no.,	"	276.0	12			
"	Chandler st. north,	"	118.5	9	8		
Park,	Trumbull to Orange,	"	116.0	18 oval	2	2	2
"	Portland to Main st.,	"	433.0	15	3	2	4
Pearl,	Main st. to 9 sewer,	"	315.0	12			
"	12 to Chestnut st.,	"	286.0	9	6		
Piedmont,	Chandler to Pleasant,	"	1079.0	30x45§	4		
Portland,	Madison to Park st.,	"	1308.0	18x27	10		
Quincy,	Austin to Chatham,	"	339.0	12	2		
Quinsigamond,	Street to Railroad,	"	245.5	18 oval			
Salisbury,	Mill Brook to Summit,	"	1421.0	27x40			
"	27 x 40 to Boynton st.,	"	826.0	20x30	15	3	3
Salem,	Near Madison north,	"	172.5	15			
"	15 to Myrtle st.,	"	199.0	12	3		
Southbridge,		"			6	6	
Sycamore,	Beacon st, west,	"	128.0	15			
"	15 to School house,	"	138.5	12	2		
Temple,	Mill Brook to Green st.,	"	787.0	15	6		
Trumbull,	Front to Park st.,	"	641.0	18 oval	6		
Union,	From Manchester to Foster,	"	182.5	18x27			
"	On curve Manchester,	"	22.0	18 oval			
"	From Manchester and Foster,	"	659.0	15 oval	11	2	2
Waldo,	Foster st north,	"	296.0	18 oval	4		
Winter,	Mill Brook to Green st.,	"	729.0	15 oval	6	2	3
Allen's Lot,	From end to Piedmont,	1870	163.0	32x48§	2		
Ash,	Washington to Summit,	"	208.5	12	2		
Austin,	Piedmont E. to Brook,	"	60.0	18x27	1	3	3
Belmont,	Curve at Brook and Hanover,	"	71.0	48x72§			
"	Hanover st. to Brook,	"	417.0	40x60§	3	4	4
"	Brook to Edward st.	"	150.5	30x45			
"	On curve at " st.,	"	27.5	20x30			
Belknap,	Plymouth st. east.	"	308.0	12	3		
Bartlett Pl.,	Cherry south to End,	"	108.0	15			
" "	" to Front st.,	"	180.0	12	4	1	1
Bowdoin,	West st to Summit,	"	1172.5	15 oval	9	4	4

§Two course.

Street.	From point to point.	Date.	Distance.	Size.	Manholes	Basins.	Inlets.
Bridge,	Mill Brook to Fulton st.,	1870	442.0	26x39	3	3	3
Carlton,	Mechanic to Front st.,	"	197.0	12	3		
Canal,	Mill Brook to Cherry st.,	"	252.0	20x30			
"	Cherry to Front st.,	"	176.5	12	5		
Hanover,	At Glenn st.,	"	25.0	48x72⅜			
"	Glenn to Belmont,	"	557.5	40x60⅜	3	3	3
Cedar,	Sever to Fruit st.,	"	340.0	20x30			
"	Fruit to West st.,	"	563.0	16x24			
"	West to Oak st.,	"	187.0	18 oval			
"	Oak to angle in st.,	"	636.0	15 oval			
"	From 15 to Chestnut st.,	"	365.0	12	17	4	4
Central,	Union to Summer st.,	"	657.0	26x39			
"	Union to Main st.,	"	724.0	20x30	10	7	7
Charlton,	Main st. east to Summit,	"	272.0	12	3	2	2
Chatham,	At Quincy st.,	"				1	1
Cherry,	Canal st. to Bartlett Pl.,	"	449.5	18 oval	3		
Church,	Mechanic to Front st.,	"	252.0	12	3		
Charles,	Blackstone to Summer st.,	"	262·0	12	3		
Chatham,	Curve at Main st.,	"	57.5	18x27	1	2	2
Cottage,	Fruit to West st.,	"	400.5	12	4	2	2
Dix,	N. Ashland to Denny st.,	"	188.0	24x36			
"	Denny st. to School House,	"	254.0	15 oval			
"	School House to Wachusett,	"	407.5	15			
"	Wachusett to Harvard,	"	291.0	12	8		
Eaton Place,	Bartlett Pl. across lot,	"	136.5	15			
" "	From 15 to Front st.,	"	275.0	12	7		
Elm,	Sever to West st.,	"	789.0	16x24			
"	From West to Summit,	"	702.5	12	12	4	4
Everett,	William to Cedar st.,	"	193.0	12	2		
Exchange,	Blackstone st. to Summer st.,	"	352.0	15	3	2	2
Foundry,	Canal to Vine st.,	"	397.0	15	3	2	2
Fruit,	Pleasant to Elm st.,	"	489.0	12	5		
Fulton,	Summer to Mulbury st.,	"	389.0	20x30	3	5	6
George,	Crossing Main st.,	"	83.5	18x27			
"	From Main st.,	"	234.0	15			
"	From 15 to Harvard st.,	"	294.0	12	5	4	6
Gold,	Washington to Summit st.,	"	169.0	12	2		
Home,	Wachusett to Wesby st.,	"	186.0	12	2		
Howard,	Blackstone to Summer,	"	244.5	15 oval	3		
John,	Sever to east of West st.,	"	983.0	27x40			
John,	From 27x40 to N. Ashland,	"	322.5	16x24			
John,	N. Ashland east,	"	560.0	15	11	3	3
Ledge,	Water St., to School House,	"	412.0	15	3		
Lilly,	Pink to N. Ashland,	"	285.5	24x36	2		
Main,	Charlton to Sycamore,	"	263.0	15 Oval			
Mechanic,	Mill Brook to Main st.,	"	1735.	26x36	8	9	9
Myrtle,	Southbridge to " "	"	224.0	20x30			
"	Portland to Rail Road,	"	245.0	12	3	2	2
N. Ashland,	Lilly to Dix st ,	"	302.0	24x36			
" "	From Dix, Lilly & Bowdoin,	"	706.5	12	10	2	2
Newbury,	At Chatham & Congress st.;	"				5	9
Oak,	Cedar to Elm st.,	"	295.0	12	3		
Pink,	John to Lilly st.,	"	182.0	24x36			

§Two course.

Street.	From point to point.	Date.	Distance.	Size.	Manholes.	Basins.	Inlets.
Pink,	Lilly to Highland,	1870	737.0	18 Oval	8	1	3
Piedmont,	Marr's House to Chandler st., and at Pleasant st.,	"	1374.0	30x45§	5	5	6
Pleasant,	Lincoln Brook to Piedmont st.,	"	856.0	40x60§			
"	Seaver to Fruit street,	"	322.5	15			
"	Fruit to West st.,	"	394.0	12	9	4	4
Plymouth,	Washington to B. & A. R. R.,	"	254.5	18x27			
"	18x27 to Orange st.,	"	209.0	18 Oval			
"	Washington to Green st.,	"	376.0	15	8		
Providence,	At Grafton st.,	"	67.0	26x39			
"	26x39 to Waverly st.,	"	918.0	18x27			
"	Waverly to Ætna st.,	"	996.0	15			
"	Ætna st., to Summit,	"	348.0	12	19	9	9
Prospect,	Summer st., east,	"	674.0	26x39			
"	On curve at Carroll st.,	"	30.0	18x27			
"	" Hanover st.,	"	34.0	18 Oval	7	8	11
Quinsigamond,	Rail Road to River,	"	172.0	18 Oval			
Sever,	Piedmont to John st.,	"	1870.0	30x45§	10		
"	John st., north,	"	179.0	27x40			
Southbridge,	Madison st., to Burnside Ct.,	"	725.0	20x30			
"	Burnside Ct., to Main st.,	"	184.0	18x27	6	6	6
Spring,	Mechanic to Front st.,	"	330.0	12	3		
Spruce,	Washington to Green st.,	"	380.0	12	3		
Sudbury,	Main to Eden st.,	"	299.5	18 Oval			
"	Eden to Chestnut st.,	"	398.0	15 Oval	7	7	7
Sycamore,	Main st., to Summit,	"	203.0	12	2	2	2
Thomas,	Union to Summer & Mill Brook	"	939.0	26x39	7	7	7
Temple,	At Mill Brook,	"	20.0	18 Oval			
"	18 to Grafton st.,	"	312.0	15	3		
Vine,	Foundry to Front,	"	350.5	12	4		
Washington,	Mill Brook to B. & A. R. R.,	"	1348.5	20x30	11		
Wachusett,	Dix st., south to end,	"	336.0	12	3	3	3
Warren,	Cherry to Front,	"	172.0	12	2		
Water,	Ledge to Grafton,	"	361.5	15 Oval	3		
West,	John to William,	"	398.0	20x30			
"	Curve at Elm,	"	37.0	16x24			
"	William to Pleasant,	"	974.5	12	13	1	1
William,	West to N. Ashland,	"	490.5	15 Oval			
"	N. Ashland to east of Everett,	"	684.0	12	9	5	5
Winter,	Mill Brook to Grafton st.,	"	411.0	40x60§	2		
Allen Street,	From Main to Mt. Pleasant,	1871	458.5	12	5	2	2
Arch,	Liberty to Carroll,	"	201.5	18 Oval			
"	Hanover to Summit west,	"	307.0	12	5	1	1
Austin,	At Main st.,	"				2	2
"	Piedmont st., to Queen,	"	327.5	18 Oval	2		
"	Queen to Lyon's Ct.,	"	214.0	15	2		
Beacon,	Jackson to Lagrange st.,	"	346.8	26x39	3	2	2
"	Lagrange to Benefit st.,	"	734.5	20x30	5	4	4
"	From Hermon st.,	"	93.0	12	6	1	1
"	From Hermon and Benefit,	"	647.5	18			
Belmont,	At Lincoln Square,	"	35.0	18x27			
"	18x27 to Carbon street,	"	272.0	18 Oval	2	2	2
"	Carbon st., to E. of Fountain,	"	425.5	15	3	2	2

§Two course.

Street.	From point to point.	Date.	Distance.	Size.	Manholes.	Basins.	Inlets.
Belknap,	Washington st., W. to Summit,	1871	147.0	12	2		
Benefit,	Main to Benefit Ct.,	"	626.0	15			
"	Benefit Ct., to Beacon st.,	"	89.0	12	7	3	3
Benefit Court,	Benefit South to end,	"	317.5	12	3	2	2
Bowdoin,	At Chestnut,	"					1
Bridge,	Mechanic to Front st.,	"	182.5	12	2		
Carroll,	Prospect to Shelby st.,	"	234.0	20x30			
"	Arch to Elliot st.,	"	103.5	18 Oval			
"	Shelby to Laurel st.,	"	277.5	15	8	6	6
"	Elliot to " "	"	187.5	12			
Cedar,	At Oak st.,	"				1	1
Central,	Near Summer st.,	"				2	2
Central Park,	Inlets for Surface Water,	"					4
Chestnut,	At Bowdoin & Pleasant st.,	"				4	4
Cherry,	At Canal st., & Bartlett Pl.,	"				3	3
Charles,	At Blackstone street,	"				2	2
Clinton,		"				1	1
Claremont,	Main to Woodland,	"	892.5	18 Oval	9		
Davis,	From Piedmont,	"	252.0	15			
"	From 15 to Queen st.,	"	125.5	12	4		
Exchange,	Cyprus st., to Bay State,	"	393.0	20x30			
"	From 20x30 to Main st.,	"	96.5	18 Oval			
"	Curve at Cyprus st.,	"	50.5	15	5	2	2
Foster,	Waldo to Main st.,	"	341.0	18x27	4	3	3
Foundry,	At Canal street,	"			1	1	
Fountain,	Arch to Belmont st.,	"	658.5	12	8		
Gertrude Av.,	Main st., west,	"	197.0	12	2		
Glenn,	Hanover to Liberty st.,	"	142.0	20x30			
"	Liberty to Edward st.,	"	474.5	15			
"	Hanover to Orchard st.,	"	189.0	15	7	3	3
Gold,	Washington street west,	"	166.5	12	2		
Grafton,	At Providence,	"				1	1
Harvard,	State to George st.	"	519.5	12	4	2	2
Hammond,	Main st., east,	"	274.0	15			
Hammond,	From 15 to Summit,	"	249.0	12	5	2	2
Hanover,	Prospect to Laurel st.,	"	375.0	12	2		
Home,	N. Ashland to Wesby st.,	"	432.0	15	5	2	2
Howard,	At Blackstone st.	"				2	2
Jackson,	Southbridge to Beacon st.,	"	574.5	26x39			
"	Beacon st., west,	"	218.5	15			
"	From 15 to Summit,	"	288.0	12	8	4	4
John,	East towards Harvard,	"	99.0	15			
"	From 15 to Harvard st.,	"	352.0	12	5	1	1
Kendall,	Auburn Place to Oak Av.,	"	236.0	18x27	1	2	2
King,	Main st., west,	"	677.0	18 Oval	6		
"	18 to Woodland street,	"	627.5	15	5		
Laurel,	At Summer st.,	"				2	2
Lagrange,	Beacon to Main st.,	"	452.0	12	4	2	2
Ledge,	At Water st.,	"				2	2
Lincoln Sq.,	Mill Brook to Belmont st.,	"	144.0	26x39			
" "	On curve to Summer,	"	90.5	18x27	4	2	2
Liberty,	Glenn to Newport,	"	258.0	18x27			
"	Newport to Palmer,	"	228.5	15			

Street.	From point to point.	Date.	Distance.	Size.	Manholes.	Basins.	Inlets.
Liberty,	Palmer to Belmont,	1871	89.5	12	6	2	2
Madison,	Portland to Orange,	"	410.0	18x27	4	5	5
Main,	Foster to Walnut st.,	"	300.5	18x27	2		
"	Mrs. Wheelock to May st.,	"	1804.0	24x36			
"	May to Claremont st.,	"	663.0	20x30			
"	Claremont to Kilby st.,	"	274.0	15	18	3	3
"	Thomas st. to Lincoln Sq.,	"	851.0	15	7	2	2
"	At Austin & Pleasant st.,	"				2	2
"	At Allen, Lagrange & Jackson,	"				3	3
Market,	Union to Main st.,	"	507.0	20x30	5		
May,	Main st., west,	"	247 0	24x36	2		
"	24x36 to Kingsbury st.,	"	216.0	20x30	2		
"	Kingsbury to Woodland,	"	685 0	18 Oval	6	2	2
"	Woodland to Clifton,	"	235.5	12	2		
Millbury,	Mill Brook to Millbury st. } (North Street.) }	"	137.0	26x39			
Millbury.	(South Street.) } Mill Brook to Millbury st. }	"	142.5	26x39	2	2	4
Mt. Pleasant,	Benefit to Allen st.,	"	284.5	12	3	2	2
N. Ashland'	At Highland st.,	"				1	1
New,	Salisbury to Highland,	"	980.0	24x36	6		
Newport,	Liberty to Edward,	"	414.5	12	4	3	3
Oak,	At Cedar st,	"				1	1
Orchard,	Glenn to Belmont st.,	"	479.0	12			
"	South of Arch st.,	"	136.0	12	6	2	2
Oread,	Main st. to Summit,	"	511.5	12	5	3	3
"	Curve at Main st.,	"	32.5	18			
"	Beacon st., west,	"	207.0	12	3	2	2
Oread Ct.,	Main st., west,	"	271.5	18 Oval	4		
Orange, _	Madison st. north,	"	150.0	15			
"	15 to Plymouth st.,	"	143.0	12	2	2	2
Palmer,	Liberty to Edward,	"	355.5	12	4	3	3
Park,	East of Salem st.,	"	50.5	15			
"	Portland to Salem st.,	"	300.0	18x27	3	2	2
Piedmont,	Near Austin st.,	"				2	2
Pleasant,	At Merrick, Russell, Main & Chestnut sts.,	"				6	6
Plymouth,	At Assonet and Belnap,	"				3	3
Providence,	At Grafton st.,	"				1	1
Salisbury,	At Lincoln Square,	"				2	2
Salem,	Park to Lynn st., & Madison st., north,	"	733.0	15			
"	Lynn to Myrtle st.,		98.5	12	7	4	4
School,	Union to Main st.,	"	609.6	18x27	6	2	2
Sever,	North to Highland st.,	"	510.0	27x40	4	2	2
Spring,						2	2
State,	Main to Harvard,	"	605.0	18 Oval	5	2	2
Summer,	From Lincoln Square,	"					
"	Market, Central & Exchange,	"	1262.0	15			
"	North of Arch st.,	"	378.0	12	14	2	2
Tremont,	Front to Mechanic st.,	"	225.5	12	3		
Union,	Near Central st.,	"				1	1
Vine,	At Cherry st.,	"				1	1

Street.	From point to point	Date.	Distance.	Size.	Manholes.	Basins	Inlets.
Washington,	Park st., to Summit,	"	452.0	15	5	9	10
"	B. & A. R. R., to Belknap, st.,	"	125.0	12	1		
Water,	At Harrison &c.,	"				8	8
Wesby,	Home to John st ,	"	179.0	12	1	2	2
Woodland,	Claremont to Summit,	"	119.0	15			
"		"	71.0	12	1	1	1

SUMMARY OF THE SEWERS NOW LAID IN THE CITY OF WORCESTER.

AMOUNT OF SEWERS LAID FROM 1867 TO 1871.

Date.	Feet of Sewers laid.	Manholes.	Catch basins.
Up to 1867	6,156	14	17
1867	5,839	19	
1868	15,863	111	68
1869	24,303	202	51
1870	43,308	333	139
1871	32,545.6	288	165
Totals,	128,014.6	967	440
	24 miles and 1294 ft.		

SCHEDULE D.

Showing the number of entrances into the present sewers, and the total number of buildings on each street where sewers are laid, January 1, 1872.

Streets.	Buildings.	Drains.	Streets	Buildings.	Drains.	Streets.	Buildings.	Drains.
Ash,	5	2	Front,	39	20	Orange,	6	5
Austin,	52	43	Fruit, .	10	5	Orchard,	15	6
Arch,	18	4	Fulton,	6	5	Oread,	8	1
Auburn Place,	7	4	George,	6	2	" Court,	9	1
Ashland,	11	7	Gertrude avenue,	3	3	Oxford	30	30
Allen,	4	4	Goddard,	8	6	" Place,	4	4
Belmont,	8	2	Gold,	14	4	Palmer,	4	
Bridge,	15	2	Glen,	11	4	Park,	16	9
Belknap,	8	2	Green,	37	9	Pearl, .	13	10
Beacon,	28	12	Grove,	20	4	Piedmont,	17	7
Boynton,	9	9	Hammond,	9	9	Pleasant,	70	50
Bowdoin,	30	13	Hanover,	13	8	Plymouth,	10	8
Burt,	10	5	Harvard,	22	11	Portland,	35	24
Blackstone,	19	7	" Court,	4	3	Prospect,	9	3
Bartlett Place,	9	3	Hermon,	13	13	Providence,	29	9
Benefit,	13	11	High,	25	8	Quincy,	6	2
Benefit Ct.	5	2	Home,	9	8	Salem,	37	18
Canal,	8	1	Houchin av.	5	5	Salisbury,	3	
Carlton,	5	1	Howard,	11	11	School,	18	7
Carroll,	16	5	Irving,	20	15	Seaver,	10	7
Causeway,	6	1	Jackson,	18	8	Southbridge,	69	34
Cedar,	12	12	John,	37	21	South Irving,	12	12
Central,	33	7	Kendall,	11	9	Spring,	11	6
Chandler,	40	34	King,	11	4	Spruce,	11	9
Charles,	11	10	Lagrange,	10	5	State,	7	1
Chatham,	35	20	Laurel,	5	1	Sudbury,	6	2
" Place,	5	3	Ledge,	1	1	Sycamore,	7	8
Charlton,	15	10	Lexington,	5	4	Summer,	25	5
Church, .	5	2	Liberty,	18	5	Temple,	29	15
Cherry,	15	2	Lilly,	2	1	Thomas,	35	4
Chestnut,	12	7	Lincoln,	9	5	Tremont,	5	
Claremont,	3	1	" Square,	6		Trumbull,	12	8
Congress,	13	8	Linden,	6	7	Union,	36	13
Cottage,	10	13	Linwood Place,	10	6	Vine,	13	7
Clinton,	13	6	Lovell's Court,	9	7	Wachusett,	5	1
Crown,	9	6	Madison,	12	12	Waldo,	6	5
Crown st. Court,	4	4	Main,	46	78	Walnut,	11	9
Cypress,	5	5	Manchester,	9	3	Warren,	6	1
Davis,	10	6	Market,	13	7	Washington,	41	12
Dix,	12	12	May,	15	5	Water,	6	6
Eaton Place.	10	6	Mechanic,	33	29	Wellington,	10	9
Eden,	1	1	Mt. Pleasant,	7	4	Wesby,	3	2
Elm,	45	30	Myrtle,	16	9	West,	24	14
Everett,	7	1	Newbury,	29	17	William,	30	19
Exchange,	34	8	Newport,	7	2	Winter,	34	24
Foster,	13	6	N. Ashland,	26	7	" st. Place	4	2
Foundry,	10		Oak,	3	1	Woodland,	4	
Fountain,	7	3						

Total buildings, 2247. Total drains, 1199. Put in in 1871, 380.

22

SCHEDULE E.

Inventory of the stock and tools for use in the Sewer Department, January 1st, 1872.

29 sets of Border stone,			4 Fish hook ropes,		$2 00
at 13.50	$391	50	7 Long h'nd'ld R. P. Shov-		
34 Inlets, at 6.50	221	00	els, 50,		3 50
1 Bbl. Cement,	2	25	5 Ames R. P. Shovels, 75,		3 75
1 Boat in Mill Brook sewer,	25	00	3 " " 75,		2 25
1 Large Tool chest,	8	00	20 feet 1 inch Gas pipe, 10,		2 00
1 Small " "	3	00	1 Hand saw,		1 50
1 Lot rope,	25	00	1 Hatchet,		75
1 Wheel barrow,	3	00	1 Stone hammer,		75
Lot Rubber boots,	18	00	2 Trowels,		1 50
15 Lanterns,	21	00	1 Brick hammer,		1 50
1 Rubber coat,	2	00	150 feet Tape measure,		50
2 Oil cloth coats,	2	00	1 Oil can,		25
5 Picks,	7	50	1 Spirit level,		2 00
3 Hoes,	1	50	3 Padlocks,		1 50
2 Steel Crow bars,	3	00	1 Cold chisel,		25
Lot of Iron bars,	2	00	1 Hooked scraper,		3 00
6 Oak pails,	2	50	1 Ladder,		1 50
2 Sewer scrapers,	8	00	100 feet Flagging,		22 00
1 " "	2	00			
160 feet small Gas pipe, 05,	8	00		$806	75

SCHEDULE F.

Inventory of Property used on Mill Brook, Jan. 1, 1872.

1 Engine and 1 6 inch Pump on Millbury st.
1 Engine at Lincoln Square.
2 6 inch Pumps on Union st. above Market.
1 4 inch Pump.
4 Picks.
4 Shovels.
2 Coal Shovels.
1 12 inch Jack Screw.
3 6 inch Belts about 46 feet long.
5 Oil Cans.
2 Vices, (one on Millbury st.)
Small tools for both Engines on Union st.
2 Tunnels.
1 Steel Bar.
Shafting and Pulleys for Pumps.

1 Counter Shaft and 2 Pulleys.
Lot of 6 inch flange Pipe for Pumps.
12 Lanterns.
1 Set of Blocks and Ropes.
Blocking and Timber under Nashua Barn.
Blocking, Timber, Boards, and joist on Mrs. Wheeler's lot, Union st.
1 Cross-cut Saw.
1 hand Saw at shop on Thomas st.
Lot of long and short bolts on Union st.
Drum and Shipper for Engine at Lincoln Square at shop on Thomas st.
25 feet 1.2 inch Rubber hose pipe and nozzle.

Report of the Water Commissioner.

To the City Engineer:

In conformity with the City Ordinance the Water Commissioner presents the following as his Fifth Annual Report, for the year ending Dec. 31, 1871.

There have been ordered to be laid during the past year distributing mains in 58 streets and avenues, of which 53 have been completed.

Bellevue one of the 5 remaining streets is unfinished on account of the regrading of the same at the crossing of Chandler street, which will be necessary when that street shall be completed. Three of the other remaining streets, Wall, Suffolk and Southbridge were ordered so late there was not sufficient time to procure and lay the pipe before the season for laying pipes had closed. Wall, one of the above streets has been worked nearly all the time since it was ordered, as we had on hand some pipe of the required size, also a large portion of it is ledge which can be excavated to nearly as good advantage in cold as in warm weather. The other remaining street, Ward, has not been laid, as the kind or size of pipe has not been decided, it being in the proposed line of the high pressure pipe now under consideration.

There have been 450 feet, 12 in. pipe relaid between the storing and distributing reservoirs, near the mill of James Smith & Co. necessitated by the regrading of the road by the town of Leicester.

The whole amount of distributing mains laid this year is 35,-438 feet. Old pipe relaid 450 feet, making a total of pipe laid this year 35,888 feet or a little more than $6\frac{3}{4}$ miles, a detailed account of which will be found in annexed table. In connection with the above pipe there has been set 80 Gates, and 30 Hydrants, also 9 Hydrants set on the old pipe, making the number of public

Hydrants at the present time 418.   Private Hydrants and shops piped for fire hose 48, making the whole number of available Hydrants 464, a list with location of same accompanying this report.   508 applications for service pipe have been made this year, of which 504 have been put in, the remaining 4 have been cancelled or withdrawn.

Sixty-six leaks have been repaired upon the pipes this year the cause of which can be seen by referring to the table on the following pages.   At present there are no leaks known, of any magnitude on the pipes which with fixtures connected with the same are in good working condition.

The appraised value of stock and tools on hand is $25,490 13, a detailed account of which will be found on following pages.

WILLIAM KNOWLES,
Water Commissioner.

Jan. 1, 1872.

SCHEDULE OF PIPE AND FIXTURES LAID IN 1871

Name of Street.	2 inch pipe	3 inch pipe.	4 inch pipe.	6 inch pipe.	8 inch pipe.	10 inch pipe.	Gates.	Hydrants.	Plugs.	Hy. branches	St. branches
Austin,					338		1				
Abbot,			462						2	1	
Adriatic,			399				1		2		1
Blossom,			670				1		2	1	
Brown,	115		275				2		1		
Belknap,	206						1				
Bluff,			479				1		1		1
Bellvue,			312				1	1	1	1	
Claremont,			504				1				
Coral,			506				2	1		1	
Clarkson,				332			2	1	1	1	
Catherine,				135			1	1	2	1	2
Channing,				332			1		1		1
Columbia,				111			1				
Cutler,				1204			1	1	2	2	1
Canterbury,			775	645			3		3	2	1
Dix,			1189				2	1		1	4
Davis,			152	60			1				1
Dover,			273				1		1		
Endicott,			422				2				
Ely,			166				1		1		
Elm,					634		1	1	2	1	1
Fountain,			714				2	1	1		
Grovesnor,			449				1		2	1	
Grand,					636		1	1	3	2	2
Goulding,			583				2				
Gates,				802			1	1	1	1	
Harris,			210				2		1		
Highland,					2138		1	3	9	3	8
Hope Cemetery,			701				1		1		
Harrington avenue,			16				1				
John,			481				2		1		
Kingsbury,			266				1		2		1
Lilly,			259				2		1		
Langdon,			543				2		1		
Lake,			1710				3	2	5	8	3
Larch,		312	178				1		2	1	2
Lancaster,			758				2				
Lyon,				514			1	1	2	1	1
Millbury,					464			1	1	1	2
Mill,				128			1		13	1	
Merrick,		26									
Oread Place,			398				1		2	1	1
Penn avenue,				763			2	1	1	1	3

Street.	2 inch pipe.	3 inch pipe.	4 inch pipe.	6 inch pipe.	8 inch pipe.	10 inch pipe.	Gates.	Hydrants.	Plugs.	Hy. branches	St. Branches
Pleasant,					1092		1	1	3	2	4
Queen,				390				1	1	1	1
Richards,			1394				1	2	2	3	
Russell,	19	7					1				
Southgate,				1182			3	1	2	2	1
Sigel,			638	57			1	1	1	1	
Shrewsbury,						627	1	1	3	2	3
Union Avenue,			678	246			3	1			
Valley,			241				1	1			
Waverly,				355			1		2		2
Wachusett,			698				3	1		1	
Washington,				604			2	1	1	1	
Worth,			460				2				
Webster,				1551	388		2	3	3	3	3
Woodland,			1151				2		2	1	1
Wall,				641					4	1	1

Totals, |340|345|17400|11111|5615|627|80|30|77|46|51

Leicester Road, old pipe relaid, 450 feet.

HYDRANTS SET ON OLD PIPE IN 1871.

Catherine street, 1; Chandler street, 2; Dewey street, 1; Jackson street, 1; John street, 1; Grand street, 1; Oak avenue, 1; Pleasant street, 1—Total, 9.

LOCATION OF HYDRANTS.

Austin Street, Flush south side, opposite High st.
    "   south east corner Irving st.
    "   south east corner Oxford st.
    "   north side, front of No. 88.
    "   south side, front of No. 103.
    "   south side, opposite Quincy st.
    "   south east corner Newbury st.
    Post, south west corner Piedmont st.
Arch Street,   "   north east corner Orchard st.
Assonet Street, "   east side, front of No. 16, 100 ft. south of Gold st.
Abbott Street, "   north west corner Chandler st.
Bloomingdale Road, Post, in front of Washburn Iron Co., Rolling Mill.
Bloomingdale Road, New Haven south side, opposite B. & A. R. R. wood shed.
Bluff Street, Post, north west corner Bellevue st.
Benefit Street, "   north side, opposite Mount Pleasant st.
    "   north east corner Beacon st.
Benefit Court, "   in center of court at south end.

Beacon Street, Flush, south east corner Lagrange st., at steamer
house.
Post, north east corner Oread st.
Bridge Street, Flush, south east corner Mechanic st.
Beach Street, "   west side, opposite Brown st.
Belmont Street, "   south west corner Orchard st.
Flush, north west corner Oak Avenue.
Bowdoin Street, Post, north side, opposite Chestnut st.
Post, south side, opposite No. 16.
"   south side, front of Palmer's carpenter shop No.
23.
Flush, south east corner North Ashland st.
Bliss Street, Flush, west side, half way between Industrial School
and Salisbury st.
Blackstone Street, Flush, north east corner Charles st.
Flush, north east corner Howard st.
"   north east corner Bridge st.
Cutler Street, Post, south west corner Vale st.
Catherine Street, Flush, north west corner Westminster st.
Post, south west corner Channing st.
Carroll Street, Post, east side, opposite Arch st.
Central Street, Flush, north side, south east corner Armsby's building.
Flush, north side, south east corner Keyes' moulding
shop.
Church Street, Flush, south west corner Mechanic st.
Columbia Street, Post, south side, opposite Blake st.
Canal Street, Flush, south west corner Cherry st.
Congress Street, Flush, north side, front of S. Bridges' lot, between
Crown & Newbury st.
Chandler Street, "   north east corner Irving st.
Flush, north east corner Oxford st.
"   north side, opposite Wellington st.
"   north east corner Newbury st.
Post, south east corner Piedmont st.
"   north east corner Queen st.
"   north west corner Mason st.
Chatham Street, Flush, south west corner Houchin Avenue.
Flush, south west corner Irving st.
"   south west corner Oxford st.
"   south west corner Crown st.
"   south east corner Quincy st.
Crown Street, "   south west corner Congress st.
Clinton Street, "   east side, opposite Park, front of T. M. Lamb's
residence No. 23.
Cedar Street, "   north west corner Everett st.
"   north side, midway between Everett and Oak st.
"   south east corner Oak st.
Chestnut Street, Post, north east corner Pearl st.
Flush, east side, opposite Cedar st.
Post, south east corner Sudbury st.

Chestnut Street, Post, east side, opposite William st.
Coral Street, " north west corner Waverly st.
" north east corner Clarkson st.
Dewey Street, " west side, front of chapel, opposite Austin st.
Dix Street, Flush, south east corner Wachusett st.
Post, north west corner Goulding st.
Edward Street " north west corner Elliott st.
" south west corner Glen st.
" north west corner Newport st.
Flush, north west corner Palmer st.
Elizabeth Street, Post, west side, opposite Farwell st.
Post, south west corner Belmont st.
Elliot Street, Flush, north side, front of Porter Davis' residence No
17.
East Worcester Street, Flush, north east corner Larkin st.
Flush, north east corner Cross st.
" north east corner Henry st.
East Central Street, Flush, south side, front of No. 66.
Flush, south side, front of No. 94.
Exchange Street, Flush, north side, front of Music Hall.
Post, north side, opposite Cypress st.
" north west corner Union st.
Flush, north side, opposite Blackstone st.
Ellsworth Street, Post, north side, midway between Millbury and
Lodi st.
Elm Street, Flush, north side, front of Church of Unity.
" north side, front of Dr. Workman's residence
No. 25.
" north west corner Chestnut st.
" north side, opposite Linden st.
Post, north side, front of Gov. Lincoln's Estate.
Flush, north west corner Oak st.
" north east corner West st.
" north east corner Fruit st.
" south west corner Seaver st.
Post, north side, 300 ft. west from Seaver st.
" south west corner Hudson st.
Front Street, Flush, north side, front of Crompton's block, west of
Rail Road track.
" north west corner Carlton st.
" north west corner Church st.
" north side, opposite Trumbull st.
" north side, opposite Bartlett Place.
" north side, opposite Vine st.
" north west corner Bridge st.
" north side, near south east corner Fobes Stone
block.
" north west corner Summer st.
Fruit Street, " south east corner Cottage st.
Foster Street, " north east corner Waldo st.

Foster Street, Flush, south west corner Cyprus st.
Franklin Street, Post, south side, west of B. & A. railroad.
        Post, north side west of canal.
        "   south east corner Milk st.
Fountain Street, Post, east side, midway between Arch and Belmont st.
Freeland Street, Post, north side, near south east corner J. H. Cole's residence.
Gardner Street, Flush, south side, front of Tainter's mill.
Garden Street, Flush, north east corner Nashua st.
Grove Street, Flush, north east corner Concord st.
        "   north east corner Lexington st.
        "   east side, near south west corner of Wire mill.
        "   east side, near entrance to Washburn & Moen's shipping room.
        "   near center of Washburn & Moen's wire mill.
        "   near north end of Washburn & Moen's wire mill.
Gold Street, Post, north side, opposite Summit st.
Gates Street,   "   north side, 400 feet from Main st.
Grand Street,   "   south west corner Hollis st.
Grafton Street, Flush, south side, front of Bradley's car shop.
        Post, south west corner Franklin st.
        "   north side, opposite Coral st.
        "   north side, opposite Penn Avenue.
        "   north side, opposite Mendon st.
        "   north west corner Wall st.
Green Street,   "   east side, opposite Franklin st.
        Flush, west side, front of Providence freight house.
        "   west side, opposite Goddard st.
        "   west side, opposite Winter st.
        "   south west corner Plymouth st.
        "   north west corner Gold st.
        "   north west corner Ash st.
        "   east side, south of Crompton's driveway.
        "   west side, front of Fox Mills.
Harrington Avenue, Post, south east corner Westminster st.
        Post, south side, corner Mount Vernon st.
        "   south east corner Windsor st.
Harrison Street, "   north west corner Coral st.
        Post, north west corner Penn Avenue.
        "   south east corner Blake st.
Home Street, Flush, north side, opposite Wesby st.
High Street,   "   north west corner Chatham st.
Hammond Street, Flush, north side, front of S. Mauhinney's residence.
        Post, north west corner Beacon st.
        "   New Haven, north side, opposite Canterbury st.
Hermon Street, Flush, north side, opposite Taylor & Farley's.
        Flush, north west corner Beacon st.

23

Hermon Street, Flush, south side, west of railroad, north east from
        Junction shop.
Harvard Street, "   north west corner Sudbury st.
      "   west side, opposite Harvard st. Court.
      "   south east corner George st.
      "   south west corner Dix st.
      "   west side, opposite State st.
Highland Street, Flush, north side opposite Harvard st.
      Flush, south east corner North Ashland st.
      Post, north side opposite West st.
      "   north side, opposite Sever st.
      "   north west corner Dover st.
Jackson Street, Flush, north east corner Harris st.
      Flush, New Haven, north east corner Beacon st.
      "   New Haven, south side, opposite south west cor-
        ner Junction shop.
John Street,   "   north side, at head of alley leading to Wachu-
        sett st.
      "   north east corner Wesby st.
King Street,   "   north east corner Queen st.
      Post, south east corner Woodland st.
Kendall Street, "   south side, opposite Auburn Place.
      Flush, north west corner Oak Avenue.
Lincoln Street, "   east side, opposite Worcester & Nashua depot.
      "   north east corner Linwood Place.
      "   north east corner Kendall st.
      Post, east side, opposite Garden st.
      Flush, south east corner Harrington Avenue.
      Post, north east corner Forest Avenue.
Linwood Place, Flush, south side front of S. J. Brimhall's residence.
Liberty Street, Post, north west corner Arch st.
      Flush, north west corner Glen st.
      "   west side, opposite Newport st.
Lyon Street,   "   north east corner Bates st.
Laurel Street, "   north east corner Hanover st.
      ,"   north west corner Carroll st.
      "   north west corner Edward st.
      "   south side, near Wilmot st.
Lunelle Street, Post, north west corner Lafayette st.
Lamartine Street, Flush, south side, front of school house,
      Flush, north side, opposite Langdon st.
      "   north side, opposite Lodi st.
      "   north side, opposite Lunelle st.
      "   south side, opposite street leading to Sargent's
        Card Co., shop.
Lagrange Street, Flush, north side, between Main and Beacon st,
Leicester Street, New Haven, east side, opposite Mill st.
      Post, north side, 100 feet west from Lake st.
      New Haven, front of Hunt's mills.
      New Haven, at Darling's mills, in yard,

Leicester Street, Two New Haven, at Ashworth & Jones mill.
    Flush, opposite Jas. Smith's mill.
    New Haven, corner Leicester st. and road leading to
        Reservoir.
Lake Street, Post, east side, opposite Baker st.
    "   south east corner Mill st.
Maple Street, Flush, west side, near corner Maple Place.
Mulberry Street, Flush, south east corner Mulberry st. Court.
    Post, west side, opposite State Lunatic Asylum barn.
Mechanic Street, Flush, south side, front of Crompton's block.
    Flush, north side, in depot platform.
    Post, south west corner Carlton st.
    Flush, south side near steamer house.
    Post, south west corner Church st.
    Flush, south west corner Spring st.
Manchester Street, Flush, south side, opposite C. Baker, & Co.'s.
    Lumber yard.
Millbury Street, Flush, west side, opposite No. 17.
    Flush, west side, opposite Foyle st.
    "   north west corner Lafayette st.
    "   north west corner Ellsworth st.
    "   north west corner Sigel st.
    Post, west side, opposite Worth st.
Myrtle Street, Flush, north side, near south east corner Stevens'
    block.
    "   north west corner Portland st.
Mason Street, Post, west side, opposite school house.
Main Street, Post, west side, at Lincoln Square, north of hay scales.
    Flush, north east corner of court to Court Mills.
    "   east side, front of No. 57.
    "   north east corner Market st. front of Exchange
        Hotel.
    "   near north east corner school st. front of No.
        125.
    "   midway between School and Thomas st. front
        of 147.
    "   near Thomas st. front of J. W. Howe & Co.'s.
        wire works.
    "   east side, front of L. R. Hudson's.
    "   east side, front of L. W. Sturtevant's tailor
        shop, No. 235.
    "   south east corner Central st.
    "   north east corner Exchange st. front of Bay
        State House.
    "   front of north west corner of Mechanic's Hall
        building.
    "   front of south west corner Union Block.
    "   North east corner Foster st., front of Blake &
        Robinson's store.

Main Street, Flush, east side, opposite Elm st., front of People's
   Insurance Block.
  " north east corner Mechanic st.
  " east side, opposite Pleasant st.
  " east side, on north line of Old South Church.
  " north east corner Park st.
  " east side, opposite Chatham st., front of
   Cheney's block.
  " north east corner Allen Court.
  " front of south end of Scott's block, No. 573.
  " north east corner Myrtle st.
  " north east corner Madison st.
  " east side, front of No. 674.
Post, north east corner Charlton st.
Flush, north west corner Wellington st.
  " north east corner Hermon st.
Post, north east corner Benefit st.
  " north east corner Hammond st.
  " east side, opposite Claremont st. front of J. H.
   Walker's.
  " east side, opposite Downing st.
  " east side, opposite Beaver st.
  " north east corner Tirrell st.
New Haven, east side, at north east corner L. Coes'
   Estate.
New Haven, at Webster Square.
May Street, Post, south side, front of No. 19.
  " south east corner Woodland st.
Maywood Street, Post north side, west of Woodland st.
North Ashland Street, Flush, north east corner John st.
   Flush, north east corner Home st.
Newbury Street, Flush south east corner Congress st.
     " south east corner Chatham st.
Orient Street, Post, north west corner Chrome st.
Orange Street Flush, east side, front of No. 25.
    " north east corner Plymouth st.
    " north east corner Madison st.
Oread Street, " north side, at south west corner Chas Wood's
   Estate.
Prescott Street, " north west corner Concord st.
    " north west corner Lexington st.
    " east side, opposite south end of Washburn &
   Moen's.
    " east side between Warren Thread Co. and
   Richardson's Shop.
    " west side at corner Washburn & Moen's drive-
   way near bridge.
    " north east corner Prescott st. Place.
    " north east corner Daniels' Court.
Post south east corner North st.
  " south side opposite Hanover st.

Prospect Street, " south side opposite No 35.
    " south west corner Mulberry st.
Plantation Street Post north west corner Orient st.
Park Street, Post south side front of No. 37.
    Flush, south west corner Salem st.
    "   south west corner Orange st.
    "   south side, front of Gates' block.
Providence Street, Flush, at junction of Providence and water st.
    Flush, west side, northeast corner S. D. Harding's Estate.
    "   north west corner Waverly st.
    "   north west corner Harrison st.
    New Haven, near north west corner Patterson st.
    Post, front of Rev J. D. E. Jones' residence No. 104.
    "   north west corner Winthrop st.
Pond Street, Flush, north west corner Beach st.
    "   north west corner of right angle in Pond st.
Portland Street, Flush east side front of No. 28.
    Flush, north east corner Madison st.
Piedmont Street, Post east side, midway between Main and Chand-
        ler st.
Pleasant Street, Flush, north side, front of west door in Rogers' block.
    ˙   Flush, north side, near south and north corner Baptist
        church.
    "   north side, opposite High st.
    "   north side, opposite Universalist Church.
    "   north side, opposite Clinton st.
    "   north west corner Linden st.
    "   north side, between Lindon and Ashland st. front
        of No. 107.
    "   north west corner Ashland st.
    "   north side, opposite Crown st.
    "   north east corner West st.
    "   north east corner Fruit st.
    "   north east corner Sever st.
    Post, north west corner Russell st.
    "   north east corner Hudson st.
    "   north side, opposite Abbott st.
Penn Avenue, Post, north west corner Clarkson, st.
    "   north west corner Ætna st.
Queen Street, " west side, opposite Davis st.
Reservoir Street, Post north west corner Elizabeth st.
Richard Street, Post, west side, 900 feet from Main st.
    Post, west side, 1300 feet from Main st. opposite Cleve-
        land's residence.
School Street, New Haven. south side, front of steamer No 3. house.
Sigel Street, Post, north side, midway between Millbury and Lodi st.
South Irving Street, Flush, west side, opposite Lovell's Court.
Summer Street, Post, east side, front of old antiquarian building.
    Post, east side, front of school house.
Summer Street, Post, east side, front of Edward Earle's residence.
    "   north east corner Arch st.

Summer Street, Flush, east side, opposite School st.
"   west side opposite Laurel st.
"   south east corner Laurel st.
Post south east corner East central st.
"   east side, opposite Exchange st.
"   east side, midway between Charles and Howard st.
"   east side, midway between Howard & Bridge st.
"   south east corner Fulton st.
Flush, north west corner Mechanic st.
Shrewsbury Street, Flush, north west corner Mulberry st.
Flush, north side, front of Dr. Brackett's, opposite
      freight house.
"   at junction of Shrewsbury and East Worcester st.
"   south side, opposite Hill st. near St. Anne's
      church.
"   south west corner Larkin st.
"   south east corner Cross st.
Post, south west corner Lyon st.
Shelby Street, "   north side, front of No. 53.
Salem Street, Flush west side, front of No. 23.
"   west side, front of No. 39.
Post, north west corner Myrtle st.
Flush, north west corner Madison st.
"   front of City Stable.
Southbridge Street, Flush. east side, at N. & W. R. R. crossing front
      of No. 66.
Post, south west corner Madison, st.
Flush, east side, front of No. 128. near planing mill.
"   south west corner Salem st.
"   east side, midway between Salem & Hermon st.
      front No. 180.
Flush, east side, opposite Hermon st.
Post, east side opposite Junction foundry.
Flush, north east corner Lafayette st.
"   north west corner Hammond st.
Sycamore Street, Flush, north west corner Beacon st.
Sudbury Street,   "   north east corner Eden st.
State Street, Flush, south west corner Main st.
Southgate Street, Post south west corner Grand st.
Post, west side, front of school house.
Thomas Street, Flush, south side, front of No. 9.
Flush, north side, front of No. 58.
"   north east corner Union st.
"   north side, east of railroad.
"   north east corner Summer st.
Temple Street, "   south side front of No 57.
Tirrell Street, Post, north side, front of Tirrell's residence No. 11.
Trumbull Street, Flush, west side midway between Front and Park st.
Union Street, Flush, at south west corner Lincoln Square.
"   east side, opposite Court Mills.
"   north west corner School st.

Union Street, Flush, south west corner Thomas st.
" north west corner Central st.
" south west corner Exchange st.
" west side, near center of Merrifield's building.
" north west corner Foster st.
" west side, opposite Manchester st. under Nashua
    R. R. bridge.
" west side, opposite south west corner of Rice,
    Barton & Co's shop.
Vine Street, Flush, north east corner Cherry st.
" north east corner Foundry st.
Vernon Street, Flush, north east corner Water st.
" corner Winthrop st.
Wall Street, Post, south west corner Suffolk st.
Water Street, Flush, west side, opposite Ledge st.
" west side, near north end of stone ware manu-
    factory.
" west side, opposite Harrison st.
" west side near north east corner of Hamilton's
    Tape factory.
" corner Green st.
Winter Street, " north side, opposite Pond st.
Ward Street, Flush, north west corner Foyle st.
Post, north west corner Taylor st.
" north west corner Grant st.
" north west corner Endicott st.
Washington Street, Flush, east side, opposite Orange st. school house.
Flush, north west corner Plymouth st.
" south west corner Gold st.
" north east corner Spruce st.
Post, north west corner Lafayette st.
Woodland Street, Post, east side, north of Oberlin st.
Post, north east corner Loudon st.
" north east corner Hawthorne st.
West Street, Flush, east side, opposite Cottage st.
" north east corner Cedar st.
Walnut Street, " south east corner Maple st.
William Street, " north side, opposite Everett st.
Post, south side, opposite North Ashland st.
Flush, north east corner West st.
Wellington Street, Flush, north west corner South Irving st.
Webster Street, New Haven, west side, front of school house.
New Haven, opposite drive way between Marble shop
    and Curtis Mill.
New Haven, west side opposite Curtis Court, south
    end of Mill.
Webster Street, New Haven, west side opposite north west corner
    Hope Cemetery.
Wilmot Street, Post, east side, opposite Shelby st.
Post, north east corner Farwell st.
" south west corner Belmont st.

Court Mills, Post corner Union street. One in Court south of mill.
Court Mills, Four inch pipe in building with hose on each floor.
W. A. Wheeler, two in foundry.
L. W. Pond, Flush in yard north side of shop.
Edward Earle, Post in yard south-west of house.
Rice, Barton & Co., Pipe in building, with hose on each floor.
Wm. Dickinson, Flush in yard, hose in building.
Crompton's foundry, Mechanic st., Hydrant with hose in foundry.
Baker's, Manchester st., pipe with hose attached in centre of building.
R. Ball & Co., Salisbury st., have hose on each floor.
Washburn & Moen, wire works, Hydrants with hose attached.
Industrial School, Flush in yard east of building.
Worcester & Nashua R. R. freight house, two places with hose at-
    tached.
Keyes' Planing Mill, Pipe with hose attached on each floor.
State Lunatic Asylum, Post in yard near south end of building.
   "   "   "   "   "   " north   "   "
Merrifield's, Hydrant with hose attached in engine room.
    "   Exchange street, Pipe in center of building with hose
         on each floor.
    "   Cypress street, Pipe in center of building with hose on
         each floor.
    "   Foster street, Pipe in west wing with hose on each floor.
B. & A. R. R. freight house, Pipe with hose attached.
Washburn Iron Co., rolling mill, Hydrant in mill.
Worcester Academy, Providence street, New Haven in yard south
    of building.
Heald & Britton, Pipe in foundry with hose attached.
New York Steam Engine Co., Flush in yard south side of shop.
Crompton's Loom Works, Green st, Flush in yard west of foundry.
Fox Mills, two post Hydrants in yard. Force pump pipe.
    "   connected with city water pipe.
Junction Shop, four Flush Hydrants east of building.
    "   " five pipes in building with hose attachen on each floor.
Allen's Fire Arms Manufactory, port in yard in rear of shop.
Union Water Meter Co., Pipe on each floor with hose attached.
Ethan Allen's estate, Main street, Flush in yard north of house.
Gas Works, three Flush Hydrants in yard.
Providence Engine House, New Haven in yard north-east of house.
Adriatic Mills, two Hydrants east of mill, with hose attached in yard.
    "   " two Hydrants in yard west of mill, with hose attached.
    "   " two places in Mill to attach hose.
Wood, Light & Co., Pipe on each floor with hose attached.
D. Tainter, Garden street, Pipe in tower of mill with hose on each
    floor.
A. H. Hammond, residence Claremont st., hose at east end of barn.
Coes' Wrench Shop, Hydrant with hose attached at boiler house.
Wright Bottomly, Leicester st., Hydrant in yard east of factory.
Mechanics' Hall, Pipe in south stairway with hose attached, one
    nozzle above the roof.
Bay State Shoe Co., Austin street, Flush in yard in rear of shop.

TABLE OF REPAIRS.

Date.	Name of Street.	Kind of pipe.	Cause of Leak.
Jan. 10	Harrison,	Cement	Joint.
" 11	Main,	Service	Solder Joint.
" 12	"	Cement	Rust.
" 12	Hammond,	"	Joint.
" 18	Brook,	"	"
" 21	Foyle,	"	"
" 21	Pond,	"	"
" 21	Millbury,	"	"
" 30	Leicester,	"	Two Joints.
Feb. 2	Henry,	"	Joint.
" 3	Lunelle,	"	"
" 6	Newton,	"	"
" 23	Mason,	"	"
" 24	Hammond,	"	"
Mar. 2	Irving,	"	Rust.
" 3	Vernon,	"	Joint.
" 6	Plymouth,	Service	Solder Joint.
" 7	Water,	Cement	Joint.
" 8	Vernon,	"	"
" 11	Maywood,	"	Two Joints.
" 17	High,	Service	Solder Joint.
" 29	Millbury,	Cement	Joint.
Apr. 8	Providence,	Service	Sewer Accident.
" 20	Madison,	"	Settling sewer trench.
" 26	Bridge,	Cement	Joint.
" 27	Salem,	Service	Settling sewer trench.
May 5	John,	"	" " "
" 5	Goddard,	"	" " "
" 6	Leicester,	Cement	Two Joints.
" 9	"	"	Two Solder Branches
" 11	Front,	"	Joint.
" 11	"	Gate	Packing Box.
" 15	John,	Service	Settling sewer trench.
" 26	Catherine,	"	Solder Joint.
" 28	Pearl,	Cement	Rust.
" 28	Myrtle,	"	"
" 28	Jackson,	"	"
" 29	Main,	Service	Settling sewer trench.
June 3	Kilby,	Cement	Rust.
" 26	Liberty,	"	Sewer Accident.
" 26	Cilfton,	"	Joint.
July 5	Millbury,	"	"
" 21	Spring,	Service	Sewer Accident.
Aug. 1	Benefit,	Cement	" "
" 7	Hammond,	Gate	Joint.
" 7	Main,	Service	Sewer Accident.

24

Date.	Name of Street.	Kind of pipe.	Cause of Leak.
" 10	Prescott,	Cement	Joint.
" 10	Main,	"	Rust.
" 18	Market,	"	Joint.
" 21	Southbridge,	"	Settling sewer trench.
Sept. 8	Main,	"	Solder Branch.
" 15	Southbridge,	Gate	Lead Joint.
" 28	"	Cement	Joint.
Oct. 2	Lamartine,	"	"
" 6	Market	"	Sewer Accident.
" 12	Irving,	"	Rust.
" 27	Beacon,	"	Sewer Accident.
Nov. 9	Green,	"	Joint.
" 23	Waldo,	"	Rust.
" 28	Southbridge,	"	Joint.
Dec. 4	Bowdoin,	Service	Solder Joint.

INVENTORY OF STOCK AND TOOLS ON HAND JANUARY 1ST, 1872.

7 feet 24 inch cast iron pipe.
20 feet 16 inch cast iron pipe.
725 feet 12 inch cast iron pipe.
23 feet 10 inch cast iron pipe.
102 feet 8 inch cast iron pipe.
437 feet 6 inch cast iron pipe.
350 feet 6 inch cast iron pipe. old.
420 feet 4 inch cast iron pipe, new.
50 feet 4 inch cast iron pipe, old.
85 feet 20 inch cement lined pipe, old.
145 feet 16 inch cement lined pipe, old.
40 feet 12 inch cement lined pipe, old.
348 feet 10 inch cement lined pipe, old.
3871 feet 8 inch cement lined pipe, new.
1897 feet 6 inch cement lined pipe, new.
2499 feet 6 inch unlined pipe.
5376 feet 4 inch cement lined pipe, new.
490 feet 4 inch cement lined pipe, old.
725 feet 3 inch cement lined pipe, new.
1176 feet 2 inch cement lined pipe, new.
7160 lbs. cast iron sleeves for cement lined pipe.
6004 feet 1 inch cement lined pipe, new.
646 feet 1 inch cement lined pipe, old.
735 feet 1¼ inch pipe not lined.
335 feet ¾ inch cement lined pipe, new.
200 feet ¾ inch cement lined pipe, old.
4713 feet ¾ inch pipe not lined.
40 feet 3 inch wrought iron pipe, old.
2 3 inch Globe valves, old.
727 lbs. cast iron bands for repairing solder branches.
2200 lbs. wrought iron rods,
532 lbs. 2 inch lead pipe,

240 lbs. 1 inch lead pipe.
227 lbs. ⅝ inch lead pipe.
211 1 inch lead connections, new.
33 ⅝ inch lead connections, new.
200 ½ inch lead connections, old.
16 24 inch cast iron sleeves.
3 16 inch cast iron sleeves.
1 12 inch cast iron sleeve.
30 8 inch cast iron sleeves.
23 6 inch cast iron sleeves.
4 5 inch cast iron sleeves.
11 4 inch cast iron sleeves.
1 24 inch bonnet.
6 8 inch bonnets.
16 6 inch bonnets.
5 4 inch bonnets.
1 12 to 8 cast iron taper.
12 8 to 6 cast iron tapers.
1 8 to 4 cast iron taper.
13 6 to 4 cast iron tapers.
3 4 to 2 cast iron tapers.
2 12 inch cast iron quarter turns.
3 8 inch cast iron quarter turns.
5 6 inch cast iron quarter turns.
22 4 inch cast iron quarter turns.
1 2 inch brass quarter turn.
1 6 inch cast iron angle.
7 4 inch cast iron angles.
2 16x6 inch cast iron branches.
5 16x4 inch cast iron branches.
2 12x12 inch four way cast iron branches.
2 12x8 inch four way cast iron branches.
2 8 inch four way cast iron branches.
3 6 inch four way cast iron branches,

2 4 inch four way cast iron branches.
2 8x6 inch four way cast iron branches.
7 10x6 inch cast iron branches.
8 10x4 inch cast iron branches.
7 8 inch cast iron branches.
4 12x4 inch cast iron branches.
7 8x6 inch cast iron branches.
19 8x4 inch cast iron branches.
20 6 inch cast iron branches.
20 6x4 inch cast iron branches.
13 4 inch cast iron branches.
1 6 inch cast iron branch, W. A. W. pattern.
5 6x4 inch cast iron branches, W. A. W. pattern.
1 5x4 inch cast iron branch, W. A. W. pattern.
4 4 inch cast iron branches, W. A. W. pattern.
2 12 inch Gates.
3 10 inch Gates.
7 8 inch Gates.
8 6 inch Gates.
10 4 inch Gates.
11 2 inch Ludlow Gates.
6 1 inch Ludlow Gates.
15 ¾ inch Ludlow Gates.
20 2 inch brass nipples long.
29 2 inch brass nipples short.
2 Meter boxes.
12 Gate boxes.
31 cast iron stop boxes and covers.
16 gate box frames—5 covers.
32 heavy gate box covers.
5 small gate box frames and covers.
10 flush hydrant boxes.
5 hydrant box frames, 23 covers.
5 flush hydrants, new.
2 flush hydrants, old.
3 post hydrants, old.
1 New Haven hydrant.
7 post hydrant boxes, new.
2 post hydrant boxes, old.
16 hydrant bowls.
16 pieces 6 inch cast iron pipe for hydrant bowls.
2 hydrant elbows with gates.
160 lbs. post hydrant box hoops.
165 lbs. post hydrant box fastenings.
1 1½ inch meter.
5 1 inch meters.
1 ¾ inch meter.
2 2 inch brass unions.
1 1½ inch brass union.
5 1¼ inch brass unions.
5 1 inch brass unions.
4 ¾ inch brass unions.
2 20 inch tapping bands.
45 16 inch tapping bands.
42 12 inch tapping bands.
65 10 inch tapping bands.
78 8 inch tapping bands.
95 6 inch tapping bands.
84 4 inch tapping bands.
20 3 inch tapping bands.
33 2 inch tapping bands.

119 lbs. back bands.
1134 lbs bolts and nuts for bands.
55 lbs. wrought iron back bands.
22 2 inch plugs.
145 1¼ inch plugs.
90 1 inch plugs.
185 ¾ inch plugs.
159 ½ inch stops for bands.
57 ½ inch stops for bands, old.
13 ¾ inch waste stops.
15 ½ inch waste stops.
24 ½ inch waste stops old.
7 hydrant waste stops.
205 ½ inch thimble couplings for iron pipe.
11 ¾ inch thimble couplings for iron pipe.
60 2 inch rubber packings for tapping bands.
37 1 inch rubber packings for tapping bands.
206 ½ inch rubber packings for tapping bands.
72 1¼ inch brass tees.
266 1 inch brass tees.
78 1 inch combination nipples.
17 ¾ inch combination nipples.
137 wrought iron bands and bolts for plugging street branches.
50 lbs. solder.
360 lbs. old brass.
700 feet 2x3 inch chestnut lumber.
1527 feet inch chestnut plank.
lot old lumber.
100 spruce pickets for reservoir fence.
9 pairs rubber mittens.
3 large tool boxes.
3 small tool boxes.
1 Knowles' rotary pump.
1 Knowles' small steam pump.
1 Knowles' large steam pump.
2 steam boilers.
2 canal barrows.
1 wheel barrow.
29 picks.
67 shovels.
12 iron bars.
3 iron tampers.
5 striking hammers.
3 stone hammers.
10 hand hammers.
1 paving hammer.
1 bit stock and bits.
6 hand saws.
1 saw set.
2 large try squares,
1 small try square.
2 planes.
1 drawing knife.
2 chisels.
2 gouges.
7 hand axes.
4 steel wedges.
400 lbs chains
1 grind stone and frame.
1 oil stone.
4 carpenters horses,

5 steam gauges.
2 cast iron sinks.
1 small stove.
3 large stoves.
1 base burner stove.
1 force pump.
3 screw drivers.
5 dies for cutting packing.
2 gal. iron boilers.
1 copper boiler.
1 tank for testing meters.
15 jack screws.
475 lbs. rosin.
75 lbs. 6 inch nails.
2 hoes.
1 spirit level,
2 desks.
5 window frames.
5 brooms.
3 platforms for laying pipe on.
10 monkey wrenches.
5 pairs long legs rubber boots.
8 brass nipples for flush hydrant tops.
1 canvas tent.
5 lbs. rubber packing cloth.
10 yards enameled cloth.
2 wagons.
1 sleigh.
1 harness.
4 office chairs.
2 hand carts.
20 lbs. hemp packing.
18 lbs. winding twine.
3 bbls. charcoal.
431 lbs. lead.
32 water pails.
1 set pulley blocks and ropes.
168 lbs. steel in drills.
5 iron spoons.
56 cold chisels.
2 ladles.
20 lead sets.
2 furnaces.
6 packing irons.
1 drill stock, clamps and drills for drilling
        iron pipe.
3 goose necks.
3 large mixing boxes.
3 small mixing boxes.
2 hand sleds.
7 stop wrenches.
11 gate wrenches.
9 hydrant wrenches.
4 wrenches for repairing hydrants.
9 malleable iron adjustable wrenches
1 pair of tongs for repairing hydrants.

1 boiler for thawing hydrants.
1 truck.
2 coal hods.
25 feet $\frac{3}{4}$ inch rubber hose.
1 copper pump.
4 oil cans.
7 oilers.
2 powder cans.
6 masons trowels.
38 lanterns.
4 tea kettles.
1 30-gallon kettle.
1 fan blower.
1 platform scales.
1 bench and press for lining service pipe.
1 14 inch cone.
1 8 inch cone.
1 6 inch cone.
2 4 inch cones.
1 3 inch cone.
1 2 inch cone.
5 sets 1 inch cones.
1 set $\frac{3}{4}$ inch cones.
2 iron vises.
1 pipe vise.
1 wood vise.
1 portable forge.
3 pairs shears.
3 soldering furnaces.
4 soldering irons and small tools.
9 files.
1 chalk line.
2 pairs $1\frac{1}{2}$ inch pipe tongs.
4 pairs $1\frac{1}{4}$ inch pipe tongs.
5 pairs 1 inch pipe tongs.
2 pairs $\frac{3}{4}$ inch pipe tongs.
2 pairs $\frac{1}{2}$ inch pipe tongs.
2 pairs $\frac{1}{4}$ inch pipe tongs.
1 No. 1. Stanwood's pipe cutter.
1 No. 1 Foster's pipe cutter.
4 No. 2. Stanwood's pipe cutter.
1 $\frac{3}{4}$ inch pipe tap.
1 $\frac{1}{2}$ inch pipe tap.
5 packed drill stocks and 21 drills,
1 nail hammer.
5 small punches.
patterns for pipe, gate and hydrant box
        frames and covers, branches &c.
lot tools for building hydrants.
128 bbls, cement.
1 handle basket.
2 paving rammers.
1 pair dividers.
1 watering trough.
1 ton coal.

FREE PUBLIC LIBRARY.

REPORTS

OF THE

DIRECTORS AND LIBRARIAN.

25

DIRECTORS IN 1872.

DIRECTORS REPORT.

To Hon. George F. Verry, Mayor, and the City Council of the City of Worcester:

The Directors of the Free Public Library respectfully present their Twelfth Annual Report:

As the most full account of the condition and operation of this trust may be found in the reports of the Committees of Directors, to whose especial care the different concerns of the Library have been entrusted, and especially in the report of the Librarian, who is led by duty and zeal to pass over the whole ground of the interests of the Library, these several reports are presented as a part of this communication. Though it would be tedious and impertinent to repeat the details of statement and important opinions and recommendations, a brief notice of prominent features in these reports may be useful. The report of Samuel S. Green Esq., of his first year as Librarian, shadows forth the earnestness and variety of the labors by which he has increased the number and the satisfaction of visitors, and has given new life and power to the Green Library of consultation, which some have been disposed to regard as dead, because it can move only in the minds of those who carry out its treasures. "In 3814 cases the Librarian has furnished information to seekers or pointed out the sources from which it might be obtained." And it is stated that it is "within the limits of probability, that half as many more persons have helped themselves" from encyclopædias and dictionaries of biography, language and other branches of knowledge, to which free access is given without the intervention of the Librarian. These shelves have a completeness that is sought in vain in some larger libraries, and much attention is given to its improvement. Here may be understood the truth of the old

Latin proverb, that to know where you may find any thing is indeed the greatest part of learning. Those who resort to this hall have been encouraged to think that they were doing the right thing by their respect for persons of all occupations whom they have met here. And they who have made an unaccustomed effort to benefit themselves by special study, as well as more practiced students, have rejoiced in the cheerful guidance of the Librarian, as he has led them to the hidden springs of wisdom. The common remark that a good librarian is the best catalogue, indicates but a part of his value. The personal aid of a man of learning, and ready sympathy with seekers for knowledge is always desirable and appreciated, and in no place more so than in a library for the various population of an industrious city. As the current of events soon submerges the most prominent men of their time, and the places that knew and depended on them will soon know them no more, it is well that the documents of this institution, that combines as its objects intellectual improvement and enjoyment, and moral and religious culture, with aid in the advancement of material wealth, should refresh the knowledge of the changing inhabitants of this city in regard to their great benefactor. In 1860 Dr. John Green, the beloved physician, consummated his gift of 7500 volumes of well selected works to the city, and reserved the right of making additions which he nobly used in more rare and costly selections, until his death on Oct. 17, 1865. He bequeathed $30,000 to be held by the city as a fund and invested, of which one-fourth of the income was to be annually added to the fund, and three-fourths of it was to be used for the purchase of books to make a part of the Green Library, which was to be kept at the expense of the city as a free public library for consultation and not for circulation. He added a bequest of 30 shares of bank stock, receivable after the decease of persons to whose use they were first devoted, and this property was to be invested to accumulate until it reached the value of $20,000, when it will constitute the Librarian Fund, and he gave other bequests for the increase of the Green Library Fund to take effect after the termination of the lives of beneficiaries. The addition of one-fourth of the income to the Green Library Fund has the advantage of a perceptible enlargement of the temporary income, to meet the needs of the city, while the future accumulation of that fund has been shown in the 8th report of this Board, to promise a larger provision for a library, than has ever existed. The three-fourths of income applied to the increase of the Green Library makes a substantial addition. But the use of the books is not the only advantage derived from it. This Library stands as a noble beacon to guide the improving course of the circulating department, which is adapted to the wishes of the larger portion of the citizens. Many circulating libraries have been established, which were sustained and useful until their collection became worn and they were left to decay and die in disuse. But while the Green Library shall shine more and more as an example, it will not be expected that the circulating department will be suffered to decay by the government and people of our city. To this active division of the Library the balance of the liberal appropriations of the city has been devoted, after payment of salaries and incidental expenses. Arrangements have been made for circulation under necesary precautions, of works of rarity and high value for mechanical uses and other objects of knowledge, requiring the opportunity of study in the shop or at home. The number of volumes given out in the eleven months ending with Nov. 30th, when it is required that the yearly account shall end, is 62,954, and the number of persons who have begun to use the Library in the same period is 2019 ; when in the twelve months of the year 1870 the number of new takers was 1654. The Librarian gives monthly statistics of the use of the circulating department which will be examined with interest. They show, as might be expected, that in the season when vegetation slumbers, and the action of animal life is obstructed and diminished, the minds of our people are roused to increased activity in the use of this institution.

Free public libraries have sometimes been commended under the name of charities, as if they were provided chiefly for those who have a limited ability to purchase books. As well might the glorious sun be called a charity, because it shines on the cottage as well as the palace, and often gives to the humble dwelling the most perfect illumination. In the pressure of the multiplicity of books, a free public library has become more than a luxury. It is a necessity. The unlimited use of money cannot ensure to a private citizen a library so valuable for all occasions, as

is a public library selected by the combined action of intelligent
citizens from the various occupations of a growing city, and ad-
ministered by a librarian who has the learning and disposition to
make it most free and effective.   The rapid increase of a library
is not an unmixed good.   It appears by the report of Dec. 1,
1871, that the Library of Congress contained 286,846 volumes.
Of the additions of the last year, 8551 volumes were obtained by
purchase, and 5640 by claim on all books to which copyright is
secured, and the librarian is a learned, able and devoted officer.
But one of our distinguished citizens who knows that library
well, has recently stated in his journal, that most of these books
are very valuable, but a portion of them is trashy and worthless,
and he recommends that the librarian should provide the room
that is desired, by getting rid of all the trash in the library by selling it, or burning it or giving it away.   He adds, put
out of it all the worthless things, and it will still be the largest
and in many respects the most valuable library in the country.
But to what human hand shall be entrusted the task to separate the
tares from the wheat ? Or is it more safe to let both grow together
until the harvest, when the reapers are the angels.   In the rota-
tion of public appointments, one reformer may cast out the dead
languages, and his successor with less scruple may send after
them the old English masters.

The Report of the Committee on the Library, consisting of
Rev. David Weston, C. B. Metcalf, Esq., Rev. William R. Huntington, Prof. Charles O. Thompson, and Nathaniel Paine, Esq.,
does not indicate the liberality and caution with which they have
performed the important duty of selecting books and presenting
them, with others proposed by other directors and takers of
books, and largely by the Librarian, for purchase by sanction of
the Board.   In their care the books are distributed to the department in which they are expected to be most useful.   The encouragement and facilities that have been given to those who use
the Library, to ask for books suited to their taste and needs have
resulted in a decided improvement of the collection and a general
satisfaction of all such demands.

The Committee on the Reading Room, Charles A. Chase, Esq.,
Dr. George E. Francis, and Henry A. Marsh, Esq., by their chairman, Mr. Chase, present a satisfactory report of the operations

of the periodical department in the past year. It has been carried on with liberality in harmony with the generosity of citizens who established it by voluntary contributions, and by the watchfulness of the Committee and their attention to the wishes of the numerous visitors, the supply has been fairly proportioned to the very active demand and the character of the publications is constantly improved.

The Report of Nathaniel Paine Esq., Treasurer of the Reading Room Fund, shows the safe investment of that fund and the faithful appropriation of the very satisfactory income.

Hon. E. B. Stoddard, Chairman, reports for the Committee on the Building, consisting of himself and George W. Russell Esq., and Charles H. Morgan Esq. The large and judicious expenditure for repairs and improvement has been rewarded by greater gratification of the eye and the taste, and an increase of comfort and convenience, that have had much effect in making the Library attractive and useful. The Committee express the hope that no great expense will be required for a long time for any outside repairs. When the building was erected it was thought to be large for its object, and no claim was made for greater size, nor for the opportunity of extension, which might then have been obtained at a moderate cost. That the growth of the city and the increased use of the books, and their necessary multiplication, have dwarfed the accommodations, is a less evil than an unfrequented repository of unvalued volumes could be. It is the duty of the directors, as it has been their endeavor in time past, to exercise such economy in regard to the building and all the concerns of the Library, that it may be considered a cheap as well as a valuable and honorable institution of the city. By the continuance of this cautious management the necessity of a larger building may be postponed.

The Committee on Finance, Hon. E. B. Stoddard, Stephen Salisbury, and Henry A. Marsh Esq., by their chairman, Mr. Stoddard, have reported in two several accounts. To this Committee is entrusted by the founder the oversight and reinvestment of the Green Library Fund, deposited in the custody of the Treasurer of the city. Twice in the last year the Committee have made thorough examinations of the accounts of George W. Wheeler, Esq., City Treasurer, concerning this fund, and they were verified and the

securities for investment were found in the City Treasury.   The
portion of the yearly income of this fund applicable to the purchase of books was $1972.76, an amount sufficient to obtain
many desirable books.

The annual appropriations of the city have been liberal and
progressive with the increased use of the Library.   The books
obtained from this source are placed in the circulating department.   On consultation with Mr. Green, the Librarian, he estimates that of the

Balance of appropriation in the City
   Treasury,   -   -   -   - $4556.02
The expenditures necessary until the
   receipt of the next appropriation,
   will be for salaries and the care of
   building,   -   -   - $1850.00
For other expenses exclusive of books,   1100.00 — $2950.00

Leaving for books for first half of this year, $1606.02

This is a larger sum than has usually been expended for books
in a half year but it has become necessary, because in the two
last years the purchases have been restricted and small on account of the large cost of improvement of the building.   Many
valuable books are now wanted.

The salaries are necessarily a large part of the cost of a public library ; such laborious, faithful and acceptable services as
those which Mrs. Emma S. Phillips, Miss Sarah F. Earle, and
Miss Jessie E. Tyler, have rendered for several years, deserve the
compensation which they have received.   Work that is well done
seldom appears to be difficult, and there is always competition to
keep down the price of such occupations.   But the Directors
have been guided by regard to the interests of the Library not
less than by justice to the deserving.   The interests of a well
qualified librarian, like those of a skillful mechanic and a superior man of general business, will take care of themselves ; and
a public library that is subject to the claims of the intelligent
citizens of Worcester, cannot afford to with-hold a fair equivalent
for the learning and talent that are required in the duties of the
Librarian.

It will be observed that the account of the Green Library Fund
states the payment of a tax on bank stock, which constituted one

fourth part of the fund given by Dr. Green. This unprecedented exaction is contrary to the policy of exemption from taxation of funds of " literary, charitable, benevolent and scientific institutions," that is sanctioned by the previous legislation of Massachusetts, and is permitted to continue as to other kinds of property, and it is opposed to the increasing generosity towards such institutions that prevails through our nation at this time. This tax was required by a law passed with little opportunity for examination, in the later busy days of the last session of the legislature. As a preventive of escape from taxation it gathered into its net all the shares of banks. The reason alleged for bringing the bank stock of these institutions under the operation of this law, is the apprehension that the Trustees might allow the treasury of this trust to be a cover to save the pockets of private citizens ; a supposition not more astonishing, as an insult to those who are selected as trustees of public institutions, than as an absurdity, because if it existed, there could be no escape from the disgrace and the severe legal penalty of such a transaction. The Directors have no disposition to resist or to question the authority of the legislature and therefore the tax was paid according to the letter of the law. But they could not neglect their duty to endeavor to protect the trust committed to them. They therefore presented to the legislature at its present session, a respectful petition, that bank stock, like other property of this Library, and other similar institutions, may be exempted from taxation, and that the money paid into the State Treasury as a tax, may be refunded ; and strong confidence is entertained that this petition will be granted, as it is supported by the general approbation of the people, and by the example of the earliest legislation of Massachusetts. In the year 1636, eight years after the first settlement of the colony, amid the alienations of a religious controversy, and in the beginning of the war with the Pequod Indians, the General Court agreed " to give £400," equal to a year's rate of the whole colony, payable in instalments, "towards a school or college." Then as now, we find education the favored object of the bounty and care of the government and the people.

The Directors of the Free Public Library, by

STEPHEN SALISBURY, *President.*

WORCESTER, JAN 16, 1872.

26

REPORT OF THE LIBRARIAN

OF THE FREE PUBLIC LIBRARY.

To *Hon. Stephen Salisbury, President of the Board of Directors of the Free Public Library.*

In conformity with our rules and regulations, I herewith transmit my first " annual report on the condition of the library. " As the financial year of the city of Worcester now closes November 30th, instead as hitherto, December 31st, it has been thought advisable that all the statistics of the library, as presented in this report, should be made to show the condition of the library for the eleven months, only, from January 1, to December 1.

Much hard work has been done by all the executive officers of the library during these months, and, in consequence, greater order in its arrangements and more efficiency in its management are apparent, and an increased confidence in the usefulness of the institution is felt by its users.

USE OF THE CIRCULATING DEPARTMENT.

62,954 volumes have been given out to holders of cards since January 1. Were the number of volumes given out in December added to this total it would appear that almost exactly the same number was issued in 1871 as in 1870.

This is remarkable when it is remembered that during the cold months at the beginning of the present year very few additions were made to the circulating department, the expenditures on the building had been necessarily so large, and also when we bear in mind that much care has been taken lately to add to the collections, in so far as practicable, only books of a high character. The method now in use with us for recording the issue of books enables me to present the following table showing how many volumes were delivered to patrons during every one of the several months.

*January, 7325	February, 6777	March,	7325
April, 6244	May, 5570	June,	4712
July, 4764	August, 4547	September,	4997
October, 5095	November, 5598		
Total,			62,954

It will be noticed that the largest number of books was taken out in the months of January, February, and March. More volumes were issued in Spring than in Autumn. The smallest numbers, of course, are those showing the use of the library in midsummer.

The circulating department has been kept open 281 days during the eleven months covered by this report. The average daily issue of volumes has been 224. During the months of June, July and August this average daily issue was 178 volumes. This fact vindicates your action in voting not to close the library for the few weeks which, until recently, it has been thought necessary to take for the examination of the library and in order to give the usual summer vacation to the officers. During the months of January, February and March, the number of books given out daily was, in the average, 281 volumes.

The largest number of books issued in any one day is 614, the number given out March 4th. It is no uncommon thing to give out 400 or 500 volumes in a single day. It is seldom that 600 are issued. During a few days in the hottest of the weather a few less than a hundred volumes were delivered to users. Most work of the kind we are considering is done Saturday afternoon and evening. Monday evening and Wednesday afternoon are busy seasons. Thursday I should judge without making a careful examination of the record is our dullest day.

It is gratifying to add that the statistics given above are more accurate than it was possible to make them in the use of the methods of previous years.

The number of persons who have availed themselves of the priviliges of the circulating department for the first time during the past eleven months or after a long disuse of them is 2,019

* Estimated in part.

against 1654 for the whole of the year 1870.   This number is distributed over the months as follows:

January,	270	February,	243	March,	251
April,	169	May,	139	June,	132
July,	130	August,	140	September,	170
October,	176	November,	199		
Total,					2,019

ADDITIONS TO THE LIBRARY.

These are as follows:

	Books,	Pamphlets & Papers.
Books given to Green Library,	349 vols.	290
Books bought for Green Library out of Green Library Fund,	311	
Books added to Green Library in other ways,	14 "	
Newspapers and Magazines bound,	309 "	
Total,	983 vols.	290
Books bought for Circulating Library,	663 "	
Books given to Circulating Library,	68 "	263
Magazines bound,	10 "	
Total,	741 "	263

Annexed to this report may be found a list of givers.   419 volumes and 545 pamphlets and papers have been given to us since the beginning of the year.   Included among the volumes are the files of the Liberator and American Anti-Slavery Standard given to us by Richard D. Webb, Esq., of Dublin, Ireland; some portion of the correspondence regarding which gift was given in the report of the library committee a year ago.

Particular mention should be made of a valuable donation of books and pamphlets from Hon. George F. Hoar.   Mr. Hoar, when in Europe last Summer, mindful as ever of the interests of this library, and alive to the importance of placing at the disposal of citizens the means of forming an intelligent opinion on social questions now under discussion, had a collection of public documents and pamphlets, on the Labor question, minority representation and some other subjects, made for presentation to us upon his return.   The gift is valuable and timely.

Fewer books have been bought for the library this year than last year.   In the case of the Green Library this is owing to two facts.   First, the purchases in 1870 were larger than they can ordinarily be, because the income of the Green library fund had been allowed to accumulate instead of being spent month by month according to our usual method of procedure. Second, large orders for books are now in London and considerable additions will soon be made to this department.

As was stated before, few additions were made to the circulating department during the early part of the year 1871, owing to a want of means. Latterly, however, books have been added in large numbers, and care has been taken so to arrange the finances of the institution that money shall always be at our disposal for the purchase of books instead of spending it in large sums at any one time.

The board of Directors is to be congratulated that the money matters of the library, thanks to the persistent efforts of the proper committees and librarian, are very well systematized and are on a sound, business footing.

It may be well to mention that among the additions to the Green Library are a set of the Scientific American, containing the rare first volume, the supplementary volume to Stuart & Revitt's Antiquities of Athens. Some valuable works on Bridges and Sewers, Spon's & Cresy's Dictionaries of Engineering, Tomlinsen's Cyclopædia of Useful Arts, some valuable State Geological Reports, good editions of Chaucer and several other poets, Jowett's Dialogues of Plato, and the rare work by the same author on some of Paul's Epistles, Thomas's Pronouncing Biographical Dictionary and the last two volumes of Allibone's Dictionary of Authors.

A considerable number of stories in the French language have been added to the circulating department. These are much used by the French portion of the population.

It is in contemplation to make additions of German books to the same department in a short time. Arrangements are making by which we expect to obtain, as issued, the new weekly volumes of "Specifications and Drawings of Patents," which the office at Washington began to issue last July. It will be remembered that these volumes contain *complete* specifications and elaborate drawings, and that, in them, the record of the issue of patents is to be kept up to date. The work will be too expensive for many individuals to own, but can be secured by Public

Libraries, under certain restrictions, by paying the cost of binding it in a certain manner. When the volumes already issued
shall have been received and others published, carrying the
record back to the time covered by the reports issued in the old
form, our facilities will be ample for showing patrons promptly
what patents have been issued by our government. We have also
subscribed to the "List of Patents," the latest number of which will
be always found on the table in the upper reading-room and all the
numbers of which, as fast as they come into our possession, can
be consulted upon application to the librarian or his assistants.

It will be noticed that the number of volumes of Magazines
and Newspapers bound since Jan 1, is 319, where as the number
reported as bound in 1870 is only 106. This large increase is to
be accounted for in two ways.

First, in February and March, we sent to the bindery 82 volumes of Magazines and Newspapers issued in 1869 and the first
half of 1870, which regularly would have been bound in the
years 1869 and 1870.

  · Second, we have bound certain volumes of the sets of the
"Massachusetts Spy" and "Palladium" which we procured last
year, and 12 volumes of Littell's Living Age, the numbers of
which had been secured in accordance with a vote of the board
to fill up our set of this periodical. The German newspapers
have not been bound until this year. Nor has the Overland
Monthly. By binding these periodicals 22 volumes were added
to the list. It may be well to remark that while we should be
careful not to spend money in binding periodicals which will not
be used, liberal expenditure is desirable in this direction. Sets
of Magazines and Reviews and files of Newspapers are very useful in such a library as ours and they must be bound to be pre-
served, and placed in a condition to be used. The cost of binding should be regarded much in the same light as an expenditure
for books. Some novels, for instance, we buy bound, some
unbound. When we buy them bound we pay for the binding at
a bookstore. When we buy them unbound we pay for the binding at a bindery. This year as hitherto many of the files of
newspapers taken in the lower reading-room have been given to
the American Antiquarian Society, on condition that they shall
be bound and with the understanding that they can be used there
by citizens who wish to consult them.

Samuel S. Green, Librarian, in account with the Directors of the Free Public Library.

DR.

To money on hand Jan. 1, 1871,	36.81
To fines collected from Jan. 1, to Dec. 1, 1871,	336.37
To catalogues sold from Jan. 1, to Dec. 1, 1871,	73.00
To set of books sold by order of Directors,	39.00
To Sundries,	19.11
	$504.29

CR.

By Wood,	14.25
By Labor,	5.97
By Dusting and Cleaning,	25.96
By Service in Circulating Department,	120.82
By Express,	15.63
By Postage and Post Office Bills,	46.46
By Advertising,	1.87
By Stationary and Books,	7.57
By Numbers of Magazines and papers purchased,	2.54
By Tools and Furniture,	28.40
By Books for which money has been refunded,	2.45
By Sundries,	19.39
By Amount due from Librarian,	212.98
	$504.29

Dec. 26, 1871. The receipts of the above account of Samuel Green, Esq., Librarian, are satisfactorily stated and the payments are well-vouched.

STEPHEN SALISBURY,

One of the Committee on Finance.

It will be noticed that the expenditure for service in the circulating department is larger, by some fifty dollars, for the eleven months of this year than for the twelve months of 1870. The reasons for this are found in the fact of the rapid and large increase of the use made of the Green library this year, which has called for the more constant presence of the librarian there; and in another fact, viz: that the busiest seasons in the circulating department are also the seasons when the demand for books and information is most active in the Green library and those in which the reading-rooms are most frequented.

It will be noticed also that the receipts from fines are very much larger than those reported last year.

GREEN LIBRARY.

This department has been the scene of much activity during the last eleven months.   We have to note here a large increase in the use of the books.   The number of applications for information and books in a single year, instead of being stated in hundreds as in previous years must now be stated in thousands.

It appears from an estimate, founded in large part upon records carefully kept, that in 3814 cases the librarian has furnished information to seekers, or pointed out the sources from which it might be obtained, during the eleven months of this year.   It is much within the bounds of probability that one-half as many more persons have helped themselves to information by the use of the Encyclopædias and Dictionaries which are provided here in such numbers, and to which free access is allowed without the intervention of the librarian.   It thus appears that in 5721 cases citizens have had the means given them of answering questions of interest or importance to them, and it is obvious to the officers of the library that where persons have sought for information from them they have almost always found it or been put in the way of obtaining it.   During several months, volumes of bound Magazines and of Illustrated Papers have been left lying upon the tables to furnish amusement to persons who did not care for study or serious reading.   Much judgment has to be used in this matter to prevent disturbance to persons using the library for its more legitimate purposes by mere pleasure seekers, still about 1600 persons, it is estimated, have been provided with recreation in this way without incommoding readers and students. Adding 1600 to 5721 we have a total of 7321 persons who have received benefit or pleasure from the use of this department of the library.   This number, of course, does not include persons who have used current numbers of periodicals in the Green library room, but only those who have used the bound volumes here.   It is gratifying to find so large a use to have grown up in less than a year of a department of the library which has been but little used hitherto.

If any persons have doubted in regard to the usefulness of a reference library, the books of which cannot be taken from the building, the experience of the past year would show them that such an institution can be made very useful by making provision for unlocking its riches in the constant presence of officers ready to help seekers obtain required information. It may be remarked that nine-tenths, probably nineteen-twentieths of the applications made to the librarian for information have been to point out where it could be obtained instead of to get certain specified books. The users of this department comprise representatives of all classes, and ages. Thus school children come in large numbers for information connected with their studies. A considerable number of young men come here regularly to prepare themselves for debates. Many carpenters and mechanics study here the principles which lie at the foundation of their trades. Newland's Carpenter and Joiner's Assistant is one of the books that have been most used during the year. Teachers make much use of the library. It is also used by editors, authors, clergymen, teachers and scholars in Sunday Schools, commercial travellers, and, in fact, by men in all departments of life. The young men of the Free Institute of Industrial Science find great assistance here in looking up particular subjects and in preparing theses.

If we were to add to the numbers already given, the number of persons who frequent the Green library room to read magazines, reviews and papers, the total number of persons using this room in the course of a year would probably appear to be upwards of 15,000.

The usefulness of the whole institution will appear when it is remembered that these figures represent the use of only one department. To show the value of the library we must consider the very large number of persons who read the daily and weekly newspapers in the lower reading-room and the 70,000 volumes issued yearly in the circulating department.

While readers have been so numerous in the Green library room there has been activity there of another kind. Much work has been done in arranging the books on the shelves according to subjects and in numbering them. The whole Green library has been roughly arranged and one half of it has been finally arranged and numbered. In the course of two or three months it is hoped that the final revision of the arrangement of the remaining one-half will be completed and the whole library numbered. This work has been done under the superintendence of

27

the librarian by Miss Sarah F. Earle. By her good judgment and intelligence in carrying out his general plans, the librarian has been relieved from much care, and the work of final revision has been rendered comparatively light.

No time has been found during the year to give to the improvement of the catalogues of the Green library, nor is it likely that time will be found at present with the number of attendants now employed here. While it is desirable that the improvements suggested in the last report of the library committee should be made sometime, it is not indispensable that they should be made now. The experience of the past year has shown that however excellent the catalogues in this department might be, they would be chiefly useful to the officers of the library. The main dependence of the users of the reference department seems to be upon the librarian and not upon catalogues. While our collection continues moderate in size the librarian can carry in his memory a sufficient knowledge of the contents of the library to enable him, with the aid of such catalogues as we have to meet the requirements of patrons. Still, if time can be found for the work, the attempt will be made to carry out some of the suggestions above referred to.

The Green library room has been insufficiently lighted until recently, so many more persons than formerly have resorted to it. Six additional brackets, designed and put up under the superintendence of Mr. Morgan, of the Building committee, have removed all cause for complaint on this score. Measures have also been taken, and it would appear successfully, to improve the ventilation of this room.

LIBRARY SERVICE.

All departments of the library have been open every day in the year with the exception of Sundays, Memorial day, and the legal holidays of Washington's Birth day, Fast Day, Fourth of July and Thanksgiving Day. Until this year the library has been closed for the two days immediately succeeding Thanksgiving Day. On legal holidays the lower reading-room has been kept open certain hours for the first time this year. The hours are from 9 A. M. to 1 P. M. and from 3 to 5 and 7 to 9 P. M. Access in these hours has been given to certain reference books and the magazines and papers in the upper reading-room upon application to an attendent.'

These arrangements have proved satisfactory. Citizens come in large numbers to the reading-room on holidays. Thanksgiving, about 150 persons read the papers. This number indicates a busy day.

The Green library room, according to the " rules and regulations " is to be kept open during the same hours as the circulating department, that is from 9 A. M. to 8 P. M. for the first five secular days in the week and from 9 A. M. to 9 P. M. Saturdays. This year, this room has really been open every evening until 9½ o'clock and the librarian has almost invariably been in attendance until that hour. Miss Earle has also remained in the lower reading-room until 9½ o'clock. The same persons have acted as assistants in the library this year as last year, namely Mrs. Emma S. Phillips and Misses Sarah F. Earle and Jessie E. Tyler. Mrs. Phillips and Miss Tyler have had charge of the circulating department and their work has consisted in finding, delivering, charging and marking off books called for by users, in keeping up the index, covering and repairing books, cataloguing, and such other things as they have been asked to do by the librarian. They have cut the leaves of all the books in the Green library whose leaves had not been cut before. They are now engaged in opening a new ledger in which to keep accounts with the users of the circulating department. They have been industrious, obliging and capable and have rendered excellent service. I am sorry to have to announce the withdrawal from the library next January of Mrs. Phillips who has served us faithfully for about six years, and whose experience has given her services a high value. I wish to unite with the board of directors in the expression of good wishes for her prosperity and happiness in the new sphere of life which she is now entering. Miss Earle has had the charge of both reading-rooms. It has been her business to go to the Post Office, put up and take down the papers, keep the files perfect, see that papers and magazines come promptly, attend to their preparation for binding, send for and hunt up indexes and missing numbers and do such other work as is required for the satisfactory working of things in this department. I have had also to rely upon her to do many errands outside of the library,

202 CITY DOCUMENT.—No. 26.

and to write many letters and look over many bills. She also keeps the list of books which the board orders to be purchased. In my absence she has given assistance to users of the Green library in finding information. As before stated the arrangement of the books in the Green library has, under general directions from the librarian, been her work. I consider her services very valuable and now that her health has become fixed and she is able to do a full day's work I wish that a moderate addition could be made to her salary. I prefer the same request in regard to Miss Tyler who has served the library several years and who will in the absence of Mrs. Phillips become under the board and librarian the head of the circulating department. There will be a considerable difference between the salary which you will probably think it wise to vote to the new assistant and the one which Mrs. Phillips has received. Recognition of this fact may enable the board to see its way clear to accede to the desires of the other assistants.

The duties of the librarian have been multifarious. Besides having a general and in some cases a particular supervision of the work carried on by the assistants he has kept records and accounts in the circulating department, records in the Green library, attended to a large correspondence, received visitors, aimed to keep informed in regard to new publications in England and America, given much assistance to the library committee in the selection of books, acted as the executive officer of this and the other committees of the board and of the board itself, purchased the books, examined accounts and watched the working of our methods and studied the working of new methods in use elsewhere. His principal work however and that which he has always remembered as of first importance has been to receive cordially all persons who are seeking information and help them to find what they wish.

MISCELLANEOUS.

The usual annual examination of the circulating department of the library has been made this year, but so recently that the results cannot be given in this report. Two new departments have been established in the circulating library which will now very soon be in operation. These have been established in accordance with suggestions in the last report of the committee on the library, in order that valuable books might be put in that department and carefully guarded against injury and loss. Some care has been taken to bring to the notice of citizens the privileges which they may enjoy here by means of notices in the daily papers, by hanging cards in a few places and by writing a notice for the City Directory. Much more might be done in this direction. It may be well to remark that the expensive books purchased last year have been much used during the present year. Efforts made early in the year to prevent the defacement of books have been moderately successful. The principal means used, in addition to watchfulness at the library, was the preparation of a circular which was read in all the public schools and printed in the daily papers setting forth the penalties under the laws of Massachusetts for making pencil marks in books or mutilating them. As a precaution against fire, a man engaged for that purpose, has slept in the library building for several months past.

I have various suggestions to make to different committees, but will reserve them until the organization of the next board of directors. Plans have also been formed for the work of the coming year, but it is unnecessary to mention them here.

It only remains for me to thank the committees of the board of directors and its president and secretary for the heartiness of their co-operation in considering and carrying out plans for the interests of the library.

Respectfully submitted,
SAMUEL S. GREEN, Librarian.

GIFTS FROM JANUARY 1 TO NOVEMBER 30, 1871.

	Books	Pamphlets and Papers		Books	Pamphlets and Papers
Argentine Minister, Wash't'n,	1		Sarah F. Earle.		7
Boston Athnæeum, Library,		15	John Eaton, Jr., Commis-		
Central Library, Syracuse,		1	sioner of Education,	1	
Free Public Library, Newton,	1		Andrew H. Green,		1
Mercantile Library Association,	1		Frank Green,		1
New York State Library,		1	Samuel A. Green.		3
Public Library, Boston,		19	Samuel S. Green,		5
" " Cincinnati,	1		Clarendon Harris,		11
" " Oxford,		1	S. N. Haskell,	3	
" " Taunton,		1	Alonzo Hill's Heirs	45	
" " Watertown,		1	George F. Hoar,	10	162
St. Louis Pub. School Library,	1		Elmer P. Howe,		59
Silas Bronson Library,		1	Charles Hudson,		1
State Library, Boston,		1	Wm. R. Huntington,		1
American Antiquarian Society,		4	A. P. Marble,	1	1
Am. Unitarian Association,		1	Frederick May,	1	
City of Worcester,		1	D. S. Messinger,	5	
Commissioner of Pensions,		1	F. A. Von Moschzisker,	1	
Commissioner of Revenue,		1	D. H. Paine,	5	
Directors St. Louis Public			Nathaniel Paine,		I
Schools,		1	H. L. Parker,		3
Mass. New Church Union,		17	Wm. J. Potter, Sec'y,		3
Institution for Blind, Mass.,		1	L. U. Reavis,		1
Smithsonian Institute,	1	1	Rice & Whiting,	1	
State of Massachusetts,	14	10	E. H. Russell,		1
United States,	40		J. Sabin & Sons,		11
Worcester ' Disrict Medical			Stephen Salisbury,	2	
Society,		1	Seaver & Francis,		1
Worcester Gazette,		2	M. Seguin, aîné		2
Young Mens' Christian As'n.		1	J. L. Sibley, Librarian,		1
Ezra Abbott,		1	Samuel Smith, City Clerk,		1
E. Adams,		2	Wm. A. Smith,		37
P. E. Aldrich,	1		Snow Brothers,	1	
E. G. Allen,		6	Charles Sumner,	13	6
Henry C. Baird,		5	C. O. Thompson,		3
Z. Baker,		2	Roger F. Upham, Sec'y,		1
Bangs, Merwin & Co.,		1	Francis A. Walker, Superinten-		
Joachin Barrande,		3	dent of Census,	1	
Edmund M. Barton,		5	Richard D. Webb,	41	
Mrs. Henry H. Chamberlin,	102	1	D. Weston,		1
George E. Chambers,		1	Caroline E. White,		1
Charles A. Chase,	1	6	Henry Wilson,	2	
Ann. K. Colton,	1	11	Samuel Woodward,	2	2
Joseph A. Denny,		1	A Friend,	83	59
Mrs. R. P. Dunn,	1		Other Friends,	15	46
Edward Earle,	3				
Henry Earle,		1	Total,	419	545

Report of the Library Committee.

To the Directors of the Free Public Library—

Gentlemen : It has been customary hitherto for the Library Committee, at the commencement of each year to appoint a secretary
by whom their report should be presented at the close of the year,
and whose report has been the general Report of the Library. The
secretary of the Library Committee has thus been obliged to keep
himself accurately informed of the whole state of the library, to
preserve a careful record of all new measures and to prepare a
long and detailed report ; duties which have demanded of him
no little time and attention.

It seemed best to your committee at the commencement of this
year that the office of secretary of the committee should be dispensed with, and that the greater part of the matter hitherto communicated in the report of the Library Committee should be presented in the report of the librarian. For the details in reference
to the working of the library during the past year, and for its
present condition, your committee would therefore refer you to
the Librarian's report.

In the judgment of your committee, the affairs of the library
have been so conducted during the past year as to secure to the
citizens of Worcester, in a larger degree than ever before, the
benefits which such an institution is designed to confer. Especial pains have been taken to ascertain and to meet the actual
wants of the patrons of the library. The public have been encouraged to present the titles of such books as have been desired and
as the library did not contain, and these, if of a character
approved by your committee have been the first recommended to
be purchased. Of other books, it has been the aim of your Committee to recommend for purchase as few as practicable of a

light and transient, and as many as practicable of a solid and permanent character.

In the Green library, it has been the aim of your committee to recommend for purchase, first, as in the circulating department, such books as have been desired by the patrons of the library for immediate use ; and, secondly, to a larger extent than in any other direction, such as will be of advantage to those engaged in mechanical and manufacturing interests, as the leading interests of our city. An attempt has been made to increase the facilities for using the Green library. The librarian has had his hours of service, seven hours each working day, definitely arranged and announced to the public, and has been expected to place all the treasures of the library and his own time and labor, so far as practicable, at the command of any one who might wish for any information which the library could afford. There is evidence that these attempts have resulted in the largely increased value of the library to the city.

Something of progress has been made in the arrangement and classification of the library and in the systematizing of its working.

Your committee have approved bills for the purchase of books to the amount of $2306.99 ; and for binding, to the amount of $655.04

Valuable gifts have been received, which, though noticed in the librarian's report, demand especial and grateful mention here. Of these, we would particularly refer to the donation of extensive and valuable document on the question of Labor Reform, from Hon. Geerge F. Hoar, and of files of the Anti-Slavery Standard and the Liberator from Richard D. Webb, Esq., of Dublin, Ireland

It should be added that the Librarian and his assistants have executed the instructions of yourcommittee and co-operated with them, cheerfully, ably, and in every way satisfactorily.

D. WESTON, *Chairman.*

REPORT OF THE COMMITTEE ON THE READING ROOM.

To the Directors of the Free Public Library.

The two branches of the Reading Room have been supplied, during the past year, with a large, varied and excellent collection of American and foreign newspapers and magazines, the greater number furnished from the income of the subscription fund established in 1865. Many valuable periodicals are contributed as the direct gift of individuals. In this class are included all of a sectarian character, to which our by-laws do not allow us to subscribe. This list has received a considerable increase during the past year, and the committee tender their thanks to the respective donors. The average daily attendance of visitors upon the rooms has steadily increased, and has apparently doubled during the past two years. The experiment of keeping the lower room open during certain hours on public holidays, has met with popular favor, and we recommend that the arrangement be maintained.

The following publications are regularly received and kept on file:

DAILY.

Albany Evening Journal.
Allgemeine Zeitung.
Boston Daily Advertiser.
  "   " Evening Transcript.
  "   " Journal.
  "   . Post
Le Charivari.
Evening Post.
Globe (Washington.)
New York Commercial Advertiser.
  "   " Daily Tribune.
  "   " Herald.
  "   " Times.
North American and U. S. Gazette.

Providence Daily Journal.
Springfield " Republican.
Worcester Daily Spy, 3 copies (one given by Publishers.)
Worcester Evening Gazette, 3 copies (one given by Publishers.)
The World.

TRI-WEEKLY.

Chicago Tribune.
L' Evénement.
The Mail.

SEMI-WEEKLY.

Cincinnati Semi-Weekly Gazette.

28

WEEKLY.

Advent Christian Times.
Appletons' Journal.
American Artisan.
Army and Navy Journal.
The Athenæum.
Bell's Life in London.
Berliner Montags Zeitung.
Boston Investigator.   Given by B. G.
  Howes.
The Chemical News.
The Christian Register.   Given by Am.
  Unit. Asso.
The Churchman.
The College Courant.
The Commercial Bulletin.
The Commonwealth.
The Connecticut Courant.
Detroit Tribune.
The Engineer.
Engineering.
L' Etendard National. Given by Pub
  lishers.
Every Saturday.
Examiner.
Fitchburg Reveille.
Friends' Review. Given by S. H. Colton.
Harper's Weekly.
Home Journal.
The Illustrated London News.
The Independent.
The   "   Statesman.
The Index.   Given by S. F. Earle.
Iron World and Manufacturer. Given by
  Publishers.
Journal of the Society of Arts.
Liberal Christian. Given by Am. Unit.
  Asso.
Littell's Living Age.
The Liverpool Weekly Mercury.
The Lowell   "   Journal.
The Maine State Press.
The Massachusetts Ploughman.
The Methodist.   Given by Rev. A. H.
  McKeown.
La Minerve.
The Mining Journal.
The Missouri Democrat.
The Montreal Herald.
The Nation.
Nature.
New England Farmer.
Notes and Queries.
The Pall Mall Budget.
Plymouth Pulpit.
Punch.

The Revolution.
The Saturday Review.
The Scientific American.
The Spectator.
The Spirit of the Times.
United Service Gazette.
The Universalist.   Given by publisher.
Washington Weekly Chronicle.
Weekly Alta California.
The Weekly Freeman's Journal.
The   "   Scotsman.
Woman's Journal. Given by S. F. Earle.
Woodhull and Claflin's Weekly.   Given
  by Publishers.
The Worcester Palladium.   Given by
  Publisher.
The World's Crisis.   Given by Samuel
  . Ayres.
The Yale Courant.
Zion's Herald.   Given by Rev. A. H.
  McKeown.

SEMI-MONTHLY.

The Academy.
American Literary Gazette and Pub-
  lisher's Circular.
Bowdoin Scientific Review.   Given by
  W. W. Rice.
Dwight's Journal of Music.
The Harvard Advocate.
Revue des Deux Mondes.

MONTHLY.

Advocate of Peace.
All the Year Round.
American Agriculturist,
  "   Journal of Numismatics.
The "   "   " Science and Arts.
The "   Naturalist.
The Art Journal.
The Artizan.
The Association Monthly.
The Atlantic Monthly.
The Bible Banner.   Mr. Higgins
Blackwoods Edinburgh Magazine.
The Book Buyer.
The   "   Seller.
The Boston Journal of Chemistry.
The Builder.
The Bureau.
Chambers Journal.
The Contemporary Review.
Cornhill Magazine.
Dublin University Magazine.
The Fortnightly Review.

Frazers Magazine.
The Galaxy.
The Gardener's Monthly.
Gentleman's Magazine.
Good Words for the Young.
Harper's New Monthly Magazine.
The Historical Magazine.
J. E. Tilton and Co's Literary Bulletin.
Journal of the Franklin Institute.
Lippincott's Magazine.
The Literary World.
London, Edinburgh and Dublin Philosophical Magazine.
Macmillan's Magazine.
The Manufactrer and Builder.
Mechanic's Magazine.
Old and New. Given by Am. Unit.Asso.
Once a Week.
Our Dumb Animals. Given by Publishers.
Our Young Folks.
The Overland Monthly.
The Philadelphia Photographer.
The Radical.   Given by Mrs. Sarah Brown.

TheReligious Magazine. Given by Am. Unit. Asso.
Sabin and Sons American Bibliopolist.
Scribner's Monthly.
Tilton's Journal of Horticulture.
The Workshop.

QUARTERLY.

Bibliotheca Sacra.
British Quarterly Review.
The Christian Quarterly   Given by A. Wilcox.
The Edinburgh Review.
The Journal of the Anthropological Institute.
Journal of Speculative Philosophy.
London Quarterly.
The Methodist Quarterly.
New England Historical and Genealogical Register.
North American Review.
The Quarterly Journal of Science.
The Westminster Review.

For the Committee,

CHARLES A. CHASE, *Chairman.*

REPORT OF THE BUILDING COMMITTEE.

To Hon. Stephen Salisbury, President of the Board of Directors of the Free Public Library.

The Building Committee submit the following report : —

The work contracted for the Building in 1870, has been completed and paid for during the year.

The stone steps have been so changed as to meet the approbation of the public. Suitable gas lights have been placed for the Library and Reading-room and a new side-walk has been laid, so that it is to be hoped no great expense will be required for a long time on any outside repairs.

New gas lights have been furnished for the Library and Reading-rooms and for the first time in many years the building has been put in complete order. It was estimated in the last report that it would require about $3500 to pay the bills for contracts then existing.

Bills during the year to the amount of $4,079 80 have been paid.

The bill for gas viz. $731 12 seems to be very large and it is to be hoped that some means will hereafter be devised by which this item can be much reduced. Probably one quarter of the expense of gas is incurred in the school-room and ought not to be charged to the expense of the library fund.

For the committee,

E. B. STODDARD.

REPORT OF FINANCE COMMITTEE.

To Hon. *Stephen Salisbury, President of the Board of Directors of the Free Public Library of Worcester:*

The Finance Committee submit the following report of the Receipts and Expenditures on account of the Free Public Library for the year 1871.

Balance of former appropriation in the Treasury, Jan. 1, 1871,	$5,073 43	
City appropriation for 1871,	8,000 00	
Dog Fund,	1,777 50	
		$14,850 93

Bills approved and payments thereon as follows:

For Books,	1,300 63	
For Printing,	99 23	
For Binding,	655 04	
For Gas,	731 12	
For Salaries and care of Building,	3,068 48	
For Wood and Coal,	206 87	
For Water,	33 24	
For Stationary,	65 21	
For Incidental Expenses,	55 29	
		$6,215 11

In addition to the above, bills have been paid for expenses incurred in the alteration of the building and laying of the side-walk as follows:

For Steam Work and Gas Fixtures,	2,083 48	
For Painting, Mason and Carpenter work,	680 51	
For Stone work on Steps,	983 99	
For Iron Fence,	156 96	
For Sidewalk,	174 86	—$10,294 91
Balance in City Treasury, Jan. 1, 1872,	4,556 02	
		—$14,850 93

For the Committee,

E. B. STODDARD, *Chairman.*

THE GREEN LIBRARY FUND.

The Finance Committee of the Free Public Library, submit the following report of the Green Library Fund, Jan. 1, 1872.

Statement of the Fund Jan. 1, 1871.

Notes secured by Mortgage,	19,748 50	
Bank stocks (par value,)	6,200 00	
Worcester City Notes,	6,536 19	—$32,484 69

Statement of the Fund Jan. 1, 1872.

Notes secured by Mortgage,	19,498 50	
Bank stocks (par value,)	6,200 00	
Worcester City Notes,	7,443 78	—$33,142 28

Income for 1871.

Interest on Mortgage Notes,	1,532 28	
Dividends on Bank Stocks,	640 00	
Interest on City Notes,	450 39	
Interest on Bank Deposit,	7 68	— $2,630 35

One quarter of Income added to Fund as per provisions of Will,	657 59	
Balance of Income appropriated for purchase of Books,	1,972 76	— $2,630 35

BOOK ACCOUNT.

Cash in hands of City Treasurer, Jan. 1, 1871,	257 69	
Appropriated for purchase of Books during year,	1,972 76	— $2,230 45

Expended for purchase of Books during year,	1,006 36	
Paid Taxes on Bank Stocks,	110 98	— $1,117 34
Balance in City Treasury, Jan. 1, 1872,	$1,113 11	

Respectfully submitted for the Finance Committee,

E. B. STODDARD, *Chairman.*

READING ROOM FUND, TREASURER'S REPORT.

NATHANIEL PAINE, *Treasurer*, in account with READING ROOM FUND, FREE PUBLIC LIBRARY.

1871.   DR.

Jan. 2, To Balance from last year, $191 60
         To Cash for interest on City Bonds,   ٬300 00
         To Cash for interest on U. S. Bonds,   377 56 — $869 16

1871.   CR.

Dec.   By Cash paid for subscriptions to
        Periodicals and Newspapers, from Jan. 2,
        1871, to Dec. 26, 1871, inclusive, $842 94
             Postage,   1 80
Dec. 26,   Balance of cash on hand,   24 42 — $869 16

INVESTMENTS.

City of Worcester, 6 per cent. Bonds, $5,000
United States, 6 per cent. Bonds,   5,650   — $10,650

Respectfully submitted,

NATHANIEL PAINE, *Treasurer of Fund.*

The above account is well-vouched and correctly stated and the securities for the investments are in the possession of the Treasurer.

STEPHEN SALISBURY,

One of the Committee on Finance.

REPORT

COMMISSION OF PUBLIC GROUNDS.

To the Honorable City Council:

By Section 21, of the Revised Charter of Worcester, the *City Council* is authorized to elect a board of three commissioners, hose powers and duties are defined at length. Section 1, of Chapter 8, of the Municipal Ordinances, establishes the official designation of those officers, providing as it does for the election, annually, in the month of January, of a " *Commissioner of Public Grounds.*" Having premised thus much, for the sake of brevity in their future communications and intercourse with the *Honorable Council*, the COMMISSION OF PUBLIC GROUNDS (and *not* of Shade Trees *and* Public Grounds!)would most respectfully submit the accompanying " Report of all their acts and doings, and of the condition of the public grounds and shade and ornamental trees thereon, and on said streets and highways and an account of receipts and expenditures for the same," for the financial year ending November 30, A. D. 1871.

The receipts of the Commission, from all sources, were as follows :

Balance On Hand January 2. A. D. 1871.	$1,048 88
Appropriation for 1872.	5,000 00
Use of Elm Park by menageries, &c.,	350 00
For removal of 500 yards Gravel, (Salem St.)	150 00
M. McGrath, Grass on Elm Park.	200 00
	$6,748 88

29

PER CONTRA—EXPENDITURES.

Paid H. & A. Palmer, labor and boxing trees (bill of 1870.) $121 92
Highway Department,Plowing,Labor and Street Scrapings, 275 10
Sewer Department—Constructing Inlets, Catch-basins, &c, 250 89
M. McGrath, labor during Five months, Excavation, &c.,
    as per Report,   3,976 22
M. McGrath, Excavation, Labor and Manure on Elm Park, 199 50
John Barnes, Felling trees, labor and hire of team,   238 33
Timothy S. Bliss, Plowing S. W. corner of Elm Park,   4 12
A. Barnes, labor,   16 00
John Goulding, labor,   15 00
M. McKenney, labor,   6 00
Jere Toomey,   do   21 50
Henry Forney, Trimming trees,   27 00
C. H. Perry,   "   "   and Fencing,   180 82
L. B. Chambelain, Setting trees (Bellevue St,)   5 00
Jonas Hartshorn,(Chandler St,)   12 00
S. Shumway, (Woodland St,)   5 00
Charles E. Stevens, (Boynton St,)   2 00
James H. Wall, (Elm St,)   5 00
James Draper, for Fifteen Hundred Young Trees,
    (Elms and Maples,) and setting same,   98 00
George Sessions & Son, 350 yards of earth at 12½ cts,   43 77
John Simmons & Son, Lumber and Boxing trees,   133 83
Willard Ward, labor and lumber,   123 64
Mann & Bigelow, stone and labor   53 50
C. O. Richardson, 58 Tons of Beach Stone at $4.00 per
    ton, $232.00 ; Freight, $72.50   304 00
L. H. Bigelow, Directory, Envelopes &c,   2 00
S. Harrington. Labor,   30 00
A. Ballou, Painting,   34 83
Dexter Rice, Signs,   22 75
J. D. Baldwin & Co, Advertising,   1 50
*S. D. Burbank, Burying Anaconda (Elm Park),   2 00
J D. Lovell, Grass Seed for Common and Elm Park,and tools, 86 42
J. Marble & Co.. Tar for Irons of Flag-Staff,   1 25
Sumner Pratt & Co., Guide line,   1 30
Snow Brothers, Printing Report for 1870, (Extra Copies).   23 32
                                           ——————
                                          $6,324 01
        Remaining unexpended $424 87

There are some bills for trimming and boxing Trees, and other work,
not presented, that will reduce if not extinguish this balance.

*Note.—Upon the departure of the " Grand Moral" Caravan of P. T. Barnum it was
found that an Anaconda had " shuffled off its mortal coil " and been left behind among
other hallowing influences. It required Two Dollars and a pretty tough stomach to
deodorize the neighborhood· The interment, behind the Old Gun House, of a " Capta-
tor Verborum," who fell a victim to a bad access of grammar, being a labor of love, was
devoid of expense to the treasury. In neither instance has there been subsequent offence,
although, in one case, the stench was overpowering before burial; and, in the other,
de-composition had become noisome.

⟍ The following enumerated work has been executed during the year, under the direction of the Commission. Forty-five (45) trees were protected with perpendicular slats. Seventeen (17) Circular Guards, with iron bands, have been allowed (in part) by the Commission and, in addition, One Hundred and Fifteen (115) common guards. Sixteen new posts have been affixed to seats in place of others that were rotten.

The property belonging to the Commission and fit for use is thus reported: Thirteen (13) seats; five (old) tree-guards; ten (10) new do: Fifty (50) slats for trees: Three Hundred and Fifty (350) Pickets, which will make Seven Hundred (700) slats; and Nine Circular Guards. There are also on hand Fifty-Eight (58) Tons of Beach-Stones, which will be used in paving gutters when the condition of the ground will admit of it. Quite a number of neat signs that had been put in position upon the Common, warning people " off the grass " are missing and were undoubtedly stolen. There is as yet no clue to the thief. Suspicion justly attaches to a stranger who betrayed remarkable interest in them and whose departure from the city was singularly coincident with the disappearance of those signs. Such forms of lunacy are usually harmless, however, beyond the loss consequent upon their manifestation; and no increase of the police force is recommended should there be a re-appearance of the same or similar depredators.

In the Report of the Commission for 1870, occurs the following paragraph:

" This Commission holds a very definite opinion of what should be done to render the COMMON attractive and ornamental; as it emphatically is neither at present. But it is not deemed expedient to ask appropriations for the decoration of an irregular and imperfect fraction, when measures have been initiated by the People to free the whole from incumbrance."

It is scarcely worth the while to explain the reasons by which the Commissioners were induced to change the policy thus indicated. Perhaps as decisive as any were the sneers indulged in by the sagacious counsel for the Railway Corporations, in the " Hearing " before the Railway Committee of the General Court. If it was true, as alleged, that, " aside from the railroads, from the dilapidated fence which encloses it, and all the surroundings of that Common, you will know by a single glance that it is not the resort of our citizens who would like a Park or Common for use," it seemed to this Commission high time that the desolation of this Public Ground should no longer supply an argument against its improvement to Ex-Mayors, of the legal profession, by whom it had been chiefly neglected. And, although the failure of their " uncultivated country eyes " to " appreciate the beauties of Worcester Common," as admitted by the blatant advocates from Fitchburg Ravine, might be largely due to their inability to discover an " *itching palm* " among our Flora, of which so conspicuous a specimen is supplied by their egregious Town (e), yet it behooved this Commission all the more to remedy deficiencies confessed by none so readily as themselves. For, be that COM-MON what it might, it was none the less precious for the reminiscences that it awakened and for the hopes which it inspired. It was small,— more's the pity ! yet such taunt came with an ill grace from those who had encroached upon its limits. Its appearance was forlorn enough, undoubtedly , but to whom was its bare and sterile aspect more attributable than to those who grudged all sums expended in its improvement, esteeming the devotion of a cent to plans of civic embellishment as an aggravated personal robbery ! The Commissioners had never lacked a keen perception of their duty in the premises : to that consciousness was now superadded a lively sense that the work of recla-. mation might no longer be postponed.

Accordingly, by way of experiment and almost exclusively as a tentative measure, the task of filling the acute triangle or delta, at the N. E. corner, was commenced. The material employed, and indeed the only one then available, was the scrapings from the public streets, of which the Highway Department was glad enough to be rid so handily. The capacity of that tract of land to swallow up dirt was the wonder of the Commission, which beheld the entire municipal force of men and teams severely tasked to establish even a tolerable grade. When the exhaustion of material at length constrained a pause, the enforced cessation of work was found to be rather a benefit than a misfortune. Since, with the first soaking rains, it quickly became apparent that the material used was not of sufficient specific gravity to maintain a definite and fixed level ; for which purpose as well as to fit it for the sustenance of a dense and sightly herbage, it would require to be mixed with richer and heavier soil. A small lot of loam was procured for a top dressing, but the quantity was altogether inadequaté to modify essentially the nature of the whole deposit. It still remained of an arid, heating character by no means favorable to the nutrition of the choicer grasses. A thorough conviction of this, however, was not reached until later in the season, when the progress of improvement, in other portions of the Common, had advanced to a degree which would admit of neither intermission nor delay. The tract had been thickly seeded, at the earliest moment practicable, and a speedy growth of tender herbage offered its pleasant verdure in exchange for a dreary waste. The frosts and snows of winter could be safely depended upon to settle the mass well together, if not to reduce it to a homogeneous whole. It was thought best therefore, to postpone, until the ensuing Spring, the final grading of that tract for 'which, meanwhile, material was steadily accumulated.

Encouraged by the evident success of this attempt, it was resolved to defer the work of improvement no longer, but to commence and complete at once what must, sooner or later, be undertaken. As the execution of this purpose involved the expenditure of considerable sums of money, it was deemed alike prudent and courteous to secure the co-operation of the *City Council*, by which body all appropriations must be made. The following Resolution was therefore submitted for the consideration of the members and, upon the 3d of April, A. D. 1871, it received the unanimous assent of both branches :

" *Resolved*,—that the CITY COUNCIL assures the Commissioners of their cordial co-operation in any effort for the improvement of the Common, and to that end will appropriate such necessary means and facilities as shall promise the most efficient and rapid execution of the work consistent with a judicious economy."

While these preliminaries were in process of arrangement, Mr. Anthony Chase signified to the Commission his willingness that earth should be taken from the high bank lying west of Main Street, where his residence was formerly situated. No more timely, and certainly no greater, assistance could have been offered than this ; not only on account of the quantity of material, but because of its proximity and facilities for excavation. The proposal of Mr. Chase was at once thankfully accepted. A bargain was made with Mr. Michael McGrath by which, for the sum of twenty (20) cents per square yard, he engaged to dig and

convey said earth to the Common. Work was begun on the
13th day of April and continued steadily, without interruption
save from the weather until the 7th day of August. Large and
almost inexhaustible as that bank of dirt had appeared to the
casual observer, it soon became evident that it would prove inadequate for the wants of the Common. Four Thousand One
Hundred and Thirty-Six (4136) yards were obtained from it
before it finally succumbed to the pick and shovel. Six Hundred
and Nine (609) yards were subsequently procured from a lot of
Mr. Chase, upon High Street and One Hundred and Ninety-Four
(194) yards from still another lot, of the same gentleman, upon
Chatham Street; all being excavated upon similar terms. It
has been complained, by the querulous gossips of the streets and
by their congeners, the snarling tattlers of corner paint shops,
that Mr. Chase derived incidental benefit from the operation.
Such is doubtless the fact; and it is one that is very gratifying
to this Commission which can conceive of an honorable transaction, between two parties, resulting in mutual advantage and of no
possible detriment to either. But even this accumulation was
insufficient. Nor was it until after the deposit of Four Hundred
and Thirty-Five (435) yards, from the new cellar of White &
Conant, upon Main Street, at an expense of fourteen (14) cents
per yard; and of Three Hundred and Fifty (350) yards, furnished by Mr. George Sessions, costing Twelve and one-half
cents (12½) per, yard, that the task of filling that yawning hollow gave token of accomplishment. Even then, small lots of
good soil were made use of, as they could be obtained, to supply
deficiencies in spots which seemed to demand unusual care to
remedy their natural barrenness. In addition to all this, a large
amount of loam was required for top-dressing; the hard-pan or
clay, of which the bulk of the filling consisted, affording but poor
encouragement for grass-seed. Thanks are due to Dr. Henry
Clarke, who allowed the Commission to take a great quantity of
quite rich dirt from the cellar of an old stable upon Waldo
Street, without which the labor of preparing a considerable portion of the ground could not have been completed. One
Hundred and Twelve (112) cords of fine loam were also obtained
from the estate of the late John C. Ripley, at a cost but slightly
exceeding Seventy-Five (75) cents per cord. Nor must credit

be omitted for the generosity of Mr. H. H. Houghton who, besides his constant encouragement during the progress of the work, permitted the gravel with which almost all the walks were built and without which their construction would have been impracticable save at greatly enhanced expense and trouble, to be taken from the cellar of his new block of buildings upon Salem Street. Aid of a similar nature, extended by Col. Levi Barker is also gratefully remembered and acknowledged. Indeed, there was scarcely an exception to the general desire and effort to promote, in all possible ways, the accomplishment of a work which, as was the concurrent opinion, had been too long delayed.

At the outset, it was not contemplated to do more than bring up to their proper level those portions of the Common that abut upon the South line of Front Street. But as the work advanced, and as the alteration wrought in the appearance of the grounds by the mere change of grade became clearly manifest, there was scarcely a dissentient from the appeal to the Commission to push on with the task to its completion. Sustained as this appeal was by the members of the City Council, with more or less of whom almost daily conferences were held, it influenced the final adoption of a resolve to finish the work. And the task was accomplished just as the last load of available material, required for its successful achievement, was exhausted.

During this whole time, the Foot-Paths, or Walks, had to be reconstructed, and that too with as little hindrance to public passage as possible. In nearly every instance, the allotted space was first ploughed and then shoveled out to a depth of about two feet, the bottom of the trench being crowded full with coarse stones that were found in the hard-pan and of which there was always a sufficiency. Over these was placed a layer of pebbles, covered in its turn with rough, and thereafter screened, gravel. Repeated rolling yielded a firm surface, although the excessive drought during the progress of this part of the work was a great hindrance to success. The walks will require careful repair, and renovation where washed, in the Spring, to make them pleasant for pedestrians. But they can never be made permanently dry until after the construction of a sewer across the Common, beneath the present short-lived location of the Railways. Into that sewer should be made to empty all the gutters that course along-side the Western and Central Foot-Paths and by it also must be drained the spot that will have to be selected for the permanent position of the Soldiers' Monument. For the gutters themselves, it will be absolutely essential that they should be paved, with a view to economy as well as neatness. That such an edging to the walks, besides protecting them from abrasion by every rain fall, may also be ornamental, a small cargo, consisting of Fifty-Eight (58) tons of small Beach-Stones, has been procured, at a total cost, (including $72.50 for railway tolls,) of Three Hundred and Four and one-half Dollars, ($304.50.) With these it has been computed that several hundred yards of gutters can be paved, narrow but of sufficient width for utility, and long enough to test the question of their cheapness. Too much pains cannot be taken to render the Foot-Paths dry. By this, it is not meant that they should be impervious to water, which would not be desirable, but merely that they shall absorb moisture rapidly, or otherwise be relieved from excess of Summer showers. There was not sufficient time, in the working season of 1871, to complete this part of the task as thoroughly as could be desired. It is hoped, however, in the early Spring, to profit by the experience of the Winter which, with its alternations of frost and thaw, is a thorough if somewhat radical leveller. When the walks shall have been elevated to their proposed height in the centre, thereby rendering them crowning instead of, as now, depressed by myriad feet ; and shall, at the same time, be effectually freed from superfluous water ; the greatest source of anxiety to the Commission will have been entirely removed.

During the progress of the work upon the Northern Path, it became necessary to settle upon the proper disposition to be made of the ancient Well that has so long and faithfully ministered to the popular necessities. The evidence was irresistible that the Well could not be dispensed with, being in use, as conclusively shown, throughout the twenty-four hours. A thorough cleansing was therefore ordered, a dense mass of fibre being removed which had been attracted from the roots of the adjacent Elms by the proximity of moisture. A huge stone was placed over the top, its edge being dressed to a level with the surrounding pathway. In the judgment of this Commission, such jobs are done cheapest when done so as to last. It is not doubted that the dwellers in the vicinity will be lulled to their virtuous slumbers, for many a year to come, by the music of that pump-handle. Upon application from this Commission, three (3) Inlets to the Front Street Sewer, with their accompanying and indispensable Catch-Basins, were constructed by the Department of Sewers, at a total cost of Two Hundred and Fifty Dollars and Eighty Nine cents ($250.89). The original intention was, to collect the entire surface drainage of the Common and discharge it, through appropriate channels, into these Inlets. But it will doubtless be found expedient to divert a part of that overflow to the main Sewer or Drain, which, as heretofore intimated, will be required for the Westerly side of the Common, including the site for the foundation of the Soldiers' Monument, the stability of which must not be left in question for a moment. The general grade of the whole tract is such, nevertheless, that the surface-water can be directed, until shorter courses are offered, into the Inlets to the Front Street Sewer. Especially is such the fact in regard to the rainfall upon the *Knoll* before which, " full high advanced," the Bigelow Monument discloses its graceful proportions.

The proper treatment of that *Knoll* occasioned as much, if not more embarrassment than any other problem which was presented for solution. A thicket of unsightly trees had been suffered to grow up, receiving no other care than the occasional pruning of a limb that had first been fractured by nature in rough but effectual fashion. Scarcely one of those trees, by itself, was worth saving. Had the Commission felt free to disregard all other considerations, consulting only the requirements of a correct taste, not a tree would have been spared which intefered with the plan of reducing the *Knoll* to the level of the Southern Plateau, continuing the Northerly grade, by an easy descent, until it was merged in the walk at its base. But it was not deemed prudent, strongly as it commended itself to the judgment, to make such thorough destruction. Few were marked for preservation, however, that did not give promise of future symmetry under the unwonted influence of air and sunlight to which they would for the first time, be directly exposed. Some that still remain are standing, merely because they were not e xpected to survive the winter and their removal could be conveniently deferred.

30

The plan of improvement, devised and so far executed, by the Commission, will be incomplete until after the construction of a FOUNTAIN or, more strictly, JET D'EAU. No City, within knowledge, enjoys equal facilities for the production of an imposing effect of this nature. A survey has already been made and the stakes are set, denoting the intended location of an Octagonal Basin, twenty feet in diameter, which is precisely one-half of the contemplated size. The finest display will be produced by a hollow column, thrown in a single, perpendicular jet to any height desirable so long as the falling spray shall be restricted to proper limits. It is believed that water enough could be spared to permit the play of the Jet upon Holidays, when it would, of itself, furnish an extraordinary attraction for the multitudes who throng our streets in search of amusement. In no other way can the City as cheaply supply so much innocent gratification. Sums, largely exceeding the utmost expense estimated by the Commission, were appropriated without grudging, in former years for evanescent shows of Fireworks. This simple, unadorned JET is within the plan of work which should be completed during the season that is rapidly approaching. A Fountain might be introduced, for ordinary occasions, in exact conformity to the original design, the spent waters of which, when played, should be conducted to the intersection of Salem Square with Front Street, at the North-East corner of the Common, there to supply a much needed convenience wherefrom the tired wayfarer and his animals may quench their thirst. No waste would then be possible of the invaluable element that has cost so much to introduce and diffuse, but which cannot be in too lavish abundance for every legitimate purpose.

The Commissioners have been led, through paragraphs in the public press as well as from informal communications to their Chairman, to expect that the eager co-operation of a portion of their fellow citizens would take the form of the contribution of a sum of money towards the construction of the proposed JET D'EAU. Such intention, if entertained seriously, appears to have been abandoned. But, as one of the earliest and most prominent features of their original plan of improvement; one indeed which could not be omitted without relinquishing every pretension to true adornment, it has not been as it never will be surrendered by this Commission. There would seem to be a propriety in some voluntary contribution by the owners of Real Estate, abutting upon or contiguous to the Common, which has been and must continue to be so largely benefited by the permanent improvement of that Public Ground, towards a method of ornamentation from which they will derive the chief delight. A timely opportunity will be afforded for the manifestation, in a substantial shape, of that liberality which is doubtless eager to be solicited. At the same time it will not be regarded as any evidence of needless extravagance, should the munificence of our fellow citizens, living remote from the Common, display a tendency in this direction.

No interchange of views has been had, as yet, between the committee to which is entrusted the erection of a Soldier's Monument and this Commission. Whensoever it shall appear to that committee that the time has arrived for the definitive assignment of a site, assuming that one will be sought upon the Common, this Commission will be prepared to entertain the subject with a cordial desire for efficient, mutual co-operation. There can scarcely be two opinions as to the precise spot to be preferred; among the Commissioners, most assuredly, there is entire harmony upon that point as upon all others. The City Council has already taken action, upon the Memorial of this Commission, to secure the removal of the Meeting-House of the First Parish, so long occupied for Town-Meetings. That the Petition of the City will be granted, by the Legislature of the Commonwealth, can no more be doubted than the undeniable fact that its Prayer is but an echo of the wishes of five-sixths of our population. The utter removal of that Meeting-House will relieve the Common from an awkward and unsightly incumbrance, of which no amount of hired advocacy can justify the continued retention. The design for the improvement of the Common has always contemplated the possibility of the construction of a Soldiers' Monument: and no change will be required in the general disposition of the grounds, by that possibility becoming a certainty. When the whole shall be completed; the Monument in position and the grounds immediately surrounding suitably graded and laid out; our citizens will have additional cause for felicitation at the emphasis with which they rejected the scheme, having nothing

but its audacity in its favor, of rearing upon the Common a
pile of Granite as ugly as it would have been absurd :—

"Monstrum horrendum, informe, ingens."

In closing this review and summary of the work upon the
Common, during the past year, it is but fair to insist for a
moment upon a consideration of the neglect under which that Public Ground, in the very heart of our City, has been allowed to lan-
guish. The theme for reproach at home and the butt of ridicule to
the traveller as he was borne swiftly by over street or Railway ;
who shall measure the amount of injury which the sight of such
municipal shiftlessness and unthrift has occasioned ? As we suffered the public property to go to waste, why might not the suspicion justly lurk that we were individually incapable of economical or
discreet conduct! In essaying a remedy for the mismanagement,
or neglect, of former years, the aim of the Commission has been
so to execute the trust confided that the work should not require
repetition. Apportion all the sums that even extravagance could
squander, much more the actual or intended modest expenditure
of the Commission, throughout the countless years during which
nothing was attempted ; and the cost of reclamation sinks into the
very absurdity of insignificance. The People, always apathetic and
usually indulgent to those whom they can induce to govern them,
sharply aroused by recent developments in more than one State
of the Republic, peremptorily insist upon economy in every municipal department. But the distinction between prudent thrift
and a griping penuriousness is kept closely defined. And, among
the monuments to their Civic Idols which they may erect, it is very
certain that no Golden Calf will perpetuate the worship of the
Official Skinflint.

Late in the summer a favorable opportunity presented itself and
was at once improved, to determine a question which had been the
source of much solicitude to this Commission. It was important,
with a view to ultimate future operations, to know upon what foundation the bed of peat, in Elm Park, rested and at what depth that
foundation must be sought. Taking advantage of the existing
drought, excavations were commenced and steadily prosecuted
until all further progress was arrested by a copious rain. Enough
was accomplished, to prove that the mass of peat is underlain
at an average depth of four (4) feet, by a layer or bed of sand

of a grit so fine as to be impalpable and of tenacity like well moulded putty. This subsoil differed, in no material particular, from that upon which the Sever street sewer is built, and it evidently belongs to the same formation. The discovery of that arenaceous deposit, no farther from the surface, assured the Commission of the entire practicability of forming the Pond or Ornamental Water, which has always been pictured to the imagination as the greatest charm of that Park when completed. It will however be impossible to execute any such design, as it would not be advisable even to make the attempt, until the drainage of the entire tract of land can be so controlled that its discharge may be regulated at will. A single shower was sufficiently copious to put a summary stop to operations, last autumn, by flooding the excavation. When the surface water can be drawn off, so that labor may be continued without interruption, there now appears to be no insuperable obstacle to the formation of an Ornamental Water that shall please in Summer and be not wholly without attraction in Winter. For the thanks of many a young lad and lass have been showered profusely upon the Commission in gratitude for even what little has thus far been effected to promote their enjoyment. The excavation of a suitable basin, not too deep for safety, will afford a much needed chance for cheerful and exhilarating exercise, upon sled and skate, to a multitude of children who, being born, have claims upon the world that begat them. Clay enough can be obtained, for puddling the bottom of such basin, from the side of the adjacent hill, whose eastern slopes have been rent and gashed by many and lawless, even if municipal, depredations. Those slopes indeed, require to be pared down, dressed to uniformity of outline, and sown thickly with congenial grass seed. It will be the good fortune of the Commission, if here, as elsewhere, the execution of what may well be done shall be instrumental towards the completion of that which is indispensable.

But a connection with the sewers of the city is a pre-requisite, without which little of a satisfactory nature can be achieved. The water in the pool, at Elm Park, on the fourth day of January, current, stood upon a level with the crown of Agricultural street. This is an evil which will go on increasing with every spadeful of dirt that goes to uplift the average grade of the Park.

Even nature will contribute to this overflow, in her silent but sure processes of filling up valleys by the abrasion of uplands and by deposits from decaying vegetation. In the judgment of this Commission, the time for action in the premises, by the City Government, cannot be postponed any longer. The construction of a sewer through Russell street and thence-forward along a portion of Elm or Agricultural streets, would be but the anticipation of a work that cannot, in any event, be neglected. It is believed that nothing but the character of the soil prevents the exhalations from the lowlands contiguous to the Park becoming a pestilential nuisance. Suffer the *excreta* of a rapidly increasing population to saturate it, and even the deodorizing and disinfecting properties of peat will not avail to preserve the health of the vicinage. It would appear to be the part of a far-sighted and discreet administration to fit the land for human habitation, in advance of settlement, rather than to delay indispensable measures until the decimation of the people sounds an alarm that can no longer pass unheeded. As it is, coterminons proprietors complain, with too much reason, that there is no artificial outlet provided for the waters which, owing to the extreme flatness of the land, are retained upon the surface after every rain: and that all the natural channels of discharge are permanently closed by the public streets.

Some misconception seems to exist concerning the condition of the Legacy bequeathed by the late Hon. Levi Lincoln for the "thorough drainage and improvement" of Elm Park. In the opinion of this Commission, it would not constitute a compliance with the intention of the bequest, to employ it in the construction of a sewer without the boundaries of the Park, beneficial as such sewer might be, even were it competent for the Commission, as such, to meddle with the Public Streets. It will be altogether better to excavate the proposed small basin or pond, directing thither and emptying therein all the underdrains that may be found necessary for the "thorough drainage and improvement" of the Park, comprehending among them, as will probably be essential, one of size sufficient to collect the discharge from the adjacent hill. That such application of this special fund would best fulfil the design of the Legacy, can be confidently assumed by the chairman of this Commission, who well recollects the commendation at the time bestowed upon an article from his pen, in the columns of the *Spy*, referring to which the Legator remarked that the formation of an open basin or ornamental water would be the greatest improvement that could be developed in the landscape. There is some consolation in knowing that, if immediate benefit is not derived from that fund, the sum of the fund itself, as a trust in the hands of the city, is swelling by the steady accumulation of interest.

The opinion heretofore communicated to the HONORABLE COUNCIL by this Commission, is reiterated, that the city should become proprietor of Newton Hill by purchase ; or, if that is not possible, by virtue of authority to be obtained from the General Court. Its propinquity lends a charm that, in its naturalness, is foreign to other Public Grounds throughout the country ; while its ownership, and consolidation with the Park, would forever prevent its destruction for the sake of the material which is so much needed in the valley that it dominates. If the entire, or even a major part of the water supply of the City is to be derived from Leicester, that hill must be invaluable in the immediate future, as the site for a reservoir which shall hold a temporary store against emergencies and also aid in equalizing the pressure throughout that broad arc in which the western suburbs are comprised and in the chord subtending which it is the most salient feature. There can be no question but what, in the time to come, that Hill will be wanted for some important public use ; whether of an exclusive Municipal nature, or not, is of slight consequence to the argument. Its seasonable possession would ensure the preservation of that symmetry by which the admiration of the casual visitor is so much excited and to which even comparative familiarity has not blunted the sensibilities of the oldest inhabitant. The more speedy its acquisition the greater the economy : since even *upland pasture* will not be likely to depreciate as the march of population closes in upon its base. " *Bis dat qui cito dat.* " He gives twice who gives quickly, says the ancient proverb. Celerity of action is the secret of all modern achievement. Now, as of yore, the Sibylline Books are forever lost to the irresolute and timid. Any dolt can call a halt ; but, to advance, demands genius of a high order. The measure recommended by the Commission—the acquisition of Newton Hill and its annexation to

Elm Park,—is advised as *a step forward.* The grasp of the speculator has already closed upon its North Eastern corner. A few years more of indecision,—of doubt as to the present expediency and skepticism as to the ultimate profit,—will probably settle the matter of such acquisition by rendering it impracticable. It may well happen that·Posterity, for which our affection is so inordinate that we are willing it should pay our Public Debt, may retort upon us that it would have preferred the lofty Hill "with verdure clad," to the polluted Sewer, had it been left the option.

The *Shade Trees* of the City, that line the public streets, have received more than ordinary attention. A few have been planted. A very large number were pruned of dead or useless limbs. And still others have been removed entirely, in cases where they threatened to become a serious hindrance to the use and enjoyment of Sidewalks, or already obstructed their establishment. So far as the setting out of new Shade-Trees is concerned, it has not appeared to the Commission to be worth the while to attempt very much. The grade of so many of the Streets is undetermined ; the very level of the grade itself is in so few intances thoroughly worked out, even when it has been decreed ; that a tree is at any instant liable to the sudden exposure of its roots by the official pickaxe or spade. The wiser policy has been preferred, of acquiring a stock of good, merchantable Trees at a minimum price ; allowing them to attain sufficient growth ; and then planting them out along such Streets as may be selected, on both sides, throughout their whole length. Adequate space can thus be ensured between each tree, while their relative position can conform to some other requirement than that of direct opposition. Moreover the work can be conducted with partial relation to a system previously adopted. With a view to the reception of a nursery of such trees, a suitable tract of land at the South Western corner of Elm Park, was ploughed in the Spring and well-manured and cultivated during the Summer. It had been designed to set out the young trees in the early Spring ; but, owing to delay in their receipt, this was found to be impracticable. Advantage doubtless accrued from a tardiness which, at first, seemed a misfortune, insomuch as the new plantation escaped exposure to the fervent heat and unwonted drought of

July and August. One Thousand (1,000) Maples and Five Hundred (500) Elms are now in the ground prepared for them, having been carefully and well placed there by Mr. James Draper, with whom a bargain had been previously made. With only ordinary good fortune, there can be no reason why a large proportion should not survive and attain maturity. It is the purpose of this Commission to have them properly cared for; transplanted when their rapidity of growth renders it necessary; and ultimately to set them out along the Public Streets, as before stated, or to issue them, in lieu of the present impolitic pecuniary bounty, to persons who will agree to plant them and look out for their future protection.

The following tabular statement will show the number and location of Trees, planted by individuals in A.' D., 1871, for which claims were made and allowed by this Commission :—

On Chandler and Tatnuck Streets, Twelve (12) Rock Maples.
On Bellevue Street, Five (5) Maples.
On Providence Street, Eight (8) Elms.
On Boynton Street, Two (2) Maples.
On Woodland Street, Five (5)
On Elm Street, Five (5) Elms.

The planting of quite a number that had been contracted for was prevented by the sudden and unexpected commencement of the present severe Winter.

A great amount of work has been done in pruning existing Trees. The giant Elms on Lincoln Street; those on the terrace at the Southern extremity of Court Hill; and the entire row which so superbly arches Front Street for a little while longer; have been one and all severely trimmed. If, in the opinion of some, too many limbs were here and there taken; the answer must be that it was designed rather to accomplish at once what was required than to spin out the work, to the annoyance of the wayfarer, throughout successive years. Frequent amputations by official highway-men had so reduced the roots of many of those lofty and massive Trees, that their impaired vitality was inadequate to the sustenance of the unrestricted top. It is believed that they will now take a new lease of life and attest, in their own peculiar fashion, that the heroic method of surgery is not necessarily fatal. In every one of these cases, the nourishment, that would have been wasted in useless development, will be directed to clothing with verdure limbs that are the nett result derived from *artificial selection.*

Public convenience has compelled the removal of quite a number of Trees of unequal value. The necessities of the Highway Department, with which this Commission is brought into close relations, have occasioned the felling of several whose destruction, under less immediate urgency, would furnish a theme for regret. The most signal examples were, — on Front Street, where the widening of the travelled way was incompatible with the continued toleration of the row of Elms lying East of Church Street; and the detached and stately specimens on Chestnut St., between Elm and Pleasant Streets. In this last case, the Commission was unanimous in the opinion that the whole four were very much in the way of pedestrians, upon a most important thoroughfare between several churches, the Post-office, and the homes of a large portion of the community desirous of their summary extirpation. It was decided, however, to take out two at that time, suffering the others to remain for the present. A distinct understanding was had, in the case of the most northerly, that its continued toleration would be contingent upon the execution of a half-formed purpose of Dr. Henry Clarke: and, in that of the other and larger, that the garden-fence of Mr. F. H. Kinnicutt should be retired upon a curve that will compensate for the seven feet of space in the side-walk monopolized by the tree. In most instances, where it was found necessary to remove trees to admit of the setting of curb-stones, their excision was productive of great advantage. Marked examples can be cited ; — one upon East Worcester Street, where Eleven (11) Elms were felled, materially benefitting the remainder; and another on Main, between Allen and Benefit Streets, in front of the Orphan's Home, at which point the removal of Twelve (12) Horse Chestnuts left suitable and much-needed room for the fine row of Maples with which they awkardly alternated. The doom of many a goodly tree, on Lincoln Street, was also sealed by the rapid growth of population and the consequent demand for sidewalks in and about that thriving portion of the Second Ward. In no instance has authority been granted to fell or remove a tree, without it first underwent a personal inspection from the Chairman of the Commission. Had greater discretion been exhibited in choosing fit locations for the Shade-Trees in our Streets, this Commission would be spared the painful duty of so frequently *grinding its axe*.

The efforts of the Commission to protect the Shade Trees of the City from mutilation have not been attended with the success that could be desired. Somewhat of this ill-fortune must be attributed to thoughtlessness which, reckless of warning or legal provision, persists in using tree-trunks and tree-guards, indiscriminately, as so much gratuitous pasture. In some flagrant cases it is believed that injury might have been prevented, or its agents punished, had not the ministers of the Law held views of their duty widely at variance with those cherished by this Commission. The Police appear to be of opinion that the citizen must detect, and, by sworn testimony, convict an offender; and that to them merely appertains the task of formal arrest, with the final ecstacy of exploring the wonders and participating in the mysteries of that new multiplication table—a Criminal Bill of Costs. The view upheld by this Commission, and cherished by a vast majority of the community, on the contrary, is that officers, even of the Law, should earn their salt; and that the labor should be exacted of those who never fail to be punctual at the Treasury. It is no assumption, to assert that a very imperfect display of vigilance would suppress the mischief in question, although it is not pretended that, by the exercise of such vigilance, the existing standard of proficiency in Draughts and Dominoes might not be sensibly lowered.

During the year which has elapsed since the publication of their last Annual Report, the Commissioners have taken especial note of the welcome accorded to their recommendation of a Boulevard or AVENUE, to environ and also develope the City. Particular gratification was afforded them by the written commendation of their former fellow-townsman, Hon. Andrew H. Green, whose signal merits have but just obtained fitting recognition, and whose long service as the virtual head of the New York Central Park Commission entitles his opinion to commanding influence. Among their fellow-citizens the reception of the project was unexpectedly favorable. Some, indeed, objected to it as a whole, who yet conceded the wisdom of rendering Lake Quinsigamond more accessible. In a solitary instance, a writer for the press to whose judgement much deference is ordinarily due and yielded, alleging the cost of the right of way as an insuperable obstacle, advised that any future consideration of the plan be postponed for two hundred years. To this it must suffice to respond that the project of the Commission is intended for the benefit of the very people who shall come into being hereafter and not for their perplexity in its consideration: and that if its adoption is deferred, as suggested, the chance is infinitesimal of its present advocates, by whom its merits are best appreciated, appearing in its behalf. But more momentous than all else is the fact, not doubted by the least sanguine and perspicacious among us, that in less than the life-time of a generation, this Worcester, that within the memory of the writer, has grown from the quiet village in which the arrival of the Boston coach was an event to the city that makes of slight account the bustle of a hundred Railway trains, will transcend the broadest limits that are contemplated for the location of that AVENUE. It is to anticipate such rapid progress;—to provide, in advance, that the Worcester of the coming century shall not have the circulation between its extremities obstructed, as is almost disgracefully the case with the Worcester of to-day;—to insure, so far as may be, the speedy opening and permanent maintenance of at least one wide thoroughfare which shall supply the means of direct intercommunication and easy traffic to, and from, and throughout the suburbs; that this commission declines to earn the meed of the unprofitable servant, "leaving undone that which ought to be done." That the exact bearing and scope of its recommendation may be clearly appreciated, the following passage from the report of the Commission for 1870, is copied at length, the importance of its subject-matter justifying the repetition of a statement in the precise expression of which there would be but slight hope of improvement.

" The broad Boulevards that encircle the fair city upon the banks of the Seine, contribute largely to the facilities of intercourse and traffic. A similar AVENUE, encompassing our own Worcester, would contribute more to the developement of the whole City, in the judgement of this Commission, than any other project that has been devised or consummated for years. The farm takes precedence of the shop; and yet, while no sum can be too great to lavish upon the intricate net work of alleys, courts and streets which separate the centre and heart of the Municipality into infinitesimal subdivisions, every dollar is grudged that is required to promote the convenience of those without whose toil man could not live.

The farm and its produce are indispensable ; the middleman and his store are not absolute necessities. Whatever, then, has a tendency to open up the surrounding country ; to develope its natural charms ; and to encourage settlement and culti- vation where now the bramble and the woodchuck hold undisputed possession ; substituting smooth lawns, neat gardens, and improved stock ; inducing the street loafer to become the independant yeoman, and attracting, by the simple aspect of rural loveliness the permanent sojourn of the chance wayfarer ; surely here, and in all this, is an object worth striving for, worth far more, in fact, than even current extravagance could possibiy make it cost in realization. With such an Avenue constructed, there would be an amount of intercommunication of the extremities of the city, as of the outlying but adjacent towns, that would astonish those whose ocular mote is Main Street. That great artery of business would be relieved of much needles yet serious incumbrance : a relief which, attempted in season, can be both cheaply and prudently afforded. As it is now, from Holden to Leicester, from Paxton to Shrewsbury, everything must pass through our one great thoroughfare, wearing out our pavements, impeding our local traffic, laming beasts used for traction and scaring into disease animals destined for consumption. All these annoyances and evils would be obviated, all those benefits and more would be derived, from the construction of the Avenue suggested. So broad as to admit of adequate and grateful shade to ample footpaths ; so thoroughly built as to be proof alike against autumnal frost or vernal flood ; a convenience for the loaded team and an attraction for the pleasure carriage ; wooing occupation of hundreds of charming dells and nooks by its ruthless exposure of rustic beauty, thereby benefiting individuals and augmenting the general valuation ; a measure which commends itself in proportion as it is considered : one which this Com. mission will advocate in season and out of season, living or dying, in the hope and faith of its ultimate consummation."

Did the conception of the proposed AVENUE originate merely in a scheme to accommodate or furnish enjoyment for those who ride in pleasure carriages, numerous as that class is rapidly be. coming, it would not be entertained for an instant by this Com. mission. Even in that case it might be desirable : but in that fact alone could be found no warrant for its adoption. It is in the necessity that exists for better and more uninterrupted ways of intercourse and traffic between the remoter suburbs ; not for. getting the wants of the adjoining Towns, whose obvious market is Worcester ; that a strong, if not convincing, reason is to be found why such an AVENUE should be opened to the public. The incentive that is offered to travel and the increase of commercial business that is developed by the construction of a first-class Highway, or Common Road, must be a matter of faith with the inhabitants of our fair City, to whom such advantages were never vouchsafed. In the light of experience our boasted Civilization

appears to have profited us but little.   Twenty-Five centuries ago,
the traveller from Brundusium to Rome could traverse almost the
entire length of the Italian Peninsula, experiencing fewer impedi-
ments, and with more actual comfort upon the Road itself than
is felt by the " free and enlightened citizen " who perils life and
limb in his weary toil through the ridges and sloughs of Worcester. Men in these days, are so apt to suffer their attention to be
arrested by the wider streams of traffic that they overlook the
little rivulets whose multitude makes up for their individual lack
of volume.   It is essential to the developement of our busy City
that the course of Railway travel shall be unimpeded. With this
object, measures were taken to secure the transfer, from the centre
to the circumference of the inhabited area, of the existing Tracks.
The Great Circle is the true key to distance by Land, not less
than by Sea.   But conceding the utmost that may be claimed for
the Railway as an agent of material prosperity, it is absolutely
vital to our very existence that the Wagon of the Farmer and the
Truck of the Teamster should possess every possible facility of
access and transit.   The power of the Elephant to pick up a needle
is more remarkable than is his ability to uproot an Oak.   Other
things being equal,—natural advantages of position, and the like,
—that community will quickly render itself master of the situation ; outstripping its rivals in the race for commercial pre-eminence; which builds and maintains a perfect system of Highways,
so thoroughly constructed as to be measurably proof against the
vicissitudes of the seasons.   In the proposed AVENUE these advantages should be secured, with the beauty of rural adornment
afforded by the suitable plantation of Shade, and other Trees,
conspicuous whether for bloom or foliage.   *Nor, even then, should
such an improvement be authorized, much more commenced, until
the Right of Way, in perpetuity, had been absolutely conveyed to
the City by the proprietors of real estate lying along the selected
Route.*   This Commission does not admit, at least in this instance,
that "to him who hath shall be given."   If greed and selfish-
ness prove too strong in one direction, let the course of the AVENUE
be changed towards some other quarter in which there is light
enough for the perception that wise liberality is not incompatible
with self-interest.   Over much of the Route that ought to be
adopted, there is already a travelled road which would simply re-

quire to be widened. For another portion, by the margin of the Lake, the public decision is likely to be anticipated by the action of individual proprietors. Throughout the entire distance no obstacles present themselves that should daunt the courage or impede the movements of a community like this. Want of space forbids more than a bare reference to the Boulevards of Chicago and St Louis, of which, in their as yet inchoate condition, we are told by shrewd observers that they promise to yield returns to the public treasury far more than commensurate with their exactions. In our own case it is only the adoption of the general plan, and the location of a Route with its definition by ineradicable metes and bounds, that is advocated without compromise or equivocation. A *Route*—while the land through which it may extend is comparatively valueless: and its *Definition* so indelibly and plainly that two thirds of the area comprehended shall not, as in the instance of Main Street, be stolen by thieves in the night! Construct it,—*after the* RIGHT OF WAY *is secured,*—when and as fast as you will ;—a foot, a rod, or a mile annually, as the popular exigency and favor shall demand. Accepting the prediction, however, from this Commission, that the design, when once entered upon, will so commend itself in execution as to enlist the popular impatience of results in behalf of its immediate completion.

Had the plan of the Commission been limited to devising a more facile and agreeable way of access to Lake Quinsigamond, it would unquestionably have met with more universal acceptance. The wish to make that lovely sheet of water of easier resort is shared by all classes of the community. And yet, for that very reason, because the charms of this portion of the Route will almost ensure its construction, have especial pains been taken to enlarge upon the imperative necessity of the more rural and secluded sections of the proposed AVENUE. It is by no means certain that the beauties of the landscape disclosed by a *suitable* Avenue, following the arc which, commencing near the City Alms House, runs by the Sears, Chamberlain, and Flagg Farms, deflecting South Easterly so as to skirt the sparkling Reservoir of the Messrs. Coes, would not take precedence even when forced into close competition with the attractions of the Lake Valley. Still, the Lake occupies a peculiar relation to the entire

project which challenges for it a brief consideration. The sub-
joined extract from their Report for 1870, will vindicate the
reputation of the Commissioners for ordinary prescience showing
that, whatever their deficiencies, they were at least not blind to
the signs of the times : —

"Above all — as indispensable to the completeness and symmetry of the
design, LAKE QUINSIGAMOND should be embraced within its scope. The eye of
covetousness already glances at that beautiful sheet of water. It may be that
the people of Worcester will consent to hold the fairest ornament of their city
at the will, or upon sufferance, of the capital ; but it is not believed that such
tame acquiescence will be prompted by any one who has the wit to foresee, in a
utilitarian sense only, the advantages that would follow upon its undisputed control. The opinion of the Commissioners is decided that the city of Worcester
should obtain, from the Great and General Court, power to occupy and possess
Lake Quinsigamond, for the purposes of a PUBLIC PARK, without prejudice to
the rights of riparian owners, whatever they may be. In this way, if in no other,
could the level of its waters be maintained at their average height, thus preserving the smooth and verdant banks which so mnch enhance its beauty. Nor can
any other method be devised, half as effectual, of forestalling future attempts to
divert the water of the Lake for the supply of metropolitan thriftlessness and
waste."

Of the soundness of the views, thus expressed, this Commission is more than ever persuaded. Lake Quinsigamond has been
acquired by us, so far as Title may be secured through the agency
of a popular vote cast under Legislative sanction. But, whether
it will be regarded as reduced to usufruct or possession, in
default of any action taken to utilize its pellucid waters, may well
be doubted. Long ages since, in the days of Æsop, the-dog-in-
the-manger performed his inglorious part. It is not likely that
Worcester, in the Nineteenth Century, can desire or would be
suffered to emulate that selfish example. Nevertheless the petition to the General Court, for sanction to the taking, by the
Metropolis, of water from any source within fifty (50) miles, is
a precious because timely warning. It tells us, in unmistakable
tones, that the talent committed to us must not be hidden in a
napkin nor lie buried in the earth. It says, almost in so many
words ; — " You claim that you must have control of Lake Quinsigamond for the sake of its supply of water. Take, then, and
use it ! If, however, you fail to avail yourselves of this conces-
sion, do not complain at its possible resumption and grant to
others ! "

This Commission has no desire to magnify its functions, nor to exceed the admitted limits of its authority. But it would omit no practicable method of preserving Lake Quinsigamond in its integrity and to that end would again advise that its recognition as the WATER PARK of Worcester be solicited from the General Court. Viewing that Lake as the one unrivalled natural charm of our landscape, it is of opinion that the most expedient and feasible way of retaining it in its present beauty, or of developing it to extreme perfection, is to be found in compelling it to minister to our urgent needs. Projects to this effect are abundant ; to none of them are the Commissioners mechanicians enough to adhere. Some would be content to try the simple method of pumping by means of steam. These are conscious of the expense ; but adduce, by way of set-off, the *quality* of the result as against quantity which is all that can be pretended, and even that with restrictions, of existing modes and appliances. Another and larger class, comprising some of the most thoughtful and practical among our citizens, more than doubting the prudence of depending exclusively upon a solitary source and conduit, incline to favor the scheme of deriving any additional supply from the Lake. Of the insuperable difficulties, mysteriously hinted at by those whose gaze is riveted so closely to the setting of the sun behind the hills of Leicester, that they are blind to discern his rise " by Shrewsbury clock " such shrewd men of action make sport as involving only the simplest problems in mechanical engineering. Granted the force : — what shall prevent its operation ! The boldest conception is theirs however, who, reminding us that the original construction of the Causeway cost less than Twenty Thousand Dollars, ($20,000 :) propose to add Fifteen or Twenty Feet to its height and thus retain the augmented volume of water above the dam so as to furnish the requisite power for its own elevation and at the same time maintain the necessary discharge at the outlet. Any inadequacy of gravitation to lift to the proper height and distance, they would supplement with the forces of Wind and Steam, held in reserve for public employment, when necessary, and leased for private occupation when their auxiliary might could be dispensed with. The annual outlay, under the most unpropitious conditions, it is claimed could hardly exceed the expense of that most curious

32

experiment at New Worcester whereby it was seriously sought to
determine how and in what proportions, chemical and all manner
of vegetable uncleanness could best be assimilated with the
numan system.   This at least would be gained — should such a
work be undertaken and prove successful — of which its advocates allege that there need be no distrust — the possession,
thenceforth unquestioned and indisputable, together with the
unwonted enjoyment of *Pure* Water in abundance.   It is understood that the engineers of the metropolis propose to raise the
dam at the outlet so as to increase the volume of the Lake by at
least Ten Feet in perpendicular measure.   The elevation of the
Causeway would thus appear to be contemplated in more than
one quarter.   If it is to be undertaken, it may well be that the
benefit should be made to enure to Worcester, within whose
territory the whole body of the Lake, at that point, is comprehended.   The division into an Upper and Lower Lake, real then
as it is now apparent, might be turned to advantage, in an
æsthetic view, by so planning the necessary additions to the
Causeway, the bald and inflexible outline of which is now so
offensive, as to obtain harmonious and symmetrical proportion
while securing the strength that would be absolutely essential.

Emphatic but not undue stress has been laid in this Report, on
the imperative necessity of insisting upon the gratuitous conces-
sion of the Right of Way, to the City and its inhabitants, so
long as the proposed AVENUE shall be maintained.   Such conces-
sion should be a fundamental condition precedent to the taking
of the first step by the City looking towards the realization of
the project.   Equally indispensable is the requirement of a Quit-
claim conveyance to the Municipality of all the land lying
between the AVENUE as it may be located and the water ; or the
execution of an agreement between all the parties in interest
covenanting that no building, of any description whatsoever,
shall be erected or suffered between the Lake and the AVENUE
save appropriate and essential boat-houses.   The AVENUE will
be constructed, if at all, for the purpose of developing the latent
charms of the Lake Valley and not for their disfigurement.
Should those pleasant hillsides and sunny slopes become peopled,
as they assuredly would, the new settlers should be made to feel
secure in their possession of a beauty without flaw.   No pre-

caution can be wasted which shall tend to preserve the integrity of the scene from the devastating greed of Mammon.

There is little reason to doubt tnat the Inter-Collegiate Regatta will hereafter resume its position as a permanent feature among the fascinations of Lake Quinsigamond. With us, that exhilarating and manly sport is at home, as it can never be with the votaries of the stable and race-course. It is no slight tribute to its attractions that Lake Quinsigamond should be preferred, out of all the charming sheets of water in New England, for the trial and decision of this exciting issue. It may be attended with annoyance and personal discomfort to those who have the care of preliminary preparation : but the immediate and contingent benefits, whereof it is fruitful, are to the public-spirited and reflecting more than an equivalent. We, too, with our sister cities, can boast the rapid stallion and lusty bull ; but, over and above them, it is our fortune to become the modern Elis, in which the flower of our youth annually contest the palm of pre-eminence in athletic sports, beneath the approving smiles of youth and beauty. Hither is drawn the transient visitor, to be converted, if we are wise, into the permanent sojourner and resident. The prosperity of every city is proportioned to its advance in population ; and that advance can best be secured by the broadest development and fullest exhibition of our natural advantages. To cite again the former Report of the Commission, —

"Once committed to. the execution of this project, the only one practicable for the immediate as well as ultimate convenience and adornment of the City, and it might not be found necessary to decline the munificent proffer of lands by their generous owners. And then, with the whole scheme fully accomplished ; with the Water-Park, the consummate masterpiece of nature, and the broad and shaded AVENUE; the perfected work of man ; each the complement of the other ; our fair City, not unmindful of its other manifold beauties, but exultant in these because the result of its later and maturer development, may safely anticipate the reward which is surely theirs who, enjoying advantages magnify them, and appreciating opportunities improve them.

* * * * * * * * *

The construction of the Avenue and the acquisition of the Water-Park, may not be accomplished. But the entire plan is so feasible ; its realization would so enure to the public utility and general comfort, if gradually and therefore economically perfected ; that the acknowledged good taste of the community must appreciate its countless prospective advantages and beauties, even though it deny itself their enjoyment.

In concluding this Report, the Commissioners desire to express, in the most explicit manner, their profound sense of gratitude for the cordial and sympathetic co-operation which they received from the Municipal authorities, with scarcely an exception, during the past official year. The courtesy and kind encouragement of their fellow citizens, manifested in equal unstinted measure, require a similar, public acknowledgment. For whatsoever criticism, grammatical or other, accorded to their efforts, the Commissioners believe that they close the year with no outstanding obligations, it having been their aim to discharge such indebtedness on the spot, as it accrued.

All which is Respectfully submitted for and in behalf of the Commission, by

EDWARD WINSLOW LINCOLN, *Chairman.*

Worcester, Massachusetts, January 26th, A. D., 1872.

THE EIGHTEENTH ANNUAL REPORT

OF THE

COMMISSIONERS OF HOPE CEMETERY,

FOR THE YEAR 1871.

To His Honor the Mayor, the Aldermen, and Common Council of the City of Worcester:

The Commissioners " make and render a report of their acts and doings, of the condition of the Cemetery, and of the receipts and expenditures for the same. "

Immediately after your election of a member of the board for the year 1871, it was organized by the election of Albert Tolman, *Chairman*, Stephen Salisbury, Jr., *Secretary*, Albert Curtis, *Superintendent* and David S. Messinger, *Assistant Superintendent*.

As early in the Spring as was practicable, the avenues and drive-ways were repaired and made passable, the rubbish that had accumulated in them cleared away and that which had been left on the grounds near lots that parties had cleared and graded in the previous Autumn was removed. The trees that had been set on the Avenues, and others of native growth which have been left standing on the grounds that have been cleared and graded, were properly trimmed. Through the year the Superintendent has given his personal attention to the work and had such clearing and cleaning done as becomes necessary from the growth of grass, weeds and the falling of leaves. This kind of work must be done each year, and will always require the expenditure of a portion of the annual receipts.

New ground has been opened on the right, after entering the gateway, and near the entrance. Beginning at the West end at the intersection of, and between Chestnut and Pine Avenues and extending South West to Willow Avenue, the ground has been cleared by cutting down trees, taking out the stumps, &c., and has been leveled and graded, and is ready to be laid out into lots as soon as the weather will allow the surveyor to do it. This clearing extends over about one acre and a half, and is large enough for One Hundred and seventy-five lots. There are two rows of lots fronting on Chestnut Avenue, most of which have been sold and the clearing of last year extends over all the remaining ground lying between the three avenues named. It is as desirable as any portion of the Cemetery, and the lots, with those unsold, in other parts of the grounds, will meet the demand for two or three years, excepting for small lots. Small lots, to meet the wants of persons living in our city but not sure they shall remain here, or with small families, were laid out a few years ago on River Avenue, it is a retired and beautiful spot and many of the lots have been taken, and more will probably be needed. We shall have more laid out early in the Spring.

The City authorities, after laying the water pipes up Webster street, extended them into the Cemetery. A four inch pipe was laid from Webster street through Cyprus Square to Chestnut Avenue, through Chestnut to Aspen, in Aspen to Crescent and to the line of Sycamore Avenue. The natural supply of water within the grounds is so limited and the soil is so dry, that this desirable improvement will be appreciated by the owners of lots and the Commissioners when planting trees, shrubs and flowers.

The sum of four hundred and fifty-four Dollars and 58 cents, ($454.58) was expended on the work we have described.

In 1871, there was received for wood sold $92 62. Interest, $31 57 and for 66 lots sold $1238 50.

Total receipts for the year,	$1362 69	
Add Fund in City Treasury,	1354 72 —	$2717 41
Expenditures 1871,		454 58
Now on Hand,		$2262 83

The account in detail is appended to this report.

We deem it proper to present some statistics gathered for the report of 1867, and continue them for future use and information. The Cemetery was opened in the year 1852, and 16 lots were sold, — in 1853, 61 lots were sold. — The accounts with the Cemetery while it was managed by the City Council do not show what was received for sales in the two years mentioned.

In the year 1854, 89 lots sold for		$1,261 50
In thirteen years following, to the year 1868, 816 lots sold for		10,344 50
Making 905 lots, for		$11,606 00
There was also sold in the year 1866, to be conveyed to persons who were interested in the removal of remains from the Pine Meadow burial ground 93 lots for		972 00
In the year 1868, 49 lots for		1186 50
1869, 59 lots for		1440 00
1870, 53 lots for		1025 00
1871, 66 lots for		1238 50
Whole number sold 1225.		
Received for 1148 sold since the year 1853,		$17,468 00

From the establishment of the commission until the year 1862 all the receipts from sale of lots, wood, and grass, were paid into the City Treasury, and small sums were appropriated for the clearing and improvement of the grounds. It was then found on the settlement of the accounts that the receipts had been *fully equal* to the first cost to the city of the purchase of the land, and all expenses for its care and improvement after it came under the charge of the Commissioners. With the sanction of the city the account was closed and a new account opened by the City Treasurer between the City and the Commissioners, giving them credit for the balance of $234.27. From that time to the present, no appropriations have been made by the city, all expenditures have been met by the current receipts. The time, labor, superintendence of work, and personal expenses of all the Commissioners for eighteen years, have been given gratuitously.

In consideration of the fact that the entire cost of Hope Cemetery previous to the year 1871, has been returned to the city, the Commissioners deem it fit and proper that the city have incurred the small expense of laying the water pipe, referred to, and they hope an abundant supply of water will be furnished hereafter.

We would also report to you the condition of the receiving Tomb. It was built when the Cemetery was first opened under the direction of a Committee of the City Council and has been from the first a source of very reasonable complaints from the undertakers, and is entirely unfit for the purpose for which it was designed. It should be rebuilt and enlarged. The cost of doing it well and permanently will be estimated and we respectfully suggest the propriety of your appropriating the sum, to be used for the work. If you make the appropriation, the fund now on hand, and the income of the year will be sufficient for much needed improvements on the avenues, banks and plots which are reserved for convenient and ornamental purposes. It will enable the Commissioners to fulfill in part, the duty imposed upon them in the Act creating the board, of "causing said Cemetery to be planted and embellished with trees, shrubs, flowers and other rural ornaments, as they shall think proper."

We intend, this year as soon as it is practicable, after clearing and repairing the avenues, to clear, grade, and improve the remainder of the ground fronting on Webster street, east of the entrance gate, and enrich by the application of fertilizers all the land fronting the street. Although the grounds are attractive for their situation and present a pleasing variety of surface and scenery, the soil is not fertile and they can only be brought into the state of high culture and garden-like appearance of most modern Cemeteries by the judicious application of means and labor and free expenditure of money.

The present owners of lots have the assurance that all money paid by them has or will be expended in improving the Cemetery, as will also all future receipts. If the city can make some appropriations in addition, proprietors will be encouraged to greater attention to the portions of ground under their care, and their efforts united with those of the Commissioners will make Hope Cemetery with its retired and quiet hills and vales, the proper resting place for the remains of our departing friends ; a place too, where the stricken mourner, in the presence of the graves of those who have gone before, of flowers, gentle breezes and singing birds, may see life and find hope full of immortality.

David S. Messinger Esq., who retires from the Board after ten years of most faithful service, and George W. Wheeler Esq., who from the first has rendered all required assistance, receive our, and deserve your cordial thanks.

ALBERT TOLMAN,
ALBERT CURTIS,
D. S. MESSINGER.
HENRY CHAPIN,
STEPHEN SALISBURY Jr.

Commissioners.

RECEIPTS AND EXPENDITURES.

Report of Receipts and expenditures for Hope Cemetery in the year 1871.

RECEIPTS.

1871. Jan.	Cash balance from 1870,		$1354 72	
	" from sixty-six lots sold,		1238 50	
	" from Interest on Deposit,		31 57	
Feb.	" from sale of Wood,		6 53	
March	" " " " "		1 75	
May	" " " " "		4 99	
Sept.	" " " " "		23 76	
Oct.	" " " " "		55 59	— 2717 41

EXPENDITURES.

1871. Jan.	Charles Hamilton, Printing,	5 50	
May	Cash paid for Tools,	10 12	
"	Labor on Grounds,	52 20	
June	Cash paid for Tools,	2 93	
"	Labor on Grounds,	33 69	
July	Cash paid for Tools,	1 75	
"	Labor on Grounds,	29 75	
Aug.	" " "	48 24	
"	Cash paid for 4 Spruce Trees,	2 00	
Sept.	Labor on Grounds,	111 58	
Oct.	" " "	91 13	
Nov.	" " "	65 69	
1872. Jan.	Balance unexpended at Interest,	2262 83	— $2717 41

STEPHEN SALISBURY, Jr.,
Secretary of Commissioners of Hope Cemetery.

ANNUAL REPORT

OF THE

OVERSEERS OF THE POOR.

Gentlemen of the City Council:

The Overseers of the Poor respectfully submit their Report for the present year, which on account of your action in closing the Financial year on the 30th of November instead of the 31st, of December, as has been customary heretofore, reduces the time covered by the report to eleven months, and as the last month is one in which the number of applications for relief are the most numerous, may account for the whole number aided being somewhat less than last year, the reduction however being mostly amongst that class who have received temporary aid.

No unusual epidemic sickness nor particular scarcity of labor, has occurred in our city during the year. Yet the numbers calling for aid, are not diminished, and you will observe that those having a military settlement increase more rapidly than all others, as it is double this year, what it was last, and double last year what it was the year before, thus plainly showing, that the effect of war is not fully, either shown or felt, when the battle is fought, but that its miseries endure for generations. The whole number of persons having a legal settlement in Worcester, who have received full support during the year, has been ninety-nine, and the average number forty-two. This is about the same as last year. The average at the City Alms House, has been a little less, while those at the Insane Hospitals, have been nearly three times as many as last year, and larger than for several years past ; the whole number has been fifteen, of which eleven were males and

four females.   The facility with which persons can be admitted
to the Insane Hospital, has a tendency to swell the number of
Insane Paupers for whom we are called upon to provide.   Some
who have been sentenced to a correctional institution for drunk-
enness, and similar offences, are transferred to the Hospitals,
and the first intimation given to the Overseers of the Poor of
the fact, is a bill for their board at the end of the quarter ; while
other persons of ample means to provide for themselves, are
placed there by sympathizing friends, and their accounts also are
charged to this department and are resisted at the risk of litiga-
gation.   One of such cases, has been referred to the City Solicitor, in order to test the validity of such claims.

Forty-five poor persons have been removed from the state to
their place of settlement, at our request, in accordance with the
general statute to that effect, by the parties through whose means
they were brought here.   This class is but little more than half
of what it numbered last year, which was the largest we have
ever had.

Fifty-seven State Paupers have been sent to the State
Alms House at Monson, and although the number has been much
less than last year, the complaints made by the superintendent
of that institution to the officers who have accompanied them
there have been full as loud, and also equally without cause ;
some who were sick and unable to walk, have been left at the
railway station in Palmer, by the Alms House team, and only
reached the institution through the attention of the station agent
there, who hired transportation to the Alms House for them, and
sent us the bill for the same, the attention of the general agent
at the State House, has been called to these cases, but no
response has yet been received from him on the subject.

Two hundred and ninety-one families composed of eight
hundred and sixty-three State Paupers, of which five hundred and
twenty-one were males, and three hundred and forty-two females,
have received temporary aid or partial support during the year.
Of these, sixty-five were too sick to be removed to a State Alms
House, and in accordance with the law passed in 1865, compelling
cities and towns to provide for such cases, have received such aid as
has been deemed necessary, and the cost of supplies so provided, has
in most cases been reimbursed, but the medical attendance being

computed on the basis of the cost of similar cases in Rainsford Island Hospital, falls far short of what is thought to be a reasonable compensation, as the circumstances where the parties are scattered all over the city are entirely different from what they would be concentrated in a single establishment.

This law is deficient inasmuch as it makes only partial provision for the member of the family, actually too sick to be moved, and leaves the remainder, also State Paupers, entirely without means, and compels the cities and towns where they happen for the time being to reside, either to provide for them without compensation or divide the family, retaining the sick father or mother and pauperizing the children entirely, by sending them to a State Alms House. This method of proceeding is of course resisted by the parents, and the result is they are provided for as a matter of charity, and the cost comes out of the city instead of the State Treasury, where it should properly fall. The attention of the Board of State Charities has been called to this fact in order to induce them if possible to make more liberal allowances in future for such cases.

Four hundred and sixty heads of families have applied for and received temporary aid or partial support during the year. Two hundred and seventy-two were males, and one hundred and eighty-eight females; of these, two hundred and eighty-two were relieved the first time, one hundred and seventy-six of them males and one hundred and six females. One hundred and one had a settlement in this city, sixty-two males and thirty-nine females. Forty of them had a military settlement, twenty males and twenty females. This class of settlements as has been before mentioned; has doubled every year. One hundred and twenty-eight had a settlement otherwise, seventy four males and fifty four females, three hundred and twenty-six resided in this city one hundred and sixty-one males and one hundred and sixty-five females. Fifteen were insane; eleven males and four females, and as has been before stated, is largely in excess of former years. Three were idiotic, all females. Sixty-eight were confirmed inebriates— fifty one were males and seventeen females, and the whole number included in the above statistics are one thousand four hundred and sixty five.

There have also been fed and lodged at the Station House, two thousand four hundred and seven vagrants, or travellers. A descriptive list and account of every one of which, is required by the Board of State Charities annually, which with the keeping account of, and classifying as above reported, being required by the Laws of the Commonwealth, make no small amount of labor to be performed, in addition to the other duties of this department.   In providing for all of these, there have been drawn at the Clerk's Office, for food, fuel, clothing, medicine and other articles eleven hundred and twenty orders on various persons ; and there has been disbursed to the several applicants, in various amounts as follows :

In Cash Allowances,	$ 189 00	
For Fuel,	732 75	
Groceries,	1404 25	
˙ Furniture and Clothing,	90 26	
Medicine Attendance and Nursing,	594 40	
Transportation of Paupers,	204 71	
Burial Expenses,	262 00	
Insane Hospital Bills,	1560 57	
Reform and Nautical School Bills,	593 18	
Books Stationary and Stamps,	117 38	
Aid to Paupers in other Towns,	185 32	
Miscellaneous Expenses,	˙ 80 10	6013 92
Salary of Clerk Eleven months,		916 66
Salary of City Physician Eleven Months,		641 66
Total Expense of City Department,		$7,572 24

A City Hospital where cases of accident and extreme sickness, can now be cared for, has been opened during the year.   And many unfortunate persons for whom no provision has heretofore been made, except what could be done for them at the Police Station, can now be comfortably attended to there, thus relieving the City Physician from what has previously constituted no inconsiderable portion of his most urgent calls.   His compensation, which is paid from the appropriation for the support of the Poor, has this year been raised by the committee on Finance of the City Council, from four hundred, the sum formerly paid, to seven hundred dollars, and upwards, of two hundred and fifty dollars, additional has been paid for medical attendance in the city, during the year ; a sum far in excess of what has heretofore been expended in that direction.

At the City Alms House and Hospital which has recently been

inspected by the full board, accompanied by several members of the past and present City Governments, everything indicates the same thrift and careful management we have been accustomed to see there under the charge of our Superintendent and Matron for several years past, and their continued efforts to do their whole duty have been duly appreciated, and our confidence in them annually expressed, during the many years they have filled their responsible position.

The Buildings are all in good condition, the old Brick house has been newly shingled during the year. A new brick smoke house has also been built in the rear of the main building and about thirty rods of double stone wall, on the line of the Farm, on the old Boylston Road. The crops raised on the Farm the past year compared favorably with those on other Farms in the vicinity. Not so much hay has been cut as usual on account of the unfavorable weather in the early part of the season, but the addition of about 25 acres recently made to the Farm will probably another year make amends for deficiencies heretofore existing.

The number of Inmates at the institution at the present time is thirty-three, which with the twenty-one Boys in the Truant School, and their Teacher, and the other members of the Superintendent's Family make in all fifty-nine, and although larger than usual now, the average as has before been stated, is not greater than last year.

The annual inventory and appraisal at the Farm has as usual just been made and is as follows:

96 Acres of Cleared Land,	$7,680 00	
100 Acres of Wood Land,	7,500 00	
26 Acres near Harlow place,	1,040 00	
30 Acres in Davidson Pasture,	1,280 00	
All the Farm Buildings,	21,000 00	
Total value of Real Estate,		$38,500 00
Stock, Tools, etc.,	7,912 30	
Furniture, Bedding etc.,	2,561 50	
Utensils, Provisions etc.,	1,475 52	
Appurtenances of Truant School,	448 00	
Total valuation,		$50,897 32
The valuation of 1870, was		50,894 07
Difference in favor of 1871,		$3 25

In making this Inventory the $600 00 recently appropriated

by the City Council at the request of the Board, for the purchase
of about 25 acres of land recently added to the Farm has not
been included, neither is the land included in the above specifica-
tion, in order to show clearly the relative expense of the present
as compared with past years.

The total expenditure has been		$4,826 84	
Receipts from Sales, and Board of Truant School,		2,471 13	
Making the Net Expense,			$2,355 71
Eleven months salary of Supt., and Matron,			666 66
Expense of Alms House Department,			3,022 37
Expense of City Department,			7,572 24
Total Expenses,			$10,594 61
And the Resources have been;			
Appropriation by the City Council,		$8,000 00	
Receipts from other Cities and Towns,		1,067 35	
Receipts from Commonwealth,		2,183 77	
Total Receipts,			$11,251 12
Total Expenses,			10,594 61
Unexpended Balance,			$656 51

A Report on the Truant School may be expected from the
Superintendent of schools, he being ex-officio, a member of this
Board, and also Chairman of the sub-committee of the Board,
on the school. The accounts have as usual, been kept separate
from those of the Alms House, and an appropriation made by
the City Council for its maintenance. The usual charge of two
and a half dollars a week, has been made for the Board of the
Teacher and each scholar, and five cents an hour allowed for
each Boys' labor, and the expense has been as follows:

Amount paid for Board,	$1,269 32	
Clothing, and other Expenses,	409 52	
Instruction and Supervision,	366 66	
Total Expenditure,		$2,045 50
Received from Boys' Labor,		93 00
Net Expense,		1,952 50
Appropriation,		3,000 00
Unexpended balance,		1,407 50
An Appraisal of the property of the School shows its Assets to be	$448 00	
In 1870, it was	393 00	
Difference in favor of 1871,		$55 00

A Table showing the monthly Disbursement of the Clerk with the amount and kind of aid provided, the number of orders drawn for the same, and total amount of bills, approved in each month, also another showing the number of Paupers in the Alms House, the total expenditure and receipts, and the net expense of each month, and one giving the number of Boys in the Truant School each month, with the amount paid for their maintenance, cost of clothing, and all other expenses, and the amount credited to them each month for their labor, is annexed to this report, to all of which your attention is most respectfully solicited.

GEORGE W. GALE, *Clerk.*

EDWARD EARLE, Mayor,
JAMES M. DRENNAN, City Marshal,
ALBERT P. MARBLE, Supt. of Schools,
GEORGE W. GALE, Clerk of the Board,
JOHN C. NEWTON,
OBEDIAH B. HADWEN,
CHARLES G. REED,
WALTER HENRY,
EDWARD KENDALL,

Overseers of the Poor.

34

ALMS HOUSE.

Monthly Accounts.	No of Paupers.	Total Expenditures.	Total Receipts.	Net Expenses.	Receipts Above Expenditures
January,	26	$385 82	$329 57	$56 25	
February,	27	272 93	173 11	99 82	
March,	33	472 16	186 44	285 72	
April,	31	680 42	143 16	537 26	
May,	26	215 37	203 59	11 78	
June,	24	340 67	171 59	169 08	
July,	21	312 43	391 18		$78 75
August,	20	196 03	111 47	84 56	
September,	23	334 81	295 32	39 49	
October,	29	477 54	203 31	274 23	
November,	33	1138 66	262 39	876 25	
		$4826 84	$2471 13	$2434 44 78 75	
				$2355 69	

TRUANT SCHOOL.

Monthly Accounts.	No of Scholars.	Cost of Board.	Clothing and other Expenses.	Teaching and Supervision.	Value of Labor.
January,	14	$143 35	$33 77		$3 00
February,	11	105 10	9 33		4 00
March,	12	126 00	91 40	$100 00	5 00
April,	10	90 32	13 63		8 00
May,	8	78 85	27 42		10 00
June,	13	106 07	3 10	100 00	15 00
July,	9	96 43	47 45		20 00
August,	8	89 67	6 50		8 00
September,	10	95 43	52 00	100 00	8 00
October,	19	140 14	5 00		10 00
November,	21	197 96	119 92	66 66	2 00
		$1269 32	409 52	$366 66	$93 00

CITY RELIEF DEPARTMENT.

Clerk's Monthly Disbursements,	No. of Orders Drawn	Paid Cash Allowances.	Cost of Fuel.	Cost of Groceries.	Furniture and Clothing.	Medicine Attendance and Nursing.	Transportation of Paupers.	Cost of Burials.	Insane Hospital Bills.	Reform and Nautical School Bills.	Postages Books and Stationary.	Paid other Towns.	Miscellaneous Expenses.	Total of Monthly Bills.
January,	196	$12 00	$200 75	$264 00	$12 00	$83 03	$33 55	$29 00	$414 97	$51 12	$32 25	$40 80	$12 25	$1183 47
February,	189	29 50	161 00	179 00	3 00	36 83	32 73	58 00	170 20	100 71	5 00	134 52	23 25	694 04
March,	153	12 00	114 00	176 00	4 50	144 38	14 00			141 67	33 03			685 50
April,	103	32 00	40 50	150 00	8 15	41 20	12 83							459 25
May,	70	12 00	31 50	80 25		26 93	15 20	60 00	8 00				6 00	236 03
June,	63	8 00	9 00	95 00	1 50	60 20	7 00	26 00	91 50		10 00			314 75
July,	58	28 00	14 00	85 00		54 28	30 10	46 00	613 85	137 19			7 50	1021 42
August,	58	8 00	2 25	95 00	7 75	46 15	5 10	18 00			5 00		15 10	206 35
September,	75	13 00	39 25	93 00	21 25	41 35	8 50	10 00	153 95		1 10			381 40
October,	62	11 50	45 00	110 00	18 26	14 75	31 25	15 00	108 10	163 49	11 50		16 00	544 85
November,	93	23 00	75 50	83 00	13 85	45 30	14 45				19 50	10 00		284 60
	1120	$189 00	$732 75	$1404 25	$90 26	$594 40	$204 71	$262 00	$1560 57	$593 18	$117 38	$185 32	$80 10	$6013 92

REPORT OF THE COMMITTEE ON THE TRUANT SCHOOL.

Gentlemen of the City Council:

The committee on the Truant School respectfully submit the following report for the eleven months ending Nov. 30, 1871. The origin and purposes of this school are set forth in the report for 1864 contained in City Document No. 19 ; and its aims are further described in the report for 1870, to which reference is here made. The observations upon its reformatory character and its reflex influence upon boys inclined to truancy, are confirmed by yearly experience. The proposition concerning a system of rewards for meritorious conduct, by which a boy is able to reduce his sentence, has been put in practice to a limited extent, with the best results. One boy has been pardoned as a reward for good conduct. The following has been added to the General Regulations : " Art. 5. Each pupil, whose deportment and scholarship have been satisfactory for one month, shall be entitled to some privilege or reward not otherwise granted ; and continuous good conduct shall be rewarded by a recommendation for pardon, one month or more before the expiration of the sentence. These regulations shall be made known to each boy when he enters the school."

By the influence of this school, and the excellent discipline of the Ungraded School on Washington street, which is, for one class of pupils, antecedent to this, the discipline of all the public schools, it is believed, has been greatly benefitted. There are records years back of wild insubordination and resistance to teachers. Each year we hope the number of these is diminishing. Scarcely a complaint of the kind has been made within a year. It has come to be understood that the whole influence of the school committee, the city government, the police and the court, and better still of the public sentiment, will sustain the teachers in the judicious exercise of all needed authority. Hence that authority is rarely questioned.

But there is an evil growing, more insidious, and if unchecked, more dangerous. Truants, we may care for. Unruly pupils can be subdued. · The children most sinned against and therefore most to be feared hereafter are such as are not sent to school at all.

To look after these and their more guilty parents and employers, and attend to the truants also, is more work than a single officer can perform. During the period covered by this report the truant officer has attended to two thousand four hundred cases of reported truancy. He has returned to school one thousand three hundred ninety-seven pupils. Four hundred children inclined to truancy have been assigned to school according to law, by the overseers of the poor. Of these forty-five persistent truants have been arrested and brought before the muncipal court. Twenty-two have been sentenced to the Truant school: the cases of others have been continued.

It will be seen that the expenses of the school for eleven months have fallen short of the appropriation for the year by $1047.50 This result is gratifying. But the city is rapidly increasing. The number of truants is variable. Other offenders may be sent to this school. We therefore respectfully recommend, that the appropriation for this school the coming year, be the same as last.

The following statistics exhibit the attendance, cost per scholar, etc., for 1871 :—

Whole number sentenced to this school since origin, Dec. 1863,	141
Number sentenced in 1871,	23
Different pupils during the year,	27
Average number in the school,	.12,27
Cases of absence,	0
do tardiness,	0
do punishment,	16
Average deportment,	83.4
Cases of sickness,	0
Cost of board, teacher and pupils, at $2.00 per week,	$1269.32
Clothing, bedding, books &c,	409.52
Tuition and supervision,	366.66
Total expenditure,	$2045.50

Value of boys' labor,	$93.00

Net expense,	$1952.50
Appropriation,	3000.00

Unexpended balance,	$1047.50
Value of school property,	448.00
Same in 1870,	393.00

Difference in favor of 1871,	$ 55.00
Cost per week for each pupil,	3.31
Same in 1870.	3.271
Total average cost per pupil, per year,	173.59
Same in 1870,	170.00

The rules and regulations adopted at the opening of this School are appended.

Respectfully submitted,

ALBERT P. MARBLE, *Supt. Schools*,

JAMES M. DRENNAN, *City Marshal*,

O. B. HADWEN, *Chairman Com. on the Farm*,

TRUANT SCHOOL COMMITTEE.

City Hall, Dec. 8, 1871.

REGULATIONS OF TRUANT SCHOOL.

SECTION I. *Article* I. The School shall be under the general direction of the Committee on the Truant School, which shall be appointed by the Mayor from the Board of Overseers of the Poor.

SEC. II. *Art.* 1. The Superintendent of the Almshouse shall keep a separate book of accounts for the Truant School, in which he shall credit all appropriations for its support, and all the labor of the boys at a price fixed by the Board of Overseers of the Poor, and he shall charge against the school all the expenses incurred for its support, including the cost of the clothing and the board of the boys, and the salary and board of the teacher.

Art. 2. It shall be the duty of the Superintendent to aid the teacher to secure prompt attendance in the school, ready obedience, good deportment and faithfulness to study.

SEC. III. *Art.* 1. It shall be the duty of the teacher of the Truant School to keep a register of attendance, in which shall be noted the date, cause and length of, and authority for, every case of tardiness or absence from the school. The teacher shall also keep a faithful record of the deportment of each scholar, with the reason for, and nature and extent of, every punishment inflicted, either personally or by the Superintendent.

Art. 2. The teacher shall make a quarterly report of the above and other matters pertaining to the interests of the school, to the Board of Overseers of the Poor, at their meeting next succeeding the close of the quarter.

Art. 3. The teacher shall labor to inspire the pupils with self-respect, and to this end, shall insist on cleanliness, and shall strive to inculcate principles of morality and justice.

Art. 4. The teacher shall assemble them every Sunday forenoon, and spend an hour with them in the reading and study of the New Testament, but shall strictly abstain from all sectarian comment.

GENERAL REGULATIONS.

Art. 1. From the 1st, of April to the 1st of October, there shall be only one session of the Truant School, each day, which shall invariably begin at 8, A. M., and close at 12, M. No boy shall be kept out of the school for any purpose whatever, except in case of emergency in the busy farming season, and every such case shall be recorded as provided in Sec. 3, Article 1, and reported by the Superintendent at the next meeting of the Board of Overseers of the Poor. It shall also enter into the next quarterly report of the teacher. From the 1st of October to the 1st of April, there shall be two daily sessions of school, from 9 A. M. to 12 M., and from 2 to 4 P. M., and on no account shall a boy be taken from the school during this season, except by permission previously obtained from the Mayor or some member of the Committee on the Truant School.

Art. 2. The use of tobacco, in any form, by the boys, is prohibited, and both the Superintendent and teacher are held responsible for the enforcement of this prohibition.

Art. 3. The teacher shall be employed and the salary fixed by the Committee on the school, subject to the approval of the Board, but no teacher shall be engaged without previously passing a satisfactory examination according to the laws of the Commonwealth and the rules of the School Committee of the City of Worcester.

Art. 4. The rate of board per week to be charged by the Superintendent against the teacher and pupils of the Truant School, shall be fixed annually by the Overseers of the Poor, at their regular meeting in January, but they may change it at any time they deem it necessary by a vote of the majority of the members of the Board. The price per hour of the services of the boys shall also be fixed at the same time and in the same manner, subject likewise to the same conditions of change.

Adopted by a unanimous vote.

JAMES B. BLAKE, *Mayor.*

GEORGE W. GALE, *Clerk.*

Worcester, Dec. 7, 1866.

35

REPORT

OF THE

COMMISSIONER OF HIGHWAYS.

WORCESTER, JANUARY 1ST, 1872.

To His Honor the Mayor, and the City Council.

Gentlemen: I have the honor herewith to present my Fifth Annual Report of the operations and condition of the Highway Department, covering a period of eleven months, ending Nov. 30th, 1871, as necessitated by the requirements of the new Ordinance on Finance, changing the end of the Financial year to that date.

The general features of the work committed to my charge have been quite like those of former years, and perhaps require no special mention. The continued prosperity and growth of the city has resulted in increased demands by citizens for new streets and the improvement of old ones, which have been met by the City Council with liberal appropriations and frequent orders on this department for the execution of work.

As will be seen by the details herewith submitted, the amount of money expended this year has been less than the previous year. In 1870 with an appropriation of $93,000 this department executed work for the city and for individuals, amounting in total expenditures to $152,454.70 and the appropriation was overdrawn by the sum of $9,459.61. In 1871 with an appropriation of $105,000, the department has executed work for the city and for individuals, amounting in total expenditures to $140,697.59 while there remains to its credit, bills for labor and material rendered the City Treasurer for collection, and the unexpended

balance of the appropriation, $28,491.36. The inventory of
stock, tools etc., also shows an increase during the year of
$3,486.24, making the actual surplus in favor of the department
$31,977.60, when the above named bills shall have been col-
lected.

In relation to the matter of purchase of materials for the use
of the department, about which there has been so much outside
criticism, I desire to make special mention, that proposals have
been solicited for the furnishing of all supplies used in the
department open to fair and honorable competition, and purchases made in every instance, at the lowest prices offered for
material suitable for the required purposes.

We have on hand ready for use early another year, and paid
for, a good supply of materials, as will be seen in detail by the
appended schedule; thus obviating the necessity of delay in
the commencement of the season's work. I would suggest therefore, that the orders for work be passed early in the year, to
enable the department to avail itself of all the advantages of the
best part of the season, as also the mutual connection which one
piece of work may have with another, and avoid as much as possible the usual troubles arising from doing work just in the commencement of Winter.

I desire again to call the attention of the City Council, as in
former reports, to the liability in which the city is involved by
allowing water spouts from various buildings to discharge upon
the sidewalks. In every instance the frequent accumulations of·
ice render the walks dangerous to pedestrians, and no amount
of care can obviate the difficulty. The frequent claims against
the city for compensation for personal injuries, by people falling
on slippery sidewalks, come mostly from this source ; and I am
satisfied that there is no safety for the city, save in their arbitrary removal.

The attention of the City Council is respectfully directed to
that portion of Main street between Chandler street and New
Worcester. The amount of travel continually passing over it,
renders impossible its satisfactory repair, with any earth material
accessible ; and I am fully of the opinion, that economy and convenience unite in the suggestion that it be"paved as soon as possible.

I would also suggest that Manchester street should be paved, for the reasons that its sunken condition and the amount of heavy travel over it, will prevent its satisfactory maintenance by any other means.

The condition of the city stables, live stock, vehicles and tools entrusted to this department, is believed to be excellent; no animal having been lost by disease or accident during the year. The steadily increasing demand for work during the last five years, has resulted in a large increase in the amount necessarily invested in stables, live stock, tools, &c. During this time, this investment has grown from $19,359.43 at the beginning of 1867 to $58,139.24 at the present beginning of 1872; all of which increase has been paid from the appropriations for the department. Notwithstanding the large increase in teams, the department is still deficient in this respect, and has been compelled to hire largely of private parties during the year: I would recommend, as I have in former reports, an increase in the number of teams owned by the city, if it is expected to continue the system of improvements which has been in progress.

BLOCK PAVING.

The permanent improvement of paving the most important streets with small granite blocks was begun last season, and has thus far given entire satisfaction to the public; as it furnishes an excellent thoroughfare in place of an imperfect and objectionable one, the cause of continual complaint and annoyance. The work has been continued the past year on the following streets: to wit:

MAIN STREET.

Order of May 24th, 1870, has been completed from Wellington street, Southwesterly: suspended in part last year to admit of construction of Sewer.

Cost of Grading,	$280 50
Carting stone, gravel and sand,	227 00
951.1 sq. yds, blocks at $2 60,	2472 86
Laying 951.1 sq. yds., at 40c.	380 44
Relaying 14.6 sq. yds., at 50c.	7 30
Relaying 21.1 yds, Cobbles at 50c.	8 56
Storage of stone,	20 00
Amounting to	$3,396 66
Average cost per sq. yd., $3 57.	

Order of June 19th, 1871, from Austin to Chandler sts., has been executed, costing :—

For Grading, $675 25
        Carting stone, gravel and sand,   356 25
        1729.6 sq. yds., blocks at $2 60,   4,496 96
        Laying 1729.6 sq. yds., at 40c.   691 84
        Storage of stone,   25 00
            Amounting to $6,245 30
        Average cost per sq., yd., $3 61.

MYRTLE STREET.

Order of June 19th, 1871, from Main to Southbridge streets, costing:
For Grading, $59 60
        Carting stone, gravel and sand,   199 75
        420 sq. yds., blocks at $2 25,   945 00
        Laying 420 yds., at 40c.   168 00
        Relaying 2 yds., at 50c.   1 00
        Storage of stone,   10 00
            Amounting to $1,383 35
        Average cost per sq. yd., $3 29.

PLEASANT STREET.

Order of June 19th, 1871, from Main to Chestnut streets has been
repaved in place of the rough cobbles ; costing :—
For Grading, Carting stone, gravel and sand, $821 95
        2156 sq. yds., blocks at $2 60,   5,605 60
        Laying 2156 yds., at 40c.   862 40
            Amounting to $7,289 95
        Less 2156 yds., Cobbles taken up at 30c.   646 80
                                                                         _____
            Net cost to the street, $6,643 15
        Average cost per sq. yd., $3 08.

UNION STREET.

Order of June 19th, 1871, under, between and fifty feet each side of
the B. & A., and W. & N., Railroad Companies bridges, costing :—
For Grading, carting stone, gravel and sand, $311 50
        722.6 sq. yds., blocks at $2 60,   1,878 76
        Laying 722.6 sq. yds., at 40c.   289 04
        35 sq. yds., cobble paving,   28 00
        Storage of stone,   15 00
            Amounting to $2,522 30
        Average cost per sq. yd., $3 49.

SUMMARY.

Of Block paving—City expense.
Total square yds., laid during the season 5979.3.
Average cost per sq. yd., $3 38.
Total amount expended under the foregoing orders, $20,190 76

FRONT STREET.

October 2d, 1871, an order was passed to pave Front street on
the North side of the street railway track, to the North line of

curb, between Church and Hibernia streets, as it will be located when it shall have been moved, under the order for widening Front street: also, to remove said track to the center of the street. The block stone were immediately contracted for, and are now on hand ; but the street was not in a condition to pave, on account of delay in removal of buildings ; most of these however have been now removed ; also the arrangements have been made with the President of the Street Railway Company, for permission to move their track ; and the block stone being secured, there seems to be nothing of importance to hinder the execution of the order early the coming Spring.

SIDEWALKS.

The special attention of the City Council has for several years been given to the matter of providing for the obvious need of more sidewalks throughout the city ; and has gradually increased the expenditures in this branch of the department, much to the comfort and satisfaction of the inhabitants, as well as the beauty and attractiveness of the city.

Your Commissioner desires the tax-payers and the public generally to understand, that neither the location nor extent of the work and consequent expenditures in this direction, are left to his disposal ; but are the result of petitions daily presented to the City Council, and by them referred to the proper committee to examine and report; and orders have been received accordingly for the execution of the work. It should be remembered by those who have felt aggrieved because their petitions were not granted, while others received a favorable consideration and report, that the applications have been exceedingly numerous, and the labors of the committee very arduous and perplexing ; and that while the committee have not felt at liberty to expend more than the liberal amount appropriated, he thinks they have intended to give all petitioners a fair consideration, and to locate the work where in their judgment it was most needed.

CURBSTONE, GUTTER AND CROSSWALKS,

have been laid upon forty-seven different streets as per order of the City Council, at the expense of the city as follows :—

Amount of New curb set,	22370 feet	
Curb reset,	6939 "	
Return curb set,	1114 "	
Circle " "	422 "	
Total No., of feet set,		30,845
Equal to 5.84 miles.		

Amount of Cobble paving, new,   10832.6 sq. yds.
       "   "   relaid,   6284.8 "   "
       Crosswalk paving, new,   2725.1 "   "
       "   "   relaid,   1057.9 "   "
   Total amount of Cobble paving laid,   20,900.4 sq. yds.
Amount of Flagstone, New,   5613.5 lin. feet
       "   relaid,   50.4 "   "
   Total amount of Flagstone laid,   5663.9 lineal feet.

   No. of long corners 68,
        short   "   101,
Entire cost to the city, $43,795 03

A part of the Return curb, Corners, Flagstone and Cobble paving have been furnished private parties and have been charged accordingly.

There have also been laid for private parties 481 Brick and Stone walks and driveways, using 1053.6 M. bricks and covering

An Area of new walk   20,073 sq. yds.
        Relaid walk   2,988 "   "

   Total,   21,630 yds., costing $32,902 45
Also 31 Concrete walks 2438 yds., costing   1,952 31

   Total cost to parties, $34,854 76

Bills of which have been returned to the City Treasurer for collection as per order of City Council. The intention has been to do the work in a thorough manner, using stock of a good quality at the lowest prices for which good articles could be obtained, and to charge the abuttors only the net cost of the labor and material furnished.

The work at the expense of the city has been done on the following streets : to wit:

FRONT STREET.

At Church Street,
   14 lineal feet, new curbstone, $11 20
   27 square yards crosswalks relaid,   11 08
    2 long corners,   12 00
      Labor,   8 40 — $42 68

WINTER STREET.

Labor on crosswalk, at Green Street,   15 00

HARVARD STREET.

68.5 sq. yds., brick walk relaid, Sudbury Street,   17 12

WATER STREET.

At] Winter Street.

89.8 lineal feet, new curbstone,	$71 84	
55 " " circular curbstone,	55 00	
68 " " flagstone,	23 80	
81.7 sq. yds., new gutter paving,	65 36	
28.5 " " " crosswalk,	22 80	
Labor,	175 90	— $414 70

CHESTNUT STREET.

Both sides from Pleasant to Walnut Streets,

538.5 lineal feet new curbstone,	$430 80	
27 " " reset "	4 05	
178.7 sq. yds., new gutter paving,	142 96	
171 " " relaid " "	68 40	
Labor,	432 65	— $1078 86

PORTLAND STREET.

Both sides from Park to Madison Street.

1734.5 sq. yds., gutter paving relaid,	$459 10	
205.2 " " brick walk relaid,	51 29	
1 long corner,	6 00	
Labor,	181 86	— $698 25

CARROLL STREET.

Both sides from Prospect to Shelby Street.

317 lin. feet new curbstone,	$253 60	
140.5 " " reset "	21 07	
89 " " new flagstone,	31 15	
201 sq. yds., new gutter paving,	160 80	
48.9 " " " crosswalk,	39 12	
2 short corners,	8 00	
Labor,	46 50	— $560 24

PARK STREET.

At Portland Street.

105 lin. feet new flagstone,	$36 75	
26.8 sq. yds., new crosswalk,	21 45	
Labor,	43 43	— $101 62

SALEM SQUARE.

Labor cutting ledge,	62 50

LAUREL STREET.

202 lin. feet curbstone reset,	$30 30	
107.5 sq. yds., gutter paving relaid,	43 00	
Labor,	10 00	— $83 30

36

PLEASANT STREET.

Both sides from Main to Chestnut Street.

612.5 lin. ft. new curbstone,	$490 00	
472 " " reset "	70 79	
25 " " " " circular,	6 25	
117 " " new flagstone,	40 95	
50 " " relaid,	4 00	
9.5 sq. yds. new gutter paving,	7 84	
240.3 " " relaid " "	112 32	
49.7 " " brick walk,	18 32	
124.3 " " new crosswalk,	72 20	
60.7 " " relaid " "	24 28	
3 long corners 18.00 2 short cor. reset 1.00	19 00	
2915 brick 46.64, Plank, sand &c. 21.44,	68 08	
Labor,	209 95	— $1143 98

South Side From Crown to Newbury Street.

12.4 lin. ft. new curbstone,	$9 92	
361.5 " " reset "	54 22	
172 sq. yds. new gutter paving,	137 60	
891.1 " " relaid " "	336 75	
42.3 " " " crosswalk,	15 65	
102.3 " " " brick "	25 57	
10.7 " " new " "	2 67	
2 long corners 12.00. 470 brick 7.52,	19 52	
Labor,	406 95	— $1008 85

HIGH STREET.

West side from Pleasant to Chatham Street.

110 lin. ft. new curbstone,	$88.00	
48.9 sq. yds. new gutter paving,	39.12	
Labor,	32.75	— $159 87

CHATHAM STREET.

Labor grading with gravel,	$22 80

PROSPECT STREET.

North side from Summer to Mulberry Streets;

219 lin. ft. new curbstone,	$176 80	
104 " " reset,	15 60	
35.6 " " new flagstone,	12 46	
72.9 sq. yds. " gutter paving,	58 32	
13.1 " " " crosswalk,	10 48	
1 long corner 6.00, 1 short corner 4.00	10 00	
Labor,	52 00	— $335 66

GREEN STREET.

At Franklin Street.

2.9 sq. yds. new gutter paving,	$2 32	
236.2 " " relaid " "	94 48	
53.4 " " " crosswalk,	21 32	
Labor,	21 80	—$139 92

WASHINGTON STREET.

West side from Park to Gold Street.

794.8 lin. ft. new curbstone,	$635 84	
321.7 sq. yds. " gutter paving,	257 36	
153 " " " crosswalk,	122 40	
44.9 " " relaid " "	17 96	
174 lin. ft. new flagstone,	60 90	
7 long corners 42.00, 1 short corner 4.00,	46 00	
Labor,	179 75	— $1320 21

PIEDMONT STREET.

Labor grading with gravel,	$14 00

GEORGE STREET.

Labor repairing,	$5 00

WEST STREET.

West side from William to John Street.

261.6 lin. ft. new curbstone,	$209 28	
16.6 " " " flagstone,	58 10	
140.8 sq. yds. " gutter paving,	112 64	
97.5 " " " crosswalk,	78 00	
1 long corner 6.00, Labor 122.75	128 75	—$586 77

WILLIAM STREET.

Including Everett Street.

22 lin. ft. new curbstone,	$17 60	
44 " " " flagstone,	15 40	
16 sq. yds. new gutter paving,	12 80	
27 sq. yds. new crosswalk,	21 60	
1 long corner 6.00, Labor 24.70	30 70	—$98 10

ELM STREET.

In front of J. H. Wall's Estate.

62 lin. ft. new curbstone,	$49 60	
10 " " reset "	1 50	
84.4 sq. yds. gutter paving relaid,	33 76	
Labor,	26 75	—111 61

FOSTER STREET.

North side.

24.4 sq. yds. new gutter paving,	$19 52

NORTH ASHLAND STREET.

Sundry Cross Walks:—

248.8 lin. ft. new flagstone,	$87 08	
24.3 sq. yds " gutter paving,	91 44	
40.9 " " relaid " "	16 36	
156.8 " " new crosswalk,	124 01	
Labor,	109 00	—$355 89

UNION STREET.

West side from Mechanic to Market Street.

1617 lin. ft. new curbstone,	$1293 60	
85.5 " " " circular curbstone,	85 50	
177.2 " " reset " "	26 57	
192 " " new flagstone,	67 20	
725.7 sq. yds. " gutter paving,	580 56	
4 " " relaid " "	1 60	
91.4 " " new crosswalk,	22 85	
51.3 " " relaid " "	20 52	
5 long corners 30.00, Labor 467.95,	497 95	—$2596 35

MYRTLE STREET.

Both sides from Portland to Salem Street.

442 lin. ft. new curbstone,	$353 60	
27 " " reset "	5 40	
201.3 sq. yds. new gutter paving,	161 04	
Labor,	143 55	—$663 59

SUMMER STREET.

At Market Street.

18.5 lin. ft. new curbstone,	$14 80	
1 long corner,	6 00	—$20 80

LINCOLN STREET.

West side from Lincoln Square to J. F. Loring's Estate.
East side from Dr. Hill's Estate to Harrington Avenue.

1005.7 lin. feet new curbstone,	$804 56	
376.7 " " reset "	58 23	
162.5 " " deep " set		
against Estate of John Goulding,	48 75	
201.2 lin. feet new flagstone,	70 42	
481.2 sq. yds., new gutter paving,	385 04	
276.3 " " relaid " "	110 52	
129.6 " " new crosswalk,	98 04	
59.6 " " relaid "	23 84	
4 long corners, 24 00, 478 ft. plank, 14 34,	38 34	
Labor, grading, raising fences, moving trees &c.	991 15	— $2,628 89

SHREWSBURY STREET.

North side from Summer to Hill Street.

1251.4 lin. feet new curbstone,	$1001 12	
27.8 " " circ. "	27 80	
138.8 " " new flagstone,	48 58	
615.2 sq. yds., new gutter paving,	492 16	
68.8 " " new crosswalk,	55 04	
2 long corners 12 00, 2 short corners, 8 00,	20 00	
Labor, grading, cartage &c.	255 85	— $1,900 55

North side from Hill to Henry Street.

527 lin. feet new curbstone,	$421 50	
237.3 sq. yds., new gutter paving,	189 84	
Labor, grading and cartage,	122 15	— $733 49

MAIN STREET.

East side from Jackson to Hammond Street.

1710.5 lin. feet new curbstone,	$1,368 40	
502.7 " " reset "	75 40	
340.5 " " new flagstone,	119 17	
748.2 sq. yds., new gutter paving,	598 56	
182.9 " " relaid gutter paving,	73 16	
144.4 " " new crosswalk,	115 52	
103.4 " " relaid "	41 36	
10 long corners, 60 00, Lowering base 45 00	105 00	
Labor, grading, cartage &c.	802 35	— $3,298 92

Both sides from Austin to Chandler Street.

37.4 lin. feet new curbstone,	$29 92	
528 " " reset "	79 20	
9.1 sq. yds., new gutter paving,	7 28	
410.6 " " relaid brick walk,	102 65	
3272 bricks 52 35, 1 long corner 6 00	58 35	
2 loads sand 2 80, 2 loads gravel 2 00,	4 80	
Labor, grading,	58 30	— $340 50

East side near Dr. Heywood's Estate.

28.7 lin. feet new curbstone,	$21 44	
12 " " " circ. curbstone,	13 20	
14 sq. yds., relaid gutter paving,	4 20	
78 " " " brick walk,	19 50	
Labor repairing, grading,	14 00	— $72 34

West side near Wm. Dickinson's Estate.

18.5 lin. feet new curbstone,	$14 80	
81.8 " " reset "	12 19	
108 " " relaid flagstone,	37 79	
790.6 sq. yds., relaid gutter paving,	319 44	
20.3 " " " crosswalk,	8 12	
78.1 " " brick walk,	19 52	
76.4 sq. yds., brick walk, relaid,	19 09	
Labor, raising flagstone,	7 25	— $438 20

SUDBURY STREET.

At Harvard Street.

38 lin. feet new curbstone,	$28 00	
27.5 " " reset "	5 50	
87.8 sq. yds., relaid gutter paving,	70 24	
1 short corner 4 00, Labor grading 42 70	46 70	— $150 44

HARRINGTON AVENUE.

North side from Lincoln to Westminster Street.

480	lin. ft. new curbstone,	$384 00
44	" " " "	15 40
222.2 sq. yds. " gutter paving,		177 76
24.7 " " " crosswalk,		19 20
1 long corner,		6 00
Labor, grading, and cartage,		230 25 —$832 61

CLINTON STREET.

East side from Pleasant to Chatham Street.

583	lin. ft. new curbstone,	$466 40
116	" " reset "	17 40
21	" " new flagstone,	7 35
263.5 sq. yds. " gutter paving,		210 80
19 " " " crosswalk,		15 92
3 long corners,		18 00
Labor, grading and cartage,		135 00 —$870 87

PROVIDENCE STREET.

West side from Grafton to Pattison Street.

2261.3 lin ft. new curbstone		1809 04
160.7 " " " circular "		160 70
57 " " reset "		8 55
421 " " new flagstone,		147 35
122 " " relaid flagstone,		12 20
1118 sq. yds. new gutter paving,		894 48
33.8 " " relaid " "		13 52
209.6 " " new crosswalk,		167 68
85 " " relaid " "		34 08
7 long corners 42.00, 72 ft. plank 2.16,		44 16
Labor, grading, finishing and cartage,		1204 85 —$4496 61

BELMONT STREET.

493	lin. ft. new curbstone,	$394 40
50	" " " flagstone,	17 50
174	sq. yds. " gutter paving,	139 20
30.5 " " " crosswalk,		24 40
2 long corners,		12 00
Labor, grading and cartage,		522 50 —$1110 00

WALNUT STREET.

Opposite Grace Church.

48	lin. ft. new flagstone,	$16 80
27.9 sq. yds. " crosswalk,		23 32
2 " " relaid brick "		50
5.5 " " gutter paving,		2 20
Labor, grading,		18 00 —$60 82

CHARLTON STREET.

Both sides from Main to Beacon Streets.

1019	lin. ft. new curbstone,	$815 20	
35	" " reset,	5 25	
100.4	" " new flagstone,	29 14	
465.3	sq. yds. " gutter paving,	372 24	
21.7	" " " crosswalk,	17 36	
26.2	" " relaid " "	20 96	
2 long corners,		12 00	
Labor, grading, .		374 43	—$1646 58

MADISON STREET.

North side from Portland to Salem Street.

218	lin. ft. new curbstone,	$174 40	
7	" " reset "	1 05	
150	" " new flagstones.	17 50	
117.3	sq. yds. " gutter paving,	93 84	
32.2	" " " crosswalk,	25 76	
1 long corner		6 00	
Labor, grading, cleaning &c.,		24 50	—$343 05

SALISBURY STREET.

East side from Lincoln Square to Grove Street.

27.3	lin. ft. new curbstone,	$21 84	
397	" " reset "	59 55	
19	" " new flagstone,	6 65	
431.8	" " relaid "	43 18	
3	sq. yds. " gutter paving,	1 20	
1 long corner,		6 00	
Labor, grading,		111 15	—$249 57

LAGRANGE STREET.

South side from Main to Beacon Street.

670	lin. feet new curbstone,	$536 00	
336.4	sq. yds., new gutter paving,	269 12	
1 long corner,		6 00	
Labor, grading and cartage,		297 30	— $1,108 42

AUSTIN STREET.

South side from Main to Oxford Street.

795.6	lin. feet new curbstone,	$636 48	
113.3	" " reset "	16 99	
45	" " new flagstone,	15 75	
388	sq. yds., new gutter paving,	310 40	
11.9	" " relaid " "	4 76	
26.1	" " new crosswalk,	20 88	
Labor, grading and cartage,		297 80	— $1,303 06

Both sides from Newbury to Piedmont Street.

146	lin. feet new curbstone,	$116 80
286	" " reset "	42 90
36	" " new flagstone,	12 60
73.3	sq. yds, new gutter paving,	58 64
111.1	" " relaid " "	44 44
20.6	" " new crosswalk,	16 48
2 long corners,		12 00
Labor, grading and cartage,		93 95 — $397 81

NEWBURY STREET.

West side from Pleasant to Chandler Street.

1233.5	lin. feet new curbstone,	$986 80
10	" " reset "	1 50
585.5	sq. yds., new gutter paving,	468 40
28.8	" " relaid " "	11 52
60.8	" " " crosswalk,	24 32
2 long corners,		12 00
Labor, grading and cartage,		433 10 — $1,937 64

CENTRAL STREET.

North side from Main to Summer Street.

731.3	lin. feet new curbstone,	$585 04
230.5	" " reset "	34 57
18.4	" " new circ. curbstone,	20 24
79	" " " flagstone,	27 65
623.2	sq. yds., new gutter paving,	498 56
5.3	" " relaid " "	2 12
56.3	" " new crosswalk,	44 80
89.3	" " relaid crosswalk,	35 72
Labor, grading, cartage &c.		395 60 — $1,644 30

THOMAS STREET.

Both sides from Main Street to Mill Brook.

143	lin. feet new curbstone,	$114 40
152.2	" " reset "	22 83
78.3	sq. yds., new gntter paving,	62 64
136	" " relaid " "	54 40
1 long corner,		6 00
Labor, grading and cartage,		84 95 — $345 22

MECHANIC STREET.

Corner of Union.

5.2	sq. yds., crosswalk relaid,	$2 08
Labor,		9 50 — $11 58

CROWN STREET.

East side from Pleasant to Chatham Street.

lin. feet new curbstone,	$391 60
" " reset "	3 97
" " new flagstone,	16 10
sq. yds., new gutter paving,	185 92
" " relaid " "	89 40
" " new crosswalk,	19 28
" " relaid brick walk,	1 40
corners,	12 00
grading and cartage,	271 45 — $991 12

VERNON STREET.

North side from Water to Pattison Street.

lin. feet new curbstone,	$731 20
" " circ. "	29 50
" " new flagstone,	23 80
sq. yds., new gutter paving,	356 80
" " " crosswalk,	29 28
" " relaid, "	6 96
corner,	6 00
grading, and cartage,	535 65 — $1,719 19

SYCAMORE STREET.

Both sides from Main to Beacon Street.

lin. feet new curbstone,	$756 56
" " " circ. curbstone,	17 00
" " reset curbstone,	5 10
" " new flagstone,	12 42
" " relaid flagstone,	21 92
sq. yds., new gutter paving,	342 88
" " " crosswalk,	29 12
corner,	6 00
grading and cartage,	452 43 — $1,643 43

OAK STREET.

Both sides from Elm to Cedar Street.

lin. ft. new curbstone,	$443 60
" " reset "	3 07
" " new flagstone,	26 25
" " relaid "	8 05
sq. yds. new gutter paving,	203 44
" " " cross walk,	. 27 44
" " relaid " "	12 20
corner 6.00, 2 short corners 8.00,	14 00
grading and cartage,	269 70 —$1007 75

37

SUNDRY SIDEWALKS.

Labor upon sundry streets.
Screening sand &c., &c., $835 38

Total to the expense of the city, $43,795 03
Leaving unexpended balance of   6,204 97

From the appropriation for year of, $50,000 00

RECEIPTS.

APPROPRIATIONS.

For Highways,	$35,000 00	
Sidewalks,	50,000 00	
Block Paving,	20,000 00—	105,000 00

SIDEWALKS—PRIVATE EXPENSE.

481 Brick and Stone Walks and Driveways,	$32,902 45	
31 Concrete walks,	1,952 31—	$34,854 76
Live Stock, Horses and Oxen sold,	$800 00	
Water Department, Labor and Material,	285 94	
Sewer " " " "	1,463 25	
Public Grounds " " "	275 10	
Public Schools " " "	2,818 90	
Poor Department for manure,	300 00	
Fire " Block Paving,	262 60	
Sundry Persons 102½ M brick,	1,004 10	
" Labor and material,	2,177 32 —	$9,387 21

APPROPRIATIONS FOR NEW STREETS.

New Worcester Hill, Labor &c.	$1,344 71	
Lafayette Street, "	1,389 05	
Wilmot " "	1,087 70	
Washington "	1,005 50	
Front "	3,556 62	
Hanover "	3,335 70	
Salisbury "	2,456 95	
Chandler "	3,698 90	
Piedmont "	734 30	
Sever	281 90	
Mechanic "	578 00	
Oak Avenue	477 65—	$19,946 98

Total receipts,	$169,188 95

Salary including clerk hire and teams for
    personal conveyance, $2,291 67
Labor pay roll,   38,807 35
Live stock, Horses and Oxen, bought and
    exchanged,   1,300 50
Hay, Grain, Straw &c.   4,379 18
Shoeing,   695 81
Tools and repairs,   3,060 65
Lumber,   1,776 01
Worcester Fire Dept., use of teams,   1,532 50
Labor, Breaking roads, moving buildings,
    hired teams, &c.   14,721 21
$18738\frac{1}{4}$ feet curbstone av. cost 53c pr. ft.   9,921 96
$425\frac{1}{4}$ feet circular curbstone av. cost 82c. pr. ft.   348 85
$179\frac{11}{12}$ feet deep curbstone, setting only, (J.
    Goulding) at $1.50,   268 87
$3549\frac{1}{4}$ feet flagstone at 25c.   887 31
750 feet No. River flagstone including freight,   244 13
Border, covering and wall stone,   311 24
$2161\frac{1}{4}$ tons cobble paving stone at $1.00,   2161 25
100 long corners,   501 50
20 short corners,   58 00
$4089\frac{8}{10}$ sq. yds., granite paving blocks at $2.60, 10,633 48
$373\frac{6}{10}$ " " " " " 2.25,   840 60
9976 pcs. " " " "   545 56
Storage of block stone,   70 00
$1156\frac{1}{10}$ M bricks (including freight) at $12.84, 14,845 95
C. O. Richardson, setting curb paving &c. 18,995 58
J. J. Randall, concrete paving,   1,834 70
Powder, Coal, Fuse &c.   128 52
Water Dept. water at the stables &c. 2 yrs,   90 00
Freight on Beach stone,   72 50
Cement pipe &c. A. B. Lovell,   253 77
Printing; Report of 1870, blanks &c.   44 60
Lime and cement,   45 50
Advertisements for paving blocks,   13 41
Expense and Receipt books,   14 00
Gas at stables,   30 34
Stationery and Postage,   11 11
Filing saws,   4 00
Medicine and attendance on stock,   30 85
Incidentals,   116 24
Amount advanced on granite paving blocks
    now on hand for use another year, to be
    measured and paid for by the sq. yd.,
    when laid,   8,518 89
        Total expenditures, $140,697 59

RECAPITULATION.

SIDEWALKS.

Amount of appropriation,	$50,000 00	
Expended,	43,795 03	
Balance unexpended,		6,204 97

ORDINARY REPAIRS.

Amount of Appropriation,	$35,000 00	
Expended,	21,910 06	
Balance unexpended,		$13,089 94

BLOCK PAVING.

Amount of Appropriation, ·	$20,000 00	
Expended,	20,190 76	
Balance overdrawn,		190 76
Total appropriations,		$105,000 00

Received for Sidewalks (private expenses)	$34,854 76	
Labor on new streets,	19,946 98	
Horses and Oxen sold,	800 00	
Brick sold,	1,004 10	
Labor and material,	2,177 32	
From other Departments,	5,405 79	
Total earnings for season,		$64,188 95
Total receipts for season,		$169,188 95

EXPENDED.

Block Paving,	$20,190 76	
Sidewalks, City expense,	43,795 03	
Sidewalks, Private expense,	34,854 76	
New Streets, ·	19,946 98	
Ordinary Repairs including cleaning cesspools,	21,910 06	
Total expenditures,		140,697 59
Balance unexpended,		28,491 36
		$169,188 95

OVERLAYINGS.

Balance unexpended,	$28,491 36	
Excess of stook at close of year,	3,486 24	
Surplus to the credit of Department,		$31,977 60

There remain on file in my office, Orders not yet executed for work as follows :

Highland Street, curb, gutter &c. estimated cost (500 ft.) $800 00
Benefit Street, curb, gutter &c. estimated cost (800 ft.)   1,350 00
Temple Street, curb, gutter &c. estimated cost (250 ft.)   325 00
Winter Street, curb, gutter &c. estimated cost (1,164 ft.)   1,400 00
Belmont Street curb, gutter &c. estimated cost (800 ft.)   1,350 00
Front Street, widening and paving only an approximate
    estimate can be offered. It being one of those
    pieces of work the cost of which is quite uncertain
    until it is completed,   15,000 00
Prescott Street, making Street, estimated cost of finishing,   700 00
Chandler Street, cutting and filling, estimated cost of
    finishing,   2,000 00
Lafayette Street, making street, estimated cost of finishing,   500 00

Total estimated expense, $23,425 00

SCHEDULE

Of the Real and Personal property belonging to the Highway Department, in the City of Worcester, Nov. 30th, 1871.

REAL ESTATE.

50,000 ft. land with city stables thereon, $21,500 00
1½ acres of land on Lamartine Street,   3,000 00
1 acre of land bought of E. Rich, on
    Pleasant Street,   150 00
Gravel pit at junction of Grove and Pratt Sts.,   150 00
Gravel pit near Paxton line,   15 00
Total of Real Estate, $24,815 00

PERSONAL PROPERTY.

LIVE STOCK.

14 Horses, $5,000 00
12 Oxen,   1,200 00 — $6,200 00

WAGONS, CARTS, SLEDS AND EQUIPMENTS.

1 four-horse wagon,	$175 00	10 ox yokes,	40 00
1 two-horse wagon,	65 00	21 neck yokes,	21 00
1 one-horse express wagon,	190 00	8 pairs ox bows,	4 00
9 two-horse carts,	1600 00	19 whiffletrees,	30 00
2 one-horse carts,	100 00	14 horse blankets,	45 50
6 ox carts,	500 00	45 meal bags,	20 00
1 tight cart,	150 00	4 surcingles,	2 00
2 sets cart wheels,	56 00	16 halters,	16 00
1 stone lifter,	225 00	14 curry combs and brushes,	28 00
1 cesspool cleaner,	200 00	8 feed baskets,	4 00
1 street roller,	200 00	8 draft chains,	18 00
1 stone truck,	40 00	6 heavy cable chains,	21 00
2 two-horse sleds,	175 00	3 scraper chains,	6 00
1 light horse sled,	40 00	15 stake chains,	10 00
2 ox sleds,	35 00	14 tie chains,	10 00
6 sets double harnesses,	300 00	4 whiffletree chains,	4 00
2 single harnesses,	50 00	2 pairs lead bars,	5 00
2 cart harnesses,	30 00		
1 lead harness,	50 00		$4,465 00

HAY AND GRAIN.

35 tons hay,	@ $35.	$1225 00	375 bushels corn,	@ 90c.	337 50
1¾ tons straw,	@ $25.	43 75			
450 bushels oats,	@ 58c.	261 00			$1,867 25

TOOLS.

2 sets tackle and falls,	$15 00	2 hay cutters,	18 00
1 grindstone,	8 00	3 grain chests,	15 00
57 good shovels,	57 00	2 feed troughs,	8 00
23 old shovels,	10 00	9 oil cans,	3 60
24 snow shovels,	24 00	Set grain measures,	1 50
5 long snow shovels,	8 00	1 spirit level,	2 00
1 ox snow shovel,	17 00	1 adze.	2 00
7 hay rakes,	1 50	3 chopping axes,	3 00
2 manure forks,	2 50	1 broad axe,	2 00
1 manure hook,	1 00	5 grub cutters,	7 50
10 hay forks,	5 00	4 ladders,	6 00
32 street hoes,	25 00	1 water pot,	1 00
4 garden rakes,	2 00	4 gravel screens,	24 00
2 spades,	2 00	1 patent scraper,	25 00
37 picks,	55 50	4 side scrapers,	16 00
4 stone drags,	12 00	6 snow scrapers,	18 00
3 side-hill plows,	30 00	4 wheelbarrows,	8 00
1 pick plow,	50 00	4 brooms,	2 00
1 snow plow,	10 00	1 oil pan,	6 00
6 plow points,	4 50	6 frost wedges,	6 00
12 crowbars,	36 00	1 iron vise,	6 00
2 pinch bars,	2 00	3 monkey wrenches,	3 00
11 stone drills,	11 00	3 stoves,	12 00
Lot of light stone tools,	5 00	Lot of rope,	3 00
7 stone hammers,	28 00	1 trowel,	1 00
7 cinder hammers,	14 00	16 water pails,	10 00
8 striking hammers,	18 00	Lot carpenter's tools,	12 00
101 lanterns,	120 00		
3 baskets,	1 00		$796 60

LUMBER &C.

12,000 feet bridge plank at $27.	$324 00	
300 feet oak plank at $40.	12 00	
300 feet pine plank at $25.	7 50	
500 feet pine boards at $25.	12 50	
17 bridge stringers at $9.	153 00	
Lot of railing and post timber,	50 00	— $559 00

STONE, BRICK, &C.

2150 feet curbstone at 70c.	1,505 00	
300 feet old curbstone at 40c.	120 00	
200 feet flagstone at 25c.	50 00	
Lot No. River flagstone,	125 00	
1,700 tons cobbles at $1.	1,700 00	
98 long corners at $5.	490 00	
62 short corners at $3.	186 00	
6 sets cesspool stone at $20.	120 00	
20 stone posts at $3.	60 00	
200 loads quarried stone at ledge,	225 00	
Lot of covering stone,	150 00	
2 M pressed brick at $30.	60 00	
155 M hard brick at $15.	2,325 00	
Amount paid for small blocks for Front Street order, to be measured after they are laid another year,	8,518 89	— $15,634 89

SUNDRIES.

Building and machinery for crushing stone,	$3,500 00	
200 feet fire hose,	150 00	
1 side lace leather,	2 00	
50 feet fuse,	50	
½ keg powder,	2 00	
Lot lead pipe,	7 00	
Lot old iron,	10 00	
Lot street signs,	20 00	
Lot arch centers, blocks, &c.,	50 00	
Office desk,	60 00	— $3,801 50

Total of Personal property,	33,324 24
Total of Real Estate,	24,815 00
	$58,139 24

Very respectfully submitted,

D. F. PARKER,

Commissioner of Highways.

ANNUAL REPORT

OF THE

Chief Engineer of the Fire Department.

To the City Council:

Gentlemen :—By the provisions of the Ordinance, establishing the Fire Department, I submit for your consideration my Third Annual Report, containing such information as will enable you to properly understand the condition and judge of the necessities of this organization, whose services can be commanded at all times, and under all circumstances to protect the property of our citizens from fire. We sometimes think these services are lightly esteemed and never fully appreciated when the risk of life, limb and injury to health are considered.

The City Council have a right to feel highly gratified with our Fire Record the past year, when they call to mind the large and destructive fires in other places.

The number of Alarms during the last Municipal year were forty-two (42) an increase of eleven (11) and it is quite probable the number will continue to increase with the growth of the city. The amount of property destroyed by fire as near as could be ascertained was fifteen thousand nine hundred and fifteen dollars ($15,915.) nearly all fully covered by insurance.

The Fire Alarm Telegraph went into operation on the 17th of last June and has worked very satisfactorily and there can be no doubt in regard to its usefulness—it was a necessity quite too long postponed and in my judgment it has already been the means of saving a larger amount of property in this city than its cost. A large number of our tax paying citizens regard it as very desirable that a Striker should be put into the bell tower of the High School House and the telegraph wire attached; it would no doubt meet with very general favor and prove useful to persons living on the west side of Main street. I think it quite as important that the bell on the School House at New Worcester should be arranged to serve the same purpose. At present we only strike there a small Gong in the house of one of the members of the Company; he if necessary rings the bell. The Department is in good condition, apparatus in good working order, companies well-organized, full ranks, unity of purpose, and harmony of action existing in, and between all the companies; and never in my opinion was this organization better able to render efficient aid to those requiring their services than at the present time. The houses in which the apparatus is kept are all in very good condition, well arranged and convenient. After the Fire Alarm was established, bedsteads and mattresses were bought for such houses as had Gongs attached, and from one to three men lodge in each house enabling those companies to make much better time at night alarms. It is very desirable that other houses should be arranged in the same manner. I am quite confident, you will agree with me, that the Hand Engine at New Worcester, with forty men, each receiving the same pay as other members, ought to be exchanged for a Steamer as a matter of economy, if for no other reason.

. It costs now about twice the amount to maintain that company that it does a Steamer company, and no fault of theirs, for they have one of the best companies and do all that duty requires of them. I wish to call your attention to the fact that a very large portion of the west part of the city is very poorly protected from fire. You will bear in mind that there is no fire apparatus west of Main Street. As the city enlarges it would be a wise provision to locate a Steamer, in the vicinity of Mason Street, and a hose carriage near the Dix street School House. Again let me ask you to consider, what could the department do should a fire occur on Union Hill? or on the hill near Grant square? The entire force would be powerless, so far as rendering any assistance and obliged to stand idle and see property burn for the want of water.

The expenses of the department for the year ending Nov.

38

30th, not including such bills as were incurred in finishing the Engine House on Beacon street, which were charged to another appropriation, were seventeen thousand three hundred and eighty eight dollars and seventy three cents ($17,388.73) and the Highway Department has allowed fifteen hundred and thirty two dollars and fifty cents ($1532.50) for the use of driver's horses and one cart belonging to the Fire Department.

I think the city would find it for their advantage to furnish Steamer No. 3. with horses and not compel us to procure them of truckmen at their own prices. There is land enough with the house on school street on which a barn could be built.

The Department for the year 1872 will be composed of the same number of men as heretofore and organized into the same companies with very few changes, either in men or officers. It will consist of the following companies, viz:

Steamer No. 1. Chas. J. Guild, Foreman, 12 men. House Bigelow court.

"   " 2. P. H. Carroll,   "   12   "   "   Beacon street.

"   " 3. Edwin Fisher,   "   12   "   "   School street.

Hose   " 1. G. N. Rawson,   "   10   "   "   "   "

"   " 2. David Boland,   "   10   "   "   Bloomingdale.

"   " 3. Geo. W. Parks,   "   10   "   "   Carlton street.

"   " 4. Samuel Knowlton, "   10   "   , "   Exchange street.

"   " 5. Daniel Hall,   "   10   "   "   Myrtle street.

Hook & Ladder, No. 1. Perry Bullard, "   20   "   "   Bigelow court.

"   "   " 2. J. Hennessey, "   20   "   "   Thomas street.

Rapid (Hand.) " 2. Chas. Bottomly, "   40   "   "   Webster street.

Drivers of steamers No. 1, & 2. 2

Board of Engineers,   5

Total   173

In addition to the above there is at Quinsigamond old Niagara No. 3. (Hand Engine) with a volunteer company of forty men in charge of Edwin L. Gates, Foreman, and would render good service if required in that village had they good facilities for obtaining water. The propriety of constructing one or more reservoirs has been suggested to which your attention is respectfully invited.

In conclusion allow me to thank the City Council and particularly the committee on Fire Department for their aid and support in seconding such efforts and measures as tender to promote the interest or efficiency of this Department. Also it affords me pleasure to acknowledge the efficient aid rendered by the City Marshal and his force by their assistance and co-operation at fires.

I am respectfully,

R. M. GOULD, *Chief Engineer.*

REPORT OF CITY MARSHAL.

MARSHAL'S OFFICE,
CITY OF WORCESTER, Dec. 1st, 1871.

To His Hon. the Mayor, and the City Council, of the City of
Worcester :

GENTLEMEN,—I have the honor to present for your consideration, my report of the business and condition of the Police Department, for the municipal year, or eleven months, ending Nov. 30th 1871.

The whole number of arrests for the above term, not including 400 made by the State Police, and in many cases assisted by our local force is 2380.

Males,	2129	Non Residents,	582
Females,	251	Minors,	453
Americans,	755	Adults,	1927
Foreigners,	1625	Committed,	697
Residents,	1798		

NATIVITY OF CRIMINALS ARRESTED.

Ireland,	1243	Nova Scotia,	19
American,	639	Italy,	2
Canada,	316	Poland,	2
England,	90	Wales,	2
Scotland,	38	West India,	2
Germany,	22	Belgium,	1
American Colored,	22	Russia,	1
Total,			2380

Whole number of Complaints made by the Marshal and Assistants in the Municipal Court during the above time 2277.

Number of Complaints made in Probate Court 94.

Discharged from Custody without Complaint for what seemed to be good and sufficient reason 73.

Comparative ages of persons are as follows :

10 years of age and under,	45
Between 10 and 20 years of age,	408
" 20 " 30 " "	869
" 30 " 40 " "	584
" 40 " 50 " "	310
" 50 " 60 " "	127
" 60 " 70 " "	34
" 70 " 80 " "	3
Total,	2380

Whole number of Lodgers accommodated at the Station House during the above time 2014.

Males,	1871	Residents,	17
Females,	143	Non Residents,	1997
Americans,	717	Minors,	370
Foreigners,	1297	Adults,	1644

NATIVITY OF LODGERS ARE AS FOLLOWS.

Ireland,	808	Wales,	9
American,	667	Denmark,	4
England,	196	Spain,	3
Scotland,	100	Italy,	2
Canada,	96	Belgium,	2
Germany,	55	Prussia,	1
American Colored,	41	Switzerland,	1
Nova Scotia,	29	Total,	2014

Whole number of Prisoners and Lodgers accommodated at the Station House during the year 4394.

The following are offences for which arrests were made during the year.

Drunkeness,	1132	Murder,	5
Assault and Battery,	165	Loafing about Theatre,	4
Larceny,	159	Bastardy,	4
Drunkeness 2nd, Conviction,	125	Common Loafer,	4
Disturbing the Peace,	95	Single Sale of Liquor,	4
Violation of City Ordinance,	66	Receiving Stolen Goods,	4
Keeping Open Shop Lord's Day,	54	Disorderly House,	3
Truancy,	45	Interfering with Officer,	3
Vagrancy,	39	Accessory to Burglary,	3
Present at Game Lord's Day,	38	Sporting on Lord's Day,	3
Insane,	29	Common Nuisance,	3
Common Drunkard,	27	Embezzlement,	3
Malicious Mischief	27	Keeping House of Illfame,	3
Breaking Glass,	27	Selling Veal under 4 weeks of age,	2
Burglary,	22	Extortion,	2
Fornication,	21	Suspicion of Larceny,	2
Breaking and Entering,	18	Disturbing Religious Meeting,	2
Assault with Dangerous Weapon,	18	Forgery,	2
Threatening,	17	Mayhem,	2
Trespass,	15	Indecent exposure of person,	2
Larceny from Building,	13	Defiling R. R. Cars,	2
Assault on Officers,	12	Ran away from Reform School,	2
Evading R. R. Fare,	11	Keeping Victualling Saloon without License,	2
Gaming on Lord's Day,	10	Keeping Liquor,	2
Adultery,	10	Selling Mortgaged Property,	2
Cruelty to Animals,	9	Horse Thief,	1
Stubborn and disobedient,	9	Arson,	1
Fast Driving,	9	Assault with intent to kill,	1
Playing Cards Lord's Day,	9	Selling Liquor,	1
Lewd and Lascivious Cohabitation,	8	Driving Away Team,	1
Ran Away from Truant School,	7	Keeping Pawn Shop without License,	1
False Pretences,	7	Pick Pocket,	1
Carrying Dangerous Weapons,	6	Escaped Prisoner,	1
Neglect of Family,	6	Selling Adulterated Milk,	1
Contempt of Court,	6	Defiling a building,	1
Ran Away from Home,	5	Detained as Witness,	1
Larceny from person,	5	Personating an Officer,	1
Peddling without License,	5	Railer and Brawler,	1
Keeping Unlicensed Dog,	5	Total,	2380
Fighting Dogs,	5		

Occupation of persons arrested during the year 1871.

Occupation	Count	Occupation	Count
Laborers,	693	Gardeners,	3
Boot & Shoe Makers,	336	Bill Posters,	3
House Keepers and Domestics,	196	Manufacturers,	3
Students,	183	Wool Sorters,	3
Machinists,	85	Reed Makers,	3
Painters,	66	Book Keepers,	2
Moulders,	49	Auctioneers,	2
Carpenters,	49	Brokers,	2
Saloon Keepers,	45	Slaters,	2
Hostlers,	44	Book Agents,	2
Farmers,	43	Porters,	2
Blacksmiths,	42	Photographers,	2
Iron and Wire Workers,	39	Stable Keepers,	2
Spinners,	37	Boarding House Keepers,	2
Teamsters,	36	Core Makers,	2
Masons,	28	Trunk Makers,	2
Brakemen,	27	Carriage Makers,	2
Weavers,	27	Lathers,	2
Pedlers,	22	Straw Workers,	2
Cyprians,	20	Jewelers,	1
Cigar Makers,	15	Sail Maker,	1
Barbers,	14	Milk Dealer,	1
Clerks,	14	Reporter,	1
Printers,	14	Waiters,	1
Loafers,	14	Gentleman,	1
Stone Cutters,	13	Producer Dealer,	1
Stone Masons,	11	Speculator,	1
Marble Cutters,	10	Pattern Maker,	1
Junk Dealers,	9	Engineer,	1
Cloth Finishers,	8	Press Man,	1
Boiler Makers,	8	Dress Maker,	1
Grocers,	8	Metalic Roofer,	1
Wool Carders,	7	Civil Engineer,	1
Sailors,	7	Last Maker,	1
Curriers,	7	File Cutter,	1
Contractors,	6	Rope Maker,	1
Plumbers,	6	Baggage Master,	1
Iron Melters,	6	Cooper,	1
Tin Smiths,	6	Tool Grinder,	1
Gun Smiths,	5	Soap Maker,	1
Hatters,	5	Seamstress,	1
Butchers,	5	Engraver,	1
Harness Makers,	4	Comb Maker,	1
Musicians,	3	Conductor,	1
Bakers,	3	Sash and Blind Maker,	1
Hack Drivers,	3	Tanner,	1
Bar Tenders,	3	Gas Fitter,	1
Wheel Wrights,	3	Loom Repairer,	1
Mercants,	3	Miner,	1
Physicians,	3	Cabinet Maker,	1
Hotel Keepers,	3	Wool Dealer,	1
Liquor Dealers,	3	Paper Maker,	1
Paper Hangers,	3	Sugar Refiner,	1
Dyers,	3	Total,	2380

Number Reported Marrried, 981.
Number Reported Single, 1399.

The resources of the Department for the year have been as follows :

Appropriation of the City Council,	$28,000	00
Fees on Warrants served by officers,	4,080	00
Witness fees of Police Officers at Municipal Court,	1,301	40
Collected for extra duty of Officers at Balls and Theatre,	192	75
Collected on Warrants for use of City Teams,	800	00
Total Resources,	$34,374	15

Expenses of the Department for the Municipal year ending Nov. 30.

Pay Roll of Police (Regular),	$25,042	70
Salary of Marshal and Assistants,	3,529	13
Teams for use of Department,	1,342	50
Special Police July 3rd and 4th,	131	98
Special Police at Convention Sept. 26, and 27,	291	62
Special Police (8 men) on duty by order of the Board since Chicago Fire,	1,078	00
Printing, Telegraphing and Postage,	158	38
Food for Prisoners and Poor Lodgers,	206	44
Cleaning Lockup, Station and Hospital,	157	11
Repairing in Station and Lockup,	83	24
Blankets for Hospital Room and Lockup,	23	25
Ice bill for the season,	19	12
Sundry Small bills,	34	84
Total Expenditures,	$32,098	31
Earnings deducted,	6,374	14
Net cost of Police Department,	25,724	16
Unexpended Balance in favor of Department,	2,275	84

A portion of the miscellaneous duties performed by the Officers during the 11 months are as follows:

Buildings found open and secured,		166
Disturbances suppressed,		110
Intoxicated persons conducted home,		105
Lost Children restored to friends,		30
Stray Teams picked up and cared for by officers,		42
Nuisances Reported,		95
Notices served,		1829
Defective Streets reported,		28
Defective Sidewalks reported,		5
Number of cases of accidents cared for at Hospital room in Station,		14
Value of stolen property reported,	$5,538	90
" " " recovered,	3,567	90
Amount of fines imposed in Municipal and Probate Courts in cases within the Department,	10,321	00

Amount of money taken from prisoners and returned,   9,494 77
The Truant Officer reports the number of delinquent
   scholars visited by him,   2400
Number returned to school,   1397
Number arrested,   45
Number committed to Truant School,   22
Number continued,   20
Number discharged without complaint,   3

In closing the Report I have to state that the discipline of the force the past year has been excellent. The conduct of its members has been exemplary; and the city has been well guarded as the small amount of property stolen by burglars and thieves. throughout the year will show in this report. The vigorous action of the force, and the prompt arrest of the different gangs of thieves and burglars during the year has without doubt prevented many heavy robberies. It will be seen that 22 arrests were made for burglary, and 13 for larceny from buildings, and 159 for other larcenies during the year.

In my former annual reports I have advocated more officers and better facilities for doing the police business of this large City; and as we grow older, and expand so rapidly as we do, these necessities are more apparant and press harder upon us. In my opinion we are at least 25 years behind the times in modern facilities for doing police business, or as compared with other cities in our vicinity.

The following table will show how we compare in some respects during the past year, with a few cities in our vicinity approximating in size to our own.

City.	Number of Inhabitants.	Number of Police Officers.	Pay of Patrol-men.	Salary of Chief.	Net Cost of Police for the year.	Total number of arrests.
Providence,	69,000	143	$2 75	$2,000	$139,000 00	6,408
Worcester,	45,000	30	2 75	1,600	25,000 00	2,282
Lowell,	43,000	38	2 50	1,600	35,000 00	2,212
Cambridge,	39,000	50	3 00	2,000	60,000 00	1,835
Charlestown,	30,000	36	3 00	2,000	41,000 00	1,330

In the above figures will be seen a very correct ratio of business done and expenses of Departments.

We are $10,000 less than Lowell in expenses.
"   "   16,000 "   "· Charlestown in expenses.
"   "   35,000 "   " Cambridge "   "
"   "   114,000 "   " Providence "   "

It will also be seen that,
Lowell   has one Police Officer to 1130 inhabitants.
Charlestown "   "   "   "   " 833   "
Cambridge   "   "   "   "   " 800   "
Providence   "   "   "   "   " 483   "
Worcester   "   "   "   "   " 1,500 "

By proper facilities for doing business I mean to say that a Station House should be above ground.   It should contain sleeping rooms for officers who come off duty at midnight instead of compelling them to go to their homes a long distance away, and if they have cases in court to return early in the morning without proper sleep.

It should have a proper drill room for officers, and bath rooms for officers and prisoners, plenty of ventilation and proper drainage and in fact all the modern improvements that can be made in such public buildings.   I would recommend that the above matters be taken into consideration by the Council.   I would also recommend that at least ten more officers be added to the regular police force of the city.   Soon after the Chicago fire, eight special officers were employed by the Marshal and placed on duty by order of the Board of Mayor and Aldermen, in order to afford better protection against fire, and better police protection for the inhabitants of the outer districts ; those men are still continued on duty.

I would respectfully suggest to the Council that the Ordinance in relation to Signs and Awnings should be amended as soon as possible, so as to compel all persons interested to conform to its provisions by the opening of spring.   I would recommend that the erection or maintaining of board Awnings or Signs over any street or sidewalk be prohibited.   I would also recommend that the law in relation to the erection of wooden buildings within the fire limits be revised, or more satisfactorily adjusted to meet the objects for which it was established.

During the seven years I have been connected with the depart-
39

ment, there have been 13,851 persons arrested 6,685 of the above number, or nearly one half, were arrested for Drunkeness.

I am placed under deep obligation to his Honor, the Mayor, the City Council, Judge Williams and the Clerk of the Municipal Court. To the chiefs of all the departments I desire to make my acknowledgements for their uniform courtesy and willingness to render assistance at all times.

To C. N. Hair and E. J. Russell, Constables of the Commonwealth I desire to express my thanks for valuable assistance rendered to the department.

For the valuable assistance of the Special Police Officers in the outer districts, I am under lasting obligation.

To Assistant Marshals Wilson and Washburn, to Captains Comings and Howe, and to the Regular Force, my thanks are especially due for their willingness in season and out of season to perform every duty.

Number of Officers in the Department (Regular Force,)   30
Special Officers doing duty,   7

Total,   37

Respectfully Submitted,

JAMES M. DRENNAN, *City Marshal.*

REPORT OF THE CITY PHYSICIAN.

WORCESTER, Dec. 28th, 1871.

To the City Council, City of Worcester :

GENTLEMEN,—The City Physician would respectfully present the following as his Annual Report:

There has been no unusual prevalence of disease in the city during the past year ; and the inmates of the Almshouse and Truant School have been remarkably free from all acute diseases.

The number of deaths of patients under my care has been fifteen (15), and are recorded as follows :

Jan. 9th, 1871, Cato Brooks (colored), aged 36. Injury to brain.

Jan. 11th, Mary Foley, aged 40. Consumption.

" 15th, Caleb Rogers, aged 72. Cancer.

" 19th, James Snow, aged 72. Bright's disease.

Feb. 15th, Eliza Gibbons, aged 60. Disease of heart.

March 4th, John McParlin, aged 62. Consumption.

April 5th, Bridget Luby, aged 52. Consumption.

May 1st, Kate Harrington, aged 18. Consumption.

April 29th, Martin Meyers, aged 55. Consumption.

May 17th, Betsey Hariot, aged 81. Injury.

" 21st, Warren E. Brewer, aged 27. Injury.

" 27th, Hiram Day, aged 43. Bright's disease.

" 31st, Michael Brannan, aged 24. Small pox.

Oct. 16th, Mary Burke, aged 60. Cancer.

Dec. 1st, Mary McCarty, aged 14. Typhoid fever.

Every Monday morning during the year an office at the City Hall has been opened from 8½ to 10 o'clock, where about one hundred and seventy-five children have been vaccinated and over fifteen hundred certificates of vaccination given. Not as many háve availed of the privilege of free vaccination, as we could have wished. There are still, in my opinion, a large number in the city, who are not protected from small pox by vaccination. It is only by constant watching to see that the people are thoroughly vaccinated, that we shall escape those terrible ravages which this much dreaded disease is making in other cities.

Twenty cases of small pox in its modified and unmodified forms have occurred in the city during the past year; two of which have died.

As soon as the disease appeared no attempt to conceal it was made, the patient was immediately isolated, all in the vicinity were vaccinated, and all necessary sanitary regulations rigidly enforced. Both the patients and their friends, in every instance excepting one, have assisted in every possible way to prevent the spreading of the disease. Though the disease has appeared at six different times during the year, by this management its increase was promptly arrested. Five patients have been sent to the Small Pox Hospital. The only case at present in the city as far as known, is the one now at the Small Pox Hospital.

The Report of the Board of Trustees of the City Hospital has shown what has been accomplished in that institution. Though it has not been in operation but a short time, it has already done much good by furnishing, comparatively, a very comfortable place for those unfortunate ones who have become sick or injured, and who have had no suitable home in which they could be properly cared for. It seems to me that it would be a wise policy to initiate at an early date a plan for establishing a city hospital on a permanent basis, which would be suited to the requirements of our rapidly growing city, and which would be a credit to the humane sentiment of the people.

All of which is respectfully submitted.

ALBERT WOOD, *City Physician.*

REPORT OF THE TRUSTEES

OF THE

WORCESTER CITY HOSPITAL,
1871.

To His Honor, the Mayor, and the City Council of the City of Worcester :—

The Board of Trustees of the City Hospital beg leave to present their first report :

The Ordinance passed by the City Council, June 26, 1871, requires that,

" Annually in the month of December, the said Board shall submit to the City Council, a report, in detail, of the expenses incurred for the maintaining and conducting of the City Hospital, during the past year, and an estimate, in detail, of the expenses of maintaining and conducting the Hospital under their charge, for the year next ensuing. "

It is also further required, that such estimates shall be accompanied by a statement of the number of the inmates of the hospital, the number of admissions thereto, of discharges therefrom, and of births and deaths therein ; and by any other information pertaining to the institution, that may be judged to be of public interest.

In this their first official communication to the municipal government, the Trustees deem it advisable to place on record a few items that may be more accessible here than elsewhere, for future reference.

The Act of the Legislature, approved May 25, 1871, authorizing the establishment of this institution, provides that the City of Worcester " may establish and maintain a hospital for the reception of persons who, by misfortune or poverty, may require relief during temporary sickness. " It would, however, be a very severe and rigid interpretation of the letter, rather than of the spirit of the law, that should close any unoccupied wards of this institution against other patients, who might be able and willing to pay for their board, and whose presence would in no way interfere with the special purposes for which the hospital was primarily and principally designed.

The aforesaid Ordinance, therefore, wisely and humanely, empowers the Trustees to receive patients other than those of the prescribed class, but only under circumstances and upon conditions against which there can be no reasonable objection.

It should not be overlooked, in this connection, that the hospital still remains in an experimental stage of existence. So far is it from resting as yet on a solid foundation, that it cannot make the slightest pretensions on the score of being equipped and furnished in every direction, with ample accommodations for all the suffering humanity that may seek to come under its roof. It may nevertheless, modestly claim to be all that the Trustees in the conscientious exercise of their authority, and in a faithful discharge of their duty, have been able to make it. Since it received its first patient, October 26, 1871, it has already been instrumental in relieving various forms of human suffering which would have been more intense and prolonged, or possibly fatal in its termination, if the patients had received even the most skillful treatment in any quarters elsewhere accessible to them ; and in one instance, at least, it has saved life which had no chance for preservation outside an institution like this. The Hospital has been successful otherwise, also, inasmch as it has abundantly demonstrated the necessity of its permanent establishment as one of the benevolent institutions of a rapidly growing city.

Having neither authority nor means to purchase real estate, the first duty devolving upon the Board of Trustees, after their organization, was " to lease suitable buildings for a hospital. " Such accommodations, centrally located, were not easily to be found ; but, after patient research in every direction where there was encouragement to make enquiry, it was finally decided with great unanimity, that, all things considered, the best accommodations obtainable would be afforded by the " Bigelow Estate," so called, situate on the corner of Front and Church streets. Accordingly, this property was rented by the Trustees, and the

venerable mansion thereon was repaired under the careful supervision of a sub-committee of the Board, and made comfortable
for the reception of eight or ten patients, such as the institution
may properly receive. The transformation of an old-style dwell-
ing-house into a modern hospital was not unattended with difficulty. Nevertheless, the undertaking was successfully planned
and executed, although requiring a considerable outlay of money.
Much of the expenditure was, however, for permanent improvements, such as the introduction of gas and city water, the construction of a bathing room, the purchase and fitting up of a
furnace, drainage into the public sewers, painting, papering &c.,
&c. Other considerable expenses had to be incurred for bedsteads, bedding, furniture for the kitchen and wards, crockery,
&c., &c. Such disbursements preparatory to the opening of
the hospital, will not have to be made again for years. The
Trustees gratefully recognize the interest felt in the institution,
as manifested by the low prices charged in several of the bills
for the above items, as well as by gifts of pictures, &c., which
will be more particularly acknowledged in another part of this
report.

Previous to the admission of any patients, a Board of consulting physicians was appointed by the Trustees, consisting of Drs.
F. H. Kelley, Merrick Bemis, and Joseph Sargent. Dr. J. G.
Park was elected Superintendent and Resident Physician, and
subsequently admitting physician of the hospital, his salary
being fixed at $700 per annum, in addition to office accommoda-
tions and board.

Twelve visiting physicians were also invited to serve gratuit-
ously, for two months each, the assignment and distribution
of their attendance having been arranged as follows:

Dr. R. Woodward and J. G. Park from the opening of the
hospital to Jan. 1, 1872. For the year 1872,—Drs. G. A. Bates
and E. Warner, from Jan. 1, to March 1 ; Drs. O. Martin and
A. Wood, from March 1, to May 1 ; Drs. H. Clarke, and J. M. Rice,
from May 1, to July 1 ; Drs. J. N. Bates and G. E. Francis,
from July 1, to Sept. 1 ; Drs. T. H. Gage and H. Y. Simpson, from
Sept. 1, to Nov. 1.

Mrs. S. W. Whiting, a lady well fitted by experience and other
qualifications, was chosen matron, and her compensation was

fixed at $25 per month, in addition to board and room in the hospital.

A cook, a laundress, and nurses, of course, must form a part of the *personnel* of the establishment; and their wages are among its necessary expenses.

The Hospital was opened for the reception of patients, on the 26th of October, 1871. The number who have received its benefits to Dec. 1st, is as follows :—

	Males.	Females.	Occupation.	Males.
Whole number,	8	8	Mechanics,	5
Of this number their			Laborers,	1
have been discharged,			Children,	1
Well,		2	Clergyman,	1
Much Improved,	1			—
Improved,		1	Total,	8
Not Improved,	1	1		Females
Died,	1		Housekeepers,	5
Remaining Dec. 1st,	5	4	Domestics,	3
	—	—		—
Total.	8	8	Total,	8

Nativity.	Males.	Females.	
Massachusetts,	3	4	
Ireland,	2	3	
England,	1		Total number of Patients from
Scotland,		1	the opening of the Hospital,
Vermont,	1		Oct. 26, to Dec. 1, 16.
N. Carolina,	1		
	—	—	
Total,	8	8	

The Trustees have the pleasure to acknowledge the receipt of several very acceptable donations, contributing, some of them to the comfort, and others to the cheerfulness, of the wards of the hospital.

From Edward L. Davis, Pictures ; from Mrs. Geo. Thrall, Bed Linen ; from J. D. Chollar, Sofa Bed ; from Dr. Geo. A. Bates, Pictures ; from Mrs. Charles A. Tenney, Pictures and Sick Chair ; from Kinnicutt & Co., Hardware ; from H. Woodward, Pictures.

Some of the above named articles are of the value of $30, or more, and whatever of them is least in a pecuniary point of view, deserves honorable mention here, as an evidence of kindly sympathy for those whom sickness or misfortune consigns to a public hospital.

From the organization of the Board of Trustees, in July last, down to the 1st of December, 1871, their expenditures have been as follows:

On the Building,	$1,428 25	
Furniture, Bedding &c.,	1,890 64 —	$3,318 89
Grocer's Bills, Oct. and Nov.	$83 39	
Provision Bills, " "	137 62	
Drugs and Medicines, Oct. and Nov.	63 00	
Pay Roll, Oct. and Nov.	214 76	
Incidentals, Oct. and Nov.	42 76 —	$541 53
Total,		$3,860 42

Small sums, for board, &c., amounting in the aggregate to less than $25, have been received by the Trustees ; but this money, having been all appropriated toward defraying the incidental expenses, as set forth above, does not require to be more formally accounted for, in this place.

The estimated expenses of the hospital, on its present basis, for the coming year, is in round numbers, $6,000.

From the exhibit, above made of the number and character of the patients who have sought admission to this institution during the few weeks that it has been open, no further demonstration of the necessity of maintaining it can be reasonably required. Its wards are already occupied almost to their full capacity, and it is a more probable contingency that they may soon be crowded, than it is that a single one of them may remain vacant for any length of time. The Trustees, indeed, are not without apprehensions that, before the close of the coming year, the accommodations may prove inadequate for the class of patients for whom, in a civilized community, it seems almost inhuman that no public provision should be made.

The future of the hospital will be what the City Council, in their wisdom, shall decide to make of it; but without overstepping the limit of their authority, the Trustees may offer suggestions and recommend measures to the municipal government, while they cherish not unreasonable hopes of beneficent aid from private sources. In the exercise of this privilege, it may be added here, as an expression of the unanimous belief of this Board, that a hospital of a capacity for not less certainly than forty patients, pleasantly situated a little retired from the noise and bustle of the city, and substantially built after such a style of

40

architecture as will admit of enlargement without disfigurement or interruption of occupation, is greatly needed in Worcester. It will be readily understood that an institution of this description, as compared with the present small establishment in the midst of the bustling uproar of the city, could be more economically managed for the treatment of its special class of patients, and would also at the same time afford extremely desirable accommodations for a considerable number of other unobjectionable persons, who would be able and willing to pay for their board, and whose admission would in no small degree, contribute to the successful, and especially to the economical, administration of the Hospital.

The conclusion at which the members of the Board have arrived, as above, is based partly on the experience of other cities where successful hospitals have been established, partly on the representations of physicians in this vicinity, but more particularly and specially on the records actually kept, in 1870, by the city physician, Dr. Wood, for the purpose of making an approximate estimate of the number of cases annually presenting themselves, as suitable for treatment in an institution like this.

Respectfully submitted for, and in behalf of the Trustees,

F. H. KELLEY, *President.*

GEORGE JAQUES, *Secretary.*

Worcester, Dec. 1, 1871.

APPENDIX.

Among gentlemen of the medical profession in Worcester, the opinion has been for years gaining strength that a public hospital here would be a highly beneficent institution. Its actual establishment, however, appears until a recent date, to have been a dream rather than an object of reasonable hope. The annually increasing expenditures of the city in every other direction had already grown oppressive, and there seemed to be slender grounds for any expectation that the timorous appeal of charity would make itself heard above the clamorous demands of public utility.

At length however, in January 1871, the City Council were induced to take into careful consideration the recommendation of Dr. Albert Wood, city physician, in his Annual Report for the year 1870, advising that a building large enough to accomodate at least twenty-five patients, and situated where it would be easily accessible, should be leased by the city, and furnished suitably for the occupation of an institution of the character of the present City Hospital.

The proceedings of the Board of Aldermen and of the Common Council, in reference thereto, resulting in a petition to the General Court for authority to take such a step, will be found in the records of these two branches of the municipal government, for the period intervening between January 1st and May 25th, 1871. It is not, however, deemed advisable to enlarge this present document, by making extracts from these records, beyond what is embodied in the following joint Report, and the Ordinance, based thereon, which was subsequently adopted:

REPORT OF THE SPECIAL COMMITTEE.

CITY OF WORCESTER,   }
IN CITY COUNCIL MAY 8, 1871. }

The Joint Special Committee of the City Council, appointed to consider and report upon the expediency of establishing a City Hospital, having carefully investigated the subject, respectfully beg leave to report as follows, viz :

The committee would call the attention of the City Council to the fact that at the present time no hospital establishment exists in Worcester, except that of the Sisters of Charity Hospital, on Shrewsbury street, which is so small and restricted in its operations as to be of but little public importance.

Hospitals, or places where the sick and those disabled by accident can resort for care and treatment, have been established and maintained in all countries from remote periods, and they are the type of the Christian civilization of any large community. There are but few cities in this country of the size of our own where there are not institutions of this kind supported either from public or private endowment. While we justly claim for Worcester respectable rank in our public schools, institutions of learning, public libraries, churches and various associations for the intellectual and moral culture of our people ; it must be acknowledged that we are sadly behind most other places in providing for those amongst us who fall victims to disease, or are overtaken by accident, and whose circumstances and means are such as to oblige them to suffer lingering illness in scanty homes or crowded boarding houses, unattended by friends, and without the care and comfort to which they are entitled by the ordinary dictates of humanity.

The municipal authorities in times past have undoubtedly waited in anticipation that this want might be supplied by the liberality of some of our wealthy citizens.   This indeed seems to be the only excuse for their not having before now, taken the matter in hand.

The late Deacon Ichabod Washburn realized the need of a hospital, and out of his princely fortune, provided in his will certain means for the establishment of such an institution ; but by necessary delay in the legal settlement of his estate, the committee are assured by the trustees of the fund that the city will not realize any benefit from this bequest for three, and possibly not for five years.   It is moreover doubtful if such a hospital as is contemplated by the will can be established and maintained with the funds provided for it, and while the city in its corporate capacity is in no manner recognized by the testator, and while there is ño special provision or inducement for the city or individuals to contribute to its support, it is thought advisable by the trustees themselves, that the city should initiate this enterprise and make an appropriation at least for a temporary hospital without delay.

To purchase a proper site, to erect suitable hospital buildings for the present and prospective wants of Worcester, to put a model institution of the kind in successful operation, and to provide for its maintenance would require an expenditure that would not be warranted in the opinion of the committee, at the present time, however desirable it might be to have it. But after full consultation with the trustees of the Washburn hospital fund, and with many of the medical profession of the city, your committee are unanimous in the belief that some plan should be devised to meet the present exigency, and afford at least temporary relief. According to a careful estimate based upon information derived from some of our leading physicians, there are annually from two hundred to two hundred and fifty persons who would be proper subjects for hospital treatment, and who would gladly avail themselves of such advantages if provided for them. Calling the total number of admittances two hundred and twenty-five or the first year, with an average treatment of three weeks to each patient, would furnish from twelve to fifteen occupants constantly. To provide temporarily for this number in a comfortable but inexpensive manner, would certainly not be a great burden upon the city. The cost of starting and supporting such an establishment for the year is estimated as follows:

Rent of some suitable dwelling house centrally located,	$1000
Salary of man and wife to superintend the hospital,	600
Cost of furnishing and fitting up for 15 beds,	3000
Help and supplies for an average of from 12 to 15 patients throughout the year,	5000
Contingencies,	400
	$10,000

It is recommended by the committee, That the sum of ten thousand dollars be appropriated as soon as the authority for the same can be had from the Legislature, if that be necessary, for the purpose of providing temporary hospital accommodations, free to such temperate and industrious persons residing in Worcester as may wish and deserve the same ; That the City Treasurer be directed to open an account under the head of City Hospital account, and charge said appropriation to such account ; That this money and all future appropriations for this object be put into the hands of seven Trustees to be expended by them under such general rules and regulations as shall be fixed by ordinance ;

That said trustees be elected by the City Council, one of them to be a member of the board of Aldermen for the time being, two to be members of the Common Council, and four to be selected from citizens at large. It is obvious that the objects of the proposed enterprise can best be attained by placing the detail of its management in the hands of an executive board who shall be under the general control of the City Council. The precise object and management of a hospital can only be stated in this report in general terms; while its benefits are intended to be free to those persons of temperate and industrious habits who by sickness or accident, require that care and attention for which they are unable to pay; yet where there is the ability, there is no reason why a just and proper amount should not be received, to aid in meeting its expenses. Many patients or their friends would prefer to pay something in proportion to their means, to prevent the feeling that they were the objects of public charity. This sentiment or desire of independence is strong among that class which the enterprise is designed to benefit; and it is one which, as the great barrier to pauperism, cannot be too highly commended and encouraged. Hence we would not have a hospital for the reception of the degraded victims of vice and intemperance, or a home for the hopeless pauper; but we would have it regarded as an asylum for the industrious and honest mechanic and laborer, who by sudden injury or disease, is temporarily prevented from laboring for the support of himself and family. We would have it a home to which may be sent, when struck down by sickness, the respectable domestic whose attic chamber cannot be made comfortable, and who cannot receive the requisite attendance, however well disposed may be the family in which she resides. We would open its doors to the stranger overtaken by disease, when absent from friends and home, and to all others, among the various classes of society, who in sickness require that comfort and medical advice which their means and homes cannot afford. It is confidently believed that if the City Council will assume the responsibility at this time, and initiate the enterprise upon the scale herein recommended, it will form a nucleus around which will grow a City Hospital that will eventually be the pride of all our people.

All of which is respectfully submitted.

F. H. KELLEY,
A. B. R. SPRAGUE,
LUTHER ROSS,
MORRIS MELAVEN,
EDWIN AMES.

Committee.

REPORT OF THE CITY TREASURER.

CITY OF WORCESTER, February 5th, 1872.

To the Honorable City Council:

GENTLEMEN:—The Treasurer has the honor and would respectfully lay before you his *twenty-second* Annual Report of the Receipts and Expenditures, Appropriations raised by tax, Abatements and Discounts, Uncollected Taxes, &c., from January 2, 1871, to January 1, 1872.

The accompanying *Cash Account* will exhibit the *Cash* transactions for the same space of time.

Cash on hand January 2d, 1871,	$28,785 28	
Received from Loans,	2,022,678 96	
Corporation tax 1871,	42, 918 97	
Highways, Sidewalks, &c.	53,321 09	
Taxes,	668,555 05	
Water Rents,	56,686 98	
All other sources,	78,515 58	—$2,951,461 91
Cash paid on Loans,	1,465,698 28	
Boston, Barre & G. R. R.	157,320 00	
Highways and Sidewalks,	140,104 29	
Schools,	120,301 35	
School Houses,	93,254 52	
Sewers,	245,657 34	
Water Works,	111,282 80	
Other departments,	534,669 64	—$2,868,288 22
Cash on hand,		$83,173 69

All of which is respectfully submitted,

GEORGE W. WHEELER,

City Treasurer for 1871.

Dr.   CITY OF WORCESTER, *in account current from Jan.* 2, 1871,

Balances, January 2, 1871 :		
Bills Receivable,	$19,000 00	
Boston, Barre, and Gardner Railroad,	104,880 00	
Interest,	33,900 00	
Lighting Streets,	9,051 99	
Military,	3.276 26	
School Houses and land for same,	139,581 53	
Sewers,	827.151 80	
Streets,	71,449 92	
War : Bounties, Contingents, and State Aid,	67,480 22	
Water Works,	649,727 90	
		$1,924,599 62
Paid Abatements,	710 71	
Boston, Barre, and Gardner Rail Road,	157,320 00	
City Hay Scales,	63 80	
City Hospital,	3,299 08	
Contingemt Expenses,	38,186 03	
Engine House,	2,047 89	
Fire Alarm Telegraph,	16,852 47	
Fire Department,	17,747 24	
Free Public Library,	10,294 91	
Fuel, Lights, and Printing,	5,889 56	
Highways, Sidewalks, &c.,	140,104 29	
Interest,	73,489 45	
Interest on Water Loan,	32,975 90	
Licenses,	324 31	
Lighting Streets,	19,767 75	
Loans,	1,465,698 28	
Military,	3,954 00	
Paupers,	14,999 86	
Police and Watchmen,	32,918 26	
Salaries,	13,833 11	
Schools,	120,301 35	
School for Truants,	2,053 60	
School Houses and land,	93,254 52	
School, State Normal,	15,028 50	
Sewers,	245,657 34	
Shade Trees and Public Grounds,	5,974 01	
Soldiers Monument,	35,000 00	
Streets, making, grading and widening,	51,554 94	
Summons,	155.39	
Tax, County,	27,639 23	
Tax, State,	51,075 00	
Tax, State on Bank Shares,	22,148 94	
War : State Aid,	11,859 50	
Water Works, (Construction,)	111.282 80	
Water Works, (Maintenance,)	24,826 20	
Six per cent. discount on $645,945 31 for prompt payment of taxes,	38,756 75	
Discount and allowance on Bank Tax,	1,828 93	
Taxes of 1871 abated by the Assessors,	1,359 16	
Taxes of 1871 uncollected,	13,497 91	
Taxes uncollected previous to 1871,	24,277 01	
Cash,	83,173 69	
		$3,031,181 67
		$4,955,781 29

to Jan. 1, 1872, *with* GEORGE W. WHEELER, *City Treasurer.* Cr.

Balances Jan. 2, 1871 :		
Loans of all kinds,		$1,899,808 04
Abatements,	$36,156 17	
Contingents,	21,437 04	
Elm Park,	940 00	
Engine House,	2,095 00	
Free Public Library,	5,073 43	
Interest on Water Loan,	170 30	
Main Street School House,	19,000 00	
Shade Trees,	1,048 88	
		$85,920 82
Received from City Scales,	350 95	
Contingent Expenses,	3,982 94	
Fire Alarm Telegraph,	3,000 00	
Fire Department,	1,555 75	
Fuel, Lights, and Printing,	400 00	
Highways, Sidewalks, &c.,	53,321 09	
Interest,	3,612 40	
Licenses,	3,558 50	
Lighting Streets,	58 76	
Loans,	2,022,678 96	
Military,	7,515 00	
Paupers,	5,750 76	
Police and Watchmen,	7,906 67	
Schools,	2,693 11	
School for Truants,	93 00	
School House on Common,	675 00	
Sewers,	85 15	
Shade Trees,	350 00	
State Aid,	13,000 00	
Streets, betterments, &c.,	14,453 70	
Summons,	412 40	
Taxes, (Corporation 1871,)	42,918 97	
Water Works, (Construction,)	8,561 49	
Water Works, (Maintenance,)	500 00	
Water Rents,	56,686 98	
		$2,254,121 58

Appropriations raised by tax :

City,	$640,500 00		
County,	27,639 23		
State,	51,075 00		
Overlayings,	12,719 52		
	$731,933 75		
Less,	45,000 00		
		$686,933 75	
Taxes, State assessed on Bank Shares,		28,997 10	
			$715,930 85
			$4,955,781 29

GEORGE W. WHEELER,
City Treasurer, for 1871.

City of Worcester, February 5, 1872.

41

Dr.   CASH ACCOUNT, *from January* 2, 1871, *to January* 1, 1872.

To Balance January 2, 1871,	$28,785 28	
Received from City Hay Scales,	350 85	
Contingent expenses,	3,982 94	
Fire Alarm Telegraph,	3,000 00	
Fire Department,	1,555 75	
Fuel, Lights, and Printing,	400 00	
Highways,	53,321 09	
Interest,	3,621 40	
Licenses,	3,558 50	
Lighting Streets,	58 76	
Loans,	2,022,678 96	
Military,	7,515 00	
Paupers,	5,750 76	
Police and Watchmen,	7,906 67	
Schools,	2,693 11	
School for Truants,	93 00	
School House,	675 00	
Sewers,	85 15	
Shade Trees,	350 00	
State Aid,	13,000 00	
Streets, (Betterments, &c.,)	14,453 70	
Summons,	412 40	
Tax on Corporations 1871,	42,918 97	
Taxes,	668,555 05	
Water Rents,	56,686 98	
Water Works, (Construction,)	8,561 49	
Water Works, (Maintenance,)	500 00	
		$2,951,461 91

CASH ACCOUNT. *from January* 2, 1871, *to January* 1, 1872.   *Cr.*

By Amount paid Abatements,	$710	71
Boston, Barre, and Gardner		
Rail Road,	57,320	00
City Hay Scales,	63	80
City Hospital,	3,299	08
Contingent Expenses,	38,186	03
Engine House,	2,047	89
Fire Alarm Telegraph,	16,852	47
Fire Department,	17,747	24
Free Public Library,	10,294	91
Fuel, Lights, and Printing,	5,889	56
Highways, Sidewalks, &c.,	140,104	29
Interest,	73,489	45
Interest on Water Loan,	32,975	90
Licenses,	324	31
Lighting Streets,	19,767	75
Loans.	1,465,698	28
Military,	3,954	00
Paupers,	14,999	86
Police and Watchmen,	32,918	26
Salaries,	13,833	11
Schools,	120,301	35
School for Truants,	2,053	60
School Houses and Land,	93,254	52
School, State Normal,	15,028	50
Sewers,	245,657	34
Shade Trees,	5,974	01
Soldiers Monument,	35,000	00
State Aid,	11,859	50
Streets, making, grading, and		
widening,	51,554	94
Summons,	155	39
Tax, County,	27,639	23
Tax, State,	51,075	00
Tax, State on Bank Shares,	22,148	94
Water Works, (Construction,)	111,282	80
Water Works, (Maintenance,)	24,826	20
By Balance to New Account,	83,173	69
	$2,951,461	91

CITY OF WORCESTER

In Board of Aldermen, Feb. 5. 1872.

Ordered, that the City Treasurer for 1871 prepare a particular account of the Receipts and Expenditures and schedule of the City Debt, to be published for the use of the inhabitants of the city, in compliance with the city charter.

A copy Attest,   SAMUEL SMITH, *City Clerk.*

City of Worcester, March 1, 1872.

To the inhabitants of the City of Worcester :

In compliance with the above order, I have prepared and would respectfully present a particular account of my report, made Feb. 5, 1871, together with a schedule of the City Debt and Water Investment.

. GEORGE W. WHEELER,

City Treasurer, for 1871.

ABATEMENTS AND DISCOUNT.

Balance undrawn January 2, 1871,	$36,156 17	
Appropriation for discount,	35,000 00	
Overlayings,	12,710 52	
		$83,875 69

EXPENDITURES.

Paid on taxes,		
Daniel W. Bemis,	$8 18	
John Blakenhorn,	8 70	
Tobias Boland,	52 34	
Anthony Cannon,	9 81	
Thomas and Michael Dowd,	14 72	
Talcott Edgerton,	3 48	
D. Franklin Estabrook,	32 71	
Goulding & Hawkins,	34 35	
John C. Grady,	16 36	
Samuel S. Green, Trustee,	16 36	
Patrick Guilfoyle,	1 64	
F. W. Harrington,	12 27	
Henry Heywood,	34 35	
F. H. Kelley,	29 44	
King & Davenport,	17 40	
C. S. Lee,	9 82	
Thomas Magennis,	14 72	
George T. Murdock,	3 27	
William F. Oakley,	6 55	
Osgood Plummer,	32 71	
Annie Smyth,	8 01	
Mary F. T. Souther,	16 38	
W. W. Sprague,	16 36	
Joanna Sweeny,	8 18	
Adin Thayer,	68 70	
Charles B. Thompson,	3 27	
Loison D. Town,	19 63	
Walker & Brown,	98 14	
A. L. Whitney & Co.,	8 18	
J. J. Williams,	96 50	
Edwin H. Wood,	8 18	
Abatement made by Assessors,	1,359 16	
Six per cent discount on $645,945.81 for prompt payment,	39,756 75	
Transfer to Contingent Expenses,	5,000 00	
		$45,826 62
Amount undrawn January 1, 1872,		$38,049 07

BOSTON, BARRE & GARDNER RAIL ROAD.

Paid Assessment in 1869,	$32,540 00	
" " 1870,	71,440 00	
" " 1871,	157,320 00	
		$262,200 00

CITY HAY SCALES.

Received for weighing:

James H. Benchly,	$301 88	
Silas Penniman,	49 07	
		$350 95

EXPENDITURES.

Paid Fairbanks, Brown & Co., repairs,	$63 80	
Transfer Contingent Expenses,	287 15	
		$350 95

CONTINGENT EXPENSES.

Balance undrawn January 2, 1871,	$21,437 04		
Appropriation,	20,000 00		
" for hydrants,	8,000 00		
Received from City Clerk, ordinances sold,	15 00		
" " fees,	963 65		
Commonwealth, armory rent,	550,00		
Commonwealth balance corporation tax 1870,	612 12		
County rent of Court room,	1,450 00		
Old South Society, heating church,	154 00		
Rail Roads, for plans,	218 00		
P. Ball, paper sold,	20 17		
Transfer from abatements,	$5,000 00		
City Scales,	287 15		
Engine House,	47 11		
Fire Alarm Telegraph,	147 53		
Licenses,	1,456 69		
Summons,	257 01		
Tax on Bank Shares,	2,938 20		
		$10,133 69	
			$63,553 67

EXPENDITURES.

Transfer to Normal School,	$28 50
Paid Committee of G. A. R. decoration of graves,	500 00
Allen & Reed, boots,	4 00
C. A. Allen, labor on plans,	130 55
Ames Plow Co., plank and stakes,	98 91
J. D. Baldwin, & Co., advertising,	23 50
Phinehas Ball, cash paid out,	27 14
John S. Ballard, matches and duster,	7 25
E. Banister, L. W. Pond and C. Baker, services,	15 00
Chas. W. and Mrs. Baker, damages,	550 00

Paid Barnard, Sumner & Co., carpets
matting &c., $621 18
Barret, Washburn & Co., pipe, hose,
labor &c., 72 55
John T. Barry, ring bell July 4th, &c., 10 00
Sarah A. Bates, damages, 150 00
N. T. Bemis, horse-hire, 7 00
L. H. Bigelow, sundries, 337 48
Boston & Albany R. R. Co., services
of commissioners, 549 65
Fred A. Brooks, services of page Com.
Council, 17 50
John J. Brosnihan, services as Asst.
Assessor, 6 00
Brown & Barnard, trucking, 40 38
W. H. Brown, labor, 3 50
Benj. Bryant, services in small-pox
hospital, 20 00
Robert P. Byrne, damages, 500 00
Chamberlain Light Battery, firing
salutes, 93 00
Joseph Chase & Co., matches, 12 95
R. H. Chase, painting and glazing &c.. 230 57
John D. Chollar, chairs and shades, 71 50
Mary L. Church, services for Assessors, 125 25
Churchill & Morse, repairing chairs, 6 50
Clark, Sawyer & Co., shade chimnies
&c., 8 68
Geo. H. Clark and Chas. Nason, rent
of land, 50 00
Wm. L. Clark, cash paid out, 14 00
J. Colbath & Co., copper ball for lib-
erty pole, 1 50
Brigham Converse, stone, 45 00
County of Worcester, costs on com-
plaints, 86 35
Cummings & Lane, repairs, 45
C. A. Cummings, repairing pipe &c., 1 35
Dawson & Guild, gas pipe &c., 4 50
Francis Defose, damages, 30 00
John Delano, mason work, 14 50
D. W. Dexter, pen and holder, 2 50
Division No. 42, sundries, 61 12
Chas. H. Dodd, labor, 32 50
Doe & Woodwell, advertising, 38 91
William Doogue, flowers, 150 00
Ella Drury, services, 16 00
S. F. Dudley, tolling bell, 3 00
Edward Earle, expenses paid in connec-
tion with union depot, 334 97

Paid J. M. Earle, services as Asst. Assessor, $30 00
E. A. Faucett, seed,   3 38
C. Foster & Co., plyers, brush &c.,   2 96
Dwight Foster, professional services,   750 00
J. C. French, labor and materials,   169 51
Thomas H. Gage, professional services,   55 00
Geo. W. Gale, Cash paid out,   19 10
Garfield & Parker, wood,   7 75
George H. Gordon, protractor,   22 00
Greene & Jordan, labor, pipe and
    sundries,   281 21
Aaron F. Greene, ringing bell, July 4th,   5 00
W. & L. E. Gurley, repairing,   33 50
Walter Hale, labor and plans,   59 94
Harkness & Fiske, posting bills,   5 00
S. R. Hathorn, labor on City Hall,   9 65
Wm. A. Hathorn, labor on City Hall,   5 75
E. Hemenway, whitening, cleaning &c.,   55 95
Abbie L. Heywood, services for Assessors, 143 25
  "   "   "   copying old Records,   30 75
  "   "   "   services for Treasurer, 57 00
E. G. & F. W. Higgins, whitening,   41 60
Highway Dept., carting ashes,   10 20
Geo. G. Hildreth, returning deaths,   12 30
J. Henry Hill, lot in Rural Cemetery,   201 00
J. P. Houghton, services as Asst. Assessor, 45 00
S. T. Howard & Co., hacking,   91 00
William Hoyle, ringing bell, July 4th,   3 00
Willard Humes, materials and labor,   940 65
G. Hutchinson, labor, paint &c.,   236 35
J. W. Jordan, labor, stove and sundries, 313 07
Journal Newspaper Co., Journal,   38 40
Margaret Keegan, damages,   100 00
John E. Kendall, Agt. Insurance,   126 00
Geo. P. Kendrick, horse hire,   3 00
Ezra Kent, ringing bell, July 4th,   5 00
Henry L. Keyes, labor for Engineer,   31 87
I. N. Keyes, boards,   10 80
Kinnicutt & Co., glass &c.,   5 52
Daniel Kinsley, care of ward room,   10 00
Asa Knowlton, damages,   3,250 94
T. M. Lamb, repairing clock,   2 50
F. W. Lincoln, Jr., & Co., Instruments, 319 00
H. F. Loomis, copy Copley's alphabets,   2 25
J. D. Lovell, axe and shovel,   2 65
Mann & Bigelow, posts,   121 00
Chauncey L. Marcy, land,   150 00
Chas. Marvin, Cash paid out,   151 41
Mathews & Chamberlain, labor, cement &c. 13 11
Wm. G. Maynard, services numbering
    streets,   556 95

Paid Edwin V. McArthur, relief vote of city
 government, $1,000 00
F. A. McClure, labor,   381 40
Thomas A. McConville, returning deaths, 42 00
Michael McKniff, damages,   660 00
H. W. Miller, stove and sundries, 28 48
F. H. Mills, labor,   385 40
W. E. Mills, labor, and cash paid out, 1,206 39
Municipal Court, costs,   116 90
T. L. Nelson, extra services,   500 00
"   "   "   Cash paid out,   375 72
F. A. Newton, services,   29 80
Maria L. Oliver, damages,   915 57
John P. K. Otis, labor for Engineer, 3 85
H. D. Parker, dinners,   92 00
Pay Roll, witnesses,   10 66
Pay Roll, services collecting statistics
 for Union Depot,   119 00
Geo. F. Peck, carpentering,   489 94
People's Club, rent of Brinley Hall, 150 00
J. L. Pinkham, oil cloth,   1 96
Willard F. Pond, damages,   70 00
Albert K. Ramsdale, damages, 100 00
Geo. Raymond, paper, tapes &c., 176 34
Charles Reed, labor,   18 75
Fred. Revere, gilding ball for flag-staff, 2 00
George Rome, damages,   100 00
J. D. Russell, pump &c.,   17 78
Patrick Ryan, damages,   79 21
Saint Paul's church use of Mechanics Hall, 60 00
Sanford & Co., books and sundries, 133 12
Joseph Santom, Jr., & Co., wood, 1 00
H. H. Samn & Son, pipe, labor &c.. 21 00
George Sessions, returning deaths,
 casket &c.,   172 90
Nathaniel Sessions, services as inspector, 360 00
R. R. Shepard, services as sealer of
 weights and measures and sundries, 483 76
Chas. Smith, brooms,   9 00
Hattie A. Smith, writing,   57 25
M. B. Smith, labor,   66 14
Samuel Smith, recording births,
 marriages, and deaths, and
 Cash paid for sundries,   592 97
T. H. Smith, labor,   6 00
W. F. Spring, ringing bell, July 4th, 5 00
Staples & Goulding, services, 25 00
State Guards, rent of Armory, 41 67
Geo. E. Stearns, services as Asst.
 Assessor,   30 00

42

Paid Martha Z. Swallow, services for Assessor, $136 50
"   "   "   copying old Records,   27 00
"   "   "   services for Treasurer, 85 50
Tateum & Horgan, monument and
        curbing,   1,295 00
Geo. Thrall, dinners,   271 00
E. A. Timme, seal,   2 00
Maria Trask, services for Assessor,   9 00
S. P. R. Triscott, labor,   379 99
N. G. Tucker, repairs,   9 39
Samuel Utley, services,   144 70
Gill Valentine, services as sealer,   25 00
Geo. F. Verry, professional services,   500 00
Wakefield & Goodnow, labor and lumber, 51 98
James H. Wall, Agt., rent of halls,   300 00
F.W.Ward, services in Treasurer's office, 825 00
W. Ansel Washburn, Cash paid out,   15 35
L. H. Wells, casting,   1 29
J. S. Wesby, binding,   3 50
Geo. W. Wheeler, services for Engineer, 1,357 21
Geo. W. Wheeler, Cash paid for
        stamps, express &c.   160 06
Geo. W. Wheeler, Jr., tolling bell,   2 00
Mary G. B. Wheeler, services for
        Treasurer,   128 00
G. Henry Whitcomb, & Co., envelopes,   14 90
Chas. Whittemore, use of ward room,   49 50
Alex. H. Wilder, furnishing list for
        Assessors,   42 50
Emery Wilson, Cash paid out,   63 85
Albert Wood, professional services,   30 00
T. M. Woodward, shades, lettering &c., 165 50
Worcester Brass Band, services,   473 00
Worcester Co., Mechanics Association,
        use of Hall,   35 00
Worcester Ice Co., Ice,   16 04
Worcester National Band, services,   200 00
Worcester Steam Boiler Works, iron
        cement and labor,   24 85
Worcester Water Works, use of water
        City Hall,   40 00
Worcester Water Works, use of water
        hydrants,   8,000 00
Worcester Water Works, use of water
        watering troughs,   245 00
Worcester Water Works, use of water
        masons use High School,   20 00
J. M. W. Yerrinton, report of hearings
        before railway committee,   230 50
                                                ————————
                                                        $38,214 53
                                                        ————————
Balance undrawn, January 1, 1872, $25,339 14
                                                        ————————

ENGINE HOUSE, Beacon Street,

Balance undrawn January 1, 1871,   2,095 00

Expenditures.

Paid Stephen Allen, Cash paid for labor,   15 00
 A. P. Cutting, plans and superintending, 70 00
 Charles H. Peck, balance of contract, 1,733 00
 Chas. H. & Geo. F. Peck, stock and
   labor,   209 13
 Water Works, putting in pipes,   20 76
 Transfer to Contingent Expenses,   47 11
                 $2,095 00

FIRE ALARM TELEGRAPH.

Appropriation.   14,000 00

Received from Bay State Fire Insurance Co.,   175 76
 Central " " " 240 77
 First National Fire " " 96 32
 Merchant and Farmers Fire
   Insurance Co.,   512 84
 Peoples Fire Insurance Co.,   529 69
 Worcester Fire Insurance Co., 1444 62
                $17,000 00

Expenditure.

Paid Gamewell & Co., putting up, $16,852 47
Transfer to Contingent Expenses,   147 53
                $17,000 00

FIRE DEPARTMENT.

Appropriation. $25,000 00
Received for Old Hose,   3 25
 From Highways for labor,   1,552 50
                $26,555 75

Expenditures.

Paid Ransom M. Gould, Chief Engineer
  salary, $550 00
 William Brophy, Engineer,   67 50
 Alzirus Brown, "   67 50
 Samuel H. Day, "   105 00
 William Knowles, "   67 50
 Members for services :
 Gov. Lincoln Co. Steamer 1, 6 mos.,   584 00
 C. J. Guild, Steward, &c.,   3 "   237 34
 Col. Davis Co., Steamer 2,   6 "   584 00
 A. B. Lovell Co., " 3,   6 "   584 00
 Stephen Allen, Steward &c., 11 "   737 92
 Rapid Engine Co., No· 2,   6 "   1,242 50
 City Hose Co., No. 1,   6 "   334 00

Ocean Hose Co., No. 2,	6	'	334 00
Eagle Hose Co., No. 3,	6	''	334 00
Niagara Hose Co., No., 4,	6	"	334 00
Yankee Hose Co., No. 5,	6	'.	329 00
Hook and Ladder Co., No. 1,	6	"	624 00
" " " " " 2,	6	"	624 00
Niagara, No. 3, Quinsigamond	6	"	60 00
Steamer 3, horse hire,			150 00
Rapid Engine Co., No. 2, horse hire,			18 00
City Hose Co., No. 1, horse hire,			26 00
Ocean Hose Co., No. 2, horse hire,			26 00
Eagle Hose Co., No. 3, horse hire,			32 00
Niagara Hose Co., No. 4, horse hire,			26 00
Yankee Hose Co., No. 5, horse hire,			36 00
Hook and Ladder Co., No. 1, horse hire,			45 00
" " " " " 2, horse hire,			45 00
William Hoyle, giving 9 alarms,			9 00
George M. Jewell, giving 10 alarms,			10 00
Wm. Stevenson, giving 13 alarms,			13 00
Geo. A. Wheeler, Jr., giving 11 alarms,			11 00
Geo. T. Aitchison, repairs,			29 90
Allen & Reed, hose, packing &c.,			28 31
Albert F. Allen, hose,			95 73
Charles Allen, labor, straps &c.,			56 96
M. B. Allen, wood,			17 42
Ames Plow Co., wheeljack,			4 00
Arcade Malleable Iron Co., castings,			26 34
Bacon & Forbes, wood,			5 30
Chas. L. Bacon, wood,			7 50
Barrett, Washburn & Co., labor, pipe and sundries,			119 87
N. T. Bemis & Co., horse hire,			3 00
Blake Brothers, labor,			8 75
James Boyd & Sons, hose,			361 80
Brown & Barnard, carting,			2 00
W. H. Brown, repairing,			271 74
J. L. Burbank, vitriol,			49 10
J. A. Carpenter, labor,			11 50
John Chaplin, repairing,			7 45
Joseph Chase & Co., dusters,			12 75
John D. Chollar, chairs and mattresses,			98 25
Corbett & Willard, repairing hose carriage,			2 65
C. A. Cummings, keys,			10 50
J. B. Cummings, ladders,			10 00
Doe & Woodwell, advertising,			75
Lyman W. Eager, driving team,			192 50
John Fay, trucking hose,			1 00
Fish & Cogger, nuts for steamer,			1 05
Henry C. Fish, rods &c.,			1 25

aid C. Foster & Có., sundries,	$47	18
Thomas D. Gard, badges,	21	60
E. L. Gates, lumber,	3	50
Josiah Gates & Sons, hose,	1,335	44
D. Gay, hay and straw,	99	10
W. H. Gay, hay and straw,	207	38
R. M. Gould, cash paid out,	8	10
Graton & Knight, repairing hose,	203	00
Greene & Jordan, pipe, labor &c.,	6	65
M. B. Greene & Co., vitriol, sulphate,		
copper &c.	94	93
H. T. Harrington, hay,	47	51
L. A. Hastings, belts and straps,	11	50
O. L. Hatch, corn and oats,	535	22
Charles Hooker, hay,	129	60
G. S. & A. J. Howe, oil,	50	67
Willard Humes, paint and labor,	8	85
B. E. Hutchinson, hose straps and belts,	19	90
Gerry Hutchinson, paper, paint, labor &c.,	57	19
Jenkins & Whitcomb, maps,	1	25
John W. Jordan, sundries,	51	52
W. H. Jourdan, coal,	45	00
John G. Kendall, Agt. insuring,	24	50
Kinnicutt & Co., lanterns &c.,	23	38
L. J. Knowles & Bro., screws,	8	00
J. B. Lawrence & Co., bed and pillows,	6	00
Learned & Clough, labor, plank &c.,	48	34
Alexander Lorimer, rope, packing &c.	62	00
A. B. Lovell, labor, pipe and sundries,	107	32
J. D. Lovell, shovel, brushes,	11	10
Jerome Marble & Co., oil,	24	56
Reynolds McAleer, straps,	4	20
H. W. Miller, springs &c.,	1	75
New York Fire Engine Hose Co., hose,	1,147	15
Henry C. Oliver, repairs and sundries,	101	24
John O'Meara, repairing,	13	00
Geo. F. Peck, carpentering,	45	86
Sumner Pratt & Co, waste and packing,	12	50
Darius Putnam, sundries,	2	14
Chas. G. Reed, wood and wheels,	22	25
T. H. Reed, labor, pipe and sundries,	40	27
Rice, Barton & Fales M. & I. Co.,		
labor, iron &c.,	444	49
John Rockwood, hay,	26	48
Samuel Ryan, "	40	80
Sanford & Co., record,	4	50
J. Santom Jr. & Co., wood,	1	35
Clark, Sawyer & Co., lantern,	1	25
James D. Shaw, labor,	20	00
William B. Shaw,	10	50

Paid Sheldon & Bartlett, stock and labor,	$9	10
Charles Shippee, services as steward,	325	00
Snow Brothers, printing,	83	85
Austin Sprague, hay,	25	90
F. G. Stiles, repairing,	61	80
Strong & Rogers, coal,	298	80
George, T. Sutton, repairing &c.,	86	49
S. Taft & Son, sundries,	51	09
R, C. Taylor, oil,	76	13
Fred A. Thomas, carting hose &c.,	7	25
A. Tolman & Co., repairs &c.,	66	10
Isaac Tower, hay,	112	61
E. J. Watson, labor,	68	88
H. B. Wellington, blacksmithing,	84	94
L. H. Wells, brass, copper &c.,	215	24
J. A. Wilkinson, labor,	15	00
T. M. Woodward, shades and fixtures,	158	25
Wor. Gas Light Co., gas,	343	36
Wor. Highway Dep't, labor and material,	471	60
Wor. Steam Boiler works, labor, iron &c.,	80	40
Wor. Water Works, use of water,	123	00
putting in pipe,	57	79

$17,747 24

Balance undrawn January, 1 1872,   8,808 41

FREE PUBLIC LIBRARY.

Balance undrawn January 2, 1871.	$5,073	43
Appropriation,	8,000	00
Amount of Dog Licenses,	1,777	50

$14,850 93

EXPENDITURES.

Paid Samuel S. Green, salary as Librarian,	$1,594	80
Sarah F. Earle, " " Assistant,	366	67
" " extra services,	50	00
Emma S. Eddy, salary as Assistant,	458	34
Jessie E. Tyler, " " "	366	67
Edward G. Allen, books,	213	55
James Austin & Co., burners,	7	25
Backus Historical Society, books,	5	00
Z. Baker, services,	66	00
Barrett, Washburn & Co., steam apparatus &c.,	1,931	52
L. H. Bigelow, books,	400	22
William Blake & Co., brackets,	61	00
Otis Bramhall, iron fence &c.,	156	96
R. H. Chase, labor,	213	43
James W. Christopher, books,	15	81
Clark, Sawyer & Co., shades, burners	15	00

Paid J. Colbath & Co., hose, pipe &c., $26 33
  Doe & Woodwell, advertising,   5 50
  Earle & Fuller, services,   38 00
  Edward R. Fiske, printing,   13 50
  C. Foster & Co., padlocks and screws,   8 35
  Hair Brothers, repairing gas fixtures,   6 57
  W. M. Hall & Sons, wood,   15 25
  Charles Hamilton, printing,   42 50
  S. D. Harris, care of building,   176 00
  R. Hollings & Co., Lanterns,   41 38
  W. R. Huntington, books,   3 00
  M. M. Joslyn, "   3 37
  W. H. Jourdan, coal,   122 22
  Kinnicutt & Co., umbrella stands,   12 50
  Little, Brown & Co., books,   268 70
  H. F. Loomis, "   15 37
  A. B. Lovell, labor and materials,   186 21
  W. N. Mansir & Co., labor,   2 00
  Mathews & Chamberlain, labor,   1 00
  H. A. Palmer, carpentering,   182 03
  Edward A. Rice, books,   10 50
  H. G. Roche, on account of contract,   983 99
  Sanford & Co., books,   376 03
  C. A. Skinner, "   12 00
  Snow Brothers, printing,   59 73
  Strong & Rogers coal,   69 40
  Stone & Downer, brokerage &c.,   16 73
  Willard Ward, labor repairing,   5 06
  J. S. Wesby, binding,   655 04
  T. M. Woodward, numbers and painting,   85 21
  Wor. Gas Light Co., Gas,   731 12
  Wor. Highways, labor and materials,   174 86
  Wor. Water Works, service pipe and
   use of water,   33 24
            $10,294 91

Balance undrawn January 1, 1872, $4,556 02

FUEL, LIGHTS, PRINTING &c.

APPROPRIATION. $6,500 00
Received of Snow Brothers, amount
   advanced them,   400 00
            6,900 00

EXPENDITURES.

Paid American Bank Note, Co., engraving
   and printing, $270 00
  Bacon & Forbes, wood,   70
  J. D. Baldwin & Co., advertising,   163 23
  L. H. Bigelow, books,   21 20
  Doe & Woodwell, advertising,   25 40

Paid W. M. Hall & Sons, wood, $1 83
   Charles Hamilton, printing,   180 45
   Harkness & Fiske, posting bills,   8 00
   W. H. Jourdan, coal,   202 05
   J. S. C. Knowlton, advertising,   71 75
   Sanford & Co., books &c.,   34 81
   Snow Brothers, printing, paper &c.,   2,478 38
   Strong & Rogers, coal,   610 21
   Tyler & Seagrave, printing,   103 53
   J. S. Wesby, binding,   63 20
   G. Henry Whitcomb, envelopes,   18 90
   Worcester Evening Gazette, advertising,   115 22
   Worcester Gas Light Co.,Gas,   1,520 70
                                                   $5,889 56

Balance undrawn January 1, 1872, $1,010 44

HIGHWAYS.

Appropriation, $35,000 00
   "   for paving,   20,000 00
   "   " sidewalks,   50,000 00
Received from Commissioner for sundries,   351 78
      Corporation and individuals
        for putting down side-
        walks, &c.   24,126 99
      St. Paul's Church, for labor,
        materials &c.,   765 12
    for Oxen,   375 00
      Brick and Stone,   1,677 76
      Wagon,   100 00
      Scrapings, earth, labor &c.,   1,016 48
    from Contingent Expenses,   10 30
      Fire Department,   471 60
      Library,   174 86
      Paupers,   500 00
      Schools,   269 90
      School House, Belmont St.,   2,043 90
      New High School House,   27 25
      Old   "   "   "   381 00
      Sewers,   737 68
      Shade Trees,   275 10
      Streets, Chandler,   3,698 90
        "   Front,   3,556 62
        "   Hanover,   3,335 70
        "   Lafayette,   1,389 05
        "   Main,   1,344 71
        "   Mechanic,   578 00
        "   Oak Avenue,   477 65
        "   Piedmont,   734 30
        "   Salisbury,   2,456 95

Received from Streets, Sever,	$281 90	
" Washington,	1,005 50	
" Wilmot,	1,087 70	
Water Works,	69 49	
		$158,321 09

EXPENDITURES.

Paid David F. Parker, salary as commis.	$2,291 67
Pay Rolls, labor of men,	38,897 35
Geo. T. Aitchison, repairing carts, wagons &c.,	629 00
Aldrich & Co., oats,	36 50
Moses B. Allen, labor,	478 87
Ames Plow Co., repairs and castings,	33 26
Andrews & Litchfield, curbstone and paving blocks,	4,716 32
C. K. Babcock, moving buildings,	987 00
W. C. Barbour & Co., paving-stones,	887 24
Wm. T. Barber, plank,	39 64
Barrett, Washburn & Co., labor, pipe &c.,	26 93
John Barry, plank,	29 56
James Bates, cobbles,	19 50
A. J. Bemis, repairing picks &c.,	4 25
James H. Benchley, hay,	203 03
H. A. Bennett, labor and use of team,	670 00
Joseph Bennett, labor, mortar &c.,	208 95
L. H. Bigelow, stationary,	20 11
Blake Brothers, crusher,	32 00
B. J. Blanchard, short corners,	30 35
Edward E. Bliss, boarding cattle,	2 00
Frank Bolio, cobbles,	8 75
J. Bond, paving stones,	11 00
J. E. Bond, exchange on oxen,	75 00
Boston & Albany R. R. Co., freight,	30 00
Boston, Barre & Gardner R. R. Co., gravel,	38 67
Boston, Hartford & Erie R. R. Co., freight,	34 13
G. M. Brackett, professional services,	7 00
J. H. Brooks, labor,	11 00
Brophy & Geer, grinding meal,	47 00
Brown & Barnard, labor, man and team,	618 50
Geo. Brown, labor,	22 80
R. W. Caine, paving stones,	185 48
John Carney, painting,	3 00
John, Cavanaugh, moving houses,	200 00
Chamberlain & Co., paving stone and lumber,	178 45
E. F. Chamberlain, paving stone,	38 55
James S. Chamberlain, curb and freight,	152 17
Lewis Chapin, removing snow,	6 00
Cheney & Gray, oil and wicks,	4 09

Paid John S. Clark & Son, corn, cement and lime,	$409	42
Cochran & Russ, brick,	384	00
E. Converse, labor, man and team,	234	50
Sumner Cook, labor,	23	30
Corbett & Willard, repairing cart &c.,	5	90
John Corless, labor,	138	88
E. B. Crane, lumber,	5	13
E. N. Cummings, brick,	3,178	00
Marcus Curtis, labor on roads,	3	50
C Dakin, cobbles,	33	00
H. W. Davis, " and labor on roads,	21	56
Rufus Davis Jr. & Co., lumber,	482	46
Dexter & Whipple, rent of land,	20	00
J. A. Dodge, hay,	432	25
Doe & Woodwell, advertising,	13	41
James Downey, cobbles,	49	13
John Doyle, labor,	45	00
S. B. Dudley, hay,	4	00
Charles Duston, brick,	27	00
Dutton and Austin, exchange of oxen	127	50
Nelson & Estey, cobbles, and labor,	289	86
Fish & Cogger, repairing gratings,	14	50
Henry C. Fish, grate bars &c.,	23	90
Charles Flannegan, labor, men and team,	990	00
Samuel Fletcher, paving blocks,	747	35
Thomas Flynn, labor with team,	706	50
N. F. Foster, labor on road,	1	00
C. Foster & Co., saw and sundries,	25	93
Garfield & Parker, lumber and labor,	1343	23
M. Garfield Estate, sundries,	25	92
John Gates & Co. lumber,	4	17
Jessie Gault, brick,	3275	50
L. Gay, straw,	99	29
Henry F. Geer, grinding corn and meal,	52	52
Graton & Knight, repairing belt &c.,	1	50
Elijah Hammond, hay,	2	50
L. B. Hapgood, one ox,	143	00
Samuel D. Harding, building wall &c.,	76	75
Stephen Harrington, curb-stone,	4	50
Jonas Hartshorn, labor on road,	9	30
O. L. Hatch, meal, corn and oats,	1078	34
Natt. & W. F. Head, brick,	3064	95
Carmi Heald, labor with team,	1279	50
William Heaton, labor on road,	2	50
A. Y. Hebard, flagging,	210	00
E. G. & F. W. Higgins, paper and labor,	9	60
Holden & Brother, potatoes,	3	00
J. W. Hooper, cobbles,	45	00

George S. Hoppin & Co., oats, feed &c., 411 25
George W. Howes, repairs of building, 4 50
Gerry Hutchinson, brick, glass, etc., 54 39
F. A. & J. N. Ingerson, flagging and
  curbing, 32 25
Jersey City Steel Co., picks and handles, 19 60
J. W. Jordan, labor, lantern globes, and
  Sundries, 126 32
Kinnicutt & Co., shovels, nails, Etc., 125 57
E. & J. Kitteredge, brick, 648 00
John Kerr, mason-work, 19 93
John Kneeland, relaying wall, 450 00
P. Langlois, repairing picks Etc., 11 15
Learned & Clough, labor, 3 50
E. G. Leathers, gravel and cobbles, 49 40
Melvin M. Lee, labor with team, 200 50
Ann K. Leonard, labor, 11 00
James L. Libbey, cobbles, 80 00
Alex. Lorimer, rope and repairing, 9 50
A. B. Lovell, pipe, lime and labor, 253 77
J. D. Lovell, shovels picks and sundries, 233 92
Daniel Mack, hay, 90 79
Mann & Bigelow, stone, 412 81
A. G. Mann, paving blocks, 15,474 08
Jerome Marble & Co., oil &c., 60 69
Loring Martin, labor with team, 261 00
Charles Marvin, writing, 33 00
D. P. Matthews, two boxes compound &c. 8 80
James Maxwell, curbstone, 614 78
William May, gravel, 1 50
W. H. Maynard & Co., corn, 362 66
Reynolds McAleer, repairing and
  sundries, 234 66
John McCarty, labor with team, 1,011 00
James McCormick, labor on road, 13 00
John McGrath, labor with team, 577 50
Michael McGrath, excavating, 263 60
Melaven & Langlois, repairing tools &c., 32 21
W. F. Merrifield, sawing, 72 99
Henry W. Miller, shovels, 34 75
G. H. Mills, labor and material for fence, 193 47
J. L. Munroe & Co., lumber, 583 75
John W. Monroe, wagon and cart, 340 00
John Murray, labor on road, 2 50
Muzzy & Co., repairing tools, 30 92
C. A. & N. M. Muzzy, blacksmithing, 383 32
Ezekiel Newton, cobbles, 342 65
Norcross Brothers, labor and materials, 250 83
A. H. Nourse, relaying wall, 280 00
W. F. Oakley, paving stones, 26 59

Paid John B. O'Leary, shoeing &c.,	$464	70
John O'Meara, cart body &c.,	20	75
A. Parker, labor and materials,	34	72
D. F. Parker, cash paid for hay and		
sundries,	475	63
Dexter H. Perry, stone drags,	27	00
Joseph S. Perry, cobbles,	51	00
J. W. & E. G. Pettigrew, potatoes,	15	60
S. W. Phetteplace, filing saws,	4	00
Willard F. Pond, hay and paving stone,	61	88
Michael Powers, excavating,	882	40
Pratt & Hammond, labor and curb,	471	12
Pratt & Inman, iron, steel and hammers,	19	25
Noah Prescott, paving blocks,	541	11
Prov. & Wor. R. R. Co., freight,	2	65
Samuel Putnam, flagstone,	241	20
Michael Quinn, blacksmithing,	44	60
J. J. Randall, laying concrete walk,	1,847	20
J. Ray, resetting fence,	5	00
David Reed, paving blocks and curb,	1,374	39
William Reed, paving blocks and curb,	1,161	23
Rice, Barton & Fales, pipe and labor,	23	00
Curtis Rice, hay,	192	78
Dexter Rice, painting signs,	1	50
S. Richards, repairing carriage,	3	50
Chas. O. Richardson, paving, setting		
curb &c.	19,075	35
F. Riley, hay,	300	86
G. L. Robbins, flagstone,	441	45
Maxcy Robbins, oats,	70	00
W. L. Robbins, relaying wall,	591	60
P. & W. Sargent, brick,	232	00
Sylvanus Sears, labor on road,	2	00
J. Q. A. Sexton, brick,	105	00
R. R. Shepard, powder,	47	49
C. W. & J. E. Smith, pair oxen,	290	00
Eli S. Smith, cleaning vault,	5	00
Snow Brothers, printing,	36	60
John P. Stockwell, straw,	85	12
L. B. Stone, labor,	125	25
Francis P. Stowell, labor,	9	00
Strong & Rogers, coal,	81	03
C. B. Sweetser, cobbles,	15	92
C. F. Sylvester, labor and cobbles,	232	53
J. M. Symonds, paving stone,	50	32
Calvin Taft, storage of paving blocks,	25	00
Stephen Taft & Son, oil and sundries,	28	99
Joseph A. Tenney, labor with team,	901	50
E. R. Thompson, running engine,	60	00
Samuel B. Thompson, curbstone,	1,463	55

Paid Town of Shrewsbury, oxen, $210 00
Tyler & Seagrave, printing,   8 00
Andrew J. Waite, labor,   73 80
E. B. Walker, curbstone,   1,153 71
Church Wallis, cleaning public market,   36 00
William Ward, keeping oxen,   6 25
H. B. Wellington, blacksmithing,   400 48
J. W. Wetherell, straw and railing,   131 39
Wm. F. Wheeler, stone crusher &c.,   18 92
A. L. Whiting & Co., picks,   21 00
Fred. G. Williams, horse,   225 00
Samuel Winslow. oats,   99 18
D. M. Woodward, labor, curbstone &c.,   668 56
Wor. Fire Dept., labor men and team,   1,552 50
Wor. Gas Light Co., gas,   56 20
Wor. & Nashua R. R. Co., freight,   6,744 85
Wor. Poor Dept., oxen,   230 00
Wor. Water Works, use of water,   90 00
"   "   "   pipe, labor &c.,   19 57
Jeptha Wright, curbstone,   295 54
                                                              $140,104 29

Balance undrawn January 1, 1872, $18,216 80

NEW STREETS.

Appropriation,   10,000 00

EXPENDITURES.

Transfer to James Street,   2,176 00
"   " Oak Avenue,   477 65
"   " Piedmont Street,   734 30
"   " Salisbury   "   2,456 95
"   " Seaver   "   281 90
"   " Washington   "   1,005 50
                                                               $7,132 30

Balance undrawn January 1, 1872, $2,867 70

BLACKSTONE STREET.

Paid Jeremiah Clifford, damages and land, $601 98
Isaac Davis,   "   "   "   687 28
Dennis Driscoll, heirs of, damages
            and land,   650 00
Daniel Foley, damages and land,   692 00
Ellen Healy, damages and land,   502 00
Martin Kilden, damages and land,   300 00
Alexander Lorimer, damages and land, 1,400 00
                                                               $4,833 26

Amount overdrawn January 1, 1872, $4,833 26

CHANDLER STREET.

EXPENDITURES.

Amount overdrawn January 2, 1871,	$9,064 40	
Paid Highway Department, labor &c.,	3,698 90	
Paid Elisha Robbins, damages,	10 000	
		$12,863 30

Amount overdrawn January 1, 1872,	$12,863 30

CHATHAM AND CORBETT STREETS.

Received for Betterments,	$5,461 66

EXPENDITURES.

Amount overdrawn January 2, 1871,	$14,000 44
Amount overdrawn January 1, 1872,	$8,538 78

FRONT STREET.

EXPENDITURES.

Paid Barrett, Washburn & Co., labor,	$2 64	
John Cavanagh, moving buildings,	4,800 00	
Hiram Fobes. damages and moving buildings,	2,650 00	
Edward Halloran & wife, damages and moving buildings,	220 00	
Highway Department, labor &c.,	3,556 62	
John Marra, damages and moving buildings,	100 00	
Mary A. Noyes, damages and moving buildings,	575 00	
Charles and Betsey Prentice, land damages and moving buildings,	5,756 00	
		$17,660 26

Amount overdrawn January 1, 1872,	$17,660 26

HANOVER STREET.

EXPENDITURES.

Paid Highway Department, grading filling &c.,	$3,335 70	
Edward Earle, land and damages,	566 25	
Stephen C. Earle, land and damages,	228 85	
Harrison G. Otis, " " "	703 60	
Gilbert Walker, " " "	583 18	
Betsey Willard and Hannah Upham, land and damages,	1,107 40	
		$6,524 98

Amount overdrawn January 1, 1872,	$6,524 98

JAMES STREET.

Transfer from New Streets, $2,176 00

EXPENDITURES.

Paid Benjamin James, making street, $2,176 00

LAFAYETTE STREET.

EXPENDITURES.

Paid Highway Department, grading and labor,			$1,389 05
Peter C. Bacon,	land and damages,		76 50
Alexander Belisle,	"	" "	34 34
Thomas Bennett and wife, land and damages,			25 90
L. Brautigam,	land and damages,		46 90
John Carroll,	"	" "	76 74
Richard Conlon,	"	" "	79 00
Abigail Creamer,	"	" "	176 96
Timothy Cummings,	land and damages,		78 13
Catharine Duffey,	"	" "	41 28
E. P. Fitzgerald,	"	" "	32 80
Patrick Hardigan,	"	" "	46 80
John Healy,	"	" "	161 20
L. C. Howard,	"	" "	91 00
Charles Huber,	"	" "	650 41
Thomas Kelley,	land and damages,		95 13
Timothy Leary,	"	" "	80 00
Patrick Maher,	"	" "	114 75
Maurice Mahony,	"	" "	107 40
Elias, Marshall,	"	" "	19 70
Alex. Monehan,	"	" "	124 50
Chas. L. Redding,	"	" "	215 60
Michael Reynolds,	"	" "	104 32
Patrick Ryan,	"	" "	92 88
C. D. Sullivan,	"	" "	111 75
Charles Wunderlich,	"	"	191 20

Amount overdrawn, January 1, 1872, $4,264 24

MAIN STREET.

EXPENDITURES.

Amount overdrawn January 2, 1871, $22,729 89
     Paid Highway Department, grading, wall &c.,   1,344 71

                              $24,074 60

Amount overdrawn January, 1 1872, $24,074 60

MECHANIC STREET.

Received for betterments, $6,303 77

EXPENDITURES.

Amount overdrawn January 2, 1872,	$11,958 28	
Paid Highway Department, grading,	578 00	
Henry C. Fish, allowance on betterment,	111 96	
Wall & Brinley, " " "	25 95	
		$12,673 19

Amount overdrawn January 2, 1872,	$6,369 42

OAK AVENUE.

Transfer from New Streets,	$477 65

EXPENDITURES.

Paid Highway Department, grading,	477 65

PIEDMONT STREET.

Transfer from New Streets,	$734 30

EXPENDITURES.

Paid Highway Department, grading,	734 30

SALISBURY STREET.

Transfer from New Streets,	$2,456 95

EXPENDITURES.

Paid Highway Department, grading &c.,	2,456 95

SEVER STREET.

Transfer from New Streets,	$281 90

EXPENDITURES.

Paid Highway Department, grading &c.,	281 90

UNION STREET.

Received of Catharine Dolan, for house,	$400 00	
" " Stephen Salisbury, " land,	1,000 00	

EXPENDITURES.

Amount overdrawn January 2, 1871,	$13,696 91	
Paid Michael Doyle, land and damages,	728 75	
Michael Early, " " "	620 70	
Jonathan Webb, heirs of, " "	941 75	
Clarissa Wellington, land and damages,	500 00	
John Winter, " " "	256 10	
		$16,744 21

Amount overdrawn January 1, 1872,	$15,344 21

WASHINGTON STREET.

Transfer from New Streets,	$1,005 50

EXPENDITURES.

Paid Highway Department, grading &c.,	1,005 00

WILMOT STREET.

EXPENDITURES.

Paid C. K. Babcock, moving house,	$75 00	
Highway Department, grading,	1,087 70	
Clara A. Lane, land and damages,	704 18	
Michael Verden, " " "	367 20	
		$2,234 08
Amount overdrawn January, 1872,		$2,234 08

WINTER STREET.

Received for Betterments,	$1,288 27

INTEREST.

Appropriation,	$90,000 00	
Received interest on taxes,	568 31	
from David S. Messinger,	1,140 00	
Wor. Safe Dep, and Trust Co.,	1,904 09	
		$93,612 40

EXPENDITURES.

Amount overdrawn January 2, 1871,	$33,000 00
Paid Josiah W. Allen, Estate of,	72 31
American Antiquarian Society,	600 00
Artemas D. Baker,	12 50
Emory Banister, Administrator,	487 08
Frederic J. Barnard,	118 00
Adaline Barnes,	83 34
E. P. B. or bearer,	1,200 00
Bearer,	617 50
B. B. & Co. or bearer,	2,250 00
Boston, Barre & Gardner R. R. Co.,	302 74
Mary Ann L. Brown,	60 50
Emeline Burnett,	37 07
Central Mut. Fire Ins. Co.,	688 72
City National Bank,	45 00
County of Worcester,	161 96
Caleb Dana, Estate of,	27 00
Isaac Davis,	387 61
Mary H. E. Davis,	46 00
Samuel DeWitt,	105 00
William Dickinson,	336 52
Daniel Farnum,	128 33
Sally Flagg,	162 00
Anna R. S. Fox.	120 00
Maria Fox,	210 00
Hannah Fowler,	50 53
J. H. Gerauld Estate of,	60 00

44

Paid William H. Gould,	$15 00
G. A. R. G. H. Ward Post No. 10,	174 53
Green Library Fund,	450 39
Eliza F. Hamilton,	180 00
Elijah Hammond,	54 00
Samuel F. Haven,	60 00
Alonzo Hill, Estate of,	98 19
Home Savings Bank,	6,140 83
Eleanor D. Knight,	60 90
Hiram Knight,	600 00
Lee Savings Bank,	720 00
D. Waldo, Lincoln Ext.	431 36
Hannah B. Lynde,	60 00
Mary G. Lynde, Estate of,	24 00
George C. Macy,	50 00
Mechanics Savings Bank,	4,487 63
Mer. & Farmers' Mut. Ins. Co.,	1,966 91
Merchants National Bank,	1,885 42
Elizabeth C. B. Miller,	196 17
New Bedford Inst. for Savings,	1,291 67
New England Mut. Life Ins. Co.,	14,500 00
John C. Newton, Treasurer,	72 00
Nathaniel Paine, Trustee,	1,187 73
David F. Parker,	267 63
Peabody Museum Fund,	397 45
People's Fire Insurance Co.,	73 88
People's Savings Bank,	927 74
Mary M. E. Pond,	36 29
H. R. or bearer,	132 00
Charles A. Rallion,	131 01
George W. Richardson, Treasurer,	258 67
H. E. Richardson,	3 13
Stephen Salisbury,	190 83
Angeline A. Sawyer,	188 40
Stephen Sawyer,	142 14
Lucie E. Smith,	27 00
Samuel Smith, Guardian,	41 09
State Mut. Life Assurance Co.,	4,765 59
Samuel V. Stone, Guardian,	15 00
Azubah H. Swallow,	66 00
Louisa H. Thompson,	113 75
Albert Tolman & Co.,	78 00
George Upham,	30 00
Gill Valentine,	12 50
Benjamin Wallace,	30 00
Erastus W. Wheeler,	37 57
Winslow & Hammond, Ext.,	30 00
Josephus Woodcock,	60 00
J. and L. Woodcock & Co.,	60 00
Jane I. Woodward,	120 00

Paid Wor. Co. Free Inst., of Industrial
    Science, $4,534 07
    Wor. Co. Inst., for Savings,   4,781 71
    Wor. Five Cents Savings Bank, 9,035 02
    Wor. Safe Dep. and Trust Co., 3,826 64
                                     ————— $106,489 45

Amount overdrawn January 1, 1872,   12,877 05

INTEREST ON WATER INVESTMENT.

Balance undrawn January 2, 1871,   170 30
Transfer from Water Rents,   32,360 78
                                     ————— $32,531 08

EXPENDITURES.

Paid Albert Ball,	36 00
Stephen Bartlett, Estate of	114 00
Joseph S. Barney, Extr.,	80 50
B. B. & Co., or bearer,	2,430 00
Bearer,	465 00
George Brown,	1,140 00
John Claflin,	60 00
Louisa Culver,	204 00
Mary H. E. Davis,	90 00
Samuel DeWitt,	135 00
Joseph B. Drury,	60 00
Clarinda S. Fiske,	60 00
Free Public Library,	300 00
Dennis Harthan,	102 00
High School Fund,	165 00
David Hitchcock,	150 00
John Jepherson,	810 00
Catharine Jones,	13 90
Hiram Knight,	180 00
Lee Savings Bank,	600 00
Charles Marvin,	60 00
Mechanics Savings Bank,	1,560 83
Mer. & Farmer's Mut. Fire Ins. Co.,	1,270 00
New Bedford Inst. for Savings,	1,066 66
Nathaniel Paine, Trustee,	100 00
Peabody Museum Fund,	270 00
People's Savings Bank,	1,200 00
John E. Phelps,	60 00
Sumner Reed,	48 00
Mary Smith,	48 17
Joseph Sprague,	780 00
Sarah D. Spurr,	39 00
State Mut. Life Assurance Co.,	9,950 00
Ethan R. Thompson,	72 00
George Upham,	230 00

Paid Edwin Waite,	$350 00	
Luther Wheelock,	300 00	
George Wight,	39 00	
Josephus Woodcock,	111 84	
Worcester Academy,	120 00	
Wor. Co., Institution for Savings,	4,830 00	
Wor. Five Cents Savings Bank,	2,855 00	
Wor. Co., Free Inst., of Ind., Science,	420 00	
		$32,975 90

Amount overdrawn January 1, 1872, $444 82

LICENSES.

Received from City Clerk,	1,756 00	
" " Co. Treasurer. dogs,	1,777 50	
" " Pomeroy E. Howland,	25 00	
		$3,558 50

EXPENDITURES.

Transfer to Free Public Library,	1,777 50	
" " Contingent Expenses,	1,456 69	
Paid Doe & Woodwell, advertising,	1 31	
John D. Chollar, chair,	14 00	
Stephen Smith, desk and book case,	300 00	
Snow Brothers, printing,	9 00	
		$3,558 50

LIGHTING STREETS.

Appropriation,	$20,000 00	
Received of E. Converse, repairing lantern,	7 25	
M. E. Daly, " "	24 07	
James Dunn, " ."	22 94	
Wilson & Rawson, "	4 50	
		$20,058 76

EXPENDITURES.

To amount overdrawn January 2, 1871,	$9,051 99	
Paid Barrett, Washburn & Co., pipe, labor, &c.,	1,226 47	
L. H. Bigelow, journal,	6 40	
Joseph Chase, & Co. matches,	54 38	
Geo. H. Clark, glass,	16 00	
E. C. Cleveland, ladders, hooks and sundries,	71 10	
C. & J. A. Colvin, lamp posts and castings,	1,290 81	
Dawson & Guild. waste,	2 40	
Henry F. Edwards, pipe, tongs and wrench,	3 25	
E. Fisher & Sons, waste,	25 00	
C. Foster & Co., shears and knife,	3 10	

Paid John Gates & Co., posts, $52 95
Green & Jordan, pipe and labor, 135 46
J. W. Jordan, lamps, wicks, labor &c., 231 97
F. A. Kirby, lighting lamps, 5,589 54
"   "   "   labor setting glass, paint-
   ing &c., 477 90
F.A. Kirby oil, alcohol, burners &c., 507 96
Jerome Marble & Co. fluid, glass &c., 492 09
Phenix Plate Co., naptha, 24 75
T. H. Reed, baskets and wicks, 15 30
I. D. Russell, lanterns, 855 50
George Waine, turning posts, 37 04
Wakefield & Goodnow, repairing, &c., 23 89
T. M. Woodward, lettering glass for
   lamps, 13 80
Wor. Gas Light Co. gas for street lights, 7,193 59
"   "   "   "   U. S. excise tax, 719 31
"   "   "   "   laying pipe, &c., 677 79
$28,819 74

Amount overdrawn January 1, 1872, $8,760 98

LOANS: FUNDED AND TEMPORARY.

Funded City Debt.
Amount due January 2, 1871, $105,000 00
Received of New England Mutual Life
   Ins., Co., 500,000 00
   Wor. County Institution
      for Savings, 12,000 00
$617,000 00

EXPENDITURES.
Paid Artemas D. Baker, $500 00
   Samuel DeWitt, 1,500 00
   George C. Macy, 2,000 00
   Wor. Co., Institution for Savings, 12,000 00
$16,000 00

Amount due January 1, 1872, $601,000 00

FUNDED SEWER DEBT.

Amount due January 2, 1871, $239,500 00
Received of Adaline Barnes, 3,000 00
   Mary A. L. Brown, 2,000 00
   Merchants & Farmers Mut.
      Fire Ins., Co., 40,000 00
   New Bedford Institution for
      Savings, 40,000 00
   Nathaniel Paine, Trustee, 5,000 00
   Charles A. Rallion, 3,000 00
   Stephen Salisbury, 5,000 00

Received of Lucia E. Smith, $1,000 00
    State Mutual Life Assurance
      Co.,   110,000 00
    Wor. Co., Free Inst. of Indus-
      trial Science,   35,900 00
    Wor. Five Cents Savings Bank,   15,000 00

Amount due January 1, 1872,   **$499,400 00**

FUNDED WATER DEBT.

Amount due January 2, 1871,   475,600 00
Received of Joseph S. Barney, Extr.,   2,300 00
    Louisa Culver,   3,400 00
    Isaac Davis,   10,000 00
    Samuel Dewitt,   3,000 00
    John R. Jordan,   2,000 00
    Mechanics Savings Bank,   50,000 00
    Merchants & Farmers Mut.
      Fire Ins. Co.,   40,000 00
    New Bedford Inst., for Savings,   35,000 00
    Nathaniel Paine, Trustee,   10,000 00
    Mary Smith.   1,000 00
    Joseph Sprague,   500 00
    State Mutual Life Assur. Co.,   133,000 00
    S. B. W. or bearer,   1,000 00
    Josephus Woodcock,   1,000 00
    Wor. Co. Inst. for Savings,   50,000 00
    Wor. Five Cents Savings Bank,   2,000 00

                              $824,300 00

EXPENDITURES.

Paid Albert Ball,   500 00
    Stephen Bartlett, Estate of   3,800 00
    E. B. or bearer,   500 00
    Louisa Culver,   3,400 00
    Mary H. E. Davis,   3,000 00
    Catharine Jones,   300 00
    Charles Marvin,   2,000 00
    Mer. & Farmers Mut. Fire Ins. Co.,   5,000 00
    Joseph Sprague,   5,000 00
    Sarah D. Spurr,   1,300 00
    Worcester Academy,   4,000 00
    Worcester Five Cents Savings Bank,   1,000 00
                             $29,800 00

Amount due January 1, 1872,   **$794,500 00**

TEMPORARY LOAN.

Amount due January 2, 1871,	$1,079,708 04
Received of Frederic J. Barnard,	6,000 00
Emory Banister, Adm'r.,	5,000 00
Central Mutual Fire Ins. Co.,	12,500 00
City National Bank,	10,000 00
Isaac Davis,	6,500 00
Mary H. E. Davis,	2,000 00
William Dickinson,	5,000 00
Daniel Farnum,	8,800 00
Charles A. Garland, Agt.,	415 00
Parley Goddard, Estate of	5,000 00
G. A. R., Post 10, Relief fund,	1,175 00
Green Library Fund,	1,315 12
Emory Holbrook, (E. E.)	3,000 00
Home Savings Bank,	210,000 00
Mer. & Farmers Mut. Fire Ins., Co.,	50,000 00
Merchants National Bank,	100,000 00
Elizabeth C. B. Miller,	5,500 00
John C. Newton, Treasurer,	1,000 00
Nathaniel Paine, Trustee,	8,200 00
David F. Parker,	3,000 00
Mary M. Pond,	700 00
Charles L. Putnam,	10,000 00
H. E. Richardson,	200 00
Stephen Salisbury,	11,000 00
Stephen Salisbury, Treasurer,	10,727 52
Angeline A. Sawyer, Guardian,	1,200 00
Sarah F. D. Spurr,	450 00
State Board of Education,	15,000 00
State Mut. Life Assurance Co.,	35,000 00
Louisa H. Thompson,	3,500 00
Asa H. Waters,	6,000 00
J. Woodcock,	4,200 00
Wor. Co. Free Inst. of Industrial Science,	22,696 32
Worcester Five Cents Savings Bank,	127,000 00
Worcester National Bank,	35,000 00
Worcester Safe Deposit & Trust Co.,	175,000 00
	$1,981,787 00

EXPENDITURES.

Paid Josiah W. Allen, Estate of	1,550 00
Emory Banister, Administrator,	5,000 00
Frederic J. Barnard,	6,000 00
Boston, Barre & Gardner Rail Road,	6,000 00
Emeline Burnett,	800 00

Paid Central Mut. Fire Insurance Co.,	$12,500 00	
City National Bank,	10,000 00	
County of Worcester,	13,000 00	
Isaac Davis,	13,000 00	
Mary H. E. Davis,	2,000 00	
William Dickinson,	12,000 00	
Daniel Farnum,	4,400 00	
Hannah Fowler,	800 00	
Charles A. Garland, Agt.,	220 00	
G. A. R., Post 10,	2,000 00	
" " " " " Relief fund,	250 00	
Elijah Hammond,	1,000 00	
Alonzo Hill, Estate of	2,500 00	
Home Savings Bank,	135,000 00	
D. Waldo Lincoln, Ex'r.,	5,522 98	
Mechanics Savings Bank,	40,000 00	
Mer. & Farmers Mut. Fire Ins., Co.,	76,504 30	
Merchants National Bank,	175,000 00	
Nathaniel Paine, Trustee,	22,600 00	
David F. Parker,	6,017 38	
People's Fire Ins. Co.,	5,000 00.	
People's Savings Bank,	28,000 00	
Mary M. E. Pond,	700 00	
George W. Richardson,	1,000 00	
H. E. Richardson, Treasurer,	200 00	
Stephen Salisbury,	11,000 00	
Stephen Salisbury, Treasurer,	12,287 30	
Angeline A. Sawyer, Guardian,	900 00	
Stephen Sawyer,	2,500 00	
Samuel Smith, Guardian,	750 00	
State Mut. Life Assurance Co.,	372,000 00	
Gill Valentine,	100 00	
Erastus W. Wheeler,	700 00	
J. & L. Woodcock & Co.,	2,000 00	
Wor. Co. Institution for Savings,	74,500 00	
Wor. Co. Free Institute of Industrial Science,	78,596 32	
Wor. Five Cents Savings Bank,	111,000 00	
Wor. Safe Deposit & Trust Co.,	165,000 00	
		$1,419,898 28
Amount due January 1, 1872,		$561,888 72

Recapitulation of Debt January 1, 1872.

Funded City Debt,	601,000 00	
Sewer Debt,	499,400 00	
Water Debt,	794,500 00	
Notes on demand,	561,888 72	
		2,456,788 72

		7,515 00
3,276	26	
615	00	
748	00	
es, 2,591	00	
		$7,230 26
		284 74
$28,000	00	
144	00	
562	77	
48	75	
2	00	
36	00	
699	00	
427	00	
4,600	80	
1,386	35	
		$35,906 67
$1,466	63	
1,054	13	
1,008	37	
131	98	
268	02	
470	25	
607	75	
1,002	00	
1,002	00	
n. $809	87	
913	00	
918	50	

Paid Ezra Churchill, on duty	220 d. and n.	$605 00
R. M. Colby,	"	297	"	816 75
Ezra Combs,	"	331	"	910 25
Benj. Cook,	"	334	"	918 50
Chas. H. Draper,	"	266½	"	732 88
J. M. Dyson,	"	333¼	"	917 13
A. P. Eaton,	"	48	..	132 00
H.E.Fayerweather,	"	234	"	918 50
J. H. Flint,	"	333½	"	917 12
T. R. Foster,	"	334	"	918 50
C. A. Garland,	"	334	"	918 50
Jaalam Gates,	"	334	"	918 50
M. S. Greene	"	334	"	918 50
J. L. Hall,	"	333	"	915 75
Louis Harper,	"	329½	"	906 12
F. H. Harris	"	334	"	918 50
P. H.Hogan,	"	333	"	915 75
J. B. Hubbard,	"	232½	"	914 37
Clark Jillson	"	113½	"	312 13
G. W. Jillson,	"	273	"	750 75
W. H. Johnson,	"	334	"	918 50
Henry M. Leland,	"	59		162 25
E. D. McFarland.	"	334	"	918 50
S. W. Ranger	"	334	"	918 50
Peter Rice,	"	135	"	371 25
S. S. Sprague,	"	327½	"	900 63

MISCELLANEOUS.

Paid Henry J. Allen, services,	$32 50
C. Arnold, soap,	6 87
J. D. Baldwin &Co., advertising,	19 25
Barnard Sumner Co., blankets,	11 25
L. H. Bigelow, books and stationery,	11 29
Mrs. E. P. Brewer, repairing flag,	4 00
John D. Chollar, chairs and matrasses,	26 00
G. P. Critcherson, pictures,	3 50
Churchill & Morse, shades and cord,	8 00
John S. Clark & Son, lime and salt,	1 70
H. H. Comings, cash paid out,	24 82
H. H. Comings Treas., mirror,	32 00
C. A. Cummings, keys and repairs,	3 25
H. W. Denny & Co., repairing	27 25
Division No. 42, groceries,	7 06
Doe & Woodwell, advertising,	12 65
James M. Drennan, cash paid out,	52 99
Henry F. Edwards, labor and materials,	42 78
E. B. Fairbanks & Co., repairing,	6 40
Wm. H. Fitton, Pictures,	5 00
T. H. Gage, professional services,	5 00
Fred. Gagnon, advertising,	10 33
Geo. D. Hall, coffee,	1 50

Paid S. T. Howard & Co., use of teams, $1,346 50
E. Hemmenway, labor, 137 42
J. W. Jordan, labor, shades &c., 15 30
J. S. C. Knowlton, advertising, 5 00
Alex. Lorimer, rope, 3 15
A. B. Lovell, labor and cement, 48 15
Marsh, Talbot & Wilmarth, cloth, 87 00
Sumner W. Ranger, handcuffs, 7 00
Chas. Shepherd, blankets, 12 00
Snow Bros. printing, 36 55
C. H. Stearns, crackers, 184 48
Taft, Bliss & Rice, meals for state police, 19 60
S. Taft & Son, soap and oil, 2 55
Talbot, Wilmarth & Co, cloth, 550 07
N. G. Tucker, repairing, 1 50
A. J. Warfield, food furnished prisoners, 20 23
W. Ansel Washburn, cash paid out, 20 60
Mrs. A. Williams, washing, 7 50
Emery Wilson postage stamps, 6 00
Albert Wood, professional service, 5 00
Worcester Ice Co., ice, 19 12

$32,918 26

Amount undrawn January 1, 1872, $2,988 41

POOR DEPARTMENT.

Appropriation, 8,000 00
Received from cities, towns and individuals
for board, provisions, wood,
coal, and sundries furnished, 859 46
Received from Commonwealth, for support,
and burials, 1,540 87
Board of State Charities,
error in account, (check
returned,) 643 00
County, board of prisoners, 79 94
G. W. Gale, Admr. of Est.,
of J. Russ, 96 73
M. McKniff, 60 00
John Farwell, articles sold, 971 44
For Oxen, 230 00
Truant School, board of boys, 1,269 32

$13,750 76

EXPENDITURES.

Paid George W. Gale, salary as clerk, 916 67
"   "   " cash paid for allow-
ances, postage, &c., 557 66
Albert Wood, salary as City Physician, 641 67
"   " extra services in care of
small-pox. 700 00

Paid Board of State Charities, support of

paupers,	$643 00
State Lunatic Hospital, Taunton board,	258 40
" " ' Worcester "	585 67
State Nautical School, board for boys,	200 56
" Reform " Westboro' board	
for boys,	322 92
State Reform School Lancaster, board	
for girls,	45 00
Tewksbury Insane Receptacle, board,	524 00
Commonwealth support of paupers,	184 50
County board of prisoners,	25 42
City of Charlestown, support of paupers,	36 30
" " Chelsea, " " "	4 50
Town of Gardner, " " "	25 00
" " Grafton, " " "	33 01
" " Oxford, " " "	10 00
" " Waltham, " " "	60 00
" " West Brookfield support of	
paupers,	16 01

For support of persons out of Alms House :

Paid Barnard, Sumner & Co., dry goods,	5 00
Bemis & Co., shoes,	10 40
N. T. Bemis & Co. horse hire,	18 00
L. H. Bigelow, pencils and sundries,	8 05
Jerome Bottomly, groceries,	25 00
Brigham & Eames, "	5 00
William Brown, care of pauper,	30 00
J. L. Burbank, medicine,	5 05
E. P. Buss, groceries,	5 00
J. E. Carlton, "	12 00
N. H. Cutting, truss,	10 00
S. N. Davis, care of pauper,	16 00
J. Dennis & Co., meat,	6 00
Division No. 42, groceries,	1,168 25
Fairbanks & Piper, medicine,	7 10
Geo. E. Francis, professional services,	3 00
T. H. Gage, consultations,	8 00
H. L. Goddard, meat,	49 88
M. B. Green & Co., medicines,	205 52
W. M. Hall & Sons, wood,	80 50
L. Harrington, groceries,	31 00
O. L. Hatch, flour,	17 00
Hildreth & Hall, burial,	8 00
Hildreth & Wilson, burials,	61 00
Holden & Brother, groceries,	108 00
John W. Hoppin, "	18 00
W. H. Jourdan, coal,	139 25
Kelley & Simpson, consultation,	15 00

Paid C. B. Knight & Co., lumber, $6 00
W. C. Lamkin, boots and shoes, 11 15
Lamson, Glazier & Co., blankets, 12 00
M. S. McConville, bandages, 4 50
T. A. McConville, burials, 68 00
J. G. Park, consultation, 9 00
Geo. F. Peck, repairing desk, 13 26
Power & McCarty, burials, 64 00
David Scott & Co., medicine, 1 95
Nelson R. Scott, " 5 00
George Sessions & Son, burials, 67 00
Snow Brothers, printing, 26 88
Stearns Brothers, groceries, 9 00
Strong & Rogers, coal, 513 00
Tyler & Seagrave, printing &c., 31 75
Ware, Pratt & Co., clothing, 6 00
Albert Wood, professional services, 202 00
Rufus Woodward " " 18 00

EXPENSES OF FARM.

Paid John Farwell, salary as Sup't., 733 34
" " cash paid for sundries, 410 34
C. D. Aldrich, fish, 11 15
Allen & Reed, boots and shoes, 80 73
Ames Plow Co., repairing plow &c., 6 29
William Arnold, washing machine, 11 00
W. E. Baker & Co., rye, essence of
coffee &c., 10 08
John D. Baldwin, Spy one year, 8 00
Barnard, Sumner & Co., dry goods, 75 31
Elliott F. Benson, labor, 50 00
L. H. Bigelow, stationery, 9 10
Joseph E. Bond, land, 600 00
Brophy & Geer, grinding, 4 64
R. Champion, wooden ware, 11 95
J. C. Chapin, carpentering, 19 37
Clark, Sawyer & Co., crockery, 99 58
J. H. Clarke & Co., dry goods, 49 09
Francis Cosgrove, shoeing, 25 50
A. G. Cutler, labor, 32 28
Avery Davis, clothing, 6 00
Silas Dinsmore, medicine, 4 00
James Draper, pears, berries &c., 34 26
Henry F. Edwards, repairing &c., 47 42
Edwin A. Fawcett, boxes &c., 12 25
G. Fletcher, fish, 2 80
C. Foster & Co., hardware, 21 48
John Gates & Co., shingles, 55 19
Geo. Geer, socks, jackets and sundries, 34 15
H. F. Geer, grinding, meal &c., 11 55

Paid H. L. Goddard, meat,	$37 79
Chas. O. Green, Tr., tax,	107 10
James Green & Co., medicines,	14 20
James Green, grass,	8 00
M. B. Green & Co., medicines,	84 94
F. Harrington, flour and grain,	90 00
O. L. Hatch, " " "	249 65
O. C. Haven, boots, shoes &c.,	42 65
Highway Dept., manure and oxen,	500 00
Hildreth & Hall, burials,	16 00
G. S. Hoppin & Co , meal &c.,	15 45
Howe Bigelow & Co., wire cloth,	2 10
W. H. Jourdan, coal,	188 07
Kendall & McClennen, hats, gloves and socks,	13 94
I. N. Keyes, planing and manure,	32 85
F. J. Kinney, apple-trees &c.,	26 24
J. B. Lawrence, furniture,	35 87
A. J. Lilley, pears and grapes,	13 38
A. B. Lovell, mortar, plaster and labor,	40 63
John D. Lovell, seeds, tools and sundries,	95 02
Jerome Marble & Co., oil and paint,	7 59
Wm. H. Maynard & Co., corn and oats,	133 01
Reynolds McAleer, blanket and sundries,	8 20
W. F. Merrifield, sawing,	28 20
Henry W. Miller, stove, zinc and sundries,	76 31
Morse & Smith, meat,	111 22
Norcross & Co., groceries,	13 95
Plaisted Brothers, crackers &c.,	42 84
Darius Putnam, groceries,	591 79
Stephen A. Reed, horse,	175 00
J. Rice, repairing saws,	3 35
Richardson Manufacturing Co., repairing,	2 35
A. K. Richmond, varnishing sleigh,	6 00
Joseph Santom, thrashing,	14 58
George Sessions & Son, burial,	8 00
R. R. Shepard & Co., groceries,	195 70
Shields & Moody, solder, labor &c.,	14 54
E. K. Spaulding, geese and duck,	3 40
Chas. Stubbs, fish,	53 18
James Taylor, tools,	11 58
A. Y. Thompson & Co., dry goods,	144 78
H. Thompson, preaching	12 00
J. Todd & Co., roasting and grinding rye,	7 28
Truant School, labor of boys,	93 00
Ware, Pratt & Co., clothing,	95 90
Mary A. Waters, labor,	16 86
H. B. Wellington, shoeing,	60 05

Paid White, Houghton & Co., scraps,	$37 50	
Young, Norcross,& Co., geese,	6 28	
		$14,999 86

Amount overdrawn January 1, 1872, $1,249 10

CITY HOSPITAL.

Appropriation, $10,000 00

EXPENDITURES.

Paid Allen & Reed, rubber goods,	14 50	
Cyrus Arnold, soap,	7 00	
Charles Belcher, meats,	95 69	
Bush & Co., drugs and medicines,	57 17	
D. J. H. Camp, alteration and repairs,	191 77	
John D. Chollar, furniture,	747 70	
Clark & Nason, plumbing, work &c.,	54 00	
Clark, Sawyer & Co., crockery,	35 80	
George H. Clark, painting,	179 84	
J. Colbath & Co., plumbing,	72 60	
C. A. Cummings, bell and repairs,	3 50	
Joseph P. Eaton, milk,	17 98	
Francestown Soap Stone Co., tubs &c.,	84 75	
M. B. Green & Co., brushes &c.,	5 83	
Hair Brothers, gas fixtures,	26 14	
Stephen Harrington, mason work &c..	360 15	
Alfred Holden & Co., coffee, tea and spices,	16 95	
John W. Jordan, furnace,	150 00	
Wm. H. Jourdan, coal	68 50	
Kinnicutt & Co., sundries,	8 08	
Knowlton Brothers, crockery,	243 80	
Lydia Lee, labor,	5 60	
W. N. Manser & Co., bath tub &c.,	37 59	
S. B. Morse, mason work,	9 00	
J. G. Park, cash paid out,	33 36	
Pay Rolls, J. G. Parks and others,	214 76	
T. H. Reed, furnace and tin ware,	399 33	
Sanford & Co., books and stationery,	47 55	
Stephen Taft & Son, groceries,	83 39	
Wm. F. Wheeler, portable grates,	20 25	
Carrie Willis, sundries,	6 50	
		$3,299 08

Amount undrawn January 1, 1872, $6,700 92

SALARIES.

Appropriation,   15,000 00

EXPENDITURES.

Paid Henry Chapin, Mayor,	$199 83	
Edward Earle, do,	1,225 00	

Paid Phinehas Ball, City Engineer, $2,291 67
   William L. Clarke, assessor,   1,466 67
   Ranson M. Gould,   do   1,103 79
   Henry Griffin,   do   1,037 79
   Charles Marvin, Auditor,   322 50
   "   "   Messenger and Janitor, 1,008 34
   Thomas L. Nelson, Solicitor,   916 67
   Henry L. Shumway, Clerk of Com.
     Council,   229 17
   Samuel Smith, City Clerk,   1,833 34
   Gill Valentine, Auditor,   90 00
   George W. Wheeler, Treasurer and
     Collector,   2,108 34
                                                                 —————— $13,833 11

Amount undrawn January 1, 1872, $1,166 89

SCHOOLS.

Appropriation, $125,000 00
Received from Commonwealth,   2,013 76
   for books,   87 57
   from B. W. Fitch, seats and
     desks sold,   236 30
   S. L. Hodges seats and
     desks,   254 43
   A. P. Marble, grammars &c.,   38 35
   S. V. Stone, sundries,   51 60
   E. Smith, schooling,   3 10
   A. W. Ward, schooling,   7 00
                                                                 —————— $127,693 11

EXPENDITURES.

Paid Albert P. Marble, salary as Supt.,   2,291 67
   Samuel V. Stone,   "   " Sec'y.,   1,558 34
   A. P. Marble, traveling expenses &c.,   197 29
   Samuel V. Stone, cash paid for postage
     stamps, express &c.,   84 87
   Geo. A. Adams,   teaching,   1,575 61
   M. E. A. Adams,   "   496 28
   E. M. Aldrich,   "   532 92
   L. M. Allen,   509 74
   Rebecca Barnard,   518 28
   A. H. Barnes,   509 74
   E. H. Barton,   170 72
   M. E. Barton,   292 68
   Florence V. Bean,   741 42
   S. A. Bigelow,   "   509 74
   H. M. Bliss,   "   463 40
   M. E. Bothwell,   "   163 64
   C. V. Bowers,   336 58

ld E. M. Boyden,	teaching,	$509	74
S. M. Brigham,	"	463	40
Annie Brown,	"	538	74
Emma Brown,		490	85
S. M. Buttrick,		378	03
M. V. Callighan,		170	72
L. S. Carter,		532	92
A. M. Chapin,		463	40
E. G. Chenery,		480	48
E. I. Claflin,		463	40
Hattie E. Clarke,		187	80
C. R. Clements,		509	74
S. W. Clements,		463	40
A. E. Clough,		551	02
E. H. Coe,		509	74
S. L. Coes,		292	68
M. P. Cole,		532	92
M. A. Collins,		463	40
E. I. Comins,		1,575	61
E. A. Cooke,		463	40
H. G. Creamer,		853	65
E. G. Cutler,		85	37
A. R. Dame,		443	89
E. E. Daniels,		480	48
T. S. Darling,		548	74
A. H. Davis,	"	2,131	80
Mary J. Davis,		474	38
L. A. Dawson,		462	18
Eliza J. Day,		348	76
Libbie H. Day,		69	80
A. S. Dunton,		532	92
Sarah E. Dyer,		42	07
M. E. Eastman,		532	92
M. L. Fitch,		532	92
Samuel E. Fitz,	"	1,575	61
C. N. Follett,		509	64
S. W. Forbes,		359	74
C. C. Foster,		1,575	71
M. T. Gale,		459	75
S. G. Gale,		459	75
E. M. Gates,	"	463	40
M. M. Geary,	"	509	74
C. A. George,	"	750	92
Orra George,		122	07
C. E. Gilbert,		514	58
L. C. Goodwin,	"	463	40
Lizzie Graham,	"	336	58
J. A. Greene,	"	507	05
A. E. Hall,	"	463	40
E. M. Halstead,	"	463	40

46

Paid V. E. Hapgood,	teaching,	$518 89
H. M. Harlow,	"	458 77
H. A. Harrington,	"	463 40
H. M. Harrington,		1,575 61
L. M. Harrington,		532 87
M. A. Harrington,	..	532 92
S. A. Harrington,		463 40
H. Hathaway,		509 74
A. F. Hemenway,		170 72
Adella Hills,		410 35
E. J. Houghton,		463 40
J. E. Howard,		549 98
Belle Y. Hoyt,		268 28
A. Hunt,		1,575 61
J. A. Hunt,		463 40
H. M. Johnson,		489 02
Rebecca Jones,		1,112 19
M. E. Kavanaugh,		463 40
E. S. R. Kendrick,		463 40
J. E. A. Kenney,		170 42
L. E. King,		509 74
M. E. D. King,		463 40
P. E. King,		597 10
Ella J. H. Knight,		292 68
Stella E. Knight,		36 48
A. F. Knowles,		509 74
B. S. Ladd,		1,009 82
M. M. Lawton,		532 92
M. J. Mack,		532 92
Clara Manley,		532 92
E. F. Marsh,		428 04
J. M. Martin,		463 40
Sarah M. Maynard,		68 29
M. E. McCambridge,		532 92
E. M. McFarland,		477 40
Kate A. Meade,		509 74
M. J. Melanefy,		463 40
Ellen Merrick,		532 92
C. H. Metcalf,		160 97
M. J. Metcalf,		136 57
N. L. Moore,		509 74
M. J. Morse,		463 40
C. H. Munger,		532 92
E. S. Nason,		1,458 53
G. A. Newton,		27 00
L. L. Newton,		635 88
S. J. Newton,		572 40
T. S. Nichols,		509 74
E. J. Norcross,		170 72
M. L. Norcross,		463 40

aid Flora J. Osgood,	teaching,	$170	72
M. J. Packard,	"	293	90
Roswell Parish,	"	1,853	66
M. Parker,		509	74
M. A. Parkhurst,		682	90
Susie A. Partridge,	..	235	35
M. E. Pease,	"	463	40
Adeliza Perry,	"	255	85
A. C. Perry,	"	509	74
L. E. Perry,		463	40
A. M. Phillips,		453	62
S. L. Phillips,		525	92
Abby Pratt,		463	40
E. J. Pratt,		451	21
E. F. Prentice,		437	79
Annie M. Prince,		10	97
A. M. Prouty,		170	72
C. E. Putnam,		463	40
A. Radcliffe,		443	90
J. P. Raymond,		417	04
A. J. Reed,		463	40
M. F. Reed,		434	75
E. M. Rice, ·		463	40
A. E. Rockwood,		147	30
E. A. Rounds,	"	547	55
H. M. Shattuck,	"	459	75
M. A. Slater,		353	94
E. B. Smith,		323	16
Hattie A. Smith,		448	76
J. F. Smith,		532	92
M. A. Smith,		532	85
S. N. Stackpole,		395	10
A. C. Stewart,		741	42
Jennie E. Stiles,		44	00
Abbie Souther,		40	00
Samuel Souther,		60	00
N. C. Thomas,		463	40
M. E. Tirrell,		304	78
Evelyn Towne,	..	463	40
C. A. Townsend,	"	140	24
M. E. Trask,	"	353	64
I. C. Upton,	"	462	20
L. Vaughn,		241	44
H. G. Waite,		609	75
E. J. Wallace,		496	31
M. H. Warren,		532	92
A. A. Wells,		463	40
M. F. Wentworth,		532	92
Myra J. Wetmore,	"	546	34
Elizabeth Wheeler,	"	204	87

Paid E. G. Wheeler,   teaching, $532 92
    M. O. Whitmore,   "   463 40
    M. F. Whittier,   "   168 72
    M. E. Wilder,   595 39
    A. C. Wyman,   456 08
    M. T. Wyman,   478 03

WOOD AND COAL.

Paid Peter Dochery, charcoal,   99 78
    Garfield & Parker, wood,   547 68
    D. F. Houghton, wood,   26 25
    W. H. Jourdan, coal,   5,375 62
    Jos. Santom, Jr., charcoal,   251 74
    Strong & Rogers, coal,   947 76

REPAIRS, WOOD AND SUNDRIES.

Paid H. Adams, repairs, wood &c.,   59 50
    S. T. Bennett, repairs,   3 00
    Sylvanus Sears, repairs, wood &c., 62 75

MAKING FIRES, SWEEPING AND CLEANING.

Paid Pay Roll for January,   391 30
  " " " February,   383 70
  " " " March,   365 75
  " " " April,   377 50
  " " " May,   271 00
  " " " June,   197 50
  " " " September,   260 75
  " " " October,   355 00
  " " " November,   396 50
    B. W. Fletcher, paid out for cleaning, 282 65
    Mary Morrissey, cleaning,   4 50
    Elizabeth Snow,   "   6 75
    Lizzie Vaughn,   "   8 00
    Gilman Wheeler,   "   &c., 87 70

MISCELLANEOUS.

Paid George I. Alden, lessons in Mechanical
        Drawing,   87 50
    Allen & Reed, springs,   264 30
    B. D. Allen, musical services,   10 00
    A. S. Allen, tuning and repairing pianos, 8 50
    Ames Plow Co., lumber,   26 46
    J. D. Baldwin, & Co., advertising, 26 75
    R. Barker, labor,   5 00
    Barnard, Sumner & Co., 27 yds., patch, 6 75
    Barrett Washburn & Co., labor, pipe &c., 5 88
    L. H. Bigelow, books, paper and sundries, 94 43
    Bill, Nichols & Co., 48 manuals, 36 00
    C. V. Bowers, allowance towards piano, 50 00
    John F. Boyce, labor,   35 10

aid B. N. Bradt & Co., desk,	$6 75
Brewer & Tileston, dictionaries and chart,	40 92
J. B. Brooks, teaming,	255 00
C. W. Burbank, surveys, plans &c.,	25 00
R. Champion, feather dusters,	4 10
John Chickering, sawing wood,	317 25
G. Childs & Son, desks,	272 50
John D. Chollar, chairs,	146 65
Clark, Sawyer & Co., burner, lighter &c.,	5 18
George H. Clark, painting and glazing,	1,439 14
E. B. Crane, lumber,	142 72
L. H. Cummings, labor,	141 00
C. A. Davis, sawing wood,	8 50
John Delano, Mason work,	21 37
Henry A. Dickerman, books,	15 50
Division No. 42, brushes, mats and sundries,	357 01
Doe & Woodwell, advertising,	1 87
Ehrgott & Krebs, demck, draw.,	11 07
G. W. Elkins, clock, repairing clocks &c.,	234 21
B. W. Fletcher, shop rent,	206 25
" " " carpenter work &c.,	1,068 99
Calvin Foster & Co., screws nails and sundries,	267 23
John Gates & Co., boards,	49 18
Nathl. P. Gates, sawing wood,	9 53
A. W. Gifford, screws,	99 83
Geo. E. Gladwin, lessons in drawing,	87 50
John R. Gow, assistance in Sec. office,	18 00
Greene & Jordan, repairs and sundries,	171 68
Hair Brothers, fitting gas pipe &c.,	230 00
Chas. Hamilton, diplomas and parchment,	38 69
J. L. Hammett, books, ink-wells and sundries,	938 45
N. R. Hapgood, labor and materials,	1386 64
W. O. Haskell & Son, school furniture,	15 17
Heald & Britton, seats and desks castings,	2013 42
E. G. & F. W. Higgins, whitening,	70 00
Milton Higgins, lessons in drawing,	96 25
S. T. Howard & Co., horse hire,	205 50
Howe Bigelow & Co., wire cloth,	4 02
F. A. & J. N. Ingerson, stone,	37 50
H. C. Jameson, blanks,	11 00
Rebecca Jones, ribbons for diplomas,	4 75
J. W. Jordan, stoves, stove-pipe, labor &c.,	3168 67
H. J. Kendall, moving buildings,	6 50
John G. Kendall, insurance,	628 90

Paid J. N. Keyes, sawing and planing, $65 02
W. F. Knight, sawing wood, 14 75
Learned & Clough, screws labor &c., 10 65
S. R. Leland, piano and cover, 307 50
H. F. Loomis, copies alphabets, 15 75
A. B. Lovell, labor, 6 50
Jerome Marble & Co., nitric and sul-
phuric acid, 3 15
Mathews & Chamberlain, repairing pipe, 3 50
Merriam, Holden & Co., settees, 60 00
C. B. Metcalf, traveling expenses, 23 00
G. W. Miles, clock, 16 00
H. W. Miller, screws, locks, nails &c., 42 03
N. P. Mulloy, keys, locks, repairs and
sundries, 134 99
C. Munger, allowance towards piano, 50 00
E. S. Nason, tuning pianos &c., 135 58
Noyes, Holmes & Co., books and slates, 88 60
John B. O'Leary, nails, bolts and hooks, 13 78
James R. Osgood, books, 15 00
Roswell Parish, cash paid out, 15 25
Peoples Fire Ins. Co., insurance, 33 75
J. S. Pinkham, carpet, 8 25
W. F. Pond, cleaning vaults, 70 00
Michael Powers, labor, powder and fuse, 193 50
Mary Pratt, ink, 124 50
George Putnam, sawing wood, 8 77
J. J. Randall, laying concrete in cellar, 176 59
T. H. Reed, brushes, basins and sundries, 58 48
Fred. Revere, numbers for school, 1 50
J. H. Ring, crash, 3 15
Geo. B. Robbins, sawing wood, 19 94
Joseph L. Ross, settees, platforms and
desks, 23 85
Geo. W. Rugg, soap, 31 50
Sanford & Co., books, paper and
sundries, 479 35
David Scott, alcoholic bottles &c., 53 98
John L. Shorey, books, 50 83
C. A. Skinner, cyclopædias, 76 80
Chas. Smith, brooms and brushes, 6 50
Snow Brothers, printing, 562 89
Jos. E. Stearns, plastering, 165 42
D. & C. P. Stevens, doors, glass and
boxes, 72 59
Wm. F. Taylor, setting glass, 2 00
Ellis Thayer, stove handles, 6 44
N. C. Thomas, services in Secretary's
office, 8 00

aid Ames Plow Co., use of pond, catch

basin, covers &c.,	$1,407	05
C. K. Babcock, labor,	142	50
Chas. Baker & Co., lumber,	468	10
J. D. Baldwin & Co., advertising,	12	25
Phinehas Ball, cash paid out,	9	50
John S. Ballard, damages and use of land,	2,790	88
Geo. C. Barney, on account of contract,	16,370	54
Barrett, Washburn & Co., labor, pipe and sundries,	79	22
Joseph Bennett, labor,	3	00
Blake Brothers, labor, iron &c.,	23	60
Harrison Bliss, brick,	60	00
Smith Bowen, damage to horse and carriage,	35	00
Brown & Barnard, carting,	632	18
A. S. Brown, lanterns, burners and reflector,	24	65
Cornelius Buckley, damages,	40	00
Geo. M. Buttrick, cement,	6	00
G. A. Carter, roofing,	115	43
Chamberlain & Co., lumber,	114	95
R. H. Chamberlain, services and use of team,	1,448	40
B. T. Chapin, labor,	847	75
R. H. Church, "	267	62
Mary L. Church, writing,	40	50
John S. Clark & Son, cement,	79	75
C & J. A. Colvin, manholes and covers,	172	49
Patrick Conner, use of land,	50	00
Cook, Rymes & Co., boxes and grates,	11	75
Corbett & Willard, sewer bars,	11	10
Corey & Duffy, pipe, iron and labor,	254	15
James Cronin, labor,	32	00
James Dailey, "	28	00
Joseph D. Daniels, damages,	225	00
Porter Davis, services &c.,	1,507	09
Dawson, Tank & Ingerson, on account of contract,	10,053	42
Patrick Day, damages,	80	00
C. M. Dodd, labor,	12	00
Doe & Woodwell, advertising,	9	83
Dennis Doyle, damages,	100	00
H. M. Dunn, labor,	748	80
H. W. Eddy, labor and cash paid out,	68	50
Fish & Cogger, repairing &c.,	2	87
H. C. Fish, "	5	39
John Fittman, labor,	333	70

Paid	Francis Flynn, damages,	$40 00
	Patrick Foley, labor,	28 00
	C. Foster & Co., hardware,	6 80
	Rufus Fuller, damages,	803 00
	John Gates & Co., lumber,	320 81
	Graton & Knight, repairing hose,	14 25
	A. T. Hubbard, flagstone,	394 61
	Geo. F. Hoar, professional services,	250 00
	D. M. Houlihan, damages,	50 00
	Howe & Hackett, oil,	30
	L. D. Hubbard, labor,	85 74
	James Hughes, "	14 00
	D. S. Jackson, brick,	31 50
	W. H. Jourdan, coal,	997 57
	Journal Newspaper Co., advertising,	13 50
	I. N. Keyes, damages &c.,	501 50
	Kinnicutt & Co., trowel,	85
	E. S. Knowles, contract, stock and labor	
	putting in sewers,	13,390 36
	Moses Laing, labor,	43 63
	Edwin Lawrence, labor,	93 75
	Leach & Co., on account of contracts,	67,031 77
	Leach & Son, " " " "	5,144 36
	Alex. Lorimer, rope, packing &c.,	71 41
	A. B. Lovell, drain pipe, labor &c.,	313 63
	J. D. Lovell, shovels and pails,	20 35
	James Mahan, damages,	300 00
	Mann & Bigelow, stone and labor,	31 62
	Jerome Marble & Co., oil, glue &c.,	43 97
	Alice McCann, damages,	50 00
	Felix McCann, labor,	318 93
	F. A. McClure "	43 75
	James McCormick, damages,	25 00
	Samuel McFadden, damages,	25 00
	H. W. Miller, nails, screws, hinges &c.,	82 10
	F. H. Mills, labor,	42 40
	James Murphy, damages,	330 00
	Vinson K. Nash, labor,	650 12
	Michael Neylon, use of land and	
	damages,	36 00
	Norwich & Wor. R. R., freight,	65 38
	Asa Nourse, labor,	165 75
	Cornelius O'Sullivan, damages,	50 00
	J. P. K. Otis, labor,	23 37
	Geo. F. Peck, carpentering.	17 11
	F. F. Phelps, manholes,	3,875 00
	A. Pike, use of derrick,	5 00
	Geo. Raymond, paper,	27 50
	J. D. Rawson, teaming,	23 00
	Rice, Barton & Fales, iron, labor &c.,	144 33

Paid J. Rice, repairing saws,	$3 75	
Stephen Rice, damages,	25 00	
Chas. O. Richardson, paving &c.,	1,124 77	
Geo. L. Robbins, stone,	3 58	
H. G. Roche, stone and labor,	3,700 12	
W. H. Sawyer, boards,	2 36	
Edward Schoolcraft, labor,	105 00	
R. R. Shepherd & Co., oil,	1 05	
Smith & Murdock, waste,	5 20	
M. B. Smith, labor,	13 50	
T. H. Smith, painting,	74 63	
Snow Brothers, printing,	73 34	
Geo. T. Sutton, pipe and labor,	22 07	
S. H. Tarbell, on acct. of contract,	36,806 56	
L. A. Taylor, services,	1,105 10	
Thompson & Hearn, plugs,	16 50	
S. Triscott, labor,	170 00	
Clarence H. Truesdell, labor,	455 68	
L. C. Trumbull, money paid back,	47 75	
Joel Upham, damages,	18 00	
E. B. Walker, on acct. of contract, &c.,	21,329 52	
Walker & Converse, on acct. of contract &c.,	39,561 85	
Wm. F. Wheeler, castings, labor, &c,,	96 51	
Jerome Wheelock, repairing,	15 00	
A. L. Whiting, pick,	1 75	
White & Conant, stone hammer,	2 00	
D. M. Woodward, labor, &c.,	147 75	
Wor. Gas Light Co., repairing and relaying pipe,	1,685 09	
Wor. Highway Dept., labor and materials,	737 68	
Wor. & Nashua R. R. Co. stock and labor,	65 30	
Wor. Steam Boiler Works, castings and labor,	24 28	
		$1,072,809 14
Amount overdrawn January 7, 1872,		$1,072,723 99

SHADE TREES AND PUBLIC GROUNDS

Balance undrawn January 2, 1871,	$1,048 88	
Appropriation,	5,000 00	
Received from City Clerk,	350 00	
		$6,398 88

EXPENDITURES.

Paid John D. Baldwin & Co., advertising,	1 50	
Amasa Ballou, painting,	34 83	

Paid John Barnes, labor,	$238 33	
Timothy S. Bliss, labor,	4 12	
Luther H. Bigelow, directory &c.,	2 00	
Silas D. Burbank, burying snake,	2 00	
Andrew Burns, labor,	16 00	
L. B. Chamberlain, setting out trees,	5 00	
James Draper, trees and labor,	98 00	
Henry Forney, labor,	27 00	
John Goulding, do.	15 00	
Stephen Harrington, grading,	30 00	
Jonas Hartshorn, shade trees,	12 00	
Highway Department, scrapings &c.,	275 10	
Elisha S. Knowles, sewer,	250 89	
John D. Lovell, grass seed &c.,	86 42	
Mann & Bigelow well stone and labor,	53 50	
Jerome Marble & Co., tar,	1 25	
Michael McGrath, teaming &c.,	3,825 72	
Michael Mc Kenney labor,	6 00	
H. & A. Palmer, stock and labor,	121 92	
C. H. Perry, boxing trees, &c.,	180 82	
Sumner Pratt & Co., cord,	1 30	
Dexter Rice, signs,	22 75	
Charles O. Richardson, beach stone,	304 50	
George Sessions & Son, earth &c.,	43 77	
Stephen Shumway, shade trees,	5 00	
John Simmons & Son, boxing trees &c.,	133 33	
Snow Brothers, printing,	23 32	
Charles E. Stevens, shade trees,	2 00	
Jeremiah Toomey, labor,	21 50	
James H. Wall, shade trees,	5 00	
Willard Ward, stock and labor,	123 64	
		$5,974 01
Amount undrawn January 1, 1872,		$424 87
ELM PARK.		
Amount of Levi Lincoln's legacy,		$940 00
SOLDIERS MONUMENT.		
Amount paid Committee,		$35,000 00
SUMMONS.		
Received for 2062 summons,		$412 40
EXPENDITURES.		
Paid, Police & Watchmen, serving,	155 39	
Transfer to Contingent Expenses,	257 01	
		$412 40
SUNDRY ACCOUNTS, (OLD).		
Amount overdrawn January, 1, 1872,		$54,140 07

TAXES ON BANK SHARES.

Amount assessed,		$28,997 10

EXPENDITUHES.

Paid State Treasurer,	$22,148 94	
Discount allowed on same,	1,828 93	
Transfer to State Tax,	2,081 03	
" " Contingent Expenses,	2,938 20	
		$28,997 10

TAXES,—COUNTY FOR 1871.

Appropriation,		$27,639 23

EXPENDITURES.

Paid Charles A. Chase, County Treasurer,		$27,639 23

TAXES,—STATE FOR 1871.

Appropriation,	51,075 00		
Less estimated Corporation Tax,	45,000 00	6,075 00	
Received of State Corp., Tax			
for 1871,		42,918 97	
Transfer from Bank Tax,		2,081 03	
			$51,075 00

EXPENDITURES.

Paid Charles Adams Jr., State Treasurer,		$51,075 00

WAR,—AID TO FAMILIES.

Received of the Commonwealth,		$13,000 00

EXPENDITURES.

Amount overdrawn January 2, 1871,	19,692 52	
Paid Soldiers and Families in January,	562 50	
" " " February,	1,037 50	
" " " March,	1,200 00	
" " " April,	934 50	
" " " May,	860 50	
" " " June,	1,016 50	
" " " July,	1,086 50	
" " " August,	900 00	
" " " September,	1,048 50	
" " " October,	963 75	
" " " November,	895 00	
" " " December,	1,354 25	
		$31,552 02
Amount overdrawn January 1, 1872,		$18,552 02

WAR,—BOUNTIES.

Amount overdrawn January 1, 1872,		$46,526 73

WAR,—Contingents.

Amount overdrawn January 1, 1872, $1,260 97

WATER RENTS.

Received for water,   48,686 98
"   "   "   for Hydrants,   8,000 00
                                                            $56,686 98

Expenditures.

Transfer to Water Interest,   32,360 78
"   "   Water Works,—Maintenance, 24,326 20
                                                            $56,686 98

WATER WORKS,—Construction Account.

Received for putting in pipes, articles sold &c., $8,561 49

Expenditures.

To amount overdrawn January 2, 1871,   649,727 90

Paid Pay Rolls, labor,   18,524 75
"   "   "   at Reservoir,   5,726 61
Allen & Reed, boots and mittens,   18 25
Charles A. Allen, labor,   293 34
Ames Plow Co., gate at reservoir &c.,   28 92
Bacon & Forbes, charcoal,   5 00
Chas. Baker & Co., lumber &c.,   246 79
Barrett, Washburn & Co., pipe and
    sundries,   3,877 80
Bemis & Co., rubber boots,   12 75
Bennett & Hixon, bricks,   182 00
H. B. Bigelow & Co., hydrants,   135 00
Boston Machine Co., water gates,   3,682 00
Bray & Hayes, cement,   222 23
Brown & Barnard, carting,   993 51
Alzirus Brown, labor and sundries,   17 32
A. S. Brown, lanterns and chimneys,   51 62
Carrie S. Burnham, land,   1,000 00
G. A. Carter, roofing boards &c.,   70 18
Edward Cassidy, labor,   27 50
S. J. Chamberlain, repairing tools,   9 13
Jason Chapin, union joints,   48 72
R. H. Church, labor,   7 00
Lemuel Coburn, old lead,   24 90
Corbett & Willard, repairing,   273 20
Francis Cosgrove,   "   9 00
Fred Drown, labor,   40 49
Edward Earle, cash paid out,   21 75
C. Foster & Co., shovels, nails and
    sundries,   157 06
Garfield & Parker, plank,   527 24
John Gates & Co., lumber,   229 47

aid Greene & Jordan, lead and pipe,	$290	89
J. W. Greene, water pipe,	12,516	21
W. H. Hackett, kerosene and wicks,	18	30
Walter Hale, services at reservoir,	190	22
W. F. Henshaw, damages,	35	00
Wm. H. Heywood, services at reservoir, &c.,	1,497	66
Emery Holbrook, land,	3,000	00
Howe, Bigelow & Co., brass cloth,	85	00
Howe & Hackett, oil and brooms,	11	50
C. Hubbard, labor,	133	00
L. D. Hubbard, labor,	78	75
Jersey City Cast Steel Tool Co., picks,	19	60
Willard Jones & Co., castings,	109	64
J. W. Jordan, water pipe, labor &c.,	425	62
D. Waldo Kent, land,	366	50
Kinnicutt & Co., trowels,	2	25
Wm. Knowles, cash paid out,	57	28
J. S. C. Knowlton, advertising,	3	50
Alexander Lorimer, cord packing,	120	80
A. B. Lovell, sand, cement, pipe &c.,	5,020	21
J. D. Lovell, grindstone, barrow, &c.,	40	63
Wm. Lucas & Son, lead,	23	78
Mann & Bigelow, stone, labor &c.,	2,995	57
Jerome Marble & Co., oil,	3	25
Henry, W. Miller, nails, locks and sundries,	129	08
C & N. M. Muzzy, repairing drills,	2	40
Norwich & Wor. R. R. Co., freight,	1	00
Asa Nourse, labor,	192	00
John P. K. Otis, labor,	49	26
H. & A. Palmer, "	3	50
F. F. Phelps, castings,	650	42
H. S. Pike, damages,	12	50
Pratt & Inman, chain, steel &c.,	58	01
Michael Quinn, repairing tools &c.,	37	70
Charles Reed, labor,	88	25
T. H. Reed, can, solder &c.,	84	12
Riley & Smith, on contract,	25,420	57
Andrew D. Rogers, labor &c.,	30	16
William Ross, windows,	23	25
Sheldon & Bartlett, hydrant boxes,	111	68
R. R. Shepard, powder and fuse,	41	21
Jesse Smith, cement,	2,995	40
Thomas Smith & Co., bolts, hooks and labor,	86	86
D. & C. P. Stevens, doors,	19	81
L. B. Stone, sand, cement and sundries,	1,018	75
G. T. Sutton, pipe, solder, labor, &c.,	752	27

Paid Union Water Meter Co. meters, pipe,
   labor, &c., $5,264 54
 E. B. Walker, stone,   711 15
 Washburn Iron Co., old iron,   17 00
 Samuel Wesson, labor,   134 69
 C. Wheaton, damages,   45 00
 Wm. F.Wheeler, castings and sundries, 7,883 52
 Benj. Willson, land,   238 70
 Wor. Gas Light Co., gas pipe, 1,576 31
 Wor. Street Railway Co. car tickets, 95 00
             ——————— $761,010 70

Amount overdrawn January 1, 1872.   752,449 21

WATER WORKS, (Maintenance Account).

Received for Boiler.   500 00
Transfer from Water Rents,   24,326 20
             ——————— $24,826 20

EXPENDITURES.

Paid William Knowles, salary, $1,100 00
 Pay Rolls, labor,   6,836 57
 Allen & Reed, boots, mittens, packing, 185 77
 Chas. A. Allen, labor,   74 20
 Ashworth, & Jones, damages, 600 00
 C. K. Babcock, raising pipe,   16 00
 Bacon & Forbes, charcoal,   10 00
 D. J. Baker, suppers,   9 80
 J. D. Baldwin & Co., advertising, 91 50
 Barrett, Wasburn & Co., pipe and
    sundries,   141 31
 S. H. Batcheller, window sashes, 3 00
 N. T. Bemis & Co., horse hire, 743 40
 Wright Bottomly, damages,   250 00
 Brigham & Emes, salt,   2 00
 Brown & Barnard, carting,   175 50
 A. S. Brown, wicks,   20
 Wm. H. Brown, repairing,   3 25
 G. A. Carter, felt, nails, labor &c., 23 48
 Wm. C. Chase, services, &c., 1,082 14
 Mary L. Church, writing,   37 50
 Corbett & Willard, repairing, tools &c., 310 11
 Francis Cosgrove, " " 27 60
 James Croan, labor,   10 00
 Albert Curtis, water pumped from
    Kettle Brook,   500 00
 Richard Curtis, use of land,   40 00
 Porter Davis, labor and cash paid out, 227 75
 Dawson, Tank & Co., guyes,   36 12
 H. W. Denny & Co., pails,   2 25

aid Doe & Woodwell, advertising,	$50 94
Fred Drown, labor,	26 55
Henry M. Dunn, labor,	216 90
Edward Earle, damages paid,	550·00
C. Foster & Co., shovels, screws &c.,	81 38
John Gates, & Co., boards,	146 12
Graton & Knight, leather,	10 33
N. S. Hale, carting,	6 00
Walter Hale, labor,	37 98
Chas. Hamilton, printing,	33 00
Thos. Harrington, boiler flues &c.,	116 95
F. B. Hartwell, use of land,	10 00
William Heaton, care of Reservoir,	133 33
Highway Department, patching paving &c.,	69 49
Howe & Hackett, kerosene &c.,	40 62
Benj. James, damages,	900 00
F. Jefts, labor,	3 22
J. W. Jordan, pipe, labor, &c.,	106 70
Wm. H. Jourdan, coal,	48 00
J. G. Kendall, Agt., insurance,	11 00
Henry L. Keyes, services in Water Office,	199 00
I. N. Keyes, sawing and planing,	29 56
Kindred Brothers, repairing picks,	5 10
Kinnicutt & Co., hatchet and sundries,	7 05
L. J. Knowles & Brother, labor &c.,	62 64
Wm. Knowles, cash paid out,	42 71
Alex Lorimer, cord rope and packing,	164 99
A. B. Lovell, cement and sand,	113 25
John D. Lovell, wheelbarrow, shovels &c.,	70 35
Wm. Lucas & Son, labor &c.,	1 55
Wm. L. Lyon & Henry L. Parker, use of land,	300 00
Mann & Bigelow, stone,	31 07
Jerome Marble & Co., oil,	17 87
Henry W. Miller, locks, screws and sundries,	19 72
Newhall & Jones, enamel cloth,	6 60
Norcross Bros., lumber, labor &c.,	829 50
Asa Nourse, labor,	22 50
John B. O'Leary, repairing,	1 20
John P. K. Otis, labor,	43 75
Patent Water & Gas Pipe Co. snips,	10 00
F. F. Phelps, castings,	70 39
M. Quinn, repairing tools,	16 00
J. D. Rawson, carting,	25 00
Charles Reed, labor,	28 05
J. H. Reed, dippers &c.,	4 70

Paid Rice, Barton & Fales, M. & I. Co.,
  steam boilers, castings &c., $2,572 38
Sanford & Co., paper and sundries, 101 08
J. Santom, Jr. & Co., coal, 23 75
C. W. & J. E. Smith, damages, 129 00
Hattie A. Smith, copying service
  returns, &c., 40 63
James A. Smith, damages, 750 00
T. H. Smith, painting, glazing &c., 50 59
Snow Brothers, printing &c., 155 81
Andrew St. André, repairing, 11 00
Strong & Rogers, coal, 1,906 31
G. T. Sutton, pipe, labor &c., 35 20
Martha Z. Swallow, writing, 9 00
E. D. Thayer, et. al., damages, 500 00
C. O. Thompson, analysis of water, 15 00
Town of Leicester, taxes, 32 13
Union Water Meter Co., meters,
  labor &c., 990 92
A. W. Ward, labor, 25 00
J. S. Wheeler, labor, 5 00
Wm. F. Wheeler, labor, iron and
  sundries, 137 62
T. M. Woodward, iron plates and
  lettering, 45 00
Wor. Gas Light Co., gas and labor, 39 27
            —————
                $24,826 20

TAXES.

Uncollected previous to 1871,   24,277 01
  " of 1871,   13,497 91

BILL RECEIVABLE.

Note, David S. Messinger, due Feb. 29, 1873, $19,000 00
Cash on hand, January 1, 1872, $83,173 69

RECAPITULATION.

Table of Cr. Balances, (Jan. 2, 1871;) Appropriations, (raised by tax 1871;) Receipts exclusive of Taxes, Transfers, each Appropriation as it stood after deducting or adding Transfers, Expenditures and Balances, from Jan. 2, 1871, to Jan. 1, 1872.

	Cr. Balances January 2 1871.	Appropriations raised by tax.	Receipts exclusive of taxes.	Transfers from.	Transfers to.	Total receipts, (including balance Jan. 2d, 1871,) after deducting or adding transfers.	Expended, including appropriations overdrawn Jan. 2, 1871 uncollected tax, cash, etc.	Dr. Balances.	Cr. Balances.
Abatements and Discount,	$36,156 17	$47,719 52		$5,000 00		$78,875 69	$40,826 62		$38,049 07
Bills Receivable,							19,000 00	$19,000 00	
Boston, Barre & Gardner R. R. Co.,							262,200 00	262,200 00	
City Hay Scales,			$350 95	287 15		63 80	63 80		63 80
Contingent Expenses,	21,437 04	28,000 00	3,982 94	28 50	$10,133 69	63,525 17	38,186 03		25,339 14
Engine House,	2,095 00			47 11		2,047 89	2,047 89		
Fire Alarm Telegraph,		14,000 00	3,000 00	147 53		16,852 47	16,852 47		
Fire Department,		25,000 00	1,555 75			26,555 75	17,747 24		8,808 51
Free Public Library,	5,073 43	8,000 00			1,777 50	14,850 93	10,294 91		4,556 02
Fuel, Lights and Printing,		6,500 00	400 00			6,900 00	5,889 56		1,010 44
Highways, Sidewalks, &c.,		105,000 00	53,321 09			158,321 09	140,104 29		18,216 80
New Streets,		10,000 00		7,132 30		2,867 70			2,867 70
Blackstone Street,							4,833 26	4,833 26	
Chandler "							12,863 30	12,863 30	
Chatham and Corbett Street,			5,461 66			5,461 66	14,000 44	8,538 78	
Front Street,							17,660 26	17,660 26	
Hanover "							6,524 98	6,524 98	
James "					2,176 00	2,176 00	2,176 00		
Lafayette "							4,264 24	4,264 24	
Main "							24,074 60	24,074 60	
Mechanic "			6,303 77			6,303 77	12,673 19	6,369 42	
Oak Avenue,					477 65	477 65	477 65		
Piedmont Street,					734 30	734 30	734 30		
Salisbury "					2,456 95	2,456 95	2,456 95		
Sever "					281 90	281 90	281 90		
Union "		1,400 00				1,400 00	16,744 21	15,344 21	
Washington Street,					1,005 50	1,005 50	1,005 50		
Wilmot "							2,234 08	2,234 08	
Winter "			1,288 27			1,288 27			1,288 27

Account									
Interest,		90,000 00	3,612 40			93,612 40	106,489 45	12,877 05	
Interest on Water Debt,	170 30			32,360 78		32,531 08	32,975 90	444 82	
Licenses,						324 31	324 31		
Lighting Streets,	20,000 00		3,558 50	3,234 19		20,058 76	28,819 74	8,760 98	
Loans, Funded and Temporary,	1,899,808 04	20,000 00	2,022,678 96			3,922,487 00	1,465,698 28		2,456,788 72
Military,			7,515 00			7,515 00	7,230 26		284 74
Police and Watchmen,	28,000 00		7,906 67			35,906 67	32,918 26		2,988 41
Poor Department,	8,000 00		5,750 76			13,750 76	14,999 86	1,249 10	
City Hospital,	10,000 00					10,000 00	3,299 08		6,700 92
Salaries,	15,000 00					15,000 00	13,833 11		1,166 89
Schools,	125,000 00		2,693 11			127,693 11	120,301 35		7,391 76
School for Truants,	3,000 00		93 00			3,093 00	2,053 60		1,039 40
School Houses,	90,000 00			90,000 00	90,000 00				
Belmont Street,			9,915 32	9,915 32	9,915 32	9,915 32	9,915 32		
High School,			59,338 21	59,338 21	59,338 21	126,170 54		66,832 33	
" " (Old)			20,411 81	20,411 81	20,411 81	20,411 81	20,411 81		
Ledge Street "			334 66	334 66		334 66	22,198 31	21,863 65	
Main "		19,000 00			19,000 00	19,000 00			19,000 00
Common,			675 00			675 00			675 00
School, (State Normal)	15,030 00			15,028 50	15,028 50	15,028 50	15,028 50		
Sewers,	5,000 00		85 15	85 15		85 15	1,072,809 14	1,072,723 99	
Shade Trees and Public Grounds,	1,048 88	5,000 00	350 00			6,398 88	5,974 01		424 87
Elm Park,	940 00					940 00			940 00
Soldiers Monument,						35,000 00	35,000 00	35,000 00	
Summons,			412 40	257 01		155 39	155 39		
Sundry (Old) Accounts,							54,140 07	54,140 07	
Taxes,—Bank Shares,	28,997 10			5,019 23		23,977 87	23,977 87		
Taxes: County	27,639 23					27,639 23	27,639 23		
Taxes: State,	6,075 00		42,918 97			51,075 00	51,075 00		
War: Aid, Bt's and Cont'gts.,	13,000 00		13,000 00	2,081 03		13,600 00	79,339 72	66,339 72	
Water Rents,			56,686 98	56,686 98		8,561 49	761,010 70	752,449 21	66,339 72
Water Works, (Construction,)	56,686 98		8,561 49			24,826 20	24,826 20		
" " (Maintenance,)	8,561 49		500 00	24,326 20		37,744 92	37,744 92	37,744 92	
Taxes, uncollected,	500 00					83,173 69	83,173 69	83,173 69	
Cash,									
	$1,985,728 86	$715,930 85	$2,254,121 58	$167,840 00	$167,840 00	$4,955,781 29	$4,955,781 29	$2,597,536 66	$2,597,536 66

$4,955,781 29

TEMPORARY LOAN, JANUARY 1, 1872.

	To whom Payable.	Amount.	Rate of Interest.	Interest paid to
1 Note,	Emory Banister, Adm'r.,	$5,000 00	6	Dec. 1, 1871.
1 "	Central Mut. Fire Insurance Co.,	12,500 00	6	May 11, 1871.
1 "	Caleb Dana, Estate of,	450 00	6	Oct. 1, 1871.
1 "	Daniel Farnum,	4,400 00	6	June 2, 1871.
1 "	Sally Flagg,	1,800 00	6	Dec. 20, 1871.
1 "	Charles A. Garland,	195 00	6	March 8, 1871.
1 "	Parley Goddard, Estate of,	5,000 00	6	April 28, 1871.
2 "	G. A. R., Geo. H. Ward, Post No. 10,	1,925 00	7	Sept. 4, 1871.
7 "	Green Library Fund,	7,443 78	7	Oct. 1, 1871.
1 "	Emory Holbrook,	3,000 00	7	Dec. 1, 1871.
3 "	Home Savings Bank,	135,000 00	7	....
1 "	Eleanor D. Knight,	1,015 00	6	April 8, 1871.
1 "	Levi Lincoln, Estate of,	1,000 00	6	May 1, 1871.
1 "	Hannah Lynde,	1,000 00	6	Sept. 1, 1871.
1 "	Mary G. Lynde,	400 00	6	Sept. 1, 1871.
5 "	Merchant & Farmer's M. F. Insurance Co.,	50,000 00	7	Jan. 1, 1872.
1 "	Elizabeth C. B. Miller,	5,500 00	6	Dec. 1, 1871.
2 "	John C. Newton, Treasurer,	2,200 00	6	July 2, 1871.
2 "	Nathaniel Paine, Trustee,	7,600 00	6	Nov. 1, 1871.
1 "	Charles L. Putnam,	10,000 00	7	Aug. 7, 1871.
3 "	Stephen Salisbury, Treasurer,	6,113 62	7	July 4, 1871.
2 "	Angeline A. Sawyer,	1,900 00	6	June 1, 1871.
1 "	Angeline A. Sawyer, Guardian,	1,200 00	6	Aug. 1, 1871.
1 "	Sarah F. D. Spurr,	450 00	6	Feb. 18, 1871.
1 "	State Board of Education,	15,000 00	No	....
3 "	State Mutual Life Assurance Co.,	30,000 00	7	Jan. 1, 1872.
1 "	Azubah H. Swallow,	1,100 00	6	Sept. 15, 1871.
1 "	Louisa H. Thompson,	3,500 00	6½	Aug. 16, 1871.
1 "	Albert Tolman & Co.,	1,200 00	6	Aug. 12, 1871.
1 "	Gill Valentine,	100 00	6	Oct. 1, 1871.
1 "	Asa H. Waters,	6,000 00	6	July 26, 1871.
1 "	Josephus Woodcock,	1,000 00	6	July 18, 1871.
1 "	John Woodcock,	4,200 00	6	Aug. 11, 1871.
4 "	Worcester County School of Industrial Science,	22,696 32	6	Jan. 1, 1872.
6 "	Worcester Five Cents Savings Bank,	127,000 00	7	Dec. 1, 1871.
2 "	Worcester National Bank,	35,000 00	..	Dec. 8, 1871.
1 "	Worcester Safe Deposit and Trust Co.,	50,000 00	No	....
		$561,888 72		

FUNDED CITY LOAN, JANUARY 1, 1872.

	To whom Payable.	Amount.	When Due.	Rate of Interest.	Interest paid to
24 Bonds	E. P. B., or bearer,	$24,000	1872—1882.	5	Dec. 1, 1871.
5 "	New England Mutual Life Insurance Co.,	500,000	July 1, 1881.	6	Jan. 1, 1872.
5 "	G. W. W., or bearer,	10,000	1874—1876.	5	Dec. 1, 1871.
13 "	Worcester County Institution for Savings,	35,000	1872—1884.	5	"
1 "	" " " " "	12,000	June 1, 1881.	6	"
10 "	Worcester Mechanics Savings Bank,	20,000	1872—1881.	5	"
		$601,000			

FUNDED SEWER DEBT, January 1, 1872.

To whom Payable.	Amount.	When Due.	Rate of Interest.	Interest paid to
1 Bond to Bearer,	$500	June 15, 1877.	6	Dec. 15, 1871.
36 Bonds to Fox Heirs,	36,000	"	6	"
4 " Institute of Industrial Science,	4,000	"	6	"
3 " Peabody Museum Fund,	2,100	"	6	"
9 " Worcester County Institution for Savings,	9,000	"	6	"
36 " Worcester Five Cents Savings Bank,	36,000	. "	6	"
10 " American Antiquarian Society,	9,000	June 15, 1878.	6	"
1 " William H. Gould,	100	"	6	"
1 " Samuel F. Haven,	1,000	"	6	"
21 " Institute of Industrial Science,	21,000	"	6	"
1 " Asahel Newton,	1,000	"	6	"
1 " Samuel V. Stone,	500	"	6	"
1 " Benjamin Wallace, estate of,	1,000	"	6	"
2 " American Antiquarian Society,	1,000	June 15, 1879.	6	"
4 " Bearer,	800	"	6	"
1 " James H. Gerauld,	1,000	"	6	"
10 " H. K or bearer,	10,000	"	6	"
4 " H. R. or bearer,	3,500	"	6	"
100 " Blake Brothers & Co., or bearer,	100,000	July 1, 1880.	6	Jan. 1, 1872.
4 " Adaline Barnes,	4,000	July 1, 1881.	6	"
3 " Mary Ann L. Brown,	3,000	" ,	6	"
4 " New Bedford Institution for Savings,	40,000	June 1, 1880.	6	Dec. 1, 1871.
1 " Nathaniel Paine, Trustee,	5,000	July 1, 1881.	6	July 1, 1871.
3 " Charles A. Rallion,	3,000	June 15, 1880.	6	Dec. 15, 1871.
1 " Stephen Salisbury,	5,000	July 1, 1881.	6	Jan. 1, 1872.
1 " Lucie E. Smith,	1,000	June 15, 1881.	6	Dec. 15, 1871.
5 " Worcester Co. Free Inst. for Ind. Science,	35,900	July 1, 1881.	6	Jan. 1, 1872.
2 " Worcester Five Cents Savings Bank,	15,000	Feb. 1, 1881.	6	"
4 " Merchant and Farmers M. F. I. Co.,	40,000	1873—1875.	6	"
11 " State Mutual Life Assurance Co.,	110,000	1872—1875.	6	"
	$499,400			

49

WATER LOAN, January 1, 1872.

To whom Payable.	Amount.	When Due.	Rate of Interest.	Interest paid to
2 Bonds Albert Ball,	$200	June 1, 1874.	6	Dec. 1, 1871.
1 " Joseph S. Barney, Extr.,	2,300	July 1, 1891.	6	"
2 " Bearer,	1,500	June 1, 1875.	6	"
19 " George Brown,	19,000	June 1, 1873.	6	"
100 " B. B. & Co., or bearer,	100,000	July 1, 1885.	6	Jan. 1, 1872.
7 " Louisa Culver,	3,400	June 1, 1876.	6	Dec. 1, 1871.
2 " A. D., or bearer,	1,500	June 1, 1872.	6	"
2 " Isaac Davis,	10,000	June 1, 1876.	6	"
3 " Samuel DeWitt,	3,000	June 1, 1876.	6	"
1 " Joseph B. Drury,	1,000	June 1, 1872.	6	"
1 " Clarinda S. Fisk,	1,000	June 1, 1878	6	"
3 " Free Public Library,	5,000	June 1, 1885.	6	"
4 " Dennis Harthan,	1,700	June 1, 1878.	6	June 1, 1871.
2 " High School Fund,	1,100	June 1, 1880.	6	Dec. 1, 1871.
3 " David Hitchcock,	2,500	June 1, 1878.	6	"
9 " John Jepherson,	9,000	June 1, 1872.	6	"
2 " John R. Jordan,	2,000	1874—1881.	6	....
3 " K., or bearer,	3,000	June 1, 1879.	6	Dec. 1, 1871.
5 " Mechanics Savings Bank,	50,000	July 1, 1886.	6	"
10 " Merchant and Farmer's M. F. Insurance Co.,	57,000	1871—1875	6	"
1 "　　"　　"　　"　　"　　"	2,000	June 1, 1873.	5	"
4 " New Bedford Institution for Savings,	35,000	June 1, 1880.	6	"
1 " Nathaniel Paine, Trustee,	10,000	July 1, 1876.	6	July 1, 1871.
8 " Peabody Museum Fund,	4,500	June 1, 1877.	6	Dec. 1, 1871.
6 " People's Savings Bank,	20,000	1873—1876.	6	"
2 " John E. Phelps,	1,000	June 1, 1878.	6	"
4 " Sumner Reed,	800	June 1, 1872.	6	"
1 " Mary Smith,	1,000	June 1, 1876.	6	"
13 " Joseph Sprague,	13,000	1875—1876.	6	"
4 " State Mutual Life Assurance Co.,	13,000	1873—1873.	5	"
36 "　　"　　"　　"　　"　　"	228,000	1872—1878.	6	"
3 " Ethan R Thompson,	1,200	June 1, 1872.	6	"
1 " George Upham,	1,000	June 1, 1874.	6	"
8 " G. W. W., or bearer,	6,500	1872—1876.	6	"
1 " G. W. W , or bearer,	500	June 1, 1879.	5	"
4 " Edwin Waite,	7,000	June 1, 1874.	5	"
1 " Luther Wheelock,	5,000	June 1, 1878.	6	"
1 Note, George Wight,	500	....	6	"
4 Bonds, "　　"	1,300	June 1, 1875.	6	"
1 " Josephus Woodcock,	1,000	June 1, 1886.	6	"
15 " Worcester County Institution for Savings,	98,000	1886—1890.	6	"
4 " Worcester Five Cents Savings Bank,	11,000	1872—1873.	5	"
12 "　　"　　"　　.　　"　　"	40,000	1875—1882.	6	"
4 " Worcester Mechanics Savings Bank,	11,000	June 1, 1875.	6	"
7 " Wor. Co. Institute of Industrial Science,	7,000	1877—1888.	6	"
2 " J. W., or bearer,	1,000	June 1, 1879.	6	"
	$794,500			

CITY DEBT FROM 1861 TO 1872.

TEMPORARY, SEWER, WAR, AND WATER.

Date.	Miscellaneous.	Sewer.	War.	Water.	Total.
1861	$67,324 25	....	....	$35,000 00	$102,324 25
1862	80,319 40	....	$14,000 00	35,000 00	129,319 40
1863	70,380 08	....	103,034 47	35,000 00	208,414 55
1864	61,451 99	....	118,307 71	35,000 00	214,759 70
1865	78,427 14	....	162,330 77	123,701 79	364,459 70
1866	61,337 50	....	161,953 98	201,127 11	424,418 59
1867	60,186 24	....	94,924 97	303,193 93	458,305 14
1868	56,050 43	$115,351 43	70,541 01	378,006 98	619,949 85
1869	59,193 07	235,939 36	68,024 47	410,123 10	773,290 00
1870	154,787 49	457,625 67	68,041 22	505,264 27	1,185,718 65

1871.

Miscellaneous,		$60,676 74
Boston, Barre and Gardner Railroad,		104,880 00
Sewer,	$827,151 80	860,151 80
Interest,	33,000 00	
School Houses,		85,441 46
Streets,		71,449 92
War,		67,480 22
Water,		649,727 90
		$1,899,808 04

1872.

Miscellaneous,	$76,622 69
Boston, Barre and Gardner Railroad,	262,200 00
School Houses,	88,695 98
Sewers,	1,072,723 99
Soldiers Monument,	35,000 00
Streets,	102,707 13
War,	66,339 72
Water Works,	752,499 21
	$2,456,788 72

SCHEDULE OF CITY PROPER

JANUARY 1, 1872.

REAL ESTATE OWNED BY THE CIT

Central Park, (Old Common,)
Elm Park and Improvements,
City Hall,
Alms House and City Hospital, farm and wood land,
Hope Cemetery and Improvements,
Burial Ground on Common,   )
     "   Mechanic street,   } Not used.
     "   Pine court,   )
Library building and lot,
City Pound lot, Pine street,
Engine House and lot, No. 2, New Worcester,
     "   3, Exchange street,
     "   4, Carlton   "
                5, Myrtle   "
                Mechanic   "
                Bigelow's Court,
     "   School street,
     "   Beacon   "
Hose-house, Bloomingdale Road,
Real Estate belonging to School Department,
     "   Highway   "
Water Shop and fixtures in " Worcester Water Works,'
Hook & Ladder House on Thomas st., with land,
Public Sewers cost,

PERSONAL PROPERTY.

Belonging to the School Department,
     "   Highway   "
     "   Police   "
     "   Fire
     "   Water   "
In the Council Chambers and the several offices in the Ci
At the Alms House and Farm,

Street lamps and fixtures,	13,000
Three City Scales,	1,000
Armory for Battery,	2,000

$159,535

REAL ESTATE BELONGING TO THE SCHOOL DEPARTMENT.

A full and detailed statement of the School Houses and land, and their value can be found in the School Committee's Report, page 102.

WORCESTER WATER WORKS.

The estate at Leicester, Bell Pond, Reservoirs, Pipes, Hydrants, and all the fixtures and tools belonging thereto, valued at $777,939.

SCHOOLS.

A full statement of all the personal property belonging to the School Department can be found in the School Committee's Report, page 103.

FREE PUBLIC LIBRARY.

A full and detailed statement of all the books and other property can be found in the Directors' Report.

REAL ESTATE BELONGING TO THE HIGHWAY DEPARTMENT.

60,000 feet of land on Salem street,	15,000
Barns and sheds on the above lot,	10,000
About 1½ acres of land on the Island,	6,000
Gravel pit at the junction of Grove and Pratt streets,	250
1 gravel pit on Geo. S. Newton's farm, and one on Pleasant st., near Paxton line,	50

$31,300

For an Inventory of the personal property belonging to the Highway Department, Nov. 30, 1871, see Highway Commissioners's Report, page 283.

STANDARD OF WEIGHTS AND MEASURES.

In charge of RUSSELL R. SHEPARD, *City Sealer,*

Office, No. 3, Pleasant st.

THREE CITY SCALES, in charge of the following persons :
James H. Benchley, Salem Square,
John W. Hoppin, at New Worcester,
Silas Penniman, at Lincoln Square.

IN POLICE COURT ROOM.

1 Salamander Safe, desks and furniture.

IN CHARGE OF JOHN FARWELL SUPERINTENDENT OF THE ALMS HOUSE AND CITY HOSPITAL.

Furniture in house, provisions etc., $4,037.03 ; stock on farm, farming tools, etc., valued by Overseers, Dec. 1, 1871, $7,912.30 ; furniture, bedding, etc., belonging to Truant School, $448.00

IN CHARGE OF THE SEVERAL ENGINE AND HOSE COMPANIES AND UNDER A GENERAL SUPERVISION OF THE ENGINEERS.

3 steam fire engines with hose-carriages attached, 2 hand engines, 5 hose carriages, 2 hook and ladder carriages, 13,000 feet of leading hose, 6 horses and harnesses, together with the apparatus necessary to fully equip the several companies.
Valued $30,000.

IN CHARGE OF F. A. KIRBY.

All the street lamps, 256 fluid, 566 gas and fixtures, valued at $15,000.

GOVERNMENT AND OFFICERS.

OF THE

CITY OF WORCESTER,

FOR 1872.

MAYOR,

GEORGE F. VERRY.

ALDERMEN.

Ward 1.—EMORY BANISTER.
"   2.—*JOSEPH BURROUGH.
"   3.—GILBERT J. RUGG.
"   4.—*SAMUEL D. HARDING.
"   5.—HORACE WYMAN.
"   6.—*HENRY H. CHAMBERLIN.
"   7.—EDWIN T. MARBLE.
"   8.—*GEORGE R. SPURR.

CITY CLERK AND CLERK OF THE BOARD OF ALDERMEN,

SAMUEL SMITH,

Office, No. 2, City Hall : Residence 10 Harvard st.

CITY MESSENGER,

CHARLES MARVIN, Office, No. 1, City Hall; Residence, No. 1, Clinton street.

COMMON COUNCIL.

President—CHARLES G. REED.   *Clerk*—Henry L. Shumway.

Ward 1.—Joseph Chase,
*Edward R. Fiske,
*John W. Howe.

Ward 2.—*Wm. Allen,
Parritt Blaisdell,
Luther Ross.·

Ward 3.—*Samuel McFadden,
*George F. Hewett,
Charles W. Wentworth.

Ward 4.—*Andrew Athy,
*Patrick D. Conlin,
Charles S. Childs.

Ward 5.—*John J. O'Gorman,
*John Cove,
Morris Melaven.

Ward 6.—Joseph H. Walker,
Charles G. Reed,
*Dorrance S. Goddard.

Ward 7.—Calvin L. Hartshorn,
*Edwin Ames,
*Amariah B. Lovell.

Ward 8.—E. H. Towne,
Sumner Pratt,
*Charles G. Parker.

PAGE TO COMMON COUNCIL,—Frederick A. Brooks.

---

*Aldermen and Council marked *, elected for two years.

JOINT STANDING COMMITTEES FOR 1872.

On Finance.—The Mayor and Aldermen Banister and Chamberlin; President of Council and Councilmen Walker, Childs, and Hewett.

On Claims.—The Mayor Aldermen Banister and Spurr; President of the Council, Councilmen Ross, Cove and Towne.

On Water.—Aldermen Marble and Rugg; Councilmen Allen, Parker and Fiske.

On Sewers.—The Mayor and Aldermen Wyman and Banister; President of Council and Councilman Hewett, Ross and Hartshorn.

On the Fire Department.—Aldermen Wyman and Chamberlin; Councilmen Athy, Wentworth and Lovell.

On Lighting Streets.—Aldermen Rugg and Spurr; Councilmen Childs, Ames and Chase.

On Education.—The Mayor and Aldermen Chamberlin and Harding; President of Council and Councilmen Pratt, Allen and Goddard.

On Printing.—Aldermen Harding and Rugg; Councilmen Howe, McFadden and Cove.

On Sidewalks.—Aldermen Marble and Burrough; Councilmen Ames, Howe and Blaisdell.

On Highways, Streets and Bridges.—The Mayor and Aldermen Spurr and Harding; President of Council and Councilmen Pratt, Fiske and Walker.

On Military Affairs.—Aldermen Burrough and Wyman ; Councilmen Melaven O'Gorman and Towne.

On Charities.—Aldermen Chamberlain and Burrough ; Councilmen Chase, Hartshorn and Melaven.

On Free Public Market.—Aldermen Harding and Wyman ; Councilmen Hartshorn, McFadden and O'Gorman.

STANDING COMMITTEES OF THE BOARD OF ALDERMEN.

On Health.—The Mayor and Aldermen Chamberlin and Spurr.

On Public Buildings.—The Mayor and Aldermen Harding and Wyman.

On Bills in Second Reading.—Aldermen Marble and Rugg.

On Enrollment.—Aldermen Banister and Burrough.

On Elections and Returns.—Aldermen Burrough and Chamberlin.

STANDING COMMITTEES OF THE COMMON COUNCIL.

On Bills in the Second Reading.—Councilmen Parker and Conlin.

On Enrollment.—Councilmen Wentworth, Blaisdell and Goddard.

On Elections and Returns.—Councilmen Lovell, Conlin and O'Gorman.

SOLICITOR.

THOS. L. NELSON.   Office, Post Office Building and City Hall.

TREASURER AND COLLECTOR.

WILLIAM S. BARTON.

Office, No. 6, City Hall : Residence, 23 High street.

AUDITOR.

HENRY GRIFFIN.   Office, No. 7, City Hall.

ASSESSORS.

Levi Barker, 3 years.

Wm. L. Clark, 2 years,   Josiah P. Houghton 1 year.

ASSISTANT ASSESSORS.

Ward 1.—John M. Earle,   Ward 5.—Levi Barker,
"   2.—George E. Stearns,   "   6.—Samuel Houghton,
"   3.—John Driscoll,   "   7.—Josiah P. Houghton,
"   4.—James McFarland,   "   8.—Alexander Marsh.

CITY ENGINEER.

PHINEHAS BALL.   Office, No. 5, City Hall.

50

COMMISSIONER OF HIGHWAYS.
THOMAS GATES.   Office, No. 3, City Hall.

WATER COMMISSIONER.
FRANK E. HALL.   Office, No. 5, City Hall.

COMMISSIONERS OF HOPE CEMETERY.
William Bush, 5 years,
Albert Tolman, 4 years,   Stephen Salisbury, Jr., 2 years,
Albert Curtis, 3 years,   Henry Chapin 1 year.

COMMISSIONERS OF SHADE TREES AND PUBLIC GROUNDS.
Stephen Salisbury, 3 years.
Edward W. Lincoln, 1 year,   O. L. Hatch, 2 years,

DIRECTORS OF THE FREE PUBLIC LIBRARY.
STEPHEN SALISBURY, *President,*   NATHANIEL PAINE, *Clerk.*

T. L. Nelson, T. E. St. John.	6 years	Caleb B. Metcalf, Henry A. Marsh.	3 years
C. H Morgan, C. O. Thompson.	5 years	George Jaques, Charles A. Chase.	2 years
Nathaniel Paine, William R. Huntington.	4 years	Stephen Salisbury, George E. Francis.	1 year

Samuel S. Green, *Librarian.*
Emma S. Eddy,
Sarah F. Earle, } *Assistant Librarians.*
Jessie E. Tyler,

SCHOOL COMMITTEE.
GEORGE F. VERRY, Mayor, Ex-Officio, President.
A. P. MARBLE, Superintendent.   Office, No. 11, City Hall.
SAMUEL V. STONE, Secretary.   Office, No. 13, City Hall.

Members whose term expires January, 1875. WARD.	Members whose term expires January, 1874.	Members whose term expires January, 1873.
1.—C. B. Metcalf.	Hartley Williams	Edward H. Hall.
2.—George W. Gale.	G. Henry Whitcomb.	Ann B. Earle.
3.—James McDermott.	Jason Chapin.	James Draper.
4.—P. J. Garrigan.	Thomas Griffin.	John F. Murray.
5.—F. J. McNulty.	M. J. McCafferty.	Samuel V. Stone.
6.—F. P. Goulding.	Loammi Harrington.	Edward H. Peabody.
7.—George Jaques.	Emerson Warner.	Charles Ballard.
8.—Emory Aldrich.	E. B. Stoddard.	Rufus Woodward.

MUNICIPAL COURT.

HARTLEY WILLIAMS, *Chief Justice.*

JOSEPH A. TITUS, } *Associate Justices.*
SAMUEL UTLEY,

THEODORE S. JOHNSON, *Clerk.*

TRUANT COMMISSIONERS..

GEO. F. VERRY, Mayor.

A. P. MARBLE, Superintendent of Schoools.

JONA. B. SIBLEY, City Marshal.

E. D. McFARLAND, Police and Truant Officer.
Office, City Hall: Residence, No. 117 Thomas street.

MARSHAL,

JONATHAN B. SIBLEY.

Office, City Hall: Residence No.23, Charlton street. -

ASSISTANT MARSHALS.

EMORY WILSON, Office, City Hall; residence, rear of Dr. Hill's church.

JAMES R. FISH, Office, City Hall; residence, No. 34 Piedmont street.

WATCHMEN AND DAY POLICE.

JOHN HOWE, Captain of Night Police; residence, Bartlett Place.

JOSEPH L. HALL, Captain of Day Police; residence No. 1, Pleasant Place.

Henry J. Allen,	Marshall S. Green,
Amos Atkinson,	Daniel Hannafin,
George V. Barker,	Louis Harper,
Jesse D. Barker,	Floyd H. Harris,
Ezra Churchill,	John G. Haskell,
Reuben M. Colby,	Lewis M. Howlett,
Harrison H. Comings,	Wm. H. Johnson,
James Conner,	Miles Joyce,
Perley Dean,	James Keegan,
Joseph M. Dyson,	Henry M. Leland,
A. P. Eaton,	James J. McLane,
Henry E. Fayerweather,	Michael O'Connell,
Joseph H. Flint,	Patrick O'Day,
Thomas R. Foster,	Stephen D. Pierce,
Cornelius French,	Patrick E. Ratigan,
Charles A. Garland,	Dwight C. Smith,
Jaalam Gates,	Solon S. Sprague.

CONSTABLES.

George W. Dillon,　　　　　　Edwin D. McFarland,
James R. Fish,　　　　　　　　John L. Utley,
Emory Wilson.

SPECIAL POLICE, WITHOUT PAY.

Sumner P. Hale, at	Western Railroad Station.
Charles W. Wentworth,	Mechanics Hall.
Horace L. Jenks,	New Worcester.
Moses P. Stearns,	South Worcester.
John Carson,	"　　"
Charles A. Clark,	B. & A. Freight Dep't.
Charles G. Parker,	Pleasant street, near West.
John P. Stockwell,	Rural Cemetery.
Henry J. Kendall,	Tatnuck.
Elisha J. Rawson,	Prov. & Wor. R. R. Station.
Samuel Knowlton,	Junction Station.
James H. Croome,	Street Lamps.
Henry Cole,	"
John Farwell,	City Alms House.
Jeremiah McNamara,	St. Paul's Church.
James Melanefy,	"　　"
Thomas McDermott,	"　　"
Sumner Bridges,	For the Banks.
Edward Jones,	At Valley Falls.
William Y. Holman,	May street.
John M. Hoppin,	Webster Square.
Andrew Patterson,	"　　"
Loring M. Blanchard,	Grove Mill.
Emerson Blanchard,	"　　"
J. Brainard Hall,	"　　"
Charles H. Lowe,	"　　"
Robert M. Reynolds,	Music Hall.
Luke Tulley,	Green and Pond street.
Benjamin Davis,	Nor. & Wor. R. R. Depot.
Samuel Putnam,	Pond District.
David F. Parker,	Commissioner of Highways.
Benjamin James,	Jamesville.
Archibald Dollen,	Cambridge street.
J. Brown Alden,	Junction Shop.
Leonard Gates,	Pleasant street.
George P. Blake,	Merrifield's Buildings.
David Braman,	Zion's Church.
Wm. Knowles,	For Worcester Water Works.
Henry Glazier,	Auction Rooms.
John Chaplin,	Union street.
George W. Gale,	Laurel Hill.
Thomas N. Baird,	Laurel St., Church.

Bancroft, Enoch   Adams Square.
Batchellor, Lyman   ʹ   Brinley Hall.
Elliott, Gustavus   John Street.
Holloway, Thomas   Church Street.
Maloney, James   Wor. & Nashua Repair Shop.
Keyes, Warren C.   Adriatic Mill.
Killelea, Thomas   Millbury Street.

TRUSTEES OF THE CITY HOSPITAL.

F. H. Kelley, *President.*   George Jaques, *Secretary.*
Emory Banister, Alderman.   F. H. Kelley, 4 years.
Sumner Pratt, } Councilmen.   Stephen Salisbury, Jr., 3 years.
Charles S. Childs, }   George Jacques, 2 years.
            Joseph Sargent, 1 year.

OVERSEERS OF THE POOR.

GEO. F. VERRY, Mayor.   }
A. P. MARBLE, Sup't., of Schools,   } Ex-Officio
JONATHAN B. SIBLEY, City Marshal,   } members.

Geo. F. Verry, *President.*   George W. Gale, *Clerk.*

George W. Gale and O. L. Hatch, 3 years.
Edward Kendall and Walter Henry, 2 years.
John W. Jordan and O. B. Hadwen, 1 year.

CITY PHYSICIAN.

ALBERT WOOD.   Office, Pearl street.

KEEPER OF ALMSHOUSE.

JOHN FARWELL.

UNDERTAKERS.

George Sessions,   George G. Hildreth,
Waldo E. Sessions,   Timothy McCarty,
Henry C. Willson.   Patrick H. Carroll.

PUBLIC WEIGHERS.

John W. Hoppin, N. Worcester,   Silas Penniman, Lincoln Square.
    James H. Benchley, Salem Square,
    Otis Stebbins, at Crompton's Loom Works.

WEIGHERS OF COAL.

F. H. Knight, at Jourdan's.   Joseph Leland, at Southbridge st.
Julius F. Knight at   "   Geo. W. Comee, at Central st.
F. W. Wellington at City Coal Yd. James Plympton, at Manchester st.
    Edwin Gleason at Rice, Barton & Co.'s Works.

MEASURERS OF WOOD AND BARK.

S. Penniman, Lincoln Square.   James H. Benchly, Salem Square.
John W. Hoppin, New Worcester. Sibley Putnam, Green st.
John K. James, Jamesville.
Alden Thayer, Pleasantville.

SURVEYORS OF LUMBER.

Henry W. Reed.   Edwin S. Pike.

FENCE VIEWERS.

J. F Manning,   George A. Brown,   Charles W. Burbank.

MILK INSPECTOR.

Russell R. Shepard, 3 Pleasant street.

FIELD DRIVER.

William L. Nichols.

POUND KEEPER—Thomas Gates.

SEALER OF WEIGHTS AND MEASURES.

R. R. Shepard.   Office No. 3, Pleasant st.

WARD OFFICERS.

Ward 1.—WARDEN, E. D. Buffington. CLERK, George W. Mirick.
    INSPECTORS, Simon Sargent, James Broadbent, Wm. T.
    Allen.
Ward 2.—WARDEN, Gilbert Walker. CLERK, Geo. W. Gale.
    INSPECTORS, S. J. Brimhall, Amos M. Eaton, Wm. H.
    Jankins.
Ward 3.—WARDEN, Lyman Brown. CLERK, Edward T. Redican.
    INSPECTORS, Wm. L. Gray, Cornelius Sullivan, Jeremiah
    Hennessy.
Ward 4.—WARDEN, P. E. Ratigan. CLERK, J. Edward Murray.
    INSPECTORS, Chas. C. McFarland, John B. Cosgrove, Jere-
    miah Foley.
Ward 5.—WARDEN, Jeremiah Murphy. CLERK, James J. McLane.
    INSPECTORS, E. D. Stocking, J. R. Laverty, James W.
    Doon.
Ward 6.—WARDEN, Charles L. Redding. CLERK, Chas. S. Chapin.
    INSPECTORS, Henry C. Rawson, Joseph R. Torrey, Charles
    P. Morse.

Ward 7.—WARDEN, Joseph A. Titus. CLERK, Lewis C. Muzzy.
INSPECTORS, Henry H. Merriam, John D. Lovell, Wm.
W. Cook.

Ward 8—WARDEN, Daniel Seagrave. CLERK, James H. Bancroft.
INSPECTORS, Henry Bacon, Charles H. Harvey, George A.
Geer.

BOARD OF ENGINEERS.

Office, No. 7, City Hall.

SIMON E. COOMBS, *Chief.*   SAMUEL H. DAY, *Clerk.*

Wm. Brophy,   } *Assistant Engineers.*   } John W. Loring,
Wm. Knowles,   }   } Samuel H. Day.

FIRE COMPANIES.

Rapid Engine Co.	No. 2, Charles S. Bottomly,	Foreman,	40	men.
Hook and Ladder Co.	No. 1, Perry Bullard,	"	20	"
"	No. 2, Jeremiah Hennessy,	"	20	"
City Hose Co.	No. 1, Gilbert N. Rawson,	:	10	'
Ocean Hose Co.	No. 2, David Boland,		10	'
Eagle "	No. 3, George W. Parks,		10	'
Niagara, "	No. 4, Samuel Knowlton,		10	'
Yankee "	No. 5, Vernon W. Lounsbury,	"	10	"
Steamer Gov. Lincoln,	No. 1, Charles Guild,	:	12	'
" Col. Davis,	No. 2, Patrick H. Carroll,		12	'
" A. B. Lovell,	No. 3, Edwin Fisher,	:	12	'
Engineers,			5	'

171

SALARIES OF CITY OFFICERS.

Mayor	$1,500
City Clerk	1,500
City Treasurer and Collector	2,500
City Engineer	2,500
City Solicitor	2,500
City Physician	800
Auditor of Accounts	1,500
City Messenger	1,100
Commissioner of Highways	2,200
Water Commissioner	1,200
Clerk of the Common Council	250
Clerk of the Overseers	1,000
One Assessor and Clerk of the Board	1,600
Two Assessors—each	1,100
Asst. Assessors—each three dollars per diem.	
Milk Inspector	25
Sealer of Weights and Measures	360
City Marshal	1,600
1st, Asst. Marshal	1,150
2d, Asst. Marshal	1,100

Capt. of Day Police, $3.00 per day.

Capt. of Night Police, $3.00 per night.

Patrolmen, $2.75 per day and night.

See Report of the School Committee for Salaries of Superintendent, Secretary and Teachers, page 104.

Engineers and Firemen not fixed.

Lightning Source UK Ltd.
Milton Keynes UK
UKHW010909231118
332790UK00008B/988/P